America Recommitted

America Recommitted

A Superpower Assesses Its Role in a Turbulent World

Second Edition

Donald E. Nuechterlein

THE UNIVERSITY PRESS OF KENTUCKY

Scholarly publisher for the Commonwealth,
serving Bellarmine College, Berea College, Centre
College of Kentucky, Eastern Kentucky University,
The Filson Club Historical Society, Georgetown College,
Kentucky Historical Society, Kentucky State University,
Morehead State University, Murray State University,
Northern Kentucky University, Transylvania University,
University of Kentucky, University of Louisville,
and Western Kentucky University.

05 04 03 02 01   5 4 3 2 1

Editorial and Sales Offices: The University Press of Kentucky
663 South Limestone Street, Lexington, Kentucky 40508–4008

Library of Congress Cataloging-in-Publication Data

Nuechterlein, Donald Edwin, 1925-
    America recommitted : a superpower assesses its role in a
turbulent world / Donald E. Nuechterlein—2nd ed.
        p.   cm.
    Includes bibliographical references and index.
    ISBN 0-8131-9005-3 (paper : alk. paper)
    1. United States—Foreign relations—1989–1993.
    2. United States—Foreign relations—1993–   I. Title.

E881 .N84 2000
327.73'009'049—dc21   00-043314

This book is printed on acid-free recycled paper meeting
the requirements of the American National Standard
for Permanence of Paper for Printed Library Materials.

Manufactured in the United States of America

To my wife, Mil

Contents

Tables

Preface to the Second Edition

When *America Recommitted: U.S. National Interests in a Restructured World* was published in June 1991, the world that we had known for forty-five years was in the midst of profound change. The Cold War was over, the Soviet Union was going through a major restructuring, America and its allies had crushed a new threat, Iraq, to the security of the Persian Gulf, Germany was reunited for the first time since 1945, China had reverted to a harsh authoritarian rule, and the United States debated whether it required large military forces in the post–Cold War era. The 1991 volume was published only a few months before the Soviet Union disintegrated and a more democratic Russia emerged as the major state in Eastern Europe. Suddenly the international environment was transformed.

In 2000 most of the world lives in a safer and more prosperous condition than it did twenty years ago. The United States, despite military cutbacks, continues to be heavily involved politically, economically, and militarily around the globe. Yet, many Americans worry about the dangers associated with the United States becoming an international policeman that has to be on call to intervene anywhere to maintain order and protect human rights. At the start of a new century I believe it is imperative that a serious national debate be held on this fundamental question: is the United States indeed willing to bear the large financial and human costs associated with taking on a role in this century similar to the one Imperial Rome exercised in the first century? Stated another way, is America prepared to be an international hegemon, or should it be an aloof but vigilant superpower that intervenes militarily only when its vital national interests are at stake? These questions, and their answers, form the basis of this new edition's final chapters.

In reviewing the earlier edition of *America Recommitted*, I concluded that most of the post–World War II events that were covered and the analysis remain essentially accurate as of 1990. Consequently, instead of updating chapters 5, 6, and 7—the assessments of U.S. interests and policies in North America, East

Asia, and Europe—I retained those chapters largely as written and added appropriate references to subsequent events. Two new chapters were added that discuss the major international events of the 1990s as they affected U.S. interests, giving special attention to America's relations with Russia and China. Chapter 8, "Post–Cold War Challenges to U.S. Interests," looks at the last two years of the Bush presidency and the first three years of the Clinton administration. Chapter 9, "Toward the New Millennium," addresses the major challenges to U.S. policy during the final years of the decade, especially America's military interventions in Bosnia and Kosovo. Chapter 10, "Role of the Aloof but Vigilant Superpower," assesses this country's national interests at the beginning of 2000 and draws conclusions about the future direction of American foreign policy.

As one who has studied and written extensively about American foreign policy, I believe that the assessments of U.S. national interests and policies contained in this second edition of *America Recommitted* will prove to be beneficial to readers who seek a clearer understanding of where the United States has been in its foreign relations since World War II and where it is likely to be going in the future, as Americans decide how their country should play its new role as the world's undisputed superpower.

Charlottesville, Virginia
March 2000

Preface to First Edition

The ideas in this book took shape in the spring of 1989 when the Soviet Union withdrew its troops from Afghanistan and began reducing its forces in Eastern Europe, and when President Bush declared on May 12 that "containment worked." In effect, the president acknowledged that forty years of Cold War between the United States and the Soviet Union were near an end and that a new era in international relations was about to begin. The astonishing events that followed in Eastern Europe, underscored by the dramatic toppling of the Berlin Wall in November, reinforced the view that the United States had won its forty-year struggle with the Soviet Union and was entering a new, less certain period in foreign policy.

This book is in some respects a sequel to one I wrote in 1985, *America Overcommitted: United States National Interests in the* 1980s. It surveyed various regions of the world where the United States had made defense commitments after World War II and assessed why certain countries were truly vital U.S. interests while others were not. This new volume is concerned with identifying and analyzing the political and economic trends in countries and regions that remain vital interests in the 1990s, including Canada, Mexico, and the Caribbean area; parts of South America; Japan, Australia, and other parts of East Asia; Western Europe and the Soviet Union; the Eastern Mediterranean; and the Persian Gulf.

Chapter 1 provides a conceptual framework for defining U.S. national interests worldwide and serves as a guide for discussion in the subsequent chapters. As one who worked in Berlin when the Cold War began in 1947 and who has remained a student and practitioner of U.S. foreign policy since then, I found it appropriate to include two historical chapters that survey U.S. interests and security policies over the period 1945–1980. Chapters 2 and 3 therefore review how seven presidents, from Truman through Carter, defined U.S. interests globally and appraise the policies they chose to defend them. Chapter 4 assesses Ronald Reagan's foreign policy and its impact on the Soviet Union's view of its own interests. Chapters 5–7 then examine U.S. interests in three large geographical areas of the world, North America, East Asia, and Europe. Chapter 8 reviews the international situation in the fall of 1990, especially in the Middle East.

Most of the book was completed before the Persian Gulf crisis erupted in August 1990, but that event did not materially change my assessment of America's long-term interests and policies in the post–Cold War period. What the Iraqi annexation of Kuwait underscored, however, was the vulnerability of the industrialized world to economic pressures resulting from growing dependence on Persian Gulf oil. The crisis also highlighted the need for collective security among the industrialized nations to ensure that no single country could control the flow of Persian Gulf oil to world markets.

An earlier version of Chapter 1 appeared in *Business in the Contemporary World* 2, no. 2 (Winter 1990): 112–20. A portion of Chapter 4 appeared in *Perspectives on Political Science* 19, no. 1 (Winter 1990): 43–52. I thank their publishers for permission to reprint the articles. I am indebted to scholars at Queen's University in Kingston, Ontario, and at the Australian National University in Canberra for sharing their views with me. I also wish to thank friends at the University of Virginia and the Woodrow Wilson Center in Washington, D.C., for helpful insights. The assessments made about US. national interests and policies since World War II and in the 1990s are, of course, my sole responsibility.

Charlottesville, Virginia
February 1991

Introduction, 1989

A Transition Year in World Politics

Historians will very likely look back on 1989 as the year when fundamental changes occurred in the international balance of power and altered the way many nations assessed their national interests—including defense needs, expectations for economic growth, prospects for world peace, and demands for individual rights. The spectacular changes of that year caused the new Bush administration to reassess America's international relations, especially the implications of Soviet President Mikhail Gorbachev's stunning revisions of Soviet society and foreign policy. Although the altered international environment in 1989 was relatively easy for political observers to describe, the long-term impact on U.S. foreign and national security policy required more time for definitive evaluation. Nevertheless, by the end of 1989 few observers doubted that many of the assumptions on which American foreign policy had been based for more than four decades were no longer valid and that international politics had entered a period of swift transformation. New concepts and new strategies were therefore required to help U.S. policymakers deal wisely with the evolving realities of the 1990s.

The Spring of 1989

The months of April, May, and June 1989 produced a series of remarkable political and economic events—in the United States, the Soviet Union, Western Europe, and East Asia—which implied significant changes in global relationships. The Cold War atmosphere that had characterized U.S.-Soviet relations for most of four decades was giving way to tacit accommodation of the superpowers' national interests. Among these events were President George Bush's reassessment of U.S.-Soviet relations; Mikhail Gorbachev's visit to the People's Republic of China, the first in thirty years by a Soviet leader; Secretary of State James Baker's inaugural meeting with Soviet leaders in Moscow; and West German Chancellor Helmut Kohl's demand for reduction and eventual elimination of short-range nuclear missiles on German soil. In addition, Bush signaled to the Japanese government his intention to act in accordance with provisions of a controversial 1988 "fair trade" law to open Japan's markets to more American products. The spring of 1989 also produced massive student demonstrations in Beijing, China, that were brutally suppressed by the People's Liberation Army.

Perhaps the most significant change was George Bush's declaration in an address at Texas A&M University on May 12 that "containment" of the Soviet empire had succeeded, after forty years of Western steadfastness against Soviet military and political pressure. "Containment worked," he claimed, "because our democratic principles, institutions, and values are sound, and always have been. It worked because our alliances were and are strong, and because the superiority of free societies and free markets over stagnant socialism is undeniable." The president went on to address the foreign policy implications of this new reality:

> We are approaching the conclusion of an historic postwar struggle between two visions—one of tyranny and conflict, and one of democracy and freedom. The review of U.S.-Soviet relations that my administration has just completed outlines a new path toward resolving this struggle. Our goal is bold—more ambitious than any of my predecessors might have thought possible. Our review indicates that 40 years of perseverance have brought us a precious opportunity. Now it is time to move beyond containment, to a new policy for the 1990s, one that recognizes the full scope of change taking place around the world, and in the Soviet Union itself.[1]

A few days later Mikhail Gorbachev became the first Soviet leader to visit China since Nikita Khrushchev's abortive journey there in 1959, which had precipitated a rupture in ties between the world's leading Communist powers. Deng Xiaoping, who became China's supreme leader in 1976, had set three key conditions for Moscow to meet before he would welcome Gorbachev: significant reductions in Soviet military forces stationed along their mutual border, removal of Soviet troops from Afghanistan, and Soviet pressure on Vietnam to withdraw its forces from Cambodia. Gorbachev met one condition in February 1989 when Soviet forces withdrew from Afghanistan. In April he began reducing the large number of Soviet troops stationed on China's border, and he then persuaded Hanoi to withdraw Vietnamese troops from Cambodia. Gorbachev commenced his visit to Beijing on May 15, but it was interrupted by student demonstrations against the Chinese government's refusal to permit greater personal freedom for the population.

A sharp reversal in China's internal affairs occurred on June 4, when its aging Communist leadership decided to put an end to six weeks of massive demonstrations and reimpose tight political and economic controls. This brought to a standstill the economic reforms inaugurated by Deng Xiaoping in 1976, which had produced growing prosperity and some political change. The government's use of the People's Liberation Army (PLA) to crush the demonstrations in Tiananmen Square, which by then involved more than one million people, shocked the world and reinforced the view that China's leaders were not willing to promote rapid economic growth if the price was acceptance of what it considered radical political reforms.

Changes in Eastern Europe

Moscow's tight political grip on Eastern Europe and the Baltic states was being relaxed in mid-1989 in response to the new economic and political realities in Poland, Hungary, Estonia, Latvia, and Lithuania. Poland's Solidarity Party, outlawed eight years earlier, now headed the new Polish government, with Moscow's blessing. In East Germany a mass exodus of tens of thousands of its citizens across Hungary and Austria to West Germany precipitated a crisis in November, which brought about the crumbling of the Berlin Wall and the ouster of the hard-line Communist leadership. Before the end of 1989, Germans on both sides of the border were calling for reunification.

Secretary of State James Baker visited Moscow in May 1989, and soon thereafter President Gorbachev announced that he planned unilaterally to withdraw five hundred short-range nuclear missiles from Eastern Europe. He indicated that Moscow wanted to negotiate an agreement with NATO to reduce Warsaw Pact conventional forces to a level corresponding to NATO's lower force level, an offer that was greeted with astonishment and pleasure throughout Europe. The Soviet leader's peace offensive, which had been in full flower since his dramatic arms reduction proposal at the United Nations in December 1988, caused some strains within NATO, particularly between the Bush administration and the West German government headed by Chancellor Helmut Kohl. He sent Foreign Minister Hans-Dietrich Genscher and Defense Minister Gerhard Stoltenberg to Washington in May to inform the State Department that Bonn wanted early NATO negotiations with Moscow to eliminate short-range (less than three hundred miles) nuclear missiles from both East and West Germany. After several intense discussions, the White House announced that the president did not agree with the German initiative. But it seemed clear that this issue would be addressed again before the West Germans held general elections in 1990.

International Economic Issues

The spring of 1989 also found the Bush administration taking a harder line than had President Ronald Reagan on what most members of Congress and the business community concluded were Japan's unfair trading practices. Despite Reagan's quiet efforts to persuade Japan to open its markets to American products, expand domestic demand, and avoid export practices that the United States considered "dumping," the trade deficit with Japan had not declined appreciably. This led Congress in 1988 to pass legislation, reluctantly approved by Reagan, known as the Omnibus Trade and Competitiveness Act. It authorized the president to take retaliatory action against any country that refused to negotiate what the United States viewed as unfair trading practices. In the spring of 1989 Japan, Brazil, and India were so labeled.

Frustrated over continuing large trade deficits and daily reminders that Japanese money was purchasing many U.S. businesses and prime real estate while Tokyo resisted Washington's demands for elimination of import restrictions, the Senate took a dramatic vote on a key trade issue: by a vote of fifty-two to forty-seven it nearly defeated an agreement negotiated by the Reagan administration for the countries to coproduce a Japanese jet fighter known as FSX. Opponents argued that Japan should have bought the American F-16, considered by experts to be a superior aircraft, instead of acquiring U.S. technology to establish a Japanese aircraft industry.

There was also increased congressional and business concern in 1989 about the European Community's plan to inaugurate a free trading system in 1993. The plan encompassed some 330 million people and envisaged a common currency and coordination of foreign policies among the twelve EC members. "Europe 1992" raised the specter of three competing trading blocs—Europe, North America, and a Japan-dominated East Asian economic group—and caused many to question whether the United States would be able to compete effectively with these emerging economic giants exhibiting impressive worldwide financial and marketing power. American concern about a protectionist Europe began to recede later in the year when U.S. Trade Representative Carla Hills reported after a week of meetings with EC officials that she had a "more positive frame of mind" about threats of restrictions on U.S. imports.

Effects of Detente on Regional Issues

Gorbachev's arms reduction proposals in 1989 had the dual effect of reducing the threat of war and also raising among Germans and other Europeans the question of why NATO needed nuclear missiles on the continent. The West German antinuclear movement, which had been defeated in 1983 when the Bonn government accepted American Pershing II and cruise missiles, reasserted itself in 1989. In fact, a danger emerged that NATO's nuclear deterrence policy, on which Western Europe's security had rested for forty years, might be undermined by pressure from the German public in response to Gorbachev's call for a nuclear-free Europe. The perceived end to the Cold War thus opened the prospect that NATO might experience a damaging split between its continental partners, led by West Germany and France, and its North Atlantic members—Britain, Canada, and the United States. The massive flight of East Germans to West Germany in the latter half of 1989 heightened pressures on the Bonn government for reunification. A rush to reunification was seen, however, as a potential complication in the process of achieving East-West agreement on mutual reductions in conventional arms, should the United States be forced to withdraw all its nuclear weapons from central Europe.

If the United States and the Soviet Union could reach understanding to avoid confrontations and instead to work toward significant arms reductions, what might this mean to their dealing with numerous regional conflicts, such as an Arab-Israeli confrontation over a Palestinian homeland, an inter-Arab war for control of Persian Gulf oil, civil wars in Afghanistan and Cambodia, a race war in South Africa, and conflict between India and Pakistan over Kashmir? And how would detente affect the efforts of the United

States and other nations to stop the international drug cartel's threat to the stability of several South American countries? If Moscow and Washington were able to agree not to confront one another in Asian, African, and Latin American countries, would these conflicts become less dangerous, or more so? One view was that if the United States relaxed its attitude on various regional tensions, some areas of the world would be more dangerous because no American "peacekeeper" would be present. A U.S. withdrawal from military positions abroad, in order to save money or respond to local political pressures, might embolden certain rulers—Iraq's Saddam Hussein, for example—to employ military force to settle regional disputes. A different view was that if Washington and Moscow refrained from aiding opposing sides in regional conflicts, the contending parties would have more incentive to reach political settlements rather than engage in warfare. Efforts toward peaceful resolution of tensions in Central America in 1989 were cited to support this view.

A relaxation of East-West political rivalry could bring intensification of economic competition among the United States, Europe, Japan, and possibly India for markets and investments and for preeminence in international finance. Implementation of the 1988 U.S.-Canada Free Trade Agreement (FTA) promised to create over ten years a North American free-trade zone involving 285 million people and a possible model for concluding a similar agreement with Mexico. The FTA ensured a deepening of trade links between Canada and the United States and a continuation of their close political relationship. Protectionist sentiment in Congress and President Bush's apparent willingness to accede to pressure on trade issues suggested that economic rivalry among the industrialized powers could grow as East-West tensions dissipated.

A fundamental national issue facing the United States in 1989 was how to reinvigorate productivity in the manufacturing sector and stimulate research and development, particularly in high-tech industries. During the 1970s and 1980s the U.S. public went on a buying spree in consumer products, while the country seriously neglected investment in and modernization of many key industries. As a result, manufacturing companies reduced production, went out of business, or moved overseas because of the high cost of doing business at home. American top management was criticized for paying itself far higher salaries and benefits than its European and Japanese counterparts received. American private savings, among the lowest in the industrialized world, were cited as a major reason for the decline in U.S. competitiveness with other countries, notably Japan and West Germany. Critics charged that unless the government took serious action to restrain U.S. consumption, increase savings and investment, and improve productivity, the continuing imbalance in the U.S. trade account would lead to a declining American living standard. Public realization of an economic decline, they argued, would produce great pressures on Congress for protectionist legislation, and growing indebtedness would lead the U.S. government to become dangerously dependent on the goodwill of other countries and foreign banks. The United States, some experts said, faced a loss of political sovereignty unless the president and Congress corrected this dangerous trend.[2]

Impact on the U.S. Defense Budget

The mood of detente also started a debate in Congress about the size of the defense budget and the armed forces. Secretary of Defense Richard Cheney reluctantly agreed in mid-1989 to accept additional cuts in the defense budget for fiscal year 1990 in order to help the president reach a budget resolution with Congress. These reductions resulted in the cancellation of several new weapons systems and modest reductions in personnel for the Army and the Air Force, plus elimination of one carrier battle group for the Navy. Earlier, Congress had reluctantly agreed to phase out two dozen military facilities in the United States, and there were plans to close more bases at home and overseas.

Growing sentiment in Congress to cut U.S. forces in Europe stemmed from two groups: those who believed that European NATO members were wealthy enough to provide a larger share of their own defense; and those who seemed convinced that in an era of detente and Soviet troop withdrawals, a U.S. standing army in Europe was an anachronism—even a detriment to good relations between Europe and the United States.[3] General Andrew Goodpaster, former Supreme Commander of NATO forces in Europe, called in April 1989 for a negotiated 50 percent reduction in American forces there by the mid-1990s. Redeploying 150,000 American military personnel to the United States over the next five years would produce savings in maintenance and transportation costs for the troops and their dependents; demobilizing those troops would greatly increase the total savings. Under this option, the Air Force would have a lesser role in Europe because its tactical air support would be reduced; the Navy's role in the Mediterranean would shrink; and some Navy and Air Force bases, notably in Greece and Spain, would be reduced or eliminated. Similarly, U.S. bases and the size of American forces in East Asia and the Western Pacific would be sure to come under increasing scrutiny by Congress, particularly bases in South Korea, Japan (including Okinawa), and the Philippines, where reductions would be justified on the grounds that these countries could now provide most of their own defense.

The international changes that occurred in 1989 raised a central question about whether the United States required nearly two million military personnel under arms in the 1990s and whether they needed to be stationed at bases and facilities around the entire globe. To question the extent of U.S. military deployments in Europe, East Asia, and the Indian Ocean region did not suggest a return to isolationism in foreign policy, but it did raise the issue of an overextension of American power and resources, to the detriment of other national needs and priorities. This dilemma was argued with considerable effectiveness by Paul Kennedy in his widely discussed book *The Rise and Fall of the Great Powers*.[4]

Redefining U.S. National Security for the 1990s

In the absence of a clear Soviet military threat to Western Europe and North America, the 1990s would likely witness a shift in American public attention to more insidious threats to national security: for example, the "invasion" of illegal drugs from Latin America and the laundering of billions of dollars in profits by international drug merchants. There could also be a growth in international terrorism sponsored by Middle East leaders who learned that this might be an effective method to influence—even intimidate—European and American governments. In the 1990s, threats to the world's physical environment—ozone depletion, acid rain, destruction of tropical rain forests, and so on—would get more attention from governments concerned about the well-being of their citizens.

None of these threats would affect "national security" under the conventional definition of that term in use since World War II. The Defense Department, in particular, needed to come to grips with the reality that if Mikhail Gorbachev delivered on his pledged reduction of defense budgets, personnel, and military equipment, many of the weapons on which the United States spent huge sums of money would not be transferable to combating drugs, fighting international terrorism, or dealing with dangers to the physical environment. To cite just one example, B-2 Stealth bombers, estimated to cost over $800 million each, had little relevance to the kind of threats to national security that would likely be prevalent in the 1990s. Yet $800 million would buy a great deal of equipment for use in apprehending the ships, planes, and trucks that smuggle huge quantities of drugs into the United States, and of facilities for rehabilitating countless drug addicts who seek help.

President Bush's war on drugs and his appointment of the administration's first drug "czar," William Bennett, focused media attention on the issue and on efforts to promote law enforcement and anti-drug education in American schools. Police officials in major American cities acknowledged, however, that these measures were not in 1989 reducing the availability of drugs on the streets or coping adequately with drug-related crimes. Designation of Washington, D.C., as the nation's "murder capital" received national and world attention, and more than half of the American public told pollsters that drug-related crime was the most important problem facing the United States. If one defined national security to include defense against any threat to the safety of American citizens directed from outside the country, then the massive quantities of drugs coming into the United States, the alarming number of drug-related killings and robberies, and the impact of drugs on the health of tens of thousands of children and adults needed to be viewed as a vital national security threat.

President Bush dramatized the high priority he accorded the anti-drug effort by making his first public address to the American people on this subject in August 1989. His campaign was assisted by President Virgilio Barco of Colombia, who appealed to American citizens to help combat a Colombian drug cartel that had, he said, "declared war" on his government: the cartel had killed more than fifty Colombian judges, had murdered a presidential candidate who opposed them, and was turning Colombia into a safe haven for international drug merchants. Bush gave Bennett wide authority to pool the efforts of many U.S. departments and agencies in the anti-drug campaign, and he allocated over $8 billion for these programs in FY 1990. Some Democratic members of Congress complained that the president was not spending enough to cope with the menace, but Bush countered that state and local authorities and private organizations as well should allocate larger resources to dealing with the crisis. In addition, Secretary of Defense Richard Cheney issued instructions to the Joint Chiefs of Staff to formulate a plan in support of the president's drug war, a move that had been resisted by former Defense Secretary Caspar Weinberger. Part of this effort was to be directed at helping Latin American countries improve their capability to stop the production and transport of cocaine and other drugs. Terrorism and hostage taking by Middle East extremist groups also was certain to get more attention from the Defense Department under the heading of "unconventional warfare."

President Bush knew in 1989 that he could not succeed in foreign policy or domestic affairs without building bridges to Congress, especially since both the Senate and the House of Representatives were controlled by the opposition Democrats. He told the leadership of both houses that he not only would inform them of his foreign policy plans and actions but would consult with them on these matters—as envisioned by the constitutional "advise and consent" provision. During his first three months in office the president was criticized by Democrats and some segments of the media for not having a clear foreign policy agenda or vision of the future, whereas some Republicans thought he had gone too far to accommodate the Democratic leadership, particularly his decision not to request further military aid for the Nicaraguan Contras. Secretary of State-designate James Baker told the Senate Foreign Relations Committee during his confirmation hearing on January 17, 1989 that he hoped Congress would support a realistic and bipartisan approach to foreign policy. He observed that despite many differences between the branches, the government must proceed and that "it is best that we do so together if we are to achieve the national interest."[5]

The key to deciding how the United States should reorient its foreign and national security policies "to achieve the national interest" lay in correctly defining those U.S. interests for the 1990s. This entailed the process of deciding what international priorities should guide the executive and legislative branches as they adopted specific policies, budgets, and personnel requirements for the Defense Department, the State Department, the Intelligence Community, and other U.S. agencies whose function is to promote American economic and business interests abroad. This process would need to engage the best minds in government, business, the academic communities, and the information media. For until the nation achieved a general consensus on what kind of world it wanted to see in the 1990s and the role the United States should play, it would not be possible to agree on a strategy and the policies needed to carry out that strategy. In sum, the Bush administration found a radically transformed world during its first year in office, and redefining U.S. national interests, therefore, was the major preoccupation of the White House during 1989.

1
Defining U.S. National Interests
An Analytical Framework

The term "national interest" has been applied by statesmen, scholars, and military planners since the Middle Ages to the foreign policy and national security goals of nation-states. American presidents and their secretaries of state have invoked the term since the beginning of the republic, and today it is widely used to define the broad purposes of U.S. foreign policy. For example, Ronald Reagan's report to Congress in 1987, titled *National Security Strategy of the United States,* included a section that described: U.S. Interests, Major Objectives in Support of U.S. Interests, and Principal Threats to U.S. Interests. This presidential statement asserted that the strategy it contained "reflects our national interests and presents a broad plan for achieving the national objectives that support those interests."[1] Although the concept is not new, however, there has been much ambiguity about the meaning of the term in scholarly writing. Most scholars have preferred to offer their own definitions of national interest rather than accept formulations proposed by others. Consequently, many definitions may be found in the international relations literature, most of them not particularly useful to clear thinking about the actual formulation of foreign and national security policies.[2]

During the early 1950s a great debate raged in academic circles between the "realist" school, epitomized by Hans J. Morgenthau, and the "idealist" view of national interests, often associated with a former president, Woodrow Wilson. The idealists believed that ethics and morals must play an important part in defining the national interest, and they rejected the realists' assertion that the pursuit of power should be the primary goal of a nation-state. Another debate emerged among the realists about whether there is an objective, unchanging national interest which a nation's leaders pursue, or whether, in American-style democracy, the definition of national interest (or interests) is the end product of a political process and thus subject to periodic change based on national experience.

In the 1960s some American scholars took issue with the "elitist" view that an objective national interest for any country can be identified and acted upon, as Morgenthau and others maintained. Dissenters argued that nations have multiple general interests and that in the American political context they are the result of long debate and negotiation between the president and Congress and among various political groups that hold different views of America's international goals. Among the most prominent of these "constitutionalists" was Paul Seabury, who published *Power, Freedom, and Diplomacy* in 1963. Seabury summed up his view this way: "We might thus conceive of the national interest as a kaleidoscopic process by which forces latent in American society seek to express certain political and economic aspirations in world politics through the highest organs of state. To comprehend this process, we must not merely understand something of the formal governmental processes by which foreign policy is made, but also penetrate into the depth of the nation itself to discern the wellsprings of thought, ideology, and smaller interests that feed into the mainstreams of American policy abroad."[3]

In 1973 I contributed to this debate in a volume titled *United States National Interests in a Changing World*. In reflecting on the intense discussion then taking place over whether Vietnam should have been considered a "vital" U.S. interest, requiring the use of large American forces, I argued that the intensity of an interest in any international dispute, particularly when a vital interest might be at stake, is ultimately decided by debate within the U.S. constitutional system and that the president has the primary, but not exclusive, role in defining the level of an interest.[4] The Vietnam experience proved that Congress possesses the power to override a president's (in this case, Lyndon Johnson's) view of the national interest, and this fact was underscored again in the 1980s when Ronald Reagan was unable to persuade Congress that his perception of a vital U.S. interest in Central America should prevail (see Chapter 4). In 1991 George Bush was successful in persuading Congress to support U.S. intervention in the Persian Gulf (see Chapter 8).

Yet another group of scholars think that "national interest" is too nebulous, too egocentric, or too outdated a concept to contribute anything significant to our understanding of an emerging interdependent world in which the nation-state is losing importance. One of the most influential skeptics in the 1970s was James N. Rosenau, who argued in his book, *The Scientific Study of Foreign Policy*, that neither the "objectivists" nor the "subjectivists," as he labeled proponents of the contending viewpoints, offered an effective rationale for using national interest as a research tool. He concluded: "Despite the claims made for the concept and notwithstanding its apparent utility, the national interest has never fulfilled its early promise as an analytic tool." Attempts by objectivists and subjectivists to use and apply it, he asserted, have proved fruitless or misleading, with the result that although "textbooks on international politics continue to assert that nations act to protect and realize their national interests, the research literature of the field has not been increased and enriched."[5]

Rosenau's criticism is partially correct: few scholars and few practitioners in the foreign policy field have looked systematically at why the United States pursues certain international objectives instead of others. It is too simple to suggest that bureaucratic politics, historical precedent, or economic determinism is the primary basis for deciding what American foreign policy should be. It is more reasonable to conclude, I suggest, that American policy-makers are influenced by geographical, cultural, political, and economic factors that are deeply embedded in the national experience and in the particular ideology of the American people. While it may be true that certain major countries in Europe seem willing to qualify their national sovereignty in the pursuit of an emergent supranational entity called the European Union, this fact refers to a process by which nations disappear and emerge but does not detract from the very notion of national interest itself. The issue here is not what constitutes interests but what constitutes a "nation." So long as any nation has the authority to refuse the demands of another state or international body, one must conclude that it is acting under some notion of what constitutes its national interest. We are now seeing the proliferation of national entities within states—Chechnya, East Timor, Quebec, and Kosovo are examples—which demand, in the name of national identity, independence from their larger countries. Furthermore, so long as political leaders continue to speak in terms of national interests and national priorities, scholars ought to accept some responsibility to help define those interests instead of ignoring the issue.

Nature and Kinds of National Interests

In simplest terms, the fundamental national interest of the United States is the defense and well-being of its citizens, its territory, and the U.S. constitutional system. National interest can be distinguished from the public interest because the latter deals primarily with the internal well-being of the society. The public interest is protected by a set of laws that elected officials are pledged to uphold. The national interest, on the other hand, deals with the external environment, and most sovereign states reserve to themselves the ultimate authority to decide how to function in the international arena—or system, as some prefer to call it. Under the U.S. constitutional system, the president has the primary responsibility to define national interests with the advice and consent of the Senate, and with financial support from the Senate and House. In matters involving the public interest, national authority is more evenly divided among the president, the Congress, and the courts. Public interest and national interest are not mutually exclusive, however. The public interest is heavily influenced by the international environment at a given time, especially during international tensions; the national interest is influenced by the degree of social stability and political unity prevailing in the country, as demonstrated by the post-Vietnam political climate in the United States.

Strategic interests are second-order interests: they are concerned with the political, economic, and military means of protecting the country against military threats. They may be defined in terms of geography, military power, availability or scarcity of resources, science and technology, and damage limitation in time of war. Occasionally, strategic interests tend to determine national interests, rather than the reverse, and in these cases confusion about goals and an overemphasis on military security may result. Private interests are those pursued by business and other organizations operating abroad and needing U.S. government support. As the United States trade deficit grew in the 1980s and 1990s, private business interests assumed a larger role in the assessment of national interests than they had during the 1960s and 1970s.

The United States, like most major powers, has both unchanging and changing national interests: some it has pursued consistently over long periods of time, and others it has followed for shorter periods and then altered because of changing world conditions or a new domestic political environment. Throughout the nation's history four long-term, enduring national interests have conditioned the way the U.S. government viewed the external world and this country's place in it:

1. (1) defense of the United States and its constitutional system;
2. (2) enhancement of the nation's economic well-being and promotion of U.S. products abroad;
3. (3) creation of a favorable world order (international security environment);
4. (4) promotion abroad of U.S. democratic values and the free market system.

For all practical purposes, defending the United States includes defending Canada, Greenland, Iceland, Mexico, and the Caribbean Basin. Within this defense perimeter the United States will exert great pressure, including the use of military force, to prevent a foreign power from establishing military bases, and it will employ covert actions as well as economic sanctions against local governments that may be tempted to ally themselves with a foreign power. President John F. Kennedy's confrontation with General Secretary Nikita Khrushchev in October 1962 over Soviet medium-range nuclear missiles in Cuba demonstrated the importance of this basic interest.

The U.S. interest in economic well-being includes the freedom of Americans to trade and invest abroad, access to foreign markets and natural resources, maintenance of the value of U.S. currency in international financial markets, and preservation of a high standard of living for American citizens. Concerns about persistent trade deficits, the impact of free trade on U.S. industrial workers, and the emergence of the United States as a major debtor country all reflect this interest.

Efforts to create a favorable world order flowed from America's disillusionment with isolationism after 1941 and its determination, following World War II, to create a new international environment in which Europe and East Asia would be peaceful and friendly to the United States. Sponsorship of the United Nations, containment of Soviet power, formation of NATO, and military interventions in Korea, Vietnam, and the Persian Gulf were results of the U.S. postwar interest in building a favorable world order within which Americans could feel secure.

Promoting democratic government and individual rights has been an objective of American diplomacy over much of its history. Between 1945 and 1975, however, this interest received little attention from policymakers, who were so preoccupied with creating a new world order that they did not care much about what kinds of governments the United States allied itself with. In the mid-1970s Congress prevailed on the president, through amendment of foreign aid legislation, to give greater emphasis to human rights when determining foreign assistance policy.

These four basic interests are long-term concerns that rise and fall in importance over decades, rather than months or years, and they compete for public attention and government resources. During the forty-year Cold War period, U.S. world-order interests dominated the time and thinking of American policymakers. In the 1990s, economic well-being and promotion of values were relatively more important than they were in the 1980s.

A National Interest Framework

A correct determination of U.S. national interests lies not primarily in identifying which of its four basic, enduring interests is involved in a given international dispute, but in assessing the intensity of the interest, or stake, the United States has in a specific issue or crisis. To differentiate levels of intensity, four additional terms are employed, as discussed below. These terms, if carefully defined, provide policymakers a clear choice when deciding what is at stake in any foreign policy issue.

"Survival" interests are rare and are relatively easy to identify. A survival interest is at stake when there is an imminent, credible threat of massive destruction to the homeland if an enemy state's demands are not countered quickly. Such crises are easy to recognize because they are dramatic and involve an armed attack, or threat of attack, by one country on another's home territory: Hitler's invasion of Poland in 1939, Germany's bombing of Britain in 1940–1941, North Korea's attack on South Korea in 1950, the Soviet Union's invasion of Afghanistan in 1979, and the U.S. bombing of Serbia in 1999. Iraq's invasion of Kuwait in August 1990 is a dramatic example of a survival interest—for Kuwait. Among the great powers that entered World War II, the United States was the only one whose survival interest was not threatened, even though some argue that Japan's attack on Pearl Harbor falls into this category. All the other powers were either invaded or, in the case of Britain, heavily bombed.

A "vital" interest differs from a survival one principally in the amount of time a country has to decide how it will respond to an external threat. It may involve economic, world-order, and ideological issues, in addition to defense of homeland, and may ultimately be as dangerous to the country as a military attack. But threats to a country's vital interests are potential, even probable, but not imminent dangers. They provide policymakers time to consult allies, to bargain with an adversary, to employ political and economic actions that may alter a trend, and to engage in a show of force warning an adversary that its course may lead to war. These were the policies pursued by President Bush toward Iraq in the summer of 1990 (see Chapter 8), and by President Clinton toward Yugoslavia, regarding Kosovo in 1999 (see Chapter 9).

A vital interest is at stake when an issue is so important to a nation's well-being that its leadership refuses to compromise beyond the point that it considers tolerable. If political leaders decide that they cannot compromise on an issue beyond a certain point and are willing instead to risk economic and military sanctions, the interest is probably vital. Examples are Harry Truman's decision in June 1950 to confront North Korea over its invasion of South Korea; John Kennedy's decision not to permit Soviet missiles in Cuba or elsewhere in the Caribbean; Richard Nixon's decision to take the United States off the gold standard in August 1971 and force U.S. trading partners to accept a devaluation of the dollar; Nixon's decision in October 1973 to alert U.S. forces when the Soviet Union threatened to send paratroopers to Egypt to defend that country against Israel; Jimmy Carter's effort in April 1980 to rescue American hostages in Iran; Ronald Reagan's decision in April 1986 to bomb Libya; George Bush's retaliation against Iraq in August 1990; and Bill Clinton's move in December 1995 to lead a NATO intervention in Bosnia. In sum, a vital stake may involve defense-of-homeland, economic well-being and world-order interests. Rarely, however, would a promotion-of-values interest by itself be viewed at the vital level.

It is important to emphasize that a vital interest is not defined by the kind of policy actions a president chooses in a crisis or serious international dispute: actions are symptoms of the interest's intensity rather than its governor. Occasionally a country's leadership will conclude after deliberation that an issue is a vital one—that is, it has reached the intolerable point—but that no dramatic action is warranted or even possible. Conversely, force may sometimes be used even though the issue involved is not viewed as intolerable, provided a realistic calculation indicates that the costs of using force will be low and the benefits considerable. This was probably the situation when President Reagan decided in October 1983 to invade the Caribbean island of Grenada. It may also have been true of his decision in the summer of 1987 to send more than thirty warships to the Persian Gulf to prevent Iran from establishing its control over shipping there, and it may have been the case when President Clinton sent troops to Haiti in 1994. Fundamentally, a vital interest exists when a country's leadership believes that serious harm will come to the country if it fails to take dramatic action to change a dangerous course of events. Such action may include using economic sanctions and/or conventional military force. The use of nuclear and other weapons of massive destruction, however, would not be authorized unless a survival interest is at stake.

A "major" interest is one that a country considers to be important but not crucial to its well-being. Major interests involve issues and trends, whether they are economic, political, or ideological, that can be negotiated with an adversary. Such issues may cause serious concern and even harm to U.S. interests abroad, but policymakers usually come to the conclusion that negotiation and compromise, rather than confrontation, are desirable—even though the result may be painful. Examples illustrating major interests for the United States have been the Arab oil embargo in 1973, which was a serious but not dangerous threat to the U.S. economy; the 1979 Sandinista revolution in Nicaragua; Moscow's invasion of Afghanistan in 1979; President Reagan's decision not to use force in Lebanon in 1983; President Bush's choice in 1989 not to request additional military assistance for the Nicaraguan Contras; and President Clinton's reluctance to send military forces to Rwanda in 1994. Each case involved a serious challenge to important U.S. interests, but in each one the president decided that the United States could live with an unsatisfactory outcome.

Deciding whether an issue is vital or major is a crucial choice for policymakers, specifically the president. In the final analysis, the difference between a major and a vital interest is what top policymakers believe to be tolerable or intolerable. If the president and his National Security Council believe they can accommodate an undesirable but nevertheless acceptable solution, the issue probably is a major interest. But if a situation becomes so distressing that they are unwilling to compromise further in order to find a solution, then the issue probably is vital. President Bush's demand that Iraq withdraw from Kuwait was that kind of choice in 1990. The same may be said of Bill Clinton's ultimatum to Yugoslavia in 1999 regarding Kosovo.

A "peripheral" interest is one that does not seriously affect the

Table 1. National Interest Matrix

Basic national interest   Intensity of interest

	Survival (critical)	Vital (dangerous)	Major (serious)	Peripheral (bothersome)
Defense of homeland				
Economic well-being				
Favorable world order				
Promotion of values				

well-being of the United States as a whole, even though it may be detrimental to the private interests of Americans conducting business abroad. These issues bear watching by the State Department and other government agencies, but they are a lower order of political, economic, and ideological magnitude. Examples are the imprisonment abroad of American citizens on drug charges, and isolated cases of infringement on U.S. business interests located abroad. The infringement of human rights in other countries was perceived as a peripheral interest by policymakers until the 1970s, when Congress insisted it be accorded a higher priority. President Carter agreed, and Presidents Reagan and Bush continued the policy, albeit with less public display. Cases in which human rights were accorded a major-interest priority involved South Africa and the Philippines, where serious human rights violations occurred in the 1970s and 1980s, and in Haiti, Bosnia, and Kosovo in the 1990s, when President Clinton elevated the importance of this issue.

Utilizing the National Interest Matrix

The core of this conceptual framework for assessing national interests is contained in the matrix shown in Table 1.[6] The policymaker's task is to determine how large a stake the United States has in a specific international issue or crisis—for each of the four basic interests—and then to estimate the intensity of interest that other principal countries have in that issue. Comparing these levels of interest for the major players involved in a dispute permits one to calculate whether the issue at hand is likely to end with negotiations or lead to armed confrontation. Estimates of the interests and intentions of leaders in other countries are, of course, subjective judgments made by diplomats, intelligence specialists, scholars, businessmen, journalists, and others possessing detailed knowledge of the nations involved. Policymakers, however, especially the president and his National Security Council, need to make the fundamental judgment about the intensity of the U.S. interest and then decide whether it is desirable to negotiate further or to threaten hostilities. In the case of a trade issue, the option would more likely be to use economic sanctions rather than military force.

The interest matrix should be viewed as a guide to making wise policy choices in a systematic manner rather than as a sure means of finding the "right" answer. Key foreign policy decisions result from a process in which political leaders make subjective judgments based on their different perceptions of reality. The real value of the interest matrix to decisionmaking is that it encourages policymakers to think through the important criteria they should take into account before deciding that an interest is vital and may therefore require the use of economic and military sanctions.

As an illustration of how the interest matrix may be used as a decisionmaking instrument, consider the Falkland Islands (Malvinas) controversy between Great Britain and Argentina in 1982. This was a case where two U.S. friends, one a NATO ally and the other a member of the Rio Pact, went to war over British-held islands in the South Atlantic. The Reagan administration had to decide whether Argentina's attack on the islands and occupation (liberation) constituted a major interest for the United States or whether the political stakes raised the controversy to the vital level. Britain had exercised sovereignty in the Falklands for 150 years, but Argentina had long pressed its claim that Britain illegally seized them in the 1830s. In April 1982, following several years of fruitless negotiations with Britain, Argentina's military government decided to use force. Britain's Prime Minister Margaret Thatcher was determined to retake the islands by force if negotiations conducted through the United States failed to persuade Argentina to withdraw its invading troops. A Royal Navy task force was quickly dispatched to the South Atlantic to demonstrate London's resolve. Once Britain and Argentina both decided that the Falklands constituted a vital national interest, and neither was willing to back down, war became inevitable.

Table 2. The Falkland Islands War, 1982

Basic interest	Intensity of interest			
	Survival	Vital	Major	Peripheral
Defense of homeland		Argentina	Britain	Venezuela U.S.
Economic well-being			Britain U.S.	Argentina Venezuela
Favorable world order		Britain U.S.	Argentina Venezuela	
Promotion of values		Britain Argentina	U.S. Venezuela	

The problem for the Reagan administration in the Falklands crisis was whether the interest of the United States was major, in which case it should serve only as "honest broker" between two allies, or whether the U.S. interest was vital and required taking sides. After a week of shuttle diplomacy to see whether a negotiated settlement was possible, Secretary of State Alexander Haig advised the president that there was no way of avoiding war when British naval forces reached the Falklands. Reagan then decided to give diplomatic and military support to Britain, despite incurring the hostility of nearly all his Latin American allies—including Venezuela, which strongly supported Argentina's position because of its own territorial claims against Britain. The outcome of this short war was victory for Great Britain, defeat for Argentina, and the ouster of its military government from power. The subsequent transition of Argentina into a constitutional democracy owes some credit to Prime Minister Thatcher, who confronted Argentina's military regime and won.

The interests of four countries with important stakes in the Falklands controversy may be described as follows. Argentina and Britain were the antagonists, and their interests were at the vital level: Argentina's for defense-of-homeland and promotion-of-values reasons, and Britain's for world-order and values purposes. Argentina believed it was defending a piece of Argentine territory as well as its national honor. Britain concluded that defeat in the Falklands would imply weakness in dealing with other world-order issues, such as those in Gibraltar and Hong Kong, and that national honor was involved because Britain viewed Argentina as a third-rate power. In effect, Argentina's occupation of the Falklands was seen by London as an intolerable act that Britain could not accept. The United States and Venezuela were nonbelligerents, but with important interests at stake.

The placement of these four countries on the interest matrix in Table 2 is an approximation of the stakes they had in the controversy. A key factor in the outcome was Reagan's decision to support Britain in this war, following Argentina's refusal to withdraw. In making his decision, the president implicitly decided that the U.S. world-order interest was vital.

Another example of how the interest matrix may be used is the Libyan crisis of April 1986. The Reagan administration had become frustrated over many months with Libyan-sponsored terrorism against American citizens in Europe and the Mediterranean. It laid the blame on Libya's leader, Muammar Khadafy, and finally decided to use military force against him. The immediate cause of the decision to bomb Libyan cities was secret evidence of Libyan complicity in the hijacking of a U.S. airliner and the subsequent bombing of a Berlin nightclub, where several American soldiers were injured. When President Reagan decided to retaliate by bombing Libyan territory, he asked his European allies, specifically Britain and France, to facilitate the mission. Both countries had experienced a growth in Arab-sponsored terrorism, but their governments were reluctant to support military action against Libya. In the end, British Prime Minister Thatcher agreed to permit the United States to use F-111 bombers based in Britain for the raid on Tripoli. France, however, refused consent to an overflight of its territory, and this denial caused Spain to object as well. These negative decisions by two European allies forced the American bombers to fly a circuitous route from Britain around the Strait of Gibraltar and through the Mediterranean to Tripoli, an exceptionally hazardous operation. (U.S. aircraft launched from carriers in the Mediterranean bombed military targets in the Benghazi area, but they were not equipped to handle the heavy bombing on military targets in Tripoli.) Despite the obstacles and many midair refuelings, however, all but one plane completed the mission.[7]

In the United States, public reaction against France was great, but Paris had decided that it had no vital interest in confronting Libya because of extensive French trade and investments there. Although the British government also had serious doubts about using force against Libya, Prime Minister Thatcher decided that

Table 3. U.S. Bombing of Libya, 1986

Basic interest	Intensity of interest			
	Survival	Vital	Major	Peripheral
Defense of homeland	Libya		U.S France Britain	U.S.S.R.
Economic well-being			Libya France U.S.S.R.	U.S. Britain
Favorable world order		U.S. Britain Libya	France U.S.S.R.	
Promotion of values		Libya	U.S. Britain France	U.S.S.R.

her government should support the United States. Some observers suggested that she took this unpopular position to repay President Reagan for his support during the Falkland Islands war. The Soviet Union was a fourth interested party to the crisis because Moscow had sold Libya much military equipment and because it was hosting hundreds of Soviet military advisers. Yet Moscow's interest was never a vital one, and the sudden departure of Soviet ships from Libyan ports before the U.S. attack suggested that Moscow did not wish to risk involvement. Libya, of course, had a survival interest at stake.

An approximation of how five governments viewed their stakes in the Libyan crisis during April 1986 is shown in Table 3. An important question for policymakers to review is this: should the Reagan administration have anticipated that France would not cooperate because its interests were not sufficiently high? A close examination of France's interests might have brought a careful analyst to the conclusion that France would not jeopardize its trade relations with North Africa and that it would not want to be seen as an accomplice of the United States in a military operation outside Europe. The Reagan administration had crossed the line into the vital interest level, however, and was determined to attack no matter what its European allies decided. If the British government had not permitted use of the F-111 bombers, U.S. carrier forces in the Mediterranean could have accomplished most of the mission, but it was politically important in Washington to show that at least one ally supported the Reagan decision to confront Libya on the terrorist issue.

In the cases described above, the president had to decide how deeply U.S. interests were involved and then select appropriate instruments of policy to defend them. In the Falklands case, strong voices were raised within the administration and Congress that the United States should confine its role to diplomacy. U.S. Permanent Representative to the United Nations Jeane Kirkpatrick publicly expressed this view, as did Senator Jesse Helms of North Carolina. In effect, they argued that the Falkland Islands issue was at best a major U.S. interest and that intervention to help the British would severely strain U.S. relations with Latin America. President Reagan, supported by Secretary of State Haig and Secretary of Defense Weinberger, believed that solidarity with Great Britain in what was clearly a vital British interest made the Falklands a derivative vital interest for the United States. In the case of Libya, the State Department had sought for a year by diplomacy to persuade its government, as well as that of Syria and the Palestine Liberation Organization, to stop terrorist acts against Americans. By April 1986 the Reagan White House had determined that the situation was intolerable: Middle East terrorism had reached the vital level and must be forcefully dealt with. The tactics of accomplishing a military strike against Libya were of secondary importance to the basic decision that the Libyan government needed to be jolted by force. The bombing raids had the desired effect—that is, terrorist acts subsided measurably thereafter—even though the hoped for toppling of Khadafy's government did not result.

Criteria for Determining a Vital National Interest

A crucial ingredient in assessing the national interests of sovereign states is appreciating the difference between a vital interest and a major one. The policy implications of choosing between them are fundamental because a country must be prepared for an armed confrontation, if other measures fail, once its leaders have decided that the issue at stake is vital. Survival interests are less difficult to identify because they are implicit in situations where an imminent danger of attack on the homeland exists. As in the Cuban Missile Crisis of 1962, a crisis atmosphere usually already exists. Similarly, policymakers generally know what issues are peripheral because they are not important enough to call for forceful action.

The most difficult decisions, then, the ones that consume the National Security Council's time, are those located on the threshold between major and vital interests. These involve deciding whether the U.S. stake in a foreign policy problem is so great and the opposing side's position so adamant that resolution through negotiation and compromise appears doubtful. If the president and his advisers conclude that additional compromise would be intolerable for the U.S. position, the issue at hand is vital.

The term "vital interest" has been used so loosely by policymakers, military planners, and politicians, however, that it may be confusing when applied to specific issues. It is highly desirable that policy planners and scholars adopt specific criteria for defining the term when they apply it to a national interest, whether to defense of homeland, economic well-being, favorable world order, or promotion of values abroad. The following definition may be helpful in promoting greater precision: *An interest is vital when the highest policymakers in a sovereign state conclude that the issue at stake is so fundamental to the political, economic, and social well-being of their country that it should not be compromised—even if this conclusion results in the use of economic and military sanctions.* In arriving at such a judgment, national leaders base their assessments on many factors, including intuition. But a more rigorous standard is required if the United States is to avoid repeating the miscalculations that occurred in the Vietnam War, the Lebanon peacekeeping operation in 1982–1983, the Iran arms-for-hostages episode in 1985–1986, and the bombing of Kosovo in 1999.

Table 4 presents sixteen criteria that may be used to ascertain whether a foreign policy issue is vital. Eight of these are "value factors" that policymakers believe are important to defending and enhancing U.S. national interests, and eight are "cost/risk factors" that too often are underestimated or ignored during crucial foreign policy deliberations. This listing does not imply a priority of relative importance; rather, it suggests that each factor should be considered in relation to a serious foreign policy matter *before* the label "vital" is attached to it.[8]

These value and cost/risk factors may be evaluated by policymakers in several ways. A simple one is to rate each factor as high, medium, or low. If the sum of the value factors is high and the sum of the cost/risk factors is low or medium, the level of

Table 4. Criteria for Determining Vital National Interests

Value factors	Cost/risk factors
Proximity of the danger	Economic costs of hostilities
Nature of the threat	Estimated casualties
Economic stake	Risk of enlarged conflict
Sentimental attachment	Cost of protracted conflict
Type of government aided	Cost of defeat or stalemate
Effect on balance of power	Adverse international reaction
National prestige at stake	Cost of U.S. public opposition
Support of key allies	Risk of congressional opposition

interest is more than likely to be vital. Numerical scores may also be attached, but some factors clearly will be more important than others in any given situation. For example, "balance of power" is more important in national security issues than in economic ones; "sentimental attachment" is more important in issues affecting ethnic minorities within the United States—such as those relating to Israel, southern Africa, Cyprus, and Mexico, for example—because of U.S. domestic political considerations. Whatever method is used, however, political leaders need to understand the potential costs of confronting another country on a political, economic, or security issue. Their failure to do so may lead to serious mistakes in deciding, for example, how to wage a war in Vietnam, how to keep peace in Lebanon, how to dislodge a Communist government in Nicaragua, how to oust a military dictator in Panama or in Iraq, and how to persuade a Yugoslav leader to withdraw from Kosovo. A careful use of the interest matrix and the criteria suggested here should lead to more effective decisionmaking in American foreign policy.

Instruments of Foreign and National Security Policy

Defining the nature and intensity of national interests in specific cases is the critical first step in formulating U.S. foreign and national security policies, and the interest matrix provides a frame-

Table 5. Instruments of Foreign and National Security Policy

Political/Economic Instruments
      1. Diplomatic relations
      2. Scientific and cultural exchanges
      3. Humanitarian assistance
      4. Technical assistance
      5. Information and propaganda
      6. Economic and financial assistance
      7. Economic and trade policy
      8. Military assistance
      9. Covert actions
      10. UN Security Council debate
      11. Trade embargo and economic sanctions
Political/Military Instruments
      12. Military show of strength
      13. Increased military surveillance
      14. Suspension or break in diplomatic relations
      15. Quarantine, blockade, or mining of ports
      16. Local use of conventional military force
      17. Mobilization and evacuation of U.S. population
      18. Local use of tactical nuclear weapons
      19. Threatened use of massive-destruction weapons
      20. Demonstration use of massive-destruction weapons

work for doing so. The policymaker's next task is to select the instruments or tools of policy appropriate to the level of interest at stake, and to resist using other instruments simply because they are available. Taking no action is also a policy and may be useful in some circumstances, but if an interest borders on vital, it is rare that no action will be taken to demonstrate serious concern. Occasionally, even when a nation's interest is high, its government may lack the means of defending it appropriately. If this occurs frequently, the country may lose its independence or simply be ignored by other states. Alliances are formed out of such national needs and vulnerabilities, as conclusion of the North Atlantic Treaty demonstrated in the case of Western European governments in 1949.

Great powers, especially superpowers, may employ a large variety of political, economic, and military measures to influence the policies of other states. These range from diplomatic recognition to preparation for and warning of the imminence of nuclear war. Table 5 lists twenty actions—policy instruments—that are available to a president and his National Security Council to deal with opportunities for and threats to U.S. national interests. They are arranged in ascending order of the influence or pressure that may be brought to bear on another country's foreign policy decisions. The first eleven actions are political/economic instruments, and the last nine are political/military actions that may be taken.[9]

In the 1980s the Reagan administration used many of the political/military instruments of policy. In 1983–1984 it even increased the likelihood of using nuclear weapons in Europe, if deterrence failed, by introducing into West Germany, Italy, and Great Britain—with NATO's consent—Pershing II and cruise missiles. Following Mikhail Gorbachev's rise to power in the Soviet Union and the detente relationship he established with Ronald Reagan in 1986–1987, the prospect of war and the use of political/military instruments in Europe receded. Increasing trade tensions between the United States and Japan and between the United States and the European Union, however, meant that in the 1990s political/economic instruments were employed more frequently to defend U.S. economic interests. The Bush administration used both economic and military instruments in toppling the dictatorship of General Manuel Noriega in Panama in 1989. An even greater challenge for U.S. national interests took place in the Middle East during the summer of 1990 when Iraq invaded and annexed neighboring Kuwait. The manner in which President Bush responded to that crisis and his employment of these instruments of policy are discussed in Chapter 8. In the mid-1990s President Clinton used both economic sanctions and military means to stop a civil war in Bosnia and contain a dangerous government in Iraq.

National Interests and Private Corporation Interests

The purpose of this chapter has been to outline a method for defining U.S. national interests in a rapidly changing world. Without going into extensive detail, I should like to suggest also that executives of U.S. international corporations may adapt this framework to their assessment of investment interests abroad. Table 6 is a revision for this purpose of the interest matrix shown in Table 1.[10] Similarly, the value and cost/risk factors outlined in Table 4 may be adapted for use by corporations when they must decide whether to make large investments in specific foreign countries.

What is suggested here is that U.S. international corporations have business interests and objectives that are comparable with,

Table 6. International Corporation Interest Matrix

Basic corporation interest	Intensity of international interest			
	Survival	Vital	Major	Peripheral
Protection of share-holders' equity				
Increase in profits on investment				
Enhancement of market share				
Advancement of corporate core values				

often complementary to, the national interests of the U.S. government. A corporation executive has as his bottom line the question of whether an investment in country X will add to the corporation's growth and profitability and enhance its market share. A U.S. foreign policymaker's principal consideration is whether a proposed policy will contribute to U.S. defense, economic well-being, and a more stable world order. In the 1990s with the Cold War over, there emerged a larger community of interest between U.S.-based international corporations and U.S. foreign policy decisionmakers to build a more favorable global economic system.

Summing Up

National interest, properly defined, is an exceptionally useful way to understand the foreign policy goals of nation-states. The conceptual framework outlined in this chapter provides an analytical tool for scholars who examine critical historical events in international politics and answer the "why" questions about the actions taken. An even more important use of the framework is in foreign policy and national security planning, because that is where the greatest need and most ambiguity lie. The interest matrix is not intended as a scientific method to produce the right answers to foreign policy dilemmas, but it does force policymakers to consider systematically the values they hope to uphold and the costs that might have to be paid to achieve an objective. In short, this is a road map for good policymaking, not a guarantee of choosing the wisest course. Foreign policy decisionmaking is an art, not a science, and human beings still make subjective judgments about what should be done in specific cases. Yet, it is desirable that we become more precise than we have been about ends and means, and more realistic about the consequences of policy decisions. This framework provides a mechanism for doing so.

2
Era of American Preeminence, 1945–1965

For twenty years after World War II the United States was the pre-eminent power in international relations, and it undertook to create a new world order in which American political, economic, and security interests would be enhanced. Like those in the 1920s and early 1930s, America's postwar leaders perceived no direct military threat to North America. They therefore adopted a strategy of forward defense, first in Europe and then in Asia, to contain an expansionist Soviet Union, which was seen as the only great power with both hostile intentions and the potential capability of threatening U.S. territory. For purposes of analysis, this twenty-year period may be divided into four distinct segments that correspond to significant changes in the international political environment and to United States responses: postwar idealism (1945–1946); first Cold War (1947–1954); experimentation with detente (1955–1960); renewed cold war (1961–1965). The perceptions of U.S. postwar interests held by four American presidents—Truman, Eisenhower, Kennedy, Johnson—and the policies they adopted to enhance them worldwide are the focus of this chapter.

Postwar Idealism, 1945–1946

The mood in the United States during the immediate postwar period may be summed up in two words: euphoria and optimism. Military victory over Nazi Germany in May 1945 and Imperial Japan three months later persuaded the American public that the United States had emerged from four years of war as an undisputed winner and that no foreign threat remained to divert the country from the domestic priorities that had been subordinated during the war. America's possession of the awesome atomic weapon reinforced a belief that the United States was the number-one power in the world, and most Americans thought it would remain so for an indefinite future. The United Nations, which the United States was instrumental in organizing in 1945, provided hope that world peace could be maintained without recourse to war. In 1945 Great Britain and the Soviet Union were viewed as good allies in helping to defeat the Fascist powers.

Only a few political voices, mainly those of conservative Republicans, expressed concern that the Soviet Union under Stalin was also a dictatorship, with the professed aim of communizing the entire world. Although Harry Truman, who entered the White House upon the death of Franklin Roosevelt in April 1945, had serious doubts during 1945 and 1946 about Stalin's intentions in Europe, he did not feel strong enough politically to express these misgivings publicly. Consequently, the euphoria and optimism of the period led to the near-dismantling of U.S. military forces, including the mightiest navy and air force the world had ever seen. It also led to the abrupt termination of the wartime Lend-Lease aid programs to Britain and the Soviet Union. Some optimists believed that the United States had entered a period of serene detachment from the cares of the world.

A principal objective of postwar U.S. policy was the destruction of German and Japanese war-making capability and a rebuilding of those societies along democratic lines. A second objective was the creation of a new world economic order that would reduce protective tariffs and exchange barriers, expand trade with Europe and Latin America, and open the way to major U.S. investment abroad. A third objective was the removal of the age-old rivalries and hostilities that had characterized prewar relations in Western Europe—among Great Britain, Germany and France—and had resulted in two world wars in a generation. The first priority in accomplishing European reconciliation was a political agreement between Germany and France to end their intense rivalry for supremacy on the continent. American policy in this postwar period therefore accorded a higher priority to accommodating France's strong need to reassert its international role than to supporting independence movements in Vietnam, Laos, and Cambodia.

The first major notice given to a potential Soviet military threat to Western Europe occurred in March 1946 when former British Prime Minister Winston Churchill delivered his famous "Iron Curtain" speech in Fulton, Missouri, in the presence of President Truman. The press and many members of Congress called

Churchill an alarmist because they saw no real evidence of hostile Soviet intentions toward Western Europe. Some Republicans deplored what they called President Roosevelt's Yalta "sellout" in February 1945 because the agreement reached by Roosevelt, Churchill, and Stalin allegedly provided U.S. acquiescence to Moscow's domination of Poland and other Eastern European countries. Yet it was exceedingly difficult in 1946 for Truman to persuade the optimistic American public that the country's wartime Soviet ally was a threat to Western Europe and needed to be confronted. Adding to the difficulty was a growing political conflict within the Democratic Party, between President Truman and Secretary of Commerce Henry Wallace, for party control. Wallace, who represented the liberal left of the Democratic Party, was far more sympathetic to the Soviet Union than was Truman and stated his views openly following Roosevelt's death. In 1946, after Wallace publicly disagreed with the president's hardening policy toward Moscow regarding Eastern Europe and Iran, Truman asked for his resignation. Wallace then campaigned vigorously against Truman's foreign policy and in 1948 became the presidential nominee of the new leftist Progressive Party.

One area beyond North America where the United States accepted a defense alliance was Latin America: in 1947 the Truman administration concluded the Rio Pact, a treaty pledging the nations of the Western Hemisphere (except Canada) to come to the aid of one another in case of an external threat to any of its signatories. In addition, the Panama Canal remained securely in U.S. hands, in accordance with a 1903 treaty specifying U.S. control in perpetuity. In the Pacific the United States gave the Philippines independence in 1946, the first colonial power to grant an Asian colony such status. In return, the Philippines provided extensive military facilities from which the United States maintained its role as a Pacific power. American occupation forces under the direction of General Douglas MacArthur were in charge of rebuilding Japan along democratic, nonmilitary lines. U.S. occupation forces were also in South Korea but were withdrawn in 1948. In Europe, U.S. occupation forces shared with Britain, France, and the Soviet Union the responsibility of controlling a defeated Germany.

Looking at this early postwar period from the perspective of the four basic U.S. interests described in Chapter 1 permits the following assessment.

Defense of Homeland. No foreign military power threatened the territory of the United States or its immediate neighbors in North America. The country possessed a monopoly on atomic weapons, and most of its armed forces could safely be demobilized while maintaining modest occupation units in Europe and East Asia. In the North American heartland the United States retained forces in Panama, Cuba, and Puerto Rico, and it continued its close wartime defense links with Canada.

Economic Well-being. In economic relations the United States ended World War II owing nearly half of the world's productive capacity and much of its wealth. The task was to stimulate world trade and promote free markets in order to help the industrial world recover from war and be able to buy American products. An international monetary system (IMF) was established under the United Nations to coordinate economic relationships among major trading countries, and a World Bank was set up to provide long-term credit and investment. American private capital invested heavily in foreign markets.

Favorable World Order. With respect to promoting a more peaceful world, the United States was the guiding force behind the establishment of the United Nations in 1945. In 1945–1946 the Soviet Union was not yet a serious threat to the stability of Western Europe or the Middle East; however, Moscow's negative response to U.S. plans to rebuild Germany's shattered economy and the ruthless incorporation of Poland into the Soviet sphere of influence made the Soviet Union a potential threat. Other important U.S. world-order interests were to encourage rapprochement between Germany and France; to help Great Britain remain a major power in East Asia, the Middle East, and Africa; and to rebuild the German and Japanese economies so that these defeated enemies would eventually be strong partners of the United States in resisting future threats to the world order.

Promotion of Values. Finally, the United States had a strong interest in building democracy in Germany, Italy, and Japan and in challenging the imposition of communism in Eastern Europe. Although Roosevelt had favored a strong anticolonial policy, the Truman administration deemphasized the traditional U.S. policy of self-determination. In effect, Truman emphasized U.S. world-order interests over promotion-of-values considerations in the conduct of his foreign policy.

U.S. interests and policies in the immediate postwar period demonstrated some ambivalence because the public preference, reflected in the attitude of Congress, was to return to a peacetime agenda, whereas President Truman viewed with growing concern Stalin's moves in Eastern Europe and the Soviet occupation zone in Germany. The public mood in the United States did not suggest a return of pre–World War II isolationism but instead a self-confident detachment based on the widespread perception that America faced no serious foreign dangers. It was a period when effective national leadership was urgently required.

The First Cold War, 1947–1954

Although Winston Churchill warned the United States in March 1946 that Stalin was determined to extend Soviet domination over Western Europe, the American public was not yet ready to hear that message. Early in 1947, however, the mood in Washington suddenly changed, as it became clear that Stalin was not only tightening Moscow's grip on Eastern Europe but also pressuring Turkey and Greece to permit the extension of Soviet influence into the Eastern Mediterranean. Stalin also refused to cooperate with Britain, France, and the United States in administering the four occupied zones of Germany and continued to demand huge German war reparations, which ultimately could be met only by large economic aid from the United States. The new secretary of state, retired General George Marshall, attended a fateful foreign ministers' meeting in Moscow in March 1947 and returned to Washington persuaded that Stalin was determined to undermine the Western position in Germany and subvert the governments of Western Europe. France and Italy had coalition governments including their Communist parties, and Communists controlled the powerful French and Italian labor federations.

The U.S. foreign policy establishment, consisting of many New York and Washington bankers, businessmen, and lawyers, exerted great influence in Congress and on the media with the warning that Western Europe, for which the United States had just fought a costly war, was in danger of economic collapse and might succumb to internal Communist and external Soviet pressures. George Kennan, a career Foreign Service officer who had been stationed in Moscow during the war, was the leading catalyst in promoting a new realism in dealing with postwar Russia. During 1946–1947 Kennan was assigned to the National War College in

Washington and delivered a series of lectures that laid out the rationale for his celebrated "containment" strategy for restraining the Soviet Union. He wrote these views in a famous "Mr. X" article for *Foreign Affairs* in its summer issue of 1947. Kennan's views fit well with the predisposition of President Truman, Secretary of State Marshall, and the military services to confront Stalin's aggressive policies with U.S. economic and military power.

Early in 1947, before President Truman had decided on a new policy for Western Europe, he faced a potential crisis in the Eastern Mediterranean with the cessation of Britain's substantial aid programs in Greece and Turkey. The Labour government of British Prime Minister Clement Attlee advised Washington that it could no longer provide aid to Greece in that country's civil war with a Soviet-supported insurgency, or help Turkey resist Stalin's demands for changes in a treaty governing the straits between the Black Sea and the Mediterranean. On March 12, 1947, Truman proposed to Congress a startling plan for emergency economic and military aid to those countries to help them resist Soviet intimidation. He justified this initiative by citing America's responsibility to defend freedom wherever it was under attack by international communism. This was the first postwar U.S. decision to commit U.S. military and economic aid outside the Western Hemisphere to contain Soviet military power. The president's policy became known as the Truman Doctrine and eventually proved to be successful in thwarting Moscow's designs on Greece and Turkey.

The Truman administration's second major foreign policy initiative in 1947 was the Marshall Plan. Designed to rebuild the war-shattered European economies, it consisted of a massive U.S. economic aid program to restore Europe's industrial infrastructure and stabilize deteriorating domestic political situations, particularly in France and Italy. An implicit understanding for receipt of Marshall Plan aid was that European governments would not include Communists. France and Italy soon reorganized their governments and excluded members of the Communist parties.

The Truman aid program for Greece and Turkey and the Marshall Plan for Western Europe underscored what had been apparent in Truman's thinking for nearly a year: wartime cooperation with Moscow would not continue into the postwar period because Stalin believed he could eventually impose his will on Western Europe as he had on Eastern Europe. European and American proponents of Marshall Plan aid initially offered participation to the Soviet Union and the countries of Eastern Europe, but Moscow rejected the plan in the summer of 1947. Czechoslo-vakia, unlike other Eastern European countries, was not under Communist control at that time and expressed interest in joining the U.S.-sponsored plan. This put its government in conflict with Moscow on a fundamental issue: Stalin's determination to seal off Eastern Europe from the capitalist economies of the West. The growing split between Moscow and Prague culminated in Febru-ary 1948 in a *coup d'etat* that put the Czech Communist Party in full control of the government. Russian troops had not remained in the country after World War II, but they were massed on the Czech border during the February crisis, poised to intervene. The coup sent shock waves throughout Europe and the United States and persuaded President Truman to ask Congress for a substan-tial increase in the military budget and an expansion of the armed forces. Britain, France, Belgium, the Netherlands, and Luxem-bourg concluded the Brussels Pact, which pledged mutual assis-tance in case of a Soviet attack. The Cold War had officially begun.

Attention then turned to Berlin, the former German capital administered by the four occupying powers—Britain, France, the United States and the Soviet Union. Located deep inside the So-viet occupation zone of Germany, Berlin was vulnerable to Soviet interference with ground transportation links to the Western zones of Germany, without which the position of British, French, and U.S. forces in Berlin would be untenable. In March 1948 Mos-cow sealed off East Berlin from the Western sectors of the city in retaliation for a currency reform instituted by the Western allies in their occupation zones. In June the Soviet military command in Germany announced a suspension of road and rail travel between Berlin and the Western zones because of "repairs." Moscow was testing Washington's resolve over Berlin and appeared willing to risk war in order to prevent the division of Germany into two political and economic systems, one Communist and the other capitalist. This division would deny Stalin his goal of exercising control over all of Germany and tying its economic power to the Soviet Union, a primary objective of Stalin.

General Lucius Clay, American commander in Germany, rec-ommended that force be used to open the highways and rails to Berlin. But President Truman decided instead on a gigantic allied airlift, not only to supply American forces in Berlin but also to sustain the West Berlin economy. Moscow finally lifted the block-ade in May 1949 because it became an embarrassment and be-cause the Western allies retaliated by imposing tight sanctions against exports from Eastern Europe. In addition, the Berlin blockade stiffened Western Europe's determination to proceed with economic rehabilitation under the Marshall Plan and to form security links with the United States through the new North Atlantic Treaty, signed in April 1949. European and American leaders also agreed to conclude a peace agreement with West Germany and eventually bring the new entity into political as well as economic association with the West.

In April 1949 the United States thus entered its first peacetime military alliance with Western Europe in order to prevent the Soviet Union from subverting the weak countries one by one. In doing so, Washington abandoned a century-old policy of eschewing entangling foreign alliances and pledged to resist a Soviet attack on Western Europe as if it were defending American territory. Although the North Atlantic Treaty Organization (NATO), with its military structure, did not come into being until 1951, the signing of the pact in 1949 left no doubt in Soviet or West European minds that U.S. military power was now irrevocably committed to the preservation of democratic governments in Western Europe. In effect, the United States was declaring that Western Europe was a vital U.S. national interest.

The year 1949 was a momentous one also in East Asia, where the Chinese Red Army defeated the Nationalist forces of General Chiang Kai-shek and on October 1 proclaimed the People's Republic of China. Chiang and his Nationalist troops fled to Taiwan (then called Formosa) and established a regime that they claimed as the legitimate government of all China. In February 1950 Communist Party Chairman Mao Zedong traveled to Moscow and concluded a military pact and mutual assistance agreement with Josef Stalin. The so-called Sino-Soviet bloc was thus formed, and the news of the deal had a profound political effect in the United States, where congressional Republicans accused Truman of "losing China." It also put an end to the State Department's "wait and see" policy toward Beijing. The United States refused to recognize officially the new regime, as Britain, Canada, and other governments had done. This sharp turn of events in Asia moved the Truman administration for the first time to provide military assistance to France for its antiinsurgency effort in Indochina, designed to defeat Communist Vietminh forces led by their Moscow-trained leader, Ho Chi Minh. Truman also launched a fundamental review of U.S. foreign policy, which became known as NSC-68. It recommended a vastly increased U.S. effort on a worldwide scale to contain not only the Soviet Union but also the potential power of the new People's Republic of China (PRC).

On June 24, 1950, North Korean troops, armed with Soviet weapons, launched a massive attack across the border into South Korea and within days captured Seoul, its capital. These Communist troops then began a drive to conquer the entire Korean peninsula and unite both parts under Hanoi's rule. President Truman quickly concluded that such an attack could not have been launched without Stalin's complicity, and he ordered U.S. troops stationed in Japan to defend South Korea. General Douglas MacArthur, the military governor in Japan, was placed in charge of U.S. forces. After the United Nations condemned the aggression and authorized member states to send forces to provide for the common defense under Article 51 of its charter, MacArthur was designated United Nations commander as well. In November 1950 China entered this undeclared war after MacArthur's troops defeated North Korea's army and then proceeded, with Truman's and the UN's concurrence, to invade North Korea and move toward the Yalu River border with China. MacArthur, who hoped to unify the entire Korean nation under a non-Communist government, had dismissed warnings that Beijing might intervene if its border was approached. China's intervention shocked Washington and the Western allies and reinforced Truman's view that Stalin was using Korea as a diversion for a potential attack on Western Europe. With congressional agreement, Truman put the United States on a wartime footing in order to prepare for a Soviet move against Berlin and, possibly, West Germany. He called World War II hero General Dwight Eisenhower out of retirement and sent him to organize Western Europe's defenses for a military confrontation with Soviet forces. The NATO countries then appointed Eisenhower Supreme Allied Commander of NATO forces in Europe.

In 1952 Eisenhower returned to the United States, again retired from the army, and became the Republican nominee for president. During the campaign he pledged to go to Korea and bring a quick end to the war there. Following his election in November, he did travel to Korea and then secretly warned the Communist powers that he would consider using atomic weapons to force a halt in the war. By the spring of 1953 the fighting in Korea had stopped, and a cease-fire was negotiated which left the country divided roughly where it had been in June 1950. A peace accord confirming the arrangement was signed in Geneva the following year.

The Korean War hastened the review of U.S. foreign policy and national security requirements for the 1950s and caused a substantial increase in the defense budget and the size of the armed forces. It also resulted in a series of defense pacts with many Asian countries as part of the new policy to contain Asian communism. Military and economic assistance were provided to non-Communist Asian states, and the U.S. military presence in the Western Pacific was substantially enlarged. A peace treaty with Japan, negotiated and approved in 1951, provided for U.S. military bases in Japan and Okinawa (which later was returned to Japanese sovereignty). The United States also signed defense treaties with Taiwan, South Korea, and the Philippines, and a pact with Australia and New Zealand that became known as ANZUS. In addition, Washington provided economic and military assistance to Thailand and substantially increased aid to French forces fighting the communists in Indochina. Indonesia, which the Truman administration had helped to obtain independence from the Netherlands in 1949, was courted by the State Department, but no military agreement was concluded because Indonesian President Sukarno wanted to remain non-aligned. Great Britain continued its colonial ties with Malaya and Singapore and the northern part of Borneo.

President Truman thus sought to forge a containment policy for China in both Southeast and Northeast Asia, and he tried to keep Britain and France fully engaged in this undertaking. In fact, containing China became as vital a U.S. interest in Asia as containment of the Soviet Union was in Europe. In just five years, from 1947 to 1952, the United States had moved from an alliance-free foreign policy to one of global military commitments.

Before Truman's containment-of-China policy was fully implemented, however, the Democratic Party lost control of the White House for the first time in twenty years. Two months after President Eisenhower's inauguration in 1953, a momentous event occurred in postwar international politics: Josef Stalin, the Soviet Union's dictator for nearly thirty years, died suddenly. His death ushered in a period of uncertainty in Soviet internal affairs, and his political heirs established a troika leadership as the Communist Party wrestled with the transition problem. Winston Churchill, who had returned as Britain's prime minister in 1951, urged Eisenhower to seize this opportunity to find ways of easing Cold War tensions with Moscow.

Eisenhower at that time had serious political problems with

the right wing of the Republican Party, led by Senator Joseph McCarthy of Wisconsin, which opposed any negotiations with Communist countries. These archconservatives fought the 1952 election campaign by blaming Truman and Secretary of State Dean Acheson for the Korean War and for the Sino-Soviet threat in Asia. They called for "rolling back the Iron Curtain" and denounced the idea of a Republican president negotiating with any Soviet leadership, which some of them said bordered on treason. They also championed the cause of the Chinese Nationalists on Taiwan against the Communist government in Beijing.

The president and his secretary of state, John Foster Dulles, were therefore not prepared in 1953 to explore potential changes in Soviet policy, and the administration's strong anti-Communist stance continued into 1954. Nevertheless, Eisenhower chose not to send U.S. military forces to Indochina to aid the French colonial troops that were under siege in early 1954 by Communist forces at Dien Bien Phu. That refusal contributed to France's decision to negotiate peace with Hanoi and to recognize, in July 1954, the creation of independent neutral states in Laos and Cambodia. Vietnam was divided into two administrative zones, with the northern half controlled by the Communist government in Hanoi and the southern part by non-Communist factions based in Saigon.

The Geneva peace accord on Indochina was a political embarrassment for the Eisenhower administration because it entailed turning over to Vietnamese Communists roughly half the territory previously controlled by France. It seemed to prepare the way for expansion of communism elsewhere in Southeast Asia, notably in Cambodia, Laos, and Thailand. The United States refused to sign the peace agreement, thus leaving open the question whether provision for elections within two years to unify the country would be honored. When Ngo Dinh Diem became de facto leader of South Vietnam in 1955, he renounced the election idea and established a separate government in the South with himself as president. Eisenhower gave him political support and substantial economic assistance.

The sequel to the U.S. humiliation over the division of Vietnam (similar to the situation in Korea) was Washington's plan to forge a Southeast Asia containment policy to prevent the further extension of Communist influence there. The vehicle was the Southeast Asia Mutual Security Pact, concluded in Manila in September 1954 by the United States, Britain, France, Australia, New

Zealand, the Philippines, Thailand, and Pakistan. The treaty pledged the signatories to defend one another against Communist aggression, and it contained a protocol providing for consultation and possible action in case Laos, Cambodia, or South Vietnam were threatened by Communist forces. The Manila Pact, later called the Southeast Asia Treaty Organization (SEATO), was the Eisenhower administration's way of telling the world that although it was unwilling to aid France militarily to retain its colonial control in Indochina, Washington would pledge its resources to prevent any other part of Southeast Asia from falling under Communist domination. Like the North Atlantic Pact for Europe, the Manila Pact was a signal that the United States considered the security of Southeast Asia to be a vital national interest and that it would use military force to uphold that interest.

The Manila Pact was also notable for the countries that did not choose to become members. Even though the agreement's purpose was to protect Southeast Asia, only two states in that region—Thailand and the Philippines—joined. Indonesia under President Sukarno chose instead to be associated with the Nonaligned Nations, and he hosted a conference of this group at Bandung in 1955. Burma also reaffirmed its neutrality policy and rejected overtures from Washington. India under Prime Minister Jawaharlal Nehru was opposed to both Western and Eastern blocs, but he accepted economic aid from both. Pakistan was more fearful of India than of China, but it joined SEATO because it believed that doing so would help it to obtain substantial amounts of military and economic aid from the United States. France was a reluctant participant because it resented Eisenhower's refusal to support its position in Vietnam; but it also desired U.S. backing for its policies in Europe and in North Africa. Britain, along with Australia and New Zealand, joined SEATO because the Commonwealth had a stake in defending Malaya, Singapore, and North Borneo from internal Communist insurgencies and from growing Indonesian aggressiveness.

Thus, a truce emerged in 1954 in the East-West struggle for power in Asia. By a separate agreement, the Communist regime in North Korea remained in its position, and a new Communist regime was established in North Vietnam after seven years of anticolonial war against the French. The United States refused to establish diplomatic relations with the People's Republic of China, however, and continued to insist that the Nationalist government on Taiwan was the legitimate leadership for all of China. Significantly, Thailand and Pakistan were added to the list of Asian countries the United States was pledged to defend, and Washington was on the verge of providing military and economic assistance to Laos, Cambodia, and South Vietnam. What had begun in 1947 as Truman's effort to save Greece from a Communist takeover had expanded, during Eisenhower's presidency, into a worldwide alliance system. The magnitude of the shift in U.S. interests and policy in only seven years was breathtaking.

At the end of 1954, nine years after the end of World War II, U.S. national interests could reasonably be assessed as follows.

Defense of Homeland. Although the Soviet Union had acquired atomic weapons and was building a thermonuclear capability, there was no direct military threat to the homelands of the United States or its North American neighbors. Canada and the United States retained a close military relationship, and Mexico was a stable, reasonably friendly country. U.S. forces in the Panama Canal Zone insured security in the Caribbean area. The only challenge to U.S. hegemony in North America—a Marxist-oriented government in Guatemala—was ousted during 1954 with covert assistance from the Eisenhower administration. It was a period when the safety of the North American region was taken for granted.

Economic Well-being. Western Europe was on its way to full economic recovery by 1954, and U.S. exports were in demand throughout the world. Japan was restoring its economy and expanding trade. The American dollar remained the primary international currency, and the World Bank, the International Monetary Fund, and other international financial institutions were heavily influenced by U.S. policy. The U.S. economy was sound and growing at a good pace.

Favorable World Order. The United States had decided in 1947 to take a leading role in shaping a new world order that would be favorable to American political, economic, and security needs. This decision included playing a major role in Western Europe (Marshall Plan), the Eastern Mediterranean (Greece and Turkey), and the Western Pacific (Philippines and Japan). By 1954, in the name of containing the new Sino-Soviet bloc, U.S. world-order interests were expanded to include Thailand and South Vietnam in Southeast Asia, South Korea and Taiwan in Northeast

Asia, Australia and New Zealand in the Southwest Pacific, and Pakistan and Iran in southern Asia. Recently independent nations such as India, Indonesia, and Egypt resisted U.S. pressure to join the anti-Communist group of states and instead formed a non-aligned group of nations and adopted anticolonialism as a major theme. Thus, the world had been divided into three groups of nations: the first world led by the United States, the second one dominated by the Soviet Union, and a third world presided over by India. It was a period in which military alliances, military assistance, and CIA covert actions dominated U.S. foreign policy priorities.

Promotion of Values.   U.S. propaganda during this period was essentially negative, emphasizing anti-communist themes. The Voice of America was created in order to carry the message of American freedom and democracy to the world, but as the Cold War intensified, the VOA and other U.S.-sponsored radio organizations proclaimed the horrors of Stalin's slave camps while extolling the American free enterprise system. One important non-political step was the creation of the Fulbright-Hays educational exchange program, which brought thousands of foreign students and teachers to the United States and permitted many Americans to study abroad.

This first period of Cold War all but ended East-West contacts and made the Iron Curtain a grim reality for Western Europeans, particularly West Germans. For the United States, 1954 was a year when its defenses had been rebuilt and its nuclear stockpile was rapidly expanding. Containment had stabilized the security situation in Europe, but the French withdrawal from Indochina and the creation of a Communist regime in Hanoi suggested that containment of Asian communism would soon be tested again.

Experimentation with Detente, 1955–1960

In 1955 the new Soviet leadership represented by Nikolai Bulganin and Nikita Khrushchev strongly hinted to Washington that it desired improved relations with the United States and would welcome a meeting with President Eisenhower. The Republican president was in no hurry to take political heat from his own party for warming up relations with the leaders of "godless Communism." With the 1954 midterm elections over, however, Eisenhower decided that if Moscow was prepared to make a major concession to ease East-West tensions, he would consider meeting with Soviet leaders to discuss additional ways of reducing conflict between the powers. An Austrian peace treaty was suggested as one way to test Soviet seriousness, and within a few months Moscow agreed in principle to a withdrawal of foreign forces from Austria, elections to form a central government, and permanent neutralization of that country. Negotiations had been held for nearly ten years to achieve an Austrian peace treaty and the withdrawal of Soviet and American occupation forces, but, as in the case of Germany, Moscow had insisted on unacceptable concessions from the West. With Stalin gone and the new Soviet leadership hoping to reinforce its authority at home by holding a meeting with the famous American president, a concession on Austria appeared to be a risk worth taking—particularly if the country were neutralized and could not be part of NATO.

The Geneva summit conference in July 1955 was hailed as the beginning of a new era in East-West relations. President Eisenhower proposed an "open skies" agreement under which each side could monitor the other's military installations, but this novel idea was not acceptable to Soviet leaders, who continued to be obsessed with internal security. Both sides expressed a desire for more exchanges between East and West, but they disagreed about free elections in all of Germany and unification of the country. Khrushchev emerged from the Geneva conference as the real power in the Soviet Union, and his meeting with Eisenhower gave him international as well as domestic prestige. Eisenhower, having managed to overcome the doubts of Secretary of State Dulles and conservative Republicans about the wisdom of meeting with the Russians, enhanced his reputation at home and abroad as a peacemaker. He revealed to congressional leaders that Khrushchev wanted to visit the United States and said this would provide an opportunity for more talks about limiting nuclear weapons.

The "Spirit of Geneva" became a label for the new feeling of hope in Europe that resulted from the July summit. Little change occurred in the political situation in Eastern Europe or in relations between East and West Germany, but the psychological mood improved markedly as the threat of war receded. Europeans for the first time in eight years could think about peace and increased communications through the Iron Curtain. It was a time of optimism on both sides of the Atlantic, even though no substantive agreements had been reached. In reality, however, this first period of detente in East-West relations was an uneasy truce, marked by tension as well as an improved atmosphere for discussions on arms control.

In October 1956 international tensions were again raised to near Cold War levels when Britain and France invaded Egypt and Soviet tanks moved into Hungary to crush the Hungarian Revolution. Egyptian President Gamal Abdel Nasser earlier had moved his country's foreign policy away from the West and toward closer ties with Moscow, and in 1955 he concluded an agreement to purchase arms in Eastern Europe and accept Soviet advisers. In 1956 he nationalized the Suez Canal, over the vehement protests of Britain and France, both of which had strong historical and financial interests in the waterway. These two powers were prepared to use military force against Nasser, but President Eisenhower objected to this reassertion of colonial power in the Middle East at a time when anticolonialism had become a major force in the United Nations. Britain and France then conspired with Israel to invade Suez without informing Washington. Infuriated by this action, Eisenhower threatened Britain with financial sanctions. At the same time Soviet leader Nikita Khrushchev, expressing outrage that Britain had used force against his Egyptian client, threatened to launch missiles against London. Under pressure from both Washington and Moscow, a shattered Prime Minister Anthony Eden ordered British forces out of Egypt. Reluctantly, France and Israel also withdrew. Eden was replaced as prime minister by Harold Macmillan, a wartime friend of Eisenhower, who was seen in London as the best person to mend relations with Washington.

While the Suez crisis was in progress, Hungary exploded politically and brought Europe again into a Cold War mood. What started out as peaceful demonstrations by students and others for more freedom grew into a mass protest against Soviet domination. The progressive Hungarian prime minister, Imre Nagy, declared that he wanted a fully independent country that would not be a member of the Warsaw Pact. Moscow, despite its desire for improved East-West relations, saw the Hungarian revolution as a threat to its vital interests in Eastern Europe. It feared that the revolution would spread to Poland and East Germany, where there had been protests against Communist rule. The Kremlin therefore used troops and tanks to crush the Hungarian uprising and replace Nagy's government with one prepared to follow Soviet policy directives.

Given the Eisenhower administration's campaign rhetoric

about "rolling back the Iron Curtain," many Hungarians and other Europeans expected the United States to do more than protest the brutal Soviet suppression in Budapest, possibly even to send armed support to the Nagy government; indeed, critics argued later that VOA broadcasts to Hungary implicitly pledged U.S. support to the "freedom fighters" in their just struggle against Soviet domination. Within days of the Soviet crackdown, however, it was clear that the United States had no intention of intervening, and the demonstrations were quickly crushed with the loss of thousands of lives. Nagy was later tried for treason and executed. Within a few weeks, the crisis in Budapest was over, and Hungary had adopted a pro-Soviet, repressive policy under the tough leadership of Janos Kadar.

Neither Suez nor Hungary shattered the "Spirit of Geneva" but did blunt much of the optimism that had been heard in Europe and liberal American circles in 1955–1956. A realization took root that Khrushchev was not unlike Stalin when it came to ensuring the Kremlin's control over Eastern Europe. Moreover, Soviet exploits in space and advances in nuclear weaponry were a growing source of anxiety. In 1957 the Soviet Union launched *Sputnik*, the first man-made satellite, and captured the imagination of the U.S. public. This feat embarrassed the Eisenhower administration because the vaunted U.S. technological superiority had been called into question by Soviet success in the space race. Khrushchev made the embarrassment worse by claiming that *Sputnik* proved the superiority of the Marxist system over the decadent capitalist model and predicting even greater glories for Soviet science and technology. In 1958 the Soviet Union tested its first ICBM, and the age of intercontinental ballistic missiles had arrived. The U.S. response was to initiate a large scientific and educational program to improve American science and technology. Greater emphasis was put on land-based and sea-launched missiles designed to enhance U.S. deterrence to Soviet aggression.

Khrushchev talked "peaceful coexistence" between the Soviet and Western systems, but he predicted that the Soviet gross national product (GNP) would surpass the U.S. level within a decade and that the capitalist system would be "buried" by its own weaknesses. The Soviet leader suggested that he would use Soviet military achievements to gain political concessions from the West. President Eisenhower concluded that Khrushchev was determined to extend Soviet influence around the world and that

Khrushchev was more clever than Stalin in the way he sought to accomplish his goal.

The spirit of Geneva, though tarnished, continued to characterize U.S.-Soviet relations during 1959 and into 1960. Khrushchev persisted in seeking an invitation to visit the United States, and in 1959 the president thought the time was right for serious talks about arms reductions and other issues. The Russian leader was accorded a warm reception at most of his stops across the United States and was visibly impressed with the productivity of American agriculture. Khrushchev succeeded in his effort to convince the American public that he was not a sinister dictator, but his constant harping on the superiority of the Soviet system and his prediction for success in overtaking the U.S. economic lead unsettled many serious observers. Eisenhower invited him to Camp David, the presidential retreat, for talks, and these were successful enough to engender what became known as the "Spirit of Camp David." But the four-power relationship in Berlin, a problem Khrushchev specifically raised because it was impeding Soviet control in Eastern Europe, was not resolved. The continuing flow of people from East Germany through West Berlin to freedom in the West frustrated Soviet leaders because it made a mockery of their propaganda about the "people's paradise" in the East.

The Berlin issue, Soviet missile development, and Moscow's assistance to the newly created Marxist government in Cuba caused Washington policymakers in 1960 to be exceptionally wary of Khrushchev's intentions and military capabilities. Eisenhower reluctantly agreed to a four-power summit in Paris in June 1960 to continue talks on reducing East-West tensions. Shortly before the meeting, however, Soviet rocket forces shot down an American U-2 spy plane, piloted by Gary Powers, deep inside Soviet territory. The initial U.S. response to the news was a cover story that the plane was on a weather reconnaissance mission and had strayed into Soviet airspace. But when Khrushchev announced that the captured pilot had verified the true nature of his mission, Washington admitted that Powers had indeed been photographing Soviet military installations—as other U-2s had done for four years—and said that the United States would continue to do so in the interest of national security. Khrushchev, enraged, leveled a withering blast against Eisenhower at the Paris summit and walked out. Thus ended the American president's efforts to reach out to the new Soviet leadership. His plans for a visit to the Soviet

Union later in 1960 were canceled, and Eisenhower left office disappointed that his efforts at detente had failed.

It had been almost precisely five years since the Geneva summit had launched a period of relaxation in East-West relations. Khrushchev was disappointed that he had not extracted more concessions from the United States during this period, believing that Soviet success in space and weaponry gave him new bargaining power. And the U-2 episode proved to be highly embarrassing to Khrushchev because it revealed that the Soviets had been unable for four years to shoot down the planes that had been providing the United States with accurate information about Soviet military weakness. Concluding that he could not get significant concessions from the West through detente, the Soviet leader decided to try tougher, riskier policies to persuade Washington to deal with Moscow as an equal world leader.

At the end of 1960 and the close of President Eisenhower's eight years in office, U.S. national interests could be assessed as follows.

Defense of Homeland. North America had become more vulnerable to Soviet bomber attacks, but Moscow's intercontinental missile capability was still negligible. The Eisenhower administration continued to espouse the threat of "massive retaliation" as a deterrent to Soviet conventional arms superiority in Europe. The U-2 spy program had exposed Soviet military limitations and confirmed the U.S. superiority in strategic power. In 1958 Canada and the United States concluded the North American Air Defense Treaty (NORAD), which established a warning system in the Canadian Arctic to detect the approach of Soviet bombers. It was later expanded to warn of Soviet missiles. However, the Communist takeover of power in Cuba in 1959 was troublesome because it opened the possibility that a Soviet military presence could be established in the Caribbean.

Economic Well-being. The U.S. economy continued to be the world's strongest, but President Eisenhower feared that it would be made vulnerable by heavy military spending and insufficient attention to investment in industrial modernization. Eisenhower believed that economic power was as important as military power in the long-term struggle with the Soviet system, and he put a high priority on maintaining a strong dollar as the international reserve currency.

Favorable World Order. The security situation in Europe improved substantially during the first period of detente because Khrushchev persuaded American leaders that he did not plan to use force against Western Europe. Britain and France became less important as American allies because of their humiliation at Suez, and France lost additional prestige by being forced out of Algeria in 1958. These foreign policy disasters, combined with its earlier defeat in Indochina, brought France to the brink of civil war and returned President Charles de Gaulle to power. In Asia, mainland China's hostility to the United States continued unabated, and Washington continued to block Beijing's demand for admission to the United Nations. The Korean peninsula remained divided into Communist and non-Communist zones, but the Southeast Asia Treaty Organization strengthened the defenses of Thailand, South Vietnam, and Malaya-Singapore (then under British colonial administration). Japan was emerging as a stable democracy and an economically prosperous ally. In the Middle East, U.S. economic and political interests were secured by the Central Treaty Organization, which included Iran and Pakistan among its members. Egypt remained a threat to Western interests, however, and in 1958 President Eisenhower dispatched U.S. Marines to Lebanon to prevent Egypt and Syria from subverting its government. Except for the U-2 episode and the souring of U.S.-Soviet relations, a reasonably stable world order existed at the end of 1960.

Promotion of Values. The U.S. government continued its anti-Communist campaign but moderated the rhetoric following the 1955 Geneva summit conference. It continued to trumpet the virtues of the free-market system under the slogan "People's Capitalism." Nevertheless, the promotion of values interest was clearly subordinated to U.S. world-order interests in the negotiation of aid programs with countries that were ruled by military dictators and authoritarian regimes. In short, security considerations dominated U.S. policy in the 1950s.

Renewed Cold War, 1961–1965

John F. Kennedy entered the White House in January 1961 knowing that Nikita Khrushchev had decided to abandon detente and would probably confront the United States in Berlin, in Southeast Asia, and in the Caribbean through his Cuban proxy, Fidel Castro. President Eisenhower told Kennedy before leaving office that

Laos was in danger of being overrun by local Communists, using Soviet arms and North Vietnamese advisers. If they moved to the Mekong River, he warned, they would threaten Thailand, a SEATO ally.

In March 1961, two months after taking office, Kennedy publicly warned Moscow that unless it used its influence to halt the Pathet Lao attack southward, the United States would honor its treaty commitments in the area. The new president thus staked his personal prestige on a warning to Khrushchev about potential conflict in Southeast Asia. As can be seen in retrospect, this proved to be a serious mistake. In April 1961 Kennedy was embroiled in the Bay of Pigs invasion of Cuba and its disastrous consequences. He decided that if the U.S. government could not prevail in a country ninety miles off the U.S. coast, he would run too great a risk in seeking to solve a civil war in Laos. Kennedy's decision to back away from confrontation in Southeast Asia and seek a negotiated settlement, which ultimately permitted the Communists to retain control of Laos's eastern provinces, shocked Thailand's government. His apparent weakness caused other Southeast Asian leaders—including Ho Chi Minh in North Vietnam and Sukarno in Indonesia—to conclude that Kennedy would not use U.S. military power to prevent communist gains in Indochina.

Kennedy and Khrushchev met in Vienna in June 1961 to discuss the world situation and try to reach an accommodation. Khrushchev, taking full advantage of Kennedy's embarrassment over the Bay of Pigs fiasco, demanded that the United States agree to alter the four-power arrangements in Berlin. He also pledged full support to Cuba in any future confrontation with the United States and warned Kennedy that the Soviet Union would support "just wars of national liberation" in many parts of the world. The meaning of this warning was clear to Kennedy: Khrushchev believed that the world balance of power was shifting in Moscow's favor, and he would use this new strength to promote insurgencies in Third World areas and defeat the capitalist and colonial powers in Asia, Africa, and Latin America. Stunned by the vehemence of Khrushchev's verbal attacks, the president returned home and alerted the country that a new Cold War was under way and that the United States urgently needed both to build its conventional military power and modernize its nuclear deterrent. Khrushchev's bold decision in August 1961 to build the Berlin Wall effectively shut off travel and communications between East and West Berlin, thereby lowering the Iron Curtain in Europe for a second time. Kennedy responded by reinforcing the U.S. garrison in Berlin, calling up reserves, and suggesting that Americans start planning for civil defense, even building home bomb shelters. He told his aides it would be a "cold winter."

The Kennedy administration also saw reasons for the United States to pay greater attention to Third World countries than it had done under Eisenhower: first, it was the area that Khrushchev had staked out for the expansion of Soviet influence; second, decolonization of European possessions in Africa and Asia had brought into the United Nations many new members whose sympathies lay with neither East nor West but with the Non-aligned Nations led by India, Egypt, Yugoslavia, and Indonesia. Kennedy made a special effort to improve relations with India, Indonesia, and several African states, and he launched an economic cooperation program for Latin America called Alliance for Progress, designed to improve the economies of the Rio Pact countries and foster closer political ties with the United States. The president rebuilt U.S. relations with France, headed by Charles de Gaulle, to repair the rift that had emerged during the Eisenhower administration. Finally, and most significantly for his future foreign policy, Kennedy decided to make a fundamental defense commitment to South Vietnam, following his indecisiveness on Laos in March–April 1961.

In November 1961 the National Security Council recommended that the United States send substantial military aid to South Vietnam, including U.S. helicopter crews and advisers in counter-insurgency warfare, to aid the Ngo Dinh Diem government's effort to defeat a growing communist insurgency supported by North Vietnam. Kennedy accepted these recommendations but rejected a larger U.S. military involvement at that time. Nevertheless, he and his advisers concluded that preventing a communist takeover of South Vietnam was vital to U.S. security interests in Asia and that the United States should be prepared to intervene with combat forces if necessary. Vice President Lyndon Johnson supported this tough stance. In 1961–1962 it appeared that large-scale aid to the South Vietnamese government would be sufficient to defeat the Viet Cong insurgency, but dispatching a U.S. expeditionary force had become an acceptable option.

Kennedy and Khrushchev had another confrontation in October 1962 after a U-2 reconnaissance flight over Cuba revealed that the Russians were building intermediate-range missile sites. Khrushchev believed the missiles would change the strategic balance of forces by bringing U.S. cities within range of Soviet nuclear power. Unlike Kennedy's handling of the situations in Laos and the Bay of Pigs, careful planning within the executive branch and with Congress enabled him to confront Moscow with the photographic evidence and to warn Khrushchev to remove the missiles or face retaliation. He imposed a blockade of Soviet ships headed for Cuba, obtained support from the Organization of American States, and threatened to invade the island if the missiles were not removed. Khrushchev reluctantly agreed to remove them but not before obtaining a commitment from Kennedy that the United States would never invade Cuba. Recent evidence shows that Kennedy also informally agreed to remove U.S. intermediate-range missiles from Turkey.

The result of the Cuban Missile Crisis was that Kennedy's reputation was much enhanced at home and abroad, while Khrushchev was humiliated and removed from power in 1964. After the crisis was over, Moscow changed its belligerent foreign policy and sought to improve relations with the United States, partially reverting to the detente tone of the Eisenhower-Khrushchev period. The United States and the Soviet Union concluded their first nuclear weapons agreement in 1963, a nuclear test-ban treaty which outlawed atomic and nuclear explosions in space. This agreement was hailed as a breakthrough in superpower relations and, like the Austrian peace treaty eight years earlier, as a demonstration of Moscow's desire to pursue good relations with Washington. Even the Berlin confrontation was defused; although the Berlin Wall still symbolized the division of Germany, the city did not again threaten to erupt in war. Having forced Moscow to back away from Khrushchev's confrontationist policies, Kennedy was free to turn his attention to Asia and the growing Cold War with China and North Vietnam.

In the spring of 1963 the political situation in South Vietnam deteriorated rapidly as Buddhist monks protested the growing authoritarian rule of President Diem and his brother, Ngo Dinh Nhu, who controlled the security police. When the government reacted forcefully by invading Buddhist temples and jailing many monks, it undermined Washington's confidence in Diem and played into the hands of the Viet Cong. President Kennedy faced a serious choice: he could continue to support Diem, even though this Vietnamese nationalist often rejected American advice on how to deal with non-communist dissidents, or he could undermine Diem's position and bring to power another group of leaders who would work closely with the United States to prevent a Viet Cong victory. Key members of the Kennedy administration did not believe that Diem, a devout Catholic, had sufficient support among the non-Catholic majority of his population to win the war against the Communists. When the American ambassador in Saigon, Frederick Nolting, disagreed, he was replaced by Henry Cabot Lodge, a Republican hard-liner who agreed that Diem had to go. Within several months the South Vietnamese Army led a coup against the Diem brothers, who were captured and murdered. From then on, South Vietnam was ruled by generals, none of whom had Diem's reputation as a nationalist leader.

Most South Vietnamese viewed the succession of military leaders who ran their government as puppets of the United States, and this perception undermined the peasantry's support of the war effort. Before President Kennedy could assess the new political situation brought about by Diem's ouster, he was assassinated on November 22 in Dallas, Texas. Vice President Lyndon B. Johnson, known as a "hawk" on Vietnam, took over the presidency and initiated stronger action to "save Vietnam."

While the United States was getting more deeply involved in Vietnam, the Commonwealth countries of Britain, Australia, and New Zealand were already engaged in an effort to counter the expansionist policies pursued by President Sukarno of Indonesia. He had decided in 1961 to improve relations with North Vietnam and the People's Republic of China, believing that they represented the wave of the future in Asia. He also calculated that he could increase Indonesia's influence in Malaya and Singapore, and perhaps the Philippines, if the Kennedy administration showed an unwillingness to back up the commitments of the Manila Pact with military force—as Kennedy had seemed to signal when he failed to remain firm after threatening to intervene in Laos. In 1963 Sukarno adopted a "confrontation" policy against the newly-established federation of Malaysia and directed heavy propaganda against the presence of British bases in Singapore, then part of Malaysia. He mistakenly believed that Britain would be no more steadfast in Malaysia than the Netherlands had been a few years earlier in West Irian (New Guinea), which Sukarno had annexed after making a large show of force. However, Britain and its Commonwealth partners sent reinforcements to defend the territories, and by 1963 Sukarno had lost his bid to annex North Borneo and dominate Singapore and mainland Malaya. Although effectively curbed, Sukarno continued to harbor ambitions of becoming the major power in the Malacca Strait area and believed he could do so in cooperation with the People's Republic of China and North Vietnam. Sukarno began a close political association with the powerful Indonesian Communist Party (PKI), which plotted to oust the army's leadership and take over political power with Sukarno's blessing. This effort resulted in an abortive coup on October 1, 1965, the decimation of the Communist Party, and the eventual ouster of Sukarno from power. The army under General Suharto then took control of Indonesia and reoriented its foreign policy toward the West.

Soon after becoming U.S. president, Lyndon Johnson sent Secretary of Defense Robert McNamara to South Vietnam to assess the security situation. His report was grim: the Viet Cong insurgency was gaining strength, and the new military-led government in Saigon lacked the capability to rally the population to resist the insurgents. Without additional U.S. military assistance, including more advisers and unconventional warfare specialists (Green Berets), South Vietnam might be cut in half, and Saigon would capitulate. Johnson visited Vietnam in the spring of 1964 and came to a similar conclusion; however, with the 1964 presidential election campaign under way, he was unwilling to take decisive policy actions to deal with the deteriorating situation. Instead, the president decided to warn North Vietnam and reassure South Vietnam that his administration would not change the Kennedy policy of steadfastness in Southeast Asia. The Tonkin Gulf incident in August 1964, in which a U.S. Navy ship was threatened with attack, provided the pretext for Johnson to order bombing of a North Vietnamese naval facility. It also supplied the political ammunition needed to persuade Congress to give him a strong vote of confidence. The Tonkin Gulf Resolution clearly authorized the president to use the armed forces to repel aggression in Southeast Asia. Johnson assured congressional skeptics that a show of political unity in Washington would dissuade Hanoi from pursuing its campaign to take over South Vietnam. The president had been persuaded that a show of strength by the United States would solve the North Vietnam threat without the introduction of combat troops.

That conclusion proved to be mistaken; in late 1964 and early 1965 the Viet Cong launched dramatic assaults on U.S. military facilities in South Vietnam in a show of defiance and a test of the American government's intentions. In March 1965 Johnson ordered the bombing of Viet Cong and North Vietnamese military installations in South Vietnam, and he also introduced combat Marines into the Danang area. A measured buildup of U.S. forces continued in the spring of 1965, and by July the president was faced with the choice of sending several hundred thousand troops to take control of the war or letting the South Vietnamese government negotiate the best terms it could get with Hanoi. Johnson was not unaware of the latent public opposition at home to American involvement in Vietnam, but he gambled that a massive display of U.S. firepower, especially the bombing of North Vietnam, would bring an early end to the war. In December 1965 he ordered a halt to the bombing, in order to get negotiations started with Hanoi, and he sought Moscow's help in this effort. But the assumption that the Hanoi leadership would negotiate rather than see North Vietnam destroyed proved to be incorrect; it demanded that Washington agree to a coalition government in Saigon, with Viet Cong participation—an arrangement unacceptable to the United States. Faced with the choice of admitting defeat or escalating the war, the president resumed the bombing. Fundamentally, the United States had decided to fight for military victory rather than negotiate a political settlement in Vietnam. That decision marked the beginning of a decline in American power and prestige around the world and the end of bipartisanship in foreign policy at home.

Assessment of National Interests

At the end of 1965, twenty years after the United States emerged from World War II as the preeminent world power, its basic national interests had been affected in substantial ways.

Defense of Homeland. The strategic balance still favored the United States, but the Soviet Union had acquired a limited ability to strike the country with nuclear weapons. This reality caused the Defense Department to rethink the massive retaliation doctrine of the 1950s and adopt the strategy of "graduated response." The Cuban Missile Crisis dramatized the vulnerability of the U.S. mainland to massive destruction, and the Kennedy administration began exploring ways to negotiate with Moscow about control of the nuclear arms race. The Soviet Union, even though it had agreed in 1962 to remove its medium-range missiles and refrain from establishing military bases in Cuba, retained a large training and military assistance program there. Castro's continued threat to the security of Caribbean and Central American countries remained.

Economic Well-being. The U.S. economy strengthened in the early 1960s, helped by tax cuts and a buildup in defense spending and associated research and development projects. Enlarged funding for the space program also contributed technological advances. U.S. trade grew at a good pace, and the United States led the way in negotiating reductions in tariffs and other barriers to trade. The dollar continued as the world's reserve currency, and U.S.-based multinational corporations expanded their investments and operations throughout the world. Although Japan greatly increased its exports because of an undervalued yen, it did not at that time pose a problem for U.S. economic well-being.

Favorable World Order. Except for Southeast Asia, U.S. security interests around the world were well protected at the end of 1965. Relations with Europe were strong; the Soviet Union had become more conciliatory after the Cuban Missile Crisis; and the Middle East remained relatively quiet. The Alliance for Progress assistance program had a beneficial effect in bringing stability to Latin America. African decolonization proceeded without major conflict except in the Belgian Congo (Zaire), where Belgium's withdrawal resulted in a brutal civil war.

Southeast Asia was a vital test of U.S. world-order interests for the Kennedy and Johnson administrations. Unlike the Soviet Union, China continued to be hostile and threatened, along with North Vietnam and North Korea, to upset the delicate web of security arrangements that Washington had put together during the 1950s. President Johnson made the fateful decision in July 1965 to send U.S. combat forces to defend South Vietnam because he believed a vital U.S. world-order interest was at stake in preventing Asian communist states from undermining their non-communist neighbors. In sum, the Johnson administration concluded that the Asian balance of power was at risk in Vietnam.

Promotion of Values. John Kennedy's administration gave more attention to promoting U.S. culture and political ideals abroad than had Eisenhower's, but it had a similar problem in justifying to its liberal constituencies why large amounts of aid were going to countries such as South Vietnam and South Korea, whose leaders were authoritarian and corrupt. Kennedy's dilemma in dealing with Buddhist demonstrations in Vietnam in 1963 underscored the trade-off his advisers had to work out between world-order and promotion-of-values interests.

Summing Up

In 1965, the United States was at the height of its postwar power and influence and was led by one of the most powerful presidents in American history. Within three years, however, the country's international influence was eroding and its population was engulfed in serious internal turmoil. Clearly, the nation had overreached in seeking a political hegemony rather than continuing the more modest, yet international role it had enjoyed in the 1950s and early 1960s. Historians will debate the reasons for this change in attitude. My own conclusion is that the outcome of the Cuban Missile Crisis gave American policymakers a feeling of omnipotence about their ability to use power successfully anywhere in the world. They were joined by a "can do" spirit among military officers who viewed a war in Southeast Asia as an opportunity to test new equipment and new concepts in unconventional warfare. It was an "arrogance of power," as Senator William Fulbright wrote in his book with that title, and the attitude produced a disastrous policy in Southeast Asia.

3
Time of Reassessment, 1966–1980

The fifteen years from 1966 through 1980 were a period of reassessment of U.S. national interests, prompted by the costs of the Vietnam intervention and serious public questioning about the increasingly costly world role that four presidents-Truman, Eisenhower, Kennedy, and Johnson—had pursued in their foreign and national security policies. This period of reevaluation and growing introspection included the tenures of Johnson, Nixon, Ford, and Carter—Johnson having presided during a three-year transition between the first and second phases of U.S. postwar foreign policy. This second phase may be divided into three segments corresponding to Lyndon Johnson's final three years in office, Richard Nixon's and Gerald Ford's combined eight-year incumbency, and Jimmy Carter's one-term presidency.

Overreaching in Southeast Asia, 1966–1968

In 1965 Lyndon Johnson had the opportunity, following his landslide election victory in 1964, to accomplish what none of his postwar predecessors had been able or willing to do in domestic affairs: engineer a breakthrough in civil rights legislation and reform the Social Security system to aid the elderly, poor, and infirm. Eisenhower did not seem interested in doing much in either area, and his attitude may have contributed to the Republican Party's defeat in the 1960 presidential election. John Kennedy and Lyndon Johnson clearly desired to emphasize the Democratic Party's liberal social agenda, and in his first year as president Johnson pushed through Congress landmark civil rights and Medicare legislation that Kennedy had been unable to achieve.

By 1966, however, foreign policy—specifically in Vietnam—had overwhelmed Johnson's domestic agenda and resulted in growing frustration and, in 1968, humiliation for a president who wanted to be remembered for his accomplishments in domestic policy. His national security team—Secretary of State Dean Rusk, Secretary of Defense Robert McNamara, CIA Director Richard Helms, Joint Chiefs of Staff Chairman Earle Wheeler, and National Security Adviser McGeorge Bundy—all believed in 1965 that a war against North Vietnam and the Viet Cong guerrilla forces in South Vietnam was in the vital national interest of the United States because the loss of Indochina to the Asian Communist powers would produce a domino effect on other countries in East Asia and eventually affect the political stability of Japan. Eisenhower had warned of this danger, and the Manila Pact was concluded in 1954 for the purpose of forestalling it. In the summer of 1965 and early 1966, when President Johnson made his decisions first to intervene in Vietnam and then escalate the bombing in both North and South Vietnam, the principal threat to U.S. interests in East Asia was no longer thought to be the Soviet Union, which had dominated national security thinking in the Eisenhower and Kennedy administrations; by 1964–1965, the threat was Communist China and its ally, the People's Republic of Vietnam.

Although Soviet weapons and other war supplies were sent to North Vietnam throughout the war, Soviet policy under the leadership of General Secretary Leonid Brezhnev and President Aleksei Kosygin, who replaced Khrushchev's government in 1964, was more moderate and cautious than before. Moscow even offered to be helpful to Johnson as an intermediary with Hanoi, with which Washington had no diplomatic relations. Contacts between Moscow and Beijing, however, were strained throughout the 1960s as a result of Mao Zedong's break with Khrushchev in 1959–1960 over foreign policy and Soviet aid. From the perspective of Lyndon Johnson's National Security Council, Soviet military intervention in Vietnam seemed far less likely than Chinese intervention. By 1966, however, many experts also doubted that China, then in the throes of its Cultural Revolution, would risk massive intervention in Vietnam, as it had in Korea in 1950, so long as Chinese territory was not threatened.

At the end of 1965, the United States had nearly 200,000 troops in Southeast Asia to prosecute the war, and many planners thought this would be sufficient to protect South Vietnam's populated areas against attacks by Viet Cong and North Vietnamese forces. Meanwhile, it was thought, the South Vietnamese army could be enlarged and strengthened so that it could participate fully in the counterinsurgency program. The United States would employ Air Force and Navy bombing in an ever increasing effort to destroy North Vietnamese supply lines to the south and military targets in the north, and thereby wear down Hanoi's capability to win and persuade it to negotiate peace on American terms. Few top U.S. policymakers believed in 1965 that Hanoi, even with Soviet and Chinese material support, could hold out for more than a year against the overwhelming military power that U.S. forces were able to concentrate in Southeast Asia. Some CIA analysts and a few Vietnam experts in the State Department voiced skepticism that Hanoi would capitulate to American military power, despite massive aerial bombardment of North Vietnam. President Johnson was persuaded, however, that increased bombing would at least cause North Vietnam to seek quiet negotiations through a third party, perhaps the Soviet Union. He was deeply disappointed in January 1966 that the month-long bombing halt had not produced such negotiations.

For the next two years, until March 1968, the war in Vietnam may be characterized as a concerted effort by the White House to inflict great physical harm on North Vietnam while avoiding actions that would cause either China or the Soviet Union to intervene militarily. Secretary of State Dean Rusk, who had been in charge of Far Eastern affairs in the State Department in 1950 when China intervened in the Korean War, wanted to avoid Truman's 1950 mistake of permitting U.S. forces to approach the Chinese border. Bombing near the Chinese border in 1966–1967 was considered too risky; President Johnson, who personally controlled U.S. bombing targets in North Vietnam, exercised restraints on the Pentagon in this regard. In the summer of 1967, however, he did authorize the bombing of targets close to the Chinese border because by then it appeared that the Cultural Revolution was having a devastating effect on the country, making it ill prepared to risk war with the United States. Nevertheless, neither expanded U.S. bombing of North Vietnam nor the introduction of several hundred thousand additional U.S. ground troops stopped North Vietnam's war effort or caused Hanoi to seek negotiations. Its price for stopping the war remained the same throughout the fighting: the Viet Cong must have a role in the government of South Vietnam, a condition unacceptable to either Saigon or Washington.

By the end of 1967, General William Westmoreland, U.S. commander in Vietnam, was asserting that his troops were making great progress in curtailing the Viet Cong insurgency and stopping North Vietnamese regular forces from expanding their operations. At the beginning of 1968, the United States had just over 500,000 military personnel in Southeast Asia, double the number that Secretary of Defense McNamara had predicted in 1961 would be required to win a war against North Vietnam, even if China intervened. The level of U.S. involvement appeared to many to be open-ended, and the Defense Department budget was expanding far beyond what anyone had anticipated in 1965.

In early 1968 President Johnson would have faced a bitter presidential election campaign had he decided to seek another term in the White House. He anticipated in 1965 that his chances for reelection would be problematical if the Vietnam War were still going on in 1968, and one of his reasons to escalate the war in 1966 and 1967 was that he needed clear evidence by early 1968 that the war was winding down, if not actually ending. Johnson, more than his NSC advisers, was conscious of the political price he would pay if the war were prolonged. Historians will speculate about whether he might have saved his reputation and won reelection had he decided in January 1968 to stop the bombing of North Vietnam, withdraw 50,000 to 100,000 troops, and "declare victory," as Senator John Aiken of Vermont suggested. Although antiwar protests in the United States were growing and Congress, particularly the Senate Foreign Relations Committee, showed much frustration over the duration and cost of the war, a majority of the public and Congress might have continued to support the war effort so long as it did not become stalemated and no additional troops were required. The White House understood that increasing casualties and the expanding call-up of draftees were the principal causes of rising public opposition at home. If the president had announced a partial troop withdrawal at the beginning of 1968, he might have retained congressional support for the war and weathered a bitter presidential election campaign.

What ruined the optimistic scenarios of 1968 was the stunning Tet offensive that the Viet Cong and North Vietnamese launched against American and South Vietnamese troops in February 1968. Most military analysts say the offensive, although dramatic, costly, and embarrassing to the U.S. command, was a military failure and that the Viet Cong infrastructure in South Vietnam was shattered. General Westmoreland said the enemy had taken an enormous gamble to topple the Saigon government and had failed. He was confident that American forces could thereafter press their offensive throughout South Vietnam and gradually force Hanoi to withdraw from the south. The problem with Westmoreland's appraisal of the post-Tet situation was that he asked Washington for an additional 200,000 troops to finish the job. That request, plus the psychological impact in the United States of the Tet offensive, was enough to cause President Johnson to reassess the whole war effort and, in effect, to ask whether Vietnam was truly a vital national interest after all. This reassessment was timely because of the diminishing military threat of China, resulting from its Cultural Revolution.

Clark Clifford, who was appointed secretary of defense early in 1968, was more willing than Robert McNamara to question the growing costs of the conflict. He asked his staff for a thorough review and eventually concluded that the war could not be won unless North Vietnam were to be invaded and its capital captured. That was a course the president had rejected in 1965 when he stated publicly that the U.S. objective was not to threaten the North Vietnamese regime but to persuade Hanoi to stop the insurgency in the South. Johnson had also offered Hanoi several billion dollars in U.S. aid if it stopped support for the Viet Cong. Secretary Clifford advised the president in March 1968 that the United States should moderate its war effort and seek a political solution. Secretary of State Dean Rusk reluctantly came to a similar conclusion after the Tet uprising. President Johnson received the same advice from a group of advisers outside the government, and on March 31, 1968, said that he was reducing the bombing of North Vietnam in anticipation of negotiations. But he also announced that he would not seek reelection as president the following November, news that stunned Washington and other world capitals and changed the U.S. political landscape.

It is useful to compare the Tet offensive in 1968 with the Viet Minh's siege of the French garrison at Dien Bien Phu fourteen years earlier. In both cases, Vietnamese Communist forces accomplished military feats that neither the French in 1954 nor the Americans in 1968 thought they were capable of achieving. In each case, the public in France and in the United States had tired of war in Indochina and was shocked by Vietnamese military actions that seemed to show no end in sight. The political results were similar: France got a new government in May 1954 which pledged to negotiate peace in Vietnam, and the United States elected a new president in 1968 who decided to end American participation in an even larger war. In both cases, Vietnam's Communist leaders, who had capitalized on the strong nationalist sentiments of the Vietnamese people, outlasted their opponents and eventually rid their country of foreign influence. Fundamentally, North Vietnam had a stronger national interest—survival—at stake than did France or the United States, and it demonstrated a tenacity of purpose that neither the European nor the North American power could muster. A contributing factor in the U.S. failure to achieve its objectives was the inability, or unwillingness, of its military commanders to understand the Vietnamese Communist forces' determination to prevail, no matter what the human and physical costs. In 1968 the reality for the Johnson White House was that even though it thought the United States had a vital world-order interest in defending South Vietnam, neither the government nor the country was willing to pay the escalating costs. On the other hand, the North Vietnamese decided that they had a survival interest in defending their homeland, and they were totally committed to achieving their goals despite enormous costs.

Although Southeast Asia consumed most of President Johnson's decisionmaking time from 1966 to 1969, five other issues also received attention: the attempted leftist revolution in the Dominican Republic in 1965, the Six Day War between Israel and Egypt in 1967, the beginning of discussions between Washington and Moscow to control nuclear weapons, North Korea's capture of the U.S. spy ship *Pueblo* early in 1968, and Moscow's military intervention in Czechoslovakia in August 1968. The relevance of those events to this discussion lies in how Johnson's National Security Council viewed them in terms of threats to U.S. interests. They form part of the transition from the post–World War II view of U.S. interests to the new perspective of the 1970s.

The massive demonstrations staged by leftist leader Juan Bosch in Santo Domingo in the spring of 1965 might not have elicited a military response from the United States except for two key factors. First, President Johnson was urged by his advisers to increase U.S. military power substantially in Vietnam. Remembering the March 1961 episode when President Kennedy had contemplated intervention in Laos but backed off after the Bay of Pigs disaster in Cuba, Johnson decided to avoid a similar episode in the Caribbean so that he could continue to focus on Southeast Asia. Second, President Johnson suspected that Fidel Castro and the Russians were involved in the Dominican uprising and feared that Republicans would chastise him for losing another important

Caribbean island to communism if it turned out that Bosch brought Communists into a new government. Not prepared to take this risk, Johnson dispatched 23,000 troops to that country to protect Americans and assist in restoring order. It was helpful that the Organization of American States (OAS) supported the president's call for peacekeeping forces and that several members sent troops. After four months, a moderate government was installed in Santo Domingo, and U.S. troops withdrew early in 1966. It may be inferred that Johnson considered a revolutionary government in the Dominican Republic to be a threat to vital U.S. world-order interests in the Caribbean.

The Six Day War between Israel and Egypt in June 1967 grew into a larger conflict when Jordan and Syria joined the hostilities. Israel launched a preemptive strike against the Egyptian Air Force after President Nasser demanded the evacuation of a UN peacekeeping force from the Gulf of Aqaba and made preparations for war. Israel won a resounding military victory over all three Arab neighbors and, as a result, occupied the Sinai Peninsula, the Gaza Strip, the Golan Heights, the West Bank territory of the Jordan River, and East Jerusalem—areas previously controlled by Egypt, Syria, and Jordan. The outcome caused the United States for the first time to consider Israel a military asset in the Middle East, and the Johnson administration did not press Israel to withdraw from the occupied lands except as part of a negotiated peace settlement in which the Arab states would recognize Israel's sovereignty within secure borders. This view reflected United Nations Resolution 242 and subsequent UN efforts to deal with the festering problem of Palestinians living in the occupied areas. Absorbed by the Vietnam War, the Johnson administration was vastly relieved that the United States was not asked to come to Israel's defense. In fact, the White House did not even condemn Israel's deliberate sinking of the U.S. spy ship *Liberty* and the loss of American lives. The president appeared to want at all costs to avoid any serious problems in the Middle East which might divert U.S. resources from Vietnam.

The Johnson White House also wanted to pursue the dialogue with Moscow on nuclear weapons which had been initiated during Kennedy's last year in office. Because the new Brezhnev leadership had embarked on a large nuclear arms buildup, Secretary of Defense McNamara and other key Washington officials believed it vital to U.S. strategic interests to reach an agreement with Moscow that would satisfy both countries' security needs and make unnecessary an expansion of the American ICBM arsenal once parity was reached. Meanwhile, U.S. strategy changed from a policy of massive retaliation to one of "flexible response," giving the president options other than launching an all-out nuclear war if Soviet conventional forces should invade Western Europe. President Johnson also wanted to demonstrate that the war in Southeast Asia need not mean serious deterioration in U.S.-Soviet relations. In fact, the two governments cooperated in 1965 to mediate an end to a short India-Pakistan war over Kashmir. Washington's efforts to continue a dialogue with Moscow led to a meeting in Glassboro, New Jersey, in August 1967 between President Johnson and Soviet Premier Kosygin, during which arms control and Vietnam were discussed. No formal agreements were reached, but Johnson expressed the hope that the meeting would lead to his own visit to Moscow during 1968 and the signing of a preliminary nuclear arms control agreement. He was disappointed in this hope when Soviet troops invaded Czechoslovakia in 1968.

North Korea's capture of the USS *Pueblo* in international waters in January 1968 and the imprisonment of its crew for eleven months nearly resulted in war with North Korea. The United States built up military forces in South Korea and Japan and talked in belligerent terms. This incident was seen by the White House as threatening vital U.S. interests in Northeast Asia and as a test of its resolve to defend U.S. interests there as well as in Southeast Asia. Although the American public was outraged, there was much reluctance in Congress and the administration to go to war against North Korea. The eighty-two American crewmen were not released until after the November 1968 U.S. elections, suggesting that North Korea may have thought they could be used to extract concessions from Washington during a presidential election year.

The Soviet intervention in Czechoslovakia in August 1968 brought an abrupt end to the liberalizing policies of Czech Communist leader Alexander Dubcek and shocked Western Europe and the United States. It also ended the budding relationship between Lyndon Johnson and the Soviet leadership. There is a striking parallel between Johnson's situation in 1968 and Eisenhower's disappointment in 1960 at not being able to attend a summit meeting in Moscow. Like Eisenhower, Johnson sought one final accomplishment in foreign policy to cap his presidency. The cancellation of a Moscow summit was especially disappointing to Johnson because, unlike Eisenhower's, his foreign policy was in shambles as a result of the Vietnam war.

Brezhnev's decision to crush an errant Communist leadership in Prague was magnified by his subsequent declaration of Moscow's duty to prevent a country that had adopted socialism from reversing that decision. This "Brezhnev Doctrine" was denounced by the Western countries as confirming that Moscow, for all its efforts to improve relations with the West, was not willing to loosen its tight control over satellite countries. A second Soviet intervention in Czechoslovakia in twenty years reinforced the opinion of those in the West who thought detente between East and West was an illusion and that a new Cold War was about to begin. The Brezhnev declaration also had a chilling effect in Communist countries throughout the world, including China.

At the end of 1968, therefore, U.S. basic national interests could be assessed in the following way.

Defense of Homeland.   The strategic balance of power had moved steadily toward parity between the United States and the Soviet Union, with each country having the capability to inflict enormous nuclear devastation on the other. It was therefore in the U.S. interest to negotiate an agreement with Moscow to limit nuclear weapons and also ensure that the United States retained a credible nuclear deterrent. Although President Johnson initiated talks to find the basis for such an understanding with Brezhnev, he left office before significant progress was achieved.

Economic Well-being.   The U.S. economy, which had been buoyant during the early part of the 1960s, was in serious difficulty because of the rising cost of the Vietnam War and President Johnson's reluctance until 1967 to raise taxes to pay for it. Budget deficits in 1967, 1968, and 1969 led to inflation at home and pressure on the dollar abroad, setting the stage for a serious balance-of-payments problem in the 1970s. Meanwhile, Japan's economy expanded greatly, and the European economies, with the exception of Britain's, were flourishing. The ingredients of a serious U.S. economic decline were present in January 1969 when Lyndon Johnson left office.

Favorable World Order.   The war in Vietnam had a serious negative effect on U.S. world-order interests. Europe felt neglected and in near-total disagreement with U.S. military involvement in Asia. President Charles de Gaulle took France out of NATO's military structure in 1966 and forced the withdrawal of U.S. forces from France. In Central America a military coup took place in Panama in 1968, and its leader, General Omar Torrijos, demanded a new treaty by which the United States would turn over the canal to his country. Britain announced that it would evacuate its military forces from the Indian Ocean, the Persian Gulf, and Southeast Asia before 1971, a serious blow to U.S. world-order interests. China remained implacably hostile. The United States, whose power and self-confidence were so visible in the early · 1960s, had overreached politically and militarily in Southeast Asia. Some observers called it a Pax Americana mentality. The reality was that the public and Congress simply were not willing to pay the cost of the president's view that the United States had a vital interest at stake in Southeast Asia.

Promotion of Values. President Johnson's effort to depict the Vietnam War as a defense of freedom against Communist tyranny caused a credibility problem at home and abroad because no one believed that democracy had taken hold in South Vietnam. Some critics charged that U.S. military tactics in Vietnam reflected a racist attitude toward Asians. This was a period when American ideals took a back seat to the government's overriding interest in upholding American power in Asia.

Renewed Detente, 1969–1976

Richard Nixon and National Security Adviser Henry Kissinger faced an awesome challenge when they took up the reins of foreign and national security policy in January 1969. The Johnson administration had started reducing U.S. military operations in Vietnam in 1968 and had inaugurated, belatedly, a "Vietnamization" program to turn over major responsibility for the ground war to South Vietnam's army. As was clear to Asia's leaders and most American officials, President Johnson had decided that a military victory in Vietnam could not be achieved without unacceptable costs and that a negotiated settlement was needed. Had Hubert Humphrey, the Democratic Party's nominee, been elected president, he would have continued and probably hastened the Johnson timetable for a negotiated settlement. The problem for Nixon was that the public's opposition to the war and pressure to withdraw was increasing and might scuttle the kind of "peace with honor" that he hoped for. An additional problem for Nixon was that he had won a close election, and both houses of Congress remained under Democratic Party control. Furthermore, he was disliked and distrusted by a significant segment of liberal opinion because of his strong anti-Communist tactics during his tenure in Congress. As a sitting vice president in 1960, he had been defeated for the presidency by John Kennedy, and political observers thought he was finished as a political force on the national scene.

The international climate in 1969 generally was not favorable to Nixon. China remained hostile; the Sino-Soviet border was on the verge of conflict; the European NATO allies were disillusioned over U.S. embroilment in Southeast Asia; and the U.S. economy was beginning to show the inflationary effects of the war. There were huge demonstrations in Washington, D.C., and other cities against the war, and Lyndon Johnson had become a highly unpopular leader. In sum, Richard Nixon faced a task that was almost as difficult as the one confronting Franklin Roosevelt when he entered the White House in 1933.

Nixon's objective was to extricate the United States from what many viewed as the "Vietnam quagmire" with the least amount of damage to its international prestige and to the domestic consensus on foreign policy. To accomplish the first goal, he needed the help of other major powers. Neither the British nor the French, the principal Western powers in Southeast Asia prior to 1950, were willing to give assistance. The Soviet Union, which acted as Lyndon Johnson's intermediary in trying to moderate Hanoi's demands, was no longer acceptable because of Moscow's invasion of Czechoslovakia. That left the People's Republic of China, a principal Asian power and a strong supporter of North Vietnam's struggle to oust foreign influence from Indochina. Nixon had written in an article for *Foreign Affairs* in October 1967 arguing that the United States could not ignore the fact of the existence of the People's Republic of China with its one billion people and of its important role in Asian affairs. He suggested that it was time for Washington to reconsider the policy of nonrecognition and find ways to open a dialogue with Beijing in order to improve relations.

While Nixon and Kissinger secretly pursued an opening to China, Nixon also enunciated a new policy regarding U.S. military interventions. During a visit to Guam in the summer of 1969, he said that in the future the United States would rely on its allies to carry the burden in local wars, particularly insurgencies, and that U.S. involvement would be limited to air and naval support.

He reassured allies that a nuclear threat on them would bring the full retaliatory power of the United States into play, and implied that a Soviet or Chinese intervention could involve U.S. ground forces as well. He restated this position, which came to be known as the Nixon Doctrine, in his 1970 "State of the World" report to Congress. Meanwhile, the president and Secretary of Defense Melvin Laird began a measured withdrawal of U.S. forces from Vietnam while Kissinger pursued secret talks in Paris with North Vietnamese representatives. Nixon deliberately cut the State Department out of these sensitive negotiations, and Kissinger became the de facto secretary of state for Asian affairs.

A major crisis in Nixon's presidency occurred in April 1970 when he permitted U.S. troops to accompany South Vietnamese forces on a raid into Cambodia to oust Hanoi's troops from a key sanctuary from which they threatened Saigon and other cities in South Vietnam. Nixon justified this "incursion" by saying that North Vietnam had long violated Cambodia's sovereignty by establishing bases along its eastern border and hindering the orderly withdrawal of American troops from Vietnam. This news created a fire storm of protest in the United States because Nixon appeared to be enlarging the war in Southeast Asia instead of winding it down, as he had pledged. Demonstrations broke out on college campuses across the country, and at Kent State University four students were killed by National Guard troops. Overnight the public support that Nixon had accumulated by his steady withdrawal of U.S. forces evaporated, and the public blamed him for expanding the conflict into a neutral Cambodia. Like the Tet offensive in 1968, the Cambodia incursion, which lasted little more than a week, shocked the American public. It deprived Nixon of the relative freedom he previously had enjoyed in attempting to extricate the United States from Vietnam with its prestige intact, and now he was criticized for not speeding up the withdrawal. The political pressure on the president did not go unnoticed in the capitals of Asia, the Middle East, and Europe. What looked in 1969 and early 1970 like an orderly retreat from an overextended political and military position now seemed about to become a humiliating rout for the United States. Nixon desperately needed somehow to change the context in which the withdrawal continued.

In July 1971 the president announced that Henry Kissinger had just completed a secret mission to Beijing to talk with Chinese leaders about opening nonofficial links and that Kissinger had also arranged for Nixon to visit China in 1972. It was a stunning political accomplishment that changed the strategic and political situation in East Asia. The Soviet Union, which had been rapidly increasing its military power while the United States was contracting its forces, was now on notice that the "China card," as some observers called it, could be played by Washington.

For its part, China was deeply concerned about Soviet military and political pressure, particularly the implications for China of the 1968 Brezhnev Doctrine and Moscow's displeasure over China's growing nuclear capability. Chinese leaders feared that Moscow might attack China to uphold its version of Communist orthodoxy, as it had done in Czechoslovakia in 1968. A fierce battle fought between Soviet and Chinese forces at the Ussuri River in 1969 had a sobering effect on China's top leaders, Mao Zedong and Zhou Enlai; thereafter, they seemed willing to consider ways to open relations with the United States—if the issue of Taiwan's sovereignty could be resolved. Nixon's opening to China also put a new complexion on negotiations to end the Vietnam War on acceptable terms. So long as China strongly supported Hanoi's view, North Vietnam had no incentive to compromise its goal of uniting Vietnam under its rule. But China might assist the peace process, Nixon calculated, by counseling a moderate approach in Hanoi, as it had done in 1954 when Vietnam was partitioned. Furthermore, China could hardly look favorably on the prospect that all of Indochina would be controlled by Hanoi. In short, China's national interests suggested a detente with the United States, if the leaders could get beyond their ideological barrier.

In March 1972 President Nixon was welcomed to China and had candid conversations with the aged Mao and other leaders. They agreed to disagree about Taiwan for the time being, although Nixon acquiesced in the transfer of China's seat on the UN Security Council from Taiwan to Beijing. They also made progress on opening diplomatic discussions and limited cultural exchange programs. The word "detente" came into common usage in the United States, and Richard Nixon was given credit, even by his detractors, for having "opened up China" after twenty-two years of estrangement. Two months later he went to the Soviet Union and officially renewed detente relations with Moscow's leadership. Nixon also signed the first Strategic Arms Limitation Agreement with Soviet President Leonid Brezhnev. In sum, Nixon had in two years recovered from the domestic backlash to his Cambodia adventure, had continued the gradual withdrawal of American forces from Vietnam, and was hailed in the United States and abroad for establishing good relations with Moscow and Beijing. By June 1972 there was little doubt that Nixon would be reelected to a second term in the fall.

North Vietnam was not ready to give up its dream of conquering all of Vietnam, however. As it negotiated the terms of a peace settlement with Henry Kissinger, its forces took advantage of declining U.S. troop strength to attack South Vietnam's troops and the remaining U.S. forces. In the spring of 1972, between Nixon's visits to China and Moscow, Hanoi stalled on peace negotiations while its troops launched a series of attacks against U.S. and Vietnamese forces guarding the gateway to Saigon. Nixon then made a startling move: he ordered the aerial mining of Haiphong Harbor, which effectively cut off nearly all Soviet and East European military supplies to North Vietnam. It was a high-risk action because it forced Moscow to decide whether to honor its defense arrangement with Hanoi or to accept the blockade and save its relations with Washington. Nixon calculated that Moscow would not cancel his summit visit, because Brezhnev now had to worry about the warming U.S. relations with China. Furthermore, Hanoi had not been the easiest client state for the Soviets to handle. For these reasons Moscow chose not to challenge the United States on the mining. Hanoi's offensive in South Vietnam abated, and its negotiators eventually compromised on a peace treaty.

Another crisis occurred at the end of 1972, however, when the South Vietnamese government refused to accept the final peace terms, especially the provision that permitted North Vietnamese troops to remain in positions they had captured in the south. Hanoi then decided to pressure Saigon by launching a new offensive and by breaking off negotiations with Kissinger. Nixon responded with power: he ordered massive bombing by B-52s of North Vietnam's military installations, including those in Hanoi and Haiphong. The decision produced outrage in the United States, and the Senate Foreign Relations Committee began deliberations on a war powers resolution that would curtail the president's authority to make war without consulting Congress. After a few weeks of intensive bombing, Hanoi and Saigon agreed to the peace settlement, and U.S. ground combat forces were withdrawn from Vietnam in March 1973. Washington then turned over the land war to South Vietnam's large and well-equipped army, while keeping U.S. air power intact.

The implication of the U.S. withdrawal of forces from Vietnam was that Washington no longer considered South Vietnam to be a vital interest, one to be fully defended with U.S. forces. This was so even though Nixon pledged to South Vietnam's President Nguyen Van Thieu that if Hanoi launched a massive attack in the south, the United States would use its air power to retaliate. When that pledge was put to the test in the summer of 1973, Nixon ordered the bombing of North Vietnamese installations in Cambodia. But Congress, outraged by what it considered Nixon's breach of an understanding about stopping the war, barred the expenditure of any military funds for the bombing. This dramatic action effectively ended the U.S. military involvement in Southeast Asia. A few months later, both houses of Congress approved the War Powers Resolution and overrode Nixon's veto. This controversial law obliged a president to withdraw U.S. troops from combat abroad unless both houses of Congress approved of their continued use.

Thus was Richard Nixon, the hero of detente in 1972, forced in a test of wills with Congress to abandon the Vietnam War in 1973. It seemed to many observers only a matter of time before South Vietnam would collapse under the relentless pressure from Hanoi to unify the country. That time came in April 1975, after a massive North Vietnamese offensive took its forces to the gates of Saigon. The United States was then obliged to withdraw completely from Cambodia and Vietnam in a humiliating manner.

During President Nixon's nearly six years in office, the U.S. economic interest came into jeopardy for the first time since World War II. The financial drain of the Vietnam War caused a strain on the U.S. dollar, which was governed at that time by a fixed exchange rate with foreign currencies. A gradual decline in U.S. gold reserves had been in progress for some years, while the European and Japanese economies grew rapidly and their exports expanded to the United States. U.S. foreign aid to many countries increased, and during the Vietnam war offshore purchases of supplies expanded dramatically. As a result, the U.S. balance of payments was under heavy pressure by 1971, and European countries began to worry that a devaluation of the dollar was imminent. Secretary of the Treasury John Connolly tried unsuccessfully to negotiate devaluation as a means of reducing imports, but these efforts were not successful. In August 1971, therefore, Nixon announced what became known as the "Nixon shocks": he raised U.S. tariffs on all imports by 10 percent, took the United States off fixed exchange rates, and encouraged trading nations to negotiate fluctuating rates and permit the dollar to reach a level of exchange based on market forces. In effect, the president declared that the threat to the U.S. economy had reached the vital interest level and that dramatic corrective measures were required. Even Canada, which thought it had a special relationship with the United States, was affected along with Japan, Britain, France, and West Germany—the principal U.S. trading partners. By the end of 1971, however, negotiations among the principal trading nations were completed, and the Smithsonian Agreement permitted the dollar to decline in value and to "float" in price. The temporary 10 percent tariffs were then removed, and the major trading states were obliged to coordinate trading policies in order to avoid confrontations.

Another economic shock came in the autumn of 1973 when Arab oil-exporting countries imposed an embargo on oil shipments to the United States and most of Western Europe in retaliation for Nixon's decision to send emergency aid to Israel during its October War with Egypt. In this case, unlike that of previous Arab embargoes in 1956 and 1967, U.S. domestic oil production was unable to make up the shortfall in Europe's supplies. A worldwide oil shortage quickly ensued and caused prices to rise dramatically, resulting in hardship on both sides of the Atlantic and necessitating rationing across the United States. By March 1974 the embargo had been lifted, but the economic repercussions in the United States were serious. Inflation rose dramatically as the drastic oil price rise made its way through the economy. The U.S. balance of payments came under even greater strain, and U.S. banks soon were awash in Arab "petrodollars" that needed to be recycled.

Politically, Americans realized the country's vulnerability to OPEC (Organization of Oil Exporting Countries), the cartel that set prices by controlling production in most of the world's oil-producing countries. Greater efforts were made to begin production of North Slope Alaskan oil, and domestic exploration expanded as the price of oil increased. Congress enacted legislation designed to curtail energy consumption, including reduced driving speeds and legal requirements for automobile companies to improve fuel efficiency. In sum, Americans began to understand in the 1970s that their country was not as powerful economically as it once had been and that even as a major oil producer the United States was increasingly dependent on foreign sources to support an expanding economy. Later, this vulnerability was reinforced during the

1978–1979 Iranian Revolution, when Iran's oil production nearly stopped.

The United States and the Soviet Union were on the verge of armed confrontation in the Sinai Peninsula during October 1973 after Brezhnev suggested to Nixon that Soviet and American troops should intervene to stop the war between Egypt and Israel. Despite initial defeats, Israel had begun to win that war following its resupply of U.S. tanks and other equipment. When Nixon declined Brezhnev's proposal, the Soviet leader made preparations to send airborne troops to defend Egypt. Nixon quickly responded by putting U.S. forces on worldwide alert and warning Moscow that its intervention might mean war. He also pressured Israel to stop its advance and agree to a cease-fire. The crisis subsided, but it showed that Moscow was prepared to test the president's willingness to act without congressional authority, particularly in view of his then deepening Watergate scandal. Nixon thus left no doubt that he would act to protect vital U.S. interests and decided that keeping Soviet forces out of the Sinai was vital.

Despite this and other tensions in U.S.-Soviet relations, Nixon hosted Brezhnev at a summit meeting in the United States in 1973 and visited Moscow for a second time in 1974 shortly before leaving office. It was important to both super power leaders to show the world that detente still worked, despite the Soviet Union's frustration that the economic benefits they expected to flow from the 1972 Moscow summit had not materialized. Congress declined to grant Most Favored Nation (MFN) treatment to the U.S.S.R. because of its refusal to permit Soviet citizens to emigrate. Kissinger, who became the secretary of state in the autumn of 1973, continued to emphasize "linkage" in U.S.-Soviet relations, and Nixon urged Moscow to avoid adventurism in Third World countries, in return for negotiations on a general European political settlement.

In the Caribbean, Nixon and Kissinger made a commitment to negotiate a new treaty with Panama to turn over the Panama Canal by the end of the century. The military value of the canal had declined because of the size of aircraft carriers and the rising political costs of maintaining the facilities indefinitely. Kissinger signed the terms-of-reference agreement in February 1974, and negotiations proceeded for two years. However, Kissinger left office before the final draft was agreed upon, and the Carter administration took up this matter early in 1977.

Gerald Ford, the only president in U.S. history who was not

elected either president or vice president, took office in August 1974 when Richard Nixon resigned under threat of impeachment for his involvement in the Watergate scandal. This was a dangerous period for U.S. foreign policy because a number of countries were prepared to take advantage of perceived U.S. weakness.

In 1974 Portugal relinquished colonial control in Angola, and civil war immediately broke out between Marxist and anti-Marxist factions. The United States provided covert aid to the non-Communist groups, one of them led by Jonas Savimbi and an organization called UNITA. When the foreign aid program for 1976 came up for approval, Congress deleted a provision for aid to the non-Communist forces and added language that prohibited covert aid as well. Fearing that Angola might become another Vietnam, the Democrat-controlled Congress decided that Angola was not a vital U.S. interest and did not warrant the involvement of the United States in its civil war. Shortly thereafter, the Soviet Union began ferrying Cuban troops to Angola and stockpiling military equipment there. Moscow also sent a large number of military advisers. Angola soon became a Marxist-controlled state, and Soviet military influence was suddenly present on Africa's Atlantic coast. The U.S. congressional action against aid for Angola was seen as a serious foreign policy defeat for the Ford administration.

The other test was the *Mayaquez* incident in May 1975 off the coast of Cambodia in the Gulf of Siam. Following the humiliating withdrawal of U.S. embassy and other personnel from Saigon and Phnom Penh in April, the new Khmer Rouge (Communist) government of Cambodia captured the U.S. commercial vessel and held its crew. The ship had been in international waters, but as in the *Pueblo* incident in 1968, that fact made no difference to the attackers. Clearly, this was a test of President Ford's ability to act decisively, and of how far the United States could be pushed while Southeast Asia's Communists celebrated Hanoi's victory in South Vietnam. Ford reacted strongly, sending U.S. Marines to retake the *Mayaquez* and its crew. It was a costly rescue, but the administration made its point: the United States would use force to repel any attack on American ships. If the North Koreans were involved in this test case, as some believed, it put them on warning that an attack on South Korea would be resisted with American force.

President Ford and Soviet President Brezhnev met at Vladivostok in January 1976 to prepare the way for another strategic arms treaty. They met again at a historic Helsinki heads-of-government meeting in 1976, during which the borders of post-war Europe were officially agreed upon. Although the United States was a reluctant participant, the NATO countries believed such an agreement would seal a detente relationship with Brezhnev and thus make Europe a safer place in which to live. The part of the Helsinki agreement dealing with human rights later gave rise in Eastern Europe and the Soviet Union to dissident movements that cited Moscow's participation as legitimating their calls for greater freedom. Although Moscow reluctantly agreed to the opening of Eastern Europe to a freer flow of information and exchanges with the West, such results occurred gradually. A provision to speed conventional arms reduction negotiations in Vienna also bore little fruit. In sum, the Helsinki Accords pleased the West Europeans, formalized the postwar boundaries of Germany and Poland, and recognized two separate German states with different political systems. Helsinki did not, however, alter the division of Europe into two ideological camps or reduce the huge accumulation of arms that each side confronted across central Europe. The agreement was a promise of peace without the concessions that were needed to end the Cold War.

At the end of the Nixon-Ford presidencies in 1976, the basic U.S. national interests could be assessed as follows.

Defense of Homeland.   The strategic balance of power had shifted during the early 1970s so that the United States and Soviet Union had what the Nixon administration described as nuclear "sufficiency": the ability of each to inflict devastation on the other's homeland. Nixon's decision in 1969 to proceed with the MIRV (Multiple Independently Targeted Reentry Vehicle) program was matched by Soviet technology and thus increased insecurity on both sides. The 1972 Strategic Arms Limitation Talks (SALT I) treaty established ceilings on a variety of nuclear weapons but did nothing to stop the production and deployment of Soviet missiles until these ceilings were reached. Meanwhile, Moscow continued its massive buildup of conventional forces, including a "blue ocean" navy that could be deployed anywhere in the world. Soviet missile submarines patrolled along the U.S. Atlantic coast and could threaten American territory. In view of the increased threat to the U.S. homeland, Nixon and Ford expended much effort to negotiate agreements with Moscow regarding the limits and characteristics of strategic nuclear weapons. But Ford left office before a SALT II treaty could be completed.

Economic Well-being. The U.S. international economic position continued to erode during the early 1970s. Rising oil prices stimulated the inflationary trends that were already in evidence because of defense spending on the Vietnam War. The balance of payments was adversely affected by a huge increase in imported goods, particularly cars and electronics from Germany and Japan. Unemployment rose as the Vietnam War came to an end, and growing U.S. budget deficits reflected the political impasse over national priorities between two Republican presidents and Democratic Congresses. Major U.S. industries such as steel, automobiles, and electronics were unable to compete with cheaper foreign products of better quality. It was in response to this deterioration that President Nixon took the United States off fixed exchange rates in 1971, but his action did not affect the basic problem of a relative decline in U.S. productivity. In sum, the United States was gradually losing its preeminent economic position in the world, and the government seemed incapable of reversing the trend.

Favorable World Order. The Vietnam War and its aftermath left the United States in a weakened international position and necessitated a change in relations with two major antagonists—the Soviet Union and China. Even though Richard Nixon accomplished a detente relationship with both countries and thereby eased the painful U.S. withdrawal from an overextended position in Southeast Asia, he and Gerald Ford were obliged to accept changes in international security relations that represented defeats for U.S. foreign policy. Most obvious were the Communist takeovers in Laos and Cambodia as well as South Vietnam. Less obvious defeats were Soviet and Cuban gains in Angola and Mozambique in Africa, and Moscow's growing relationship with the radical Arab states: Syria, Iraq, and South Yemen in the Middle-East, and Libya in North Africa. One positive development was the turnabout in Egypt's political orientation following the death of President Nasser in 1970 and its ill-fated October War with Israel in 1973. The new Egyptian president, Anwar Sadat, decided to terminate Soviet military assistance and seek a new security relationship with the United States. On the other hand, Great Britain's decision to withdraw military forces from the Indian Ocean, the Persian Gulf, and Southeast Asia left a power vacuum in those areas which the United States, in the aftermath of its Vietnam experiences, was unwilling to fill—as President Truman had done twenty-five years earlier when Britain gave up its security role in Greece and Turkey. Instead, Nixon made a tacit agreement with the Shah of Iran that he should assume a major security role in the Persian Gulf; in return, the United States sold Iran highly sophisticated military equipment. Following Nixon's resignation in 1974 and the final U.S. evacuation from Vietnam in 1975, the United States was in a weakened world-order as well as economic well-being position. When the country celebrated its bicentennial in July 1976, it had good reason to be proud of its two hundred-year-old democracy and political stability; but in terms of its prestige and international power, the United States was clearly weaker than it had been at any time since World War II.

Promotion of Values.   An important result of the Vietnam War was the serious questioning by the American public and Congress of the values underlying U.S. foreign policy that were used to justify its military and economic commitments abroad. Disillusioned with supporting authoritarian regimes in Vietnam, Korea, the Philippines, and Latin America, Congress reacted and added to U.S. foreign assistance legislation a provision requiring the State Department to take account of a recipient government's record in human rights. This sentiment grew rapidly in the mid 1970s and was debated in the presidential campaign of 1976. In short, the national emphasis on promotion of values increased as opposition to the costly U.S. world-order role of the 1960s hardened.

A National Malaise, 1977–1980

Jimmy Carter won the presidency in November 1976 because the American people were disillusioned with the way the federal government, under both Democratic and Republican administrations, had handled the Vietnam War. In addition, Nixon was denounced for the Watergate affair, and Ford was blamed for pardoning him. Carter spent two years campaigning as the outsider who would go to Washington with clean hands and rid the nation's capital of corruption and arrogance in the use of power. His inexperience in national politics was seen by many Americans as a virtue because he had been unsullied by the established power elites that had brought the country Vietnam and Watergate, a weakened economy, and a deteriorating physical environment.

President Carter was critical of the secretive way in which foreign policy had been made by Nixon and Kissinger, and he vowed to make the State Department, now headed by Cyrus Vance, the principal vehicle for formulating and explaining his policy. Part of the new emphasis was the creation of an office of assistant secretary of state for human rights affairs with responsibility for ensuring that human rights considerations were taken into account in formulating economic and military assistance programs abroad. Within a short time South Africa became a focal point of Carter's new look in foreign policy, and Vice President Walter Mondale was given special authority to inform Pretoria of the administration's displeasure with its apartheid policies. Military-led governments in Latin America came under new scrutiny; in fact, Brazil reacted so negatively to what it considered American meddling in its internal affairs that it canceled a military assistance program that had been in effect for thirty years. President Carter, his wife, Vice President Walter Mondale, and many senior members of the administration took an active role in publicly pressing Carter's human rights program worldwide.

Jimmy Carter's administration had three notable foreign policy achievements to offset a series of failures that ultimately turned public opinion against the president. One success was the conclusion of two Panama Canal treaties in 1977; the second was the Camp David Accords in 1979, which brought a peace agreement between Israel and Egypt; and the third was the opening of formal diplomatic relations with the People's Republic of China.

The Panama Canal treaties were a monumental undertaking, which Carter had made a priority during his first days in office. Much of the negotiation had been done during the Ford administration, but Carter had to decide the final provisions. Congress insisted on guarantees that U.S. security interests would be protected even after the canal was turned over to Panama in 1999. Unlike most treaties, these agreements not only needed a two-thirds vote in the Senate for ratification but required implementing legislation from both the Senate and the House of Representatives. Secretary of State Vance and the White House legislative affairs staff together shepherded this legislation through Congress, and in 1977 the two treaties narrowly won Senate approval.

Few foreign policy issues have generated such intensive public debate as this one. What made success possible was that it became essentially a bipartisan issue: the Defense Department had determined in the early 1970s that although the canal was strategically important, it was no longer vital to U.S. security interests; and President Nixon had made the basic decision early in 1974 that a new arrangement with Panama was needed to replace the outmoded 1903 treaty, which gave the United States control over the Canal Zone "in perpetuity." President Carter took considerable criticism from right-wing Republicans and some Democrats for signing the treaties and bringing them up for ratification, but he marshaled his resources superbly and finally won an important change in the U.S. relationship with a key Latin American ally. Had he not accomplished this task, U.S. relations with all of Latin America would have been deeply strained.

In 1978 and 1979 President Carter personally persevered, after others had given up hope, and achieved a peace agreement between Egypt's President Anwar Sadat and Israel's Prime Minister Menachem Begin. Although the final document was ambiguous on the important Palestinian homeland issue, which Sadat insisted should be part of the peace treaty, the Camp David Accords effectively ended the state of war between Israel and the largest Arab state. By this agreement, Israel withdrew from the Sinai, and Egypt acknowledged Israel's sovereignty as a state. The two countries agreed never to go to war again, and this pledge greatly improved Israel's defense situation. The United States thereafter promised increased military and economic aid to Israel, including the construction of two new air bases to replace two that were turned over to Egypt as part of the Sinai withdrawal. Washington also undertook to provide Egypt with large economic and military assistance. In sum, this was a notable political achievement for Jimmy Carter, although it did not bring peace to other Israeli-occupied territories.

President Carter and Secretary of State Vance also brought to fruition several years of negotiations with Beijing to resolve the Taiwan issue and establish full diplomatic relations with the People's Republic of China. Over the protests of far-right conservatives in Congress, Carter withdrew U.S. diplomatic recognition from the Republic of China's government on Taiwan and transferred it to Beijing, including a formal exchange of ambassadors. A nondiplomatic U.S. Interest Office was established in Taipei to handle U.S. relations with the Nationalist government of Taiwan, and the United States pledged to continue to provide the island government with military assistance for its self-defense. The United States reaffirmed Nixon's 1972 assertion that there was only one China and that its government was in Beijing, but it also insisted that Taiwan and China should work out a peaceful resolution of their differences. This action, a major shift in U.S. diplomatic relations with mainland China after a hiatus of thirty years, facilitated numerous additional arrangements between the two countries, including economic and military cooperation. At a time when the Soviet Union was beginning to demonstrate its growing military power and an expanded world role, the U.S.-China rapprochement was an important factor in advancing both the defense-of-homeland and world-order interests of the United States. It was potentially important also for U.S. economic well-being, but only marginally so for promotion of values.

Against the foreign policy successes of the Carter years, a number of failures, or at least reverses, must be weighed: Vietnam's occupation of Cambodia in 1978 and the imposition there of a Hanoi-dominated government; the reversal of Ethiopia's policy of cooperation with the United States and its new military cooperation with Moscow; the victory of a Marxist-led Sandinista revolution in Nicaragua; the Iranian revolution of 1979 and the emergence in Tehran of an anti-American Islamic republic; and the Soviet Union's invasion of Afghanistan in December 1979. Added to these reverses was Carter's failure to achieve Senate ratification of the SALT II treaty he had negotiated with Moscow, resulting from widespread concern that it was too favorable to Soviet strategic interests. Carter and Brezhnev had met in Vienna in 1979 to sign this treaty, but after Moscow invaded Afghanistan, the president withdrew it from ratification. Like Lyndon Johnson, Jimmy Carter had his hopes for a summit conference in Moscow dashed because of the Kremlin's decision to invade a neighboring country on the pretext of protecting Soviet security interests.

The most politically damaging foreign policy problem for Carter personally and for the country's international prestige was the Iran hostage crisis. In the course of a few months, the most important and seemingly durable U.S. ally in the Middle East, the Shah of Iran, was deposed in a revolution that brought to power the Ayatollah Khomeini, a fanatical Islamic cleric who vowed to rid Iran of foreign influence. Whether this turn of events could have been avoided, or at least modified, is a question that will engage scholars for many years, but available evidence indicates the Carter administration's tardiness in recognizing that by 1978 the Shah's power was in serious jeopardy. In fact, critics charged that Carter's public harping on human rights abuses in Iran contributed to the Shah's declining authority among the educated elites and played into the hands of Islamic fundamentalists.

In the autumn of 1978 the U.S. government could not decide whether to encourage Iran's military—a largely U.S.-trained and equipped force—to step in and prevent the collapse of the Shah's regime, even though he was ill and probably would have gone abroad for extended treatment. President Carter finally came to the conclusion that there was nothing the United States should do to prevent the Shah's abdication, and he decided to take his chances with the new regime installed by Ayatollah Khomeini, who had just returned in triumph from exile in France. Carter's decision was not unlike the one Truman made in the autumn of 1949 when he waited to see what the new Communist government in Beijing would do after proclaiming the People's Republic of China. A few months into 1979 it was clear that Iran's new regime was executing many military officers and politicians who had been friendly to the United States. Minor incidents at the U.S. Embassy were signals that Americans might not be immune from attack by the fanatical Revolutionary Guards. In November 1979 the embassy was stormed by a mob, and fifty-two American diplomatic personnel were taken prisoner. Six weeks later, on December 29, Soviet troops invaded Afghanistan, and Moscow installed a puppet Communist government in Kabul. These two events shocked Washington and caused President Carter to impose economic sanctions on both Iran and the Soviet Union.

Carter's inability to get the American diplomatic hostages released and his initial unwillingness to use force against Iran contributed to the American public's frustration over this major international humiliation. The failure of a military rescue effort in April 1980 only deepened Carter's political vulnerability at home and harmed his reelection campaign that summer and fall. The Iran hostage issue severely hampered his effort to defeat Republican candidate Ronald Reagan, who urged a return to a forceful American foreign policy with military power to support it. When Iran and Iraq went to war in September 1980, many Americans thought Tehran might release the hostages and seek renewal of U.S. military assistance. The U.S. diplomats were finally released, but only on the day Jimmy Carter left office and Ronald Reagan assumed the presidency in January 1981. Iran's leaders were concerned that the new president would indeed use massive force if the hostages were held longer.

President Carter's relations with the European NATO allies became strained as a result of both his personality and his policies. Europeans did not appreciate his public pronouncements on human rights and on their responsibilities to increase defense spending. The German government in particular was displeased with his handling of economic issues and his decision to cancel a neutron bomb project after pressing Bonn to accept it. When Iran's revolution occurred in 1978–1979, oil production dropped and OPEC again raised its prices, putting renewed strains on the Western economies. Europeans were unhappy with the American response and began to make their own deals with OPEC.

During the Carter years the U.S. economic position declined further as inflation, interest rates, and unemployment all climbed to unprecedented levels. The value of the dollar abroad was under constant pressure; it was saved from even greater depreciation by the willingness of other countries' central banks to hold excess dollars and by foreign purchases of U.S. securities and property. The combination of economic and political problems facing his administration caused President Carter to comment in 1979 that the country was in a "malaise," a phrase Ronald Reagan used to great advantage during the 1980 election campaign.

An irony of Carter's frustration was that even though the Democratic Party controlled both houses of Congress, its leaders seemed unwilling to cooperate with this Democratic president on many important issues, particularly the economy. Political observers concluded that Carter never understood, perhaps never cared, how Washington politics operates, particularly White House relations with Congress. For those who had thought that a new president, untainted by previous exposure to the power struggles of Washington, could make government function more effectively for the American people, Jimmy Carter's performance was a disappointment. By 1980 it was clear to a majority of the public that a stronger leader was needed at the steering wheel of government, and the Republican candidate, Ronald Reagan, looked like that person.

Assessment of National Interests

At the end of 1980, then, after fifteen years of reevaluation of the nation's foreign policy priorities by several presidents, U.S. basic national interests could be appraised as follows.

Defense of Homeland.   The Soviet Union, despite the hopes and even predictions of many experts, continued to build an awesome stockpile of nuclear and chemical weapons, plus a delivery capability, taking advantage of ambiguities in the SALT I treaty

and the unratified (but adhered to) SALT II agreement. Conservatives argued that Brezhnev wanted a clear strategic superiority
over the United States and intended to use it—as Khrushchev had
attempted to do during the Cuban Missile Crisis—to extract political concessions from the West. Moderates, including Defense
Secretary Harold Brown, believed that the United States possessed
sufficient nuclear retaliatory capability to make deterrence credible and that building new strategic systems, such as the B-1
bomber, would be redundant and unduly costly. President Carter
canceled production of the expensive B-1 for this reason. In effect,
the Carter administration decided that there had to be a limit on
the acquisition of strategic power. Nevertheless, the massive Soviet buildup of both conventional and strategic forces frightened
many Europeans, who began to question whether any American
president would use strategic weapons to retaliate against a Soviet conventional thrust into Western Europe. The issue was not
whether a U.S. defense-of-homeland interest was threatened at the
vital level by the growing Soviet strategic nuclear capability;
rather, it was how a perceived change in the strategic balance between the superpowers would affect the regional balance of
power in Europe, the Middle East, and the Western Pacific—a
question of world-order interest to the United States.

Economic Well-being. The U.S. economy was declining,
relative to those of Japan, Germany, and France; and the relative
change was reflected in growing U.S. imports, declining exports,
and large domestic unemployment. The U.S. agricultural export
program, which had cushioned the balance of trade decline in the
1970s, was damaged by President Carter's grain embargo of the
Soviet Union, following its invasion of Afghanistan, and by the
reality that former food-importing countries such as India and
China were becoming self-sufficient in agriculture. The earlier
trend of U.S. industrial losses to foreign competition persisted and
even accelerated. Japan in particular continued to take advantage
of an undervalued yen exchange rate and its many institutional
barriers to imports, thus increasing its balance-of-payments sur-
pluses with the United States. The trend in U.S. international economic relationships was not favorable, and the oil price increases
of 1978–1979 underscored U.S. vulnerability.

Favorable World Order. Although the United States had
formalized diplomatic relations with China, brought about peace

between Israel and Egypt, and defused a dangerous political situation in Panama by agreeing to relinquish the canal in 1999, the overall trend in U.S. world-order interests was not favorable either. The Persian Gulf was vulnerable to Soviet encroachment after the demise of the Shah, and Central America and the Caribbean were less secure after the triumph of the Marxist Sandinista regime in Nicaragua. Thailand and other Southeast Asian states were apprehensive following Vietnam's occupation of Cambodia, and the Soviet Union seemed prepared to take large risks to extend its influence into Africa, the Arabian peninsula, and Southwest Asia (Afghanistan). In 1980 many experts feared that Moscow would use its military bases in Afghanistan to pressure Pakistan and Iran to grant it access to facilities on the Indian Ocean. Moscow also increased military aid to Syria after President Carter negotiated the Camp David Accords in 1979.

The NATO allies, which had not entirely recovered from their dismay at seeing the Watergate scandal destroy a president, Richard Nixon, whom they genuinely respected, were perplexed and apprehensive about a political system that could send to the White House in 1977 an inexperienced governor, Jimmy Carter, from a relatively minor state and confer on him leadership of the Western alliance. To compound European concerns, the Republican Party nominated as their candidate in 1980 a former Hollywood movie actor, Ronald Reagan, who had been governor of California and who was, like Carter, lacking in national and international experience. In short, Western Europe began to doubt the capability of the U.S. political system to produce statesmen of the Truman, Eisenhower, and Nixon caliber, leaders who understood Washington politics and knew how to deal effectively with international affairs.

Promotion of Values.   President Carter brought to the forefront of foreign policymaking one basic interest—human rights—that had been submerged for most of the post–World War II era by Washington's concentration on building a favorable world order. This new emphasis was so widely supported in the 1970s by the public and Congress that it was continued, albeit in quieter tones, by the Reagan administration. Even though Carter may have failed in some aspects of foreign policy, he succeeded handsomely in giving the promotion-of-values interest a much higher priority in U.S. policymaking.

Summing Up

The period of reassessment of U.S. national interests that began in 1966 was primarily an outgrowth of the United States' failure to prevail in Vietnam, but it was exacerbated by a growing political impasse between the executive and legislative branches of government over who should decide foreign policy priorities. For twenty years after 1945 the president was generally accorded this responsibility because the international environment was dangerous and Congress felt ill equipped to decide when U.S. national interests were seriously threatened. Furthermore, the president was the commander-in-chief and in charge of diplomatic relations with other countries. Dwight Eisenhower had consulted regularly with Congress about military actions he was contemplating, with the result that the House and Senate grew accustomed to supporting the president on his assessment of world-order interests as well as defense-of-homeland matters.

Beginning in 1965, however, as a result of Lyndon Johnson's inability to obtain a quick solution in Vietnam, many members of Congress and opinion leaders began to question the president's claim that a vital U.S. interest was at stake in Southeast Asia. As the costs—both human and financial—of defending that interest grew, the public turned against the war, and Congress took up legislation to curb presidential authority to use the armed forces in conflicts abroad. These efforts culminated in the War Powers Resolution of 1973, which Nixon vetoed but Congress then passed again by a two-thirds vote in each house. The resulting ambiguity as to the president's authority to define and defend U.S. interests caused uncertainty among America's European and Asian allies and gave Moscow and other adversaries an incentive to test American policy in Asia, Africa, the Middle East, and Central America.

Presidents Nixon, Ford, and Carter had considerable difficulty in trying to deal with foreign threats to U.S. interests because congressional critics were able to prevent actions that might have forestalled trouble in Cambodia, Angola, Afghanistan, Nicaragua, and Iran. Carter's vacillation over how to deal with the revolution in Iran in 1978–1979 resulted partly from his own inexperience in handling crises but also from constraints imposed by a Congress that seemed more concerned about avoiding armed conflict abroad than about defending important U.S. interests. The capture and holding of fifty-two American diplomats in Tehran by Iranian Revolutionary Guards became a key test of executive authority and will. American voters decided in November 1980 that they wanted a stronger foreign policy, and they chose a new president, Ronald Reagan, who promised to reverse what he saw as the dangerous drift of the 1970s.

4

Resurgent American Power, 1981–1990

The presidential election of November 1980 marked a watershed in American politics and in U.S. foreign policy. President Ronald Reagan and Vice President George Bush came to office in January 1981 with a mandate for radical change in both foreign and domestic policy. Reagan was greatly assisted in his new direction for America when the Republican Party also captured control of the Senate for the first time in three decades. From the time of his inauguration it was clear that the new president intended to make the United States more powerful abroad and economically stronger at home, and to reverse five decades of growth in the federal government. Critics charged that he planned to return the country to the 1920s and that his conservative program would be rejected by the voters. After his eight years in office, however, few political observers doubted that Ronald Reagan, only the fourth president in the twentieth century to serve two full terms, had worked a minor revolution in American politics and in the government's economic role. He also vastly expanded American military power and increased U.S. influence abroad, particularly in relations with America's Cold War adversary, the Soviet Union. It may be said that the Reagan presidency had a profound effect on the direction of both U.S. and Soviet foreign policy. This chapter assesses the major foreign policy initiatives of Reagan's eight years in office and the first two years of the Bush administration, specifically the views of the two presidents on U.S. national interests and the policies they pursued to protect and advance them.

Reagan's First-Term Policy toward the Soviet Union

Ronald Reagan came to the White House convinced that most of America's international problems could be traced to the Soviet

Union's determination to expand its influence worldwide through military pressure and Communist-led revolutions. In his first news conference after taking office in January, he responded to a question about his view of Soviet intentions: "I know of no leader of the Soviet Union, since the revolution and including the present leadership, that has not repeated in the various Communist Congresses they hold, their determination that their goal must be the promotion of world revolution and a one world Socialist or Communist state—whichever word you want to use." He added: "Now, as long as they do that and as long as they at the same time have openly and publicly declared that the only morality they recognize is what will further their cause: meaning they reserve unto themselves the right to commit any crime, to lie, to cheat, in order to obtain that and that is moral, not immoral, and we operate on a different set of standards, I think when you do business with them—even at a detente—you keep that in mind."[1]

In a subsequent discussion with five journalists at the White House, Mr. Reagan reaffirmed his suspicion of Soviet intentions and tactics but also said he was prepared to negotiate with Moscow regarding nuclear weapons: "I've told the State Department that I have no timetable with regard to discussions that might lead toward future negotiations because, as I said all through the campaign, anytime they want to sit down and discuss a legitimate reduction of nuclear weapons, I'm willing to get into such negotiations."[2] Early in his administration, therefore, the president served notice that although he was deeply suspicious of Soviet aims, he was willing to negotiate arms reductions with Moscow.

During Reagan's first term the Soviet leadership changed from Leonid Brezhnev to Yuri Andropov to Konstantin Chernenko, and over this four-year period the president maintained his hardline rhetoric about the Soviet Union—once referring to it in a Florida speech as an "evil empire." Concurrently, he launched a massive military expansion program, as John Kennedy had done twenty years earlier, to impress on Soviet leaders that he intended to deal with them from a position of strength—in Europe and Asia, in Africa, where they had made significant gains in Angola, Mozambique, and Ethiopia, and in Central America, specifically Nicaragua. In sum, Reagan's view of U.S. world-order and promotion-of-values interests in the early 1980s was that while Moscow had alarmingly expanded its influence into new parts of the world during the previous decade, the United States had become introspective and indecisive in its foreign policy following the

Vietnam experience. Reagan believed he had a clear mandate from the American people to reverse this trend—to make America strong and decisive again and to deal harshly with terrorism and Communist-sponsored insurgencies wherever they occurred.

When he took office, Soviet forces had occupied Afghanistan for over a year, and Soviet troops were poised to intervene in Poland if the government there could not cope with widespread disorders caused by the outlawed labor union, Solidarity. In Iran, the government released fifty-three Americans on Reagan's inauguration day after holding them hostage for fourteen months. Vietnamese troops continued to occupy Cambodia after intervening in December 1978, with Soviet help, and nearly 50,000 Cuban troops with Soviet advisers were entrenched in Angola. But the most serious extension of Soviet influence, in Reagan's opinion, was the successful Sandinista revolution in Nicaragua in 1979 and its Marxist orientation. Soon after taking power in Managua, a hard-core Communist element within the Sandinista coalition consolidated its control of the government, supported by large Cuban, Soviet, and Eastern European advisory teams and huge supplies of Soviet weapons. The Reagan administration considered this to be a serious security threat because of Nicaragua's proximity to other Central American countries and the Sandinistas' pledge to help Communist insurgents elsewhere, particularly in El Salvador.

In 1981 El Salvador seemed destined to fall to Communist guerrillas who were armed and supported by Nicaragua and Cuba. One of the Reagan administration's first foreign policy debates was how to prevent the collapse of El Salvador's moderate government, headed by President Jose Napoleon Duarte. Alexander Haig, then secretary of state, recalls in his memoirs that the National Security Council discussed Central America regularly during early 1981 and debated how to save El Salvador. The president was willing to take tough measures, Haig believed, but his advisers were fearful of getting into "another Vietnam," a situation that might engender negative public opinion and divert Congress from enacting Reagan's domestic agenda. After describing the arguments against taking action, Haig relates: "In the other camp, which favored giving military and economic aid to El Salvador while bringing the overwhelming economic strength and political influence of the United States, together with the reality of its military power, to bear on Cuba in order to treat the problem at its source, I was virtually alone."[3] In reality, Reagan's National

Security Council never seriously considered using U.S. forces in Central America or against Cuba. Instead, it chose to deal with the Communist menace through covert operations conducted by the Central Intelligence Agency, whose director, William Casey, had been one of Ronald Reagan's closest advisers during the 1980 election campaign. Casey's wide experience in clandestine operations dated back to World War II.

During Reagan's first term, the most serious East-West political confrontation occurred in Europe over NATO's decision to implement a 1979 plan to deploy American Pershing II and cruise missiles in West Germany, and cruise missiles in Italy, Great Britain, Belgium, and the Netherlands. These weapons were meant to counter the earlier deployment of Soviet SS-20 medium-range missiles in Eastern Europe. Despite Moscow's vehement opposition to these NATO moves and its decision to suspend strategic arms negotiations with Washington in protest, several Western European parliaments voted in 1983 to accept these American weapons, which were capable of hitting Soviet targets from European soil. This demonstration of NATO unity in 1983 strengthened the alliance at a crucial juncture in East-West relations and contributed to ending the Cold War six years later.

Moscow's serious political defeat in Europe came at a time when its leadership was in transition. In March 1985 Mikhail Gorbachev was selected as general secretary of the Communist Party, and Soviet policy slowly began to change. Moscow eventually agreed to dismantle its medium-range missiles in Europe in exchange for U.S. withdrawal of Pershing and cruise missiles—a proposal it had rejected when President Reagan offered it in 1981. It also returned to the Strategic Arms Reduction Talks (START). Clearly, Western steadfastness had paid off.

Reagan's Second-Term Detente Policy toward Moscow

President Reagan shifted policy toward the Soviet Union during his second term, for two reasons. First, he was convinced, particularly after his first meeting with Gorbachev at Geneva in November 1985, that Moscow was prepared to make major concessions in order to bring about a detente in East-West relations. Second, Reagan's impressive reelection victory in November 1984 persuaded him that he could take the political risk of moving away from the anti-Soviet policy of his first term and negotiate a meaningful nuclear arms reduction agreement. White House Chief of Staff Donald Regan, who replaced James Baker in February 1985, provides illuminating insight into Reagan's thinking. In his book *For the Record* he states: "From the first days of his presidency, Ronald Reagan clearly understood that he had to undertake some great initiative toward world peace in order to be sure of his place in history. With his instinct for simplification and the big story, he also understood that only one such action could achieve the desired result: a treaty with the Russians that would dramatically reduce the number of strategic nuclear missiles deployed by the two superpowers." Citing Alexander Haig's comment (from his book *Caveat*) that President Reagan changed the name of the arms control negotiations from SALT to START because "it implied that the numbers of weapons would be systematically reduced, instead of limited, or reduced in selected categories," Regan continued:

> Reagan's every action in foreign policy—the dramatic and very costly buildup in U.S. military power; the steadfast support of America's allies in large matters and small; the overt and covert resistance to Soviet adventurism in the small but murderous "wars of liberation" that Moscow sponsored around the world; the public rhetoric of confrontation and the private signals of conciliation directed toward the Soviets; the dogged Geneva arms talks, and, above all, the Strategic Defense Initiative (SDI) . . . had been carried out with the idea of one day sitting down at the negotiating table with the leader of the U.S.S.R. and banning weapons of mass destruction from the planet.[4]

Chief of Staff Regan recalled that he talked with the president about the economic aspects of East-West relations before Reagan met with Gorbachev for the first time, outside Geneva in 1985. He told the president to be tough with Gorbachev because he believed that the Soviet leader was driven by domestic economic problems to seek an arms treaty and that he would continue to return to the negotiating table until he got an agreement. Regan relates that Reagan said, "I've been thinking along the same lines."[5]

The Geneva meeting between Reagan and Gorbachev, on November 19 and 20, 1985, laid the groundwork for later nuclear arms reduction agreements, and the two leaders agreed to meet again both in Washington and in Moscow. In October 1986, a special working meeting was hastily arranged in Reykjavik, Iceland, at Gorbachev's request. After intense discussions, attended by only a few aides, he and Reagan agreed to eliminate all intermediate range missiles (INF) in Europe and to negotiate a 50 percent reduction in strategic nuclear weapons. Finally, they instructed their teams to try again to find a basis for reducing NATO and Warsaw Pact conventional arms in Europe.

Ronald Reagan described his first meeting with Gorbachev at Geneva in his memoirs, *From an American Life,* published in 1990. The following excerpts are taken from *Time* magazine's feature article, entitled "American Dreamer," on November 5, 1990: "I had looked forward to this day for more than five years. For weeks I'd been given detailed information about the Soviet Union, nuclear-arms control and the new man in the Kremlin. In my diary the night before, I wrote, 'Lord, I hope I'm ready. George Shultz told me that if the only thing that came out of this first meeting with Mikhail Gorbachev was an agreement to hold another summit, it would be a success. But I wanted to accomplish more than that. I believed that if we were ever going to break down the barriers of mistrust that divided our countries, we had to begin by establishing a personal relationship between the leaders of the two most powerful nations on earth." Reagan said he was determined to meet alone with Gorbachev and to convince him "that we wanted peace and that they had nothing to fear from us." He recalled that the private meeting lasted for an hour and a half and "when it was over I couldn't help thinking that something fundamental had changed in the relationship between our countries. Now we had to keep it going."[6]

Ronald Reagan's legacy in American foreign policy will largely be determined by the long-term success of the detente relationship he established with the Soviet Union through direct negotiations with Mikhail Gorbachev. Reagan left office before the full results of the changes in Soviet policy could be known, but there is little question that his decision to encourage Gorbachev's efforts to alter Soviet domestic and foreign policy were widely applauded in Europe and the United States. President Bush, in his foreign policy speech on May 12, 1989, (in which he claimed that "containment worked,") applauded the accomplishment of Ronald Reagan, Margaret Thatcher, Helmut Kohl, and Francois Mitterrand, who had been firm in the face of Moscow's threats. Bush then added, "It is time to move beyond containment, to a new policy for the 1990s, one that recognizes the full scope of change taking place around the world, and in the Soviet Union itself."[7] Historians will debate whether internal Soviet tensions or Reagan's awesome military buildup in the early 1980s was more important in causing Moscow to change course dramatically beginning in 1987. If Bush was correct in his assessment that U.S. policy had succeeded after forty years—in effect, that the West had won the Cold War—a large share of the credit for inducing the change in Soviet policy should go to Ronald Reagan.

Successes and Failures in Reagan's Foreign Policy

The other foreign policy achievements, and failures, of the Reagan administration pale by comparison with the fortieth president's success in helping to bring about a fundamental shift in Soviet foreign policy. Nevertheless, there ware notable failures as well as achievements during his two terms in the White House.

A major achievement was the reestablishment of a strong relationship with NATO. When Reagan came to office, European governments mistrusted the United States because of what they perceived as President Carter's indecisiveness in foreign policy and excessive moralizing about human rights. Reagan reversed those perceptions, even though he shocked Europeans with his strong anti-Soviet rhetoric. NATO leaders applauded his defense buildup and the forceful way he handled the decision to proceed with INF deployments—despite intense Soviet pressure against the move and massive demonstrations in Europe by anti-nuclear groups.

Reagan established a particularly strong relationship with British Prime Minister Margaret Thatcher by supporting her effort to regain control of the Falkland Islands in 1982. He did so in the face of strong opposition from Washington's Latin American allies and some opposition within his own administration. Reagan also laid the basis of a good relationship with West German Chancellor Helmut Kohl, who came to power in 1982 and spearheaded the political drive in Western Europe to accept the deployment of Pershing II and cruise missiles. Reagan persuaded France to reestablish informal military links to NATO's defense planning, even though President Francois Mitterrand insisted that France should not rejoin NATO's military command. Finally, Reagan reassured European leaders that America's nuclear deterrence policy was realistic and firm. If Jimmy Carter erred on the side of raising doubts among many Europeans regarding his steadfastness in defense policy, Ronald Reagan probably erred on the side of too much toughness toward Moscow. His stance spurred the European peace movements and contributed to the strong antinuclear sentiment in Europe and America. The final result, however, was positive because Reagan demonstrated during his second term a readiness to negotiate serious arms reductions with Moscow while protecting the security interests of the NATO allies. Some experts complained that Reagan nearly bungled the Reykjavik summit because he seemed unprepared for Gorbachev's sweeping arms proposals. Nevertheless, Reagan set in motion a process of arms reductions in Europe that continued after he left office and may prove to be his most important legacy.

A second notable achievement, although far less newsworthy, was Reagan's agreement with Canadian Prime Minister Brian Mulroney to inaugurate a free-trade pact between the United States and Canada. This agreement was reached after several years of intensive negotiations with the Canadian government and with Congress, and despite powerful opposition from two of Canada's major parties—the Liberals and New Democrats. Canada held a general election on this issue late in 1988, and the Conservative government's pro-pact view prevailed. A large share of the credit for the historic agreement must be accorded to Prime Minister Mulroney, who persevered in the face of considerable opposition. Mulroney succeeded in reassuring many wavering Canadians that their country would not experience an erosion of political sovereignty by joining this comprehensive trade pact with what many of them saw as the "colossus to the south." The agreement ensured that the United States and Canada, the world's largest trading partners, would compete more effectively in the 1990s with the European Community and with Japan's potential trading bloc in Asia.[8]

A third achievement was Reagan's pressure on the governments of South Korea, the Philippines, Brazil, Argentina, and South Africa, among others, to abandon authoritarian and repressive internal policies and institute democratic constitutional reforms. The most notable of these changes occurred in the Philippines, where the Reagan team helped to bring about the removal of President Ferdinand Marcos and his replacement by Corazon Aquino, who restored constitutional government. Some may argue that the Reagan administration was slow to move against the corrupt Marcos "monarchy" because it feared jeopardizing vital American military bases in the Philippines. But the president wished to avoid another Iran-style debacle in East Asia.

Finally, Reagan gets some credit for persuading revolutionary Iran in 1988 to stop its war with Iraq and its harassment of Persian Gulf shipping. Historians will argue over how much approval the United States should receive for bringing this vicious eight-year war to an end, and how much blame it should get for accidentally shooting down an Iranian passenger plane over the Persian Gulf, with the loss of many lives. It may plausibly be argued that if the United States had not sent some thirty warships to the area in 1987 to keep the sea lanes free from Iranian attacks, the Ayatollah Khomeini's government would have instigated even greater disruption of oil exports and would not have taken the "poison potion" of defeat—as Khomeini characterized his decision to accept a cease-fire. Since the United States and the industrialized world remain dependent on the free flow of Persian Gulf oil for their economic well-being, the potential disruption to that flow posed by Iran in 1986–1987 was a near-vital interest and called for at least a show of military force on the part of the Reagan administration. In sum, Reagan's decision to send a naval task force to the Persian Gulf in 1987 made it virtually impossible for Iran to continue its stalled "holy war" against Iraq and provided Khomeini with the excuse he apparently needed to end it.[9]

Reagan's foreign policy record also indicates several notable failures, the first being a Lebanon peacekeeping operation in 1982–1984. The president sent about eight hundred U.S. Marines to Beirut in August 1982 to assist in ending a short war between Israel and the Palestine Liberation Organization, which had used Lebanon as a base camp for terrorist operations against Israel. After the PLO agreed to withdraw its troops from Lebanon, Reagan withdrew the Marines. However, following the assassination of Lebanon's new president, Bashir Gemayel, by Muslim extremists and the retaliatory slaughter of PLO dependents by Christian militia, Reagan sent 1,700 Marines back to Beirut in September to help prevent civil war between Christians and Muslims and to support a new unity government in Beirut. He also persuaded the British, French, and Italian governments to send their own peacekeeping forces. Secretary of State George Shultz sought during 1983 to negotiate a peace agreement among Israel, Syria, and the warring Lebanese political factions—looking toward the withdrawal of all foreign troops from Lebanon. But these negotiations failed, and during the summer of 1983 the Marines came under fire from Lebanese Muslim factions, which charged that Washington was conspiring with Israel to partition the country. After bombing incidents at the U.S. Embassy in Beirut and continuing sniper fire on U.S. Marines stationed at the city's airport, the Marine barracks there was shattered by a terrorist car bomb in October 1983, causing 241 deaths.

This incident shocked the American public and produced a strong reaction against the peacekeeping mission. President Reagan then had the choice of either sending a large combat force to Lebanon to occupy the greater Beirut area, or withdrawing the Marine unit under what would be seen as humiliating conditions because they were under fire. He eventually chose the latter course, and the Marines were evacuated in February 1984. The withdrawal had a negative effect on the European allies and on friendly governments in the Middle East, not least on Israel. But the Lebanon debacle had little impact on Ronald Reagan's large popularity at home because he was applauded by many for having cut his losses in time. Most Americans thought Reagan had done the prudent thing, and in November 1984 he was reelected by a huge majority.

Another failure, also in the Middle East, was Reagan's inability to resolve the Palestinian homeland issue and bring about peace between Israel, Jordan, and other Arab states. On September 1, 1982, in a foreign policy speech in California, Reagan proposed that Israel relinquish major portions of the West Bank and Gaza to Jordanian sovereignty, under which the 1.6 million Palestinians residing there would retain the right of home rule. The president voiced opposition to creation of an independent Palestinian state, but he also made it clear that he opposed Israel's annexation or control of the entire West Bank and Gaza Strip: "It is the firm view of the United States that self-government by the Palestinians of the West Bank and Gaza in association with Jordan offers the best chance for a durable, just and lasting peace. We base our approach squarely on the principle that the Arab-Israeli conflict should be resolved through negotiations involving an exchange of territory for peace."[10]

Israel strongly objected to Reagan's proposal and soon approved new Jewish settlements in the Occupied Territories. Following four years of fruitless efforts to bring about negotiations on the Reagan plan, Jordan's King Hussein decided in July 1987 that he was no longer interested in sponsoring a Palestinian homeland under Jordanian sovereignty and that only the Palestinians could negotiate their future. A Palestinian uprising (Intifada) began later in 1987, and when Reagan left office in January 1989, this widespread rebellion against Israeli rule was increasing in intensity. Unlike Jimmy Carter, who helped negotiate peace between Israel and Egypt at Camp David in 1979, Ronald Reagan left office with almost nothing to show for eight years of effort to arrange a peace settlement between Israel and its other neighbors.

Probably the most significant failure in Reagan's foreign policy occurred closer to home, in Central America. Failure there resulted more from the administration's excessive expectations than from a striking reversal such as occurred in Lebanon. In 1981 the problem for Reagan's National Security Council was how to save El Salvador from Nicaraguan and Cuban armed support of local Communist guerrillas. Reagan decided early that American troops should not be used, but he authorized covert operations to stem the flow of arms to Salvadoran insurgents and to organize resistance forces in Nicaragua. Large amounts of economic and military aid were provided to the government of President Jose Napoleon Duarte, a Christian Democrat, who had brought the right-wing death squads largely under control and begun the process of beating back the Communist insurgency. By the time Reagan left office, he could claim some success in El Salvador because Duarte's government had remained in power despite the continuing guerrilla war and attacks from the right-wing, antidemocratic elements that had controlled the country during the 1970s.

But Reagan's objectives in Central America went further: he apparently decided in 1981 to instigate the ouster of the Marxist government in Nicaragua because he believed that it posed a serious security threat to all the countries in the region and constituted a potential military base for Moscow and Havana. To a conservative administration such as Reagan's, it was anathema to permit the Soviet Union to establish a foothold on the North American continent and promote Cuban-style regimes so close to U.S. borders. The fact that Congress, especially the Democrat-dominated House of Representatives, did not share Reagan's fear of Nicaragua became a source of great tension between the two branches and led to a severe controversy over administration support for the Nicaraguan Contras (anti-Marxist forces) after Congress passed the Boland Amendment in 1984, prohibiting any aid to them. Had Reagan decided to cut his losses in Nicaragua in

November 1984, as he had done in Lebanon nine months earlier, his Central America policy might have been judged less harshly. But the dogged determination of CIA Director William Casey and others to keep the covert operation against the Marxist Sandinista government alive during Reagan's second term produced a political near-disaster for the president around the Iran-Contra episode in 1986–1987 (see below).

The Reagan Doctrine: Its Origins and Legacy

The origin of the Reagan Doctrine is not entirely clear, but most experts believe the ideas were generated early in Reagan's second term when Congress rebuffed his efforts to continue aid to the Nicaraguan Contras, despite his reelection in November 1984 by a large majority. When Congress refused to renew funding for covert activities against the Nicaraguan government because of the exposure of questionable CIA operations—including the mining of a Nicaraguan harbor—hard-line anti-Communists within the Republican Party could not accept any compromise with a Marxist regime and looked for ways to bypass congressional restrictions.

Alexander Dallin suggests that the Reagan Doctrine can be traced to a speech on March 1, 1985, in which the president spoke of the Nicaraguan Contras as "freedom fighters." He quotes from Reagan's speech: "They are our brothers, these freedom fighters, and we owe them our help. . . . They are the moral equivalent of the Founding Fathers and the brave men and women of the French Resistance. We cannot turn away from them. For the struggle is not right versus left, but right versus wrong."[11]

Bob Woodward, in his book *Veil: The Secret Wars of the CIA,* believes that the ideas for the Reagan Doctrine were already in CIA Director William Casey's mind in 1984, when Congress increased funding for covert aid to the Afghanistan resistance forces and approved small amounts of aid for the non-Communist Cambodian factions and anti-Marxist groups in Ethiopia. Woodward calls Casey the ultimate anti-Communist crusader in the administration and says that in 1984 "he saw the anti-Communist resistance movements as a unit—Nicaragua, Afghanistan, Angola, Ethiopia and Cambodia were the battleground. This was the 'Reagan Doctrine.'" Woodward also recalls that Casey, in a speech to the Metropolitan Club in New York in May 1985, after Reagan lost a close vote in the House of Representatives on a bill to provide $14 million in nonlethal aid to the Contras, labeled that rejection outrageous. Casey asserted that the United States was engaged in a worldwide war with the Soviet Union for the control of strategically important countries and compared the times to the 1930s when the world failed to take Hitler seriously. Woodward says that he let loose with this rhetorical volley: "In the occupied countries—Afghanistan, Cambodia, Ethiopia, Angola, Nicaragua—in which Marxist regimes have been either imposed or maintained by external force . . . [there] has occurred a holocaust comparable to that which Nazi Germany inflicted on Europe some forty years ago." Casey intended to confront Communist governments in all five countries because he believed they operated as surrogates of Moscow's worldwide revolutionary effort.[12]

Stephen Rosenfeld of the *Washington Post* thinks the Reagan Doctrine, which he dates from July 1985, was different from all the other foreign policy "doctrines" enunciated by postwar presidents. Whereas the Truman, Eisenhower, and Nixon doctrines were all "defensive" in their theory and practice, as part of "containment" of the Soviet Union, he suggests, the Reagan Doctrine was an "offensive" policy in theory and practice: it was designed to overthrow Communist regimes that had been imposed by Soviet troops (Afghanistan) or helped to power through military aid to Communist factions (Nicaragua, Cambodia, Ethiopia, Angola).[13]

On the basis of developments that occurred during 1989–1990, certain tentative conclusions may be drawn about the long-term effects of the Reagan Doctrine. First, it was an outgrowth of several covert action programs that had previously been approved by Congress to aid the Afghan resistance in its fight against Soviet troops in Afghanistan, and to arm the Nicaraguan resistance in its efforts against the Sandinista regime. In 1985 Congress lifted its own ten-year-old restriction on covert aid to UNITA resistance forces in Angola, and President Reagan quickly authorized CIA funding for that organization, headed by Jonas Savimbi. The president also authorized modest covert aid to non-Communist factions in Cambodia, and he provided a small amount of nonlethal aid for resistance groups in Ethiopia.

Second, the Reagan Doctrine was successful in persuading the Soviet Union and its allies to remove foreign troops from three of the countries on which the plan concentrated its efforts. Soviet forces withdrew from Afghanistan in February 1989, Vietnamese forces evacuated Cambodia in September 1989, and Moscow and

Havana made a commitment that Cuban forces would leave Angola in 1990. In each of these cases, it should be noted, the Marxist government whose tenure the Communist troops were sent to support remained in power after the Soviet, Vietnamese, and Cuban troops, respectively, withdrew. That opens the question of whether the Reagan Doctrine was designed only to remove the foreign troops, or really was intended to oust Marxist governments from power. If the objective was removal of foreign troops, the policy was successful; if it was to overthrow five Marxist governments, it cannot be viewed as successful—except, possibly, in the case of Nicaragua. This country, the most important of the five for U.S. interests, was a great disappointment for Reagan because the Sandinistas remained in power after he left office in 1989. A year later, however, they were voted out of office in relatively free elections (see Chapter 5).

President Reagan was unable to accomplish his goal in Nicaragua for two reasons: unlike Congress's decision to support covert operations in the other four countries covered by the Reagan Doctrine, it voted not to continue military aid for the Contras after 1984; and, unlike the anti-Communist resistance in Afghanistan and Angola, the Nicaraguan Contras never showed that they were capable of seriously challenging the authority of the Sandinista government in power. These two factors reinforced each other during the deliberations in Congress because many senators and congressmen who strongly opposed the Sandinistas were reluctant to continue military aid to the Contras unless they displayed a serious chance of overthrowing the government. At a minimum, they expected the Contras to gain control over a significant portion of territory (as had the Afghan and Angolan resistance), declare themselves a rival government, and request open American support. The result of their failure to do so was that Congress prohibited military aid to the Contras for the years 1985–1986, and President Reagan then had to decide whether to admit defeat in Nicaragua or press on by other means.

In judging the Reagan Doctrine as applied to Nicaragua, it is well to recall the president's extraordinary effort in the spring of 1983 to persuade the American people that Nicaragua constituted a threat to U.S. vital interests. On April 27 he addressed a special joint session of Congress—a rare occurrence except in wartime—to warn the country of the growing danger in Central America: "The national security of all the Americas is at stake in Central America," he asserted. "If we cannot defend ourselves there, we

cannot expect to prevail elsewhere. Our credibility would collapse, our alliances would crumble and the safety of our homeland would be put in jeopardy. We have a vital interest, a moral
duty and solemn responsibility. This is not a partisan issue. It is a
question of our meeting our moral responsibility to ourselves, our
friends and our posterity."[14]

In view of his strong commitment to fight communism in
Central America, it was probably a foregone conclusion that
Ronald Reagan would try to enlist the support of other countries
to aid the Contras until he could persuade Congress to reverse its
1984 decision. Under prodding from CIA Director Casey and National Security Adviser Robert McFarlane, the president solicited
aid from private donors in the United States, and from foreign
governments, among them Saudi Arabia, Israel, Taiwan, and
Brunei, which had expressed support for the Contra cause.

Reagan's passion to keep the Contra effort alive despite the
congressional ban eventually led to the Iran-Contra diversion
scandal. Casey, Lt. Col. Oliver North (a National Security Council
aide), and newly appointed National Security Adviser John
Poindexter decided—apparently without the president's knowledge—to use profits from the clandestine sale of U.S. arms to Iran
to aid the Contras. When this news broke in November 1986,
members of Congress charged that the White House had fla-
grantly disregarded the congressional ban on Contra military aid,
and for a short time the possibility existed that impeachment
charges might be brought against the president. Reagan tried to
recoup by replacing those responsible for the diversion of funds
(Poindexter and North) and eventually accepting the resignation
of White House Chief of Staff Donald Regan. Regan stated that he
had not been aware of the Iranian funds diversion, but he was
nevertheless held responsible for not keeping a closer watch on
the National Security Council staff. William Casey entered the
hospital soon after the scandal broke and died of cancer a few
months later.

The Reagan administration's ideological campaign to unseat
the Sandinista government of Nicaragua nearly brought ruin to
Reagan's foreign policy and marred his last two years in office. A
somewhat parallel situation had occurred fourteen years earlier,
in 1972, when subordinates of Richard Nixon committed the
Watergate burglary and brought his second term in office to an
ignominious end—after impeachment proceedings were initiated
against him. One reason Congress treated Reagan more kindly in

1987–1988 than it did Nixon in 1973–1974 was that Reagan, despite the furor created by the Iran-Contra episode, remained a popular figure with the American public, whereas Nixon had never been popular.

Appraising the Reagan Foreign Policy

In an early appraisal of Ronald Reagan's foreign policy, written for the January 1989 issue of *Foreign Affairs*, Robert Tucker argues that the Reagan Doctrine was "a substitute" for a policy of military intervention abroad and that Reagan accepted the limitations on the employment of American military power that were underscored by the Vietnam experience: "The attractiveness of the Reagan Doctrine was, in large measure, its apparent compatibility with these limitations. In contrast to global containment, which led to Vietnam, this version of globalism would require very little treasure and, even more significant, no American blood at all." Tucker thinks that the U.S. attacks on Libya and Grenada were "scarcely impressive" demonstrations of military power but were designed by Reagan to impress Moscow that he was prepared to use force when the need arose: "Taken together with the harsh rhetoric of the 'second cold war' of the early 1980s and the Reagan administration's rearmament effort, the effects on the Soviet government appear to have been considerable." Tucker concludes: "There is perhaps no more venerable a tradition in American foreign policy than that of willing ambitious ends while refusing to entertain the necessary means. What distinguished Mr. Reagan in this respect was that he carried a very old tradition to new heights. To an extent that is probably without precedent, he has severed the connection between ends and means in foreign policy."[15]

That judgment seems harsh. To the extent that Reagan appreciated the reality that the American public is not willing to accept large casualties resulting from inconclusive interventions abroad, Tucker is correct. But Reagan did not tell the public that there would be no costs. His administration made clear from the start that the huge defense increases of the early 1980s would be paid for by cutting back drastically on social programs. This shift in priorities was part of Reagan's election mandate, and it certainly was an acknowledged "cost" of his defense buildup. Furthermore, neither Vietnam nor Lebanon proved that the American public is unwilling to pay the costs of foreign interventions; the real issue for the public since 1945 had been the inconclusiveness of armed interventions—as Korea, Vietnam, and the 1982–1983 Lebanon peacekeeping operation showed. The lesson, as Ronald Reagan appreciated, was not that most Americans are opposed to military interventions abroad but that they expect the president to achieve an early resolution of the conflict when U.S. forces are involved. This did not happen in Korea, Vietnam, or Lebanon. It did happen in Grenada in 1984, however.

Defense Secretary Caspar Weinberger underlined this point in a widely quoted National Press Club speech on November 28, 1984, "The Uses of Military Power." He cited six conditions that must be met before the United States commits its troops to battle in foreign crises, among them positive answers to these questions: "Is this conflict in our national interest? Does our national interest require us to fight, to use force of arms?" He felt strongly that if there is a decision to use force to support national interests, "we must support those forces to the fullest extent of our national will for as long as it takes to win."[16]

Ronald Reagan's legacy in foreign policy will probably be this: Following a decade of national self-doubt about America's international role, he rebuilt American military power and the nation's self-confidence. He will receive credit for helping persuade Moscow's leadership to change course from Brezhnev's concerted drive to expand Soviet power abroad and instead to concentrate on restructuring its bankrupt socialist system. Reagan helped restore the unity and strength of the NATO alliance, and he began the process of reducing all types of nuclear weapons. Further, Reagan continued Carter's emphasis on promoting U.S. democratic values in Latin America, East Asia, and South Africa. Except for his failure to unseat the Marxist government in Nicaragua and his inability to advance the peace process between Israel and its Arab neighbors, Reagan achieved nearly all his foreign policy objectives. If his detente with Mikhail Gorbachev proved to be an enduring relationship between Washington and Moscow, Ronald Reagan may well be remembered as one of the most successful American presidents of his era.[17]

George Bush's Foreign Policy, 1989–1990

George Bush became the first sitting vice president in 140 years to be elected president, and his inauguration in January 1989 occurred at a time when continuity in American foreign policy was essential if the changes then taking place in the Soviet Union and

Eastern Europe were to be managed peacefully and not become
threatening to the security interests of the Soviet Union. It was
perhaps symbolic that in December 1988 Bush and President
Reagan had posed with Soviet President Gorbachev in New York
for a photo outlining the Statue of Liberty in the background. The
scene showed the world that the detente policies initiated during
Reagan's second term would be continued by the Bush administration, and that Mikhail Gorbachev could proceed with his restructuring policies at home and troop reductions in Europe
without fear that the United States would threaten Soviet vital interests.

Eighteen months after George Bush took over the White
House, the record was not entirely clear on whether his tenure
was essentially a continuation of the Reagan foreign policy or
whether the new president intended to carve out his own niche in
international relations. As noted earlier, Bush started by seeking
bipartisanship in foreign policy. Except for his disagreement with
Congress on policy toward China, his first year and a half in office exhibited more harmony between Congress and president on
foreign policy than was the case during Ronald Reagan's administration. Two important political realities faced President Bush in
1989: first, both the Senate and the House of Representatives were
controlled by Democrats; second, a declining Soviet military
threat caused an erosion in U.S. public support for his defense
budget and, potentially, his ability to maintain a worldwide security role for the United States. By July 1990, despite Bush's notable
diplomatic achievements in Europe, East Asia, and the Soviet
Union, the Democratic Congress seemed determined to force
larger cuts in the defense budget than he believed prudent. Then,
in August, the Persian Gulf crisis erupted and caused a reevaluation of defense priorities and a new debate about reductions in
domestic programs. Few observers doubted that the outcome of
this foreign policy crisis, precipitated by Iraq's seizure of Kuwait
and its determination to control Persian Gulf oil prices, would be
a decisive factor for the Bush presidency (see Chapter 8).

George Bush, like other world leaders, could not have
guessed the extraordinary pace of changes that would occur in
international relations during 1989–1990. His foreign policy team,
headed by Secretary of State James Baker, spent its first few
months in office studying the policy implications of changes that
had occurred in the Soviet Union. They also assessed the challenges to America's economic well-being that were opened by

Japan's emergence as a world economic power and by the European Community's decision to move toward economic and monetary union by 1993. The new administration was criticized by the Democratic majority in Congress for responding too slowly to Gorbachev's calls for arms reductions and lowered economic barriers between Eastern and Western Europe. Some Democrats called the president "timid" because of his delay in deciding on foreign policy priorities; he was also accused by some of lacking a foreign policy "vision." But Bush carefully cultivated the Washington media representatives and held far more press briefings than had Reagan. In the spring of 1990 his public approval rating (70–75 percent) was higher than that of any president in memory, at a similar point in his incumbency.

Events in Eastern Europe and China moved more rapidly in the spring of 1989 than anyone had anticipated. In Poland, the Communist Party began to lose its grip on absolute power when the Solidarity labor movement pressed for radical changes in the political and economic system. The Communist government in Warsaw decided to allow significant political reforms, with the apparent acquiescence of Soviet President Mikhail Gorbachev. The results were Eastern Europe's first non-Communist government and the emergence of a multi-party political system in Poland. In China a liberalizing movement led by students at Beijing University was permitted to demonstrate for six weeks while the aged Communist Party leadership, headed by Deng Xiaoping, debated whether it should crush the pro-democracy movement. On June 4 the government sent tanks into Tiananmen Square and brutally suppressed the student demonstrations. As a result the Bush administration found itself mired in a disagreement over China policy and also pushed by its European allies to be more responsive to Soviet calls for economic and military concessions. On China policy, the president was caught between his deep-seated concern that Beijing would again turn inward, perhaps becoming a threat to the Asian balance of power, and congressional demands that he impose tough economic sanctions on China for its abysmal human rights record and continuing suppression of the student-led reform movement. Although debate on the administration's China policy was overshadowed in the autumn of 1989 by the tumultuous events then taking place in Eastern Europe, the issue resurfaced in December after the White House announced that National Security Adviser Brent Scowcroft and Deputy Secretary of State Lawrence Eagleburger had been in China, meeting with its top leadership. The stated purpose of the trip was to brief China's leaders on Bush's summit meeting with Gorbachev at Malta a few days earlier, but a chorus of critics, both liberal and conservative, charged that the president had "kowtowed" to Deng Xiaoping's repressive government. The president's statement that he wanted China's leaders to know how deeply the United States felt about their human rights violations, as well as to maintain normal relations with a nation of one billion people, was met with skepticism and even scorn by many commentators. Bush vetoed legislation mandating tough sanctions on China, and in a close vote in January 1990 the Senate upheld his veto. But public and congressional opinion remained opposed to his view of the U.S. national interest in China. (See Chapter 8.)

In contrast with his policy toward China, the president adopted a strong human rights approach to Eastern Europe. He encouraged rapid political change in Poland and Hungary and offered economic assistance to both new non-Communist governments. He applauded Mikhail Gorbachev's changes in the Soviet Union without, however, encouraging independence movements in the Baltic states and Ukraine. But the president's advisers, like most observers in Western Europe, underestimated the growing momentum for change in the East. What started in August as a trickle of East German tourists seeking asylum in West German embassies in Budapest and Prague suddenly exploded into a rush of East Germans taking advantage of Hungary's decision to open its border with Austria. This permitted tens of thousands of refugees to enter West Germany, where they were welcomed as fellow Germans. Within a month, the Communist East German government was under siege from its own citizens and was forced to oust the party's leadership and eventually accept a coalition government with representatives of reform groups.

The destruction of the Berlin Wall, beginning on November 9, 1989, had an electrifying effect on East and West Germans and led to the ouster of the hard-line Communist dictatorship in East Berlin. It also caused political changes throughout Eastern Europe and led to a bloody confrontation in Romania between an intransigent Communist regime and Romanians demanding reform. The "Berlin earthquake" of November thus set in motion a series of political events in Eastern Europe that had profound implications for Western Europe, particularly for German reunification and for the NATO alliance (see Chapter 7).

Amid these astonishing changes in Eastern Europe and the

growing frustration within the Soviet Union over the fruits of *perestroika*, George Bush and Mikhail Gorbachev held a summit meeting December 2–3, 1989, aboard a Soviet ship off Malta in the Mediterranean. They discussed an array of East-West issues, including the need to reach a conventional arms reduction agreement in Europe and a loosening of U.S. trade restrictions toward the Soviet Union. Bush remarked during a joint news conference: "We stand at the threshold of a brand new era of U.S.-Soviet relations." Gorbachev responded, "The world leaves one epoch of Cold War and enters another epoch," adding that it was "just the beginning" of a long road to a long-lasting peaceful period.[18]

Following the Malta summit, Bush met with Western European leaders in Brussels and reassured them that the United States would continue to be fully involved in European affairs. He cautioned against a rush to German reunification and suggested that it should be a gradual process in which all European countries were involved. He said that unification should be a result of German self-determination, with a united Germany's commitment to the Western alliance and "due regard" to the legal role of the allied powers. This reference to the responsibilities of the World War II Allies—Britain, France, the Soviet Union, and the United States—was designed to allay the fears of Gorbachev, who had expressed opposition to a rapid movement toward reunification of the two German states. Bush also reiterated his call for a conventional arms reduction agreement during 1990 but cautioned against unilateral troop reductions among the NATO members.

The following week, Secretary of State James Baker met in Berlin with the new East German prime minister, Hans Modrow, and West German Chancellor Helmut Kohl. Baker took the occasion to view the results of the Berlin Wall's penetration several weeks earlier and on December 12, in a major address to the Berlin Press Club, he attempted to slow down the momentum toward German reunification. He reiterated the president's earlier statement that the World War II Allies had a continuing responsibility for Europe's future political configuration following an end to the Cold War:

> As Europe changes, the instruments for Western cooperation must adapt. Working together, we must design and gradually put into place a new architecture for a new era. This new architecture must have a place for old foundations and structures that remain valuable—like NATO—

while recognizing that they can also serve new collective purposes. The new architecture must continue the construction of institutions—like the E.C.—that can help draw together the West while also serving as an open door to the East. . . . This new structure must also accomplish two special purposes. First, as a part of overcoming the division of Europe, there must be an opportunity to overcome through peace and freedom the division of Berlin and of Germany. The United States and NATO have stood for unification for 40 years, and we will not waver from that goal. Second, the architecture should reflect that America's security—politically, militarily, and economically—remains linked to Europe's security. The United States and Canada share Europe's neighborhood.[19]

On economic relations between Europe and North America, Baker observed that as Europe moved toward economic integration and its new institutions evolved, the link between the United States and the European Community would become even more important. He proposed that the EC and the United States work together to achieve "a significantly strengthened set of institutional and consultative links." Finally, Baker addressed the sensitive "German Question" in a future Europe. I quote his remarks at length because of their insight into the Bush administration's thinking on this fundamental question of Europe's future.

A new Europe, whole and free, must include arrangements that satisfy the aspirations of the German people and meet the legitimate concerns of Germany's neighbors. . . . At last week's NATO summit, President Bush reaffirmed America's long-standing support for the goal of German unification. He enunciated four principles that guide our policy . . . : One, self-determination must be pursued without prejudice to its outcome. We should not at this time endorse nor exclude any particular vision of unity. Two, unification should occur in the context of Germany's continued commitment to NATO and an increasingly integrated European Community and with due regard for the legal role and responsibilities of the Allied powers. Three, in the interests of general European stability, moves toward unification must be peaceful, gradual, and part of a step-by-step process. Four, on the question of borders, we should reiterate our support for the principles of the Helsinki Final Act.[20]

The meaning of Baker's address was clear: German unification needed to satisfy the security needs of the four powers that had occupied Germany after World War II, and Germany needed to be tied politically and economically to Western Europe. It was implicit in Baker's remarks that a *neutral* unified Germany was not acceptable. The United States seemed to have an understanding with its allies that German unification should be a slow, deliberate process and that the security concerns of all European countries should be taken into account, particularly the Soviet Union and Poland. The results of this policy are discussed in Chapter 7.

At the end of this momentous year, in December 1989, President Bush decided to take military action in the Caribbean area in response to repeated provocations by Panama's self-proclaimed dictator, General Manuel Noriega. Noriega's troops had intimidated members of the U.S. military force that was stationed in Panama under a 1977 treaty governing control of the canal until the year 2000. Several failed coup attempts against Noriega, the latest in October 1989, had made the Bush administration appear indecisive about how to handle the deteriorating security situation regarding the Canal Zone that resulted from Noriega's cancellation of the May 1989 election results and his assumption of dictatorial powers. The December 20 invasion followed the shooting death of one U.S. officer and beatings inflicted on another officer and his wife by Panamanian police. The president's action in Panama received bipartisan support in Congress and wide approval in the U.S. media. Although this intervention, the largest U.S. military operation since Vietnam, was successful in its objective of toppling the Noriega dictatorship, it brought the disapproval of many Latin American countries, including Mexico. The impact of the U.S. intervention is discussed in Chapter 5, but it should be noted here that the Panamanian people strongly supported the ouster of the Noriega junta and reinstitution of constitutional government. Because of its short duration, the Panama intervention was viewed as a foreign policy victory for George Bush.

Appraisal of Basic U.S. Interests, 1990

At the beginning of 1990, it was important to reflect on the fundamental changes that had occurred during the previous decade and to draw some conclusions about how basic U.S. national interests had been affected by the confrontation of, and subsequent detente relationship with, the Soviet Union. These may be summarized as follows.

Defense of Homeland. It is not an overstatement to conclude that by the end of 1989 the danger to North America from nuclear attack and other forms of overt aggression on the United States was far less than it had been when Ronald Reagan and George Bush were inaugurated in January 1981. In the early 1980s the Soviet missile threat to Western Europe, the huge increase in Soviet ICBM capability, and the rapid expansion and deployment of the Soviet navy around the world suggested to many that the strategic balance of power might be shifting in Moscow's favor. However, the massive buildup of U.S. strategic and conventional power during President Reagan's first term and NATO's adamant refusal to be intimidated by Moscow's intense political pressure in 1982–1983 ultimately led to the Kremlin's decision to accept an INF agreement and to negotiate significant reductions in strategic nuclear arms. By the end of the decade the newly elevated Soviet president, Mikhail Gorbachev, had commenced the reduction of Soviet conventional forces in Eastern Europe and cuts in the Soviet navy. In sum, the military threat to the U.S. defense-of-homeland interest was greatly decreased.

At another level, however, U.S. borders were less secure because of the huge increase in illegal drugs flowing into the United States from the south, mainly through Colombia, Panama, and, to a lesser extent, Mexico. President Bush's invasion of Panama in December 1989 effectively slowed the flow through that country, but the drug cartel's operations in Colombia and Peru and the flood of drugs entering U.S. cities continued unabated. Considering the impact of this illicit trade on U.S. crime rates and the huge amounts of money it diverted from the U.S. economy, illegal drugs constituted a threat to the security of the United States itself and a drain on the U.S. economy.

Economic Well-being. The U.S. international economic interest suffered major deterioration during the 1980s because of massive expenditures on Reagan's arms buildup and large income tax cuts in 1981–1982. During the first Reagan administration the White House argued that an economic expansion resulting from tax cuts, deregulation, and increased private investment would stimulate the sluggish economy and produce enough additional revenues to balance the budget. This assumption of "Reaganomics" proved to be erroneous: by the end of the decade the United States had become the world's biggest debtor country and was running its largest ever fiscal deficits.[21] Nevertheless, during the last half of the 1980s the country enjoyed essentially full employment, a modest rate of inflation, and interest rates far lower than they had been in 1980. Although from an objective viewpoint one might conclude that U.S. economic well-being was seriously eroded during the 1980s, the signs were not visible to most Americans and were not taken seriously by a majority in Congress or by the president. On the trade side, Congress did persuade a reluctant president in 1988 to sign a modest trade protection bill designed to pressure Japan into opening its markets and engaging in "fair trade." But the outlook at the end of 1989 was that the huge trade deficits with Japan, which had leveled off at just under $50 billion annually, would not be substantially reduced except through a much greater devaluation of the dollar or additional voluntary trade restrictions, such as those Japan practiced with its automobile exports.

Favorable World Order. This was the interest most powerfully advanced during the latter part of the 1980s, largely because of the turnaround in Soviet military deployments and foreign policy in Europe, Asia, Africa, and Central America. Moscow's troop withdrawals from Afghanistan and Angola and its pressure on Vietnam to withdraw from Cambodia had a beneficial effect during 1989 on the international climate in the Middle East, East Asia, and Africa. U.S. naval intervention in the Persian Gulf in 1987–1988 stopped the war between Iraq and Iran and led, temporarily, to an improved security situation in the Gulf region. The reduction of Soviet forces in Eastern Europe and the democratic changes that swept the Warsaw Pact countries completely changed the security situation in Europe. The opening of the Berlin Wall was the symbol of a totally changed security climate on the continent after forty years of Cold War. Moscow's decision not to use its troops to prop up hard-line Communist dictatorships in East Germany, Czechoslovakia, and Bulgaria led to the violent overthrow of the Nicolae Ceausescu regime in Romania. It also resulted in a decision by all the Eastern European governments to share power with non-Communist parties, and by the Communist Party in Poland to relinquish power altogether.

In two regions of the world, however, the world-order interests of the United States were not improved by the end of the decade. China's decision in June 1989 to crush a pro-democracy movement reversed what had been a liberalizing trend there and strained that nation's relations with its neighbors as well as with the United States. Israel's refusal to permit Palestinians to exercise self-government, despite Prime Minister Menachem Begin's pledge in the Camp David Accords in 1979, made the Middle East a continuing threat to peace. Overall, however, the world order was far more favorable to U.S. interests in 1990 than it had been a decade earlier. This fact caused some members of Congress to suggest that President Bush should "declare victory" in the Cold War and begin withdrawing U.S. forces from many parts of the world.

Promotion of Values.   The Reagan and Bush administrations took credit for promoting democracy in South Korea, the Philippines, Argentina, Brazil, Peru, and Central America during the 1980s. Congressional critics pressured Reagan to impose economic sanctions on South Africa for not changing its apartheid system and chided him for not being tougher with the Pinochet dictatorship in Chile. Nevertheless, by 1990 even South Africa was gradually changing its harsh system of racial segregation,[22] and Chile had moved toward constitutional government for the first time since 1972.

Given these improvements and the trend toward more open government in Eastern Europe and the Soviet Union, the Bush administration in 1990 could proclaim that democracy and the free-market system were expanding worldwide and that communism was in retreat everywhere except Cuba.

Summing Up

In 1990, in three of its four basic national interests, the United States was in a markedly better situation than it had been for twenty-five years. Only in its economic well-being was the U.S. position worse than in 1980. Nevertheless, some economists argued that the United States could correct its international trade position in a few years by cutting the federal deficit, stimulating productivity and enacting laws to induce saving instead of borrowing by American consumers. The 1990s opened with the American government and public in an optimistic mood, in contrast to the pessimism that had prevailed only ten years earlier.

Historians may well look back on the late 1980s as one of the most dramatic periods of international change for the better in the twentieth century and as a vindication of NATO's steadfastness in the face of Soviet aggressiveness. They may also give much credit for this favorable outcome of the Cold War to Ronald Reagan and George Bush.

5
U.S. Interests and Policies in North and South America, 1990

The United States is the only great power in the twentieth century to take on major security responsibilities outside its geographic area and simultaneously ignore the other major states constituting its own "neighborhood." From 1945 until 1980, Canada and Mexico—two of America's largest trading partners—were taken for granted by Washington policymakers while successive presidents were preoccupied with building military alliances and bases around the world as part of the government's worldwide Soviet containment policy.

Washington's neglect of Latin America was shattered in 1960 by Fidel Castro's rise to power in Cuba and by President John Kennedy's subsequent military confrontation with the Soviet Union during the Cuban Missile Crisis. After Moscow removed its missiles from Cuba, Washington's attention turned elsewhere, this time to the Communist threat in Southeast Asia. Castro's revolutionary regime remained in power, however, as a result of Kennedy's bargain with Nikita Khrushchev to end the missile crisis, and Cuba continued to promote Communist revolutions in Central and South America.

After Ronald Reagan became president in 1981, Washington adopted a strong anti-Communist policy in Central America. His administration also gave more attention to economic and political developments in Mexico. Its debt crisis in 1982, resulting from a plunge in world oil prices, brought immediate help from the United States in the form of loans to assist Mexico in implementing austerity measures designed to stabilize its currency. Over the following decade, U.S.-Mexico relations improved significantly.

U.S. relations with South America were adversely influenced

by President Reagan's backing of the British government in its 1982 Falkland Islands war with Argentina. However, the United States gained prestige because of its strong support for democratic forces in South America, and during the 1980s many of the governments there—notably in Argentina, Brazil, and Uruguay—rejected authoritarian rule and adopted democratic, constitutional systems. At the end of the 1980s, even the Pinochet dictatorship in Chile had been ended through free elections and a return to democratic government.

Canada received increased attention from Washington in the 1980s, for both economic and political reasons. The province of Quebec, which was governed by the separatist Parti Quebecois until 1985, threatened to secede from Canada. A provincial referendum held in May 1980 to determine whether the French-speaking province should be politically separate from but economically linked with Canada resulted in a defeat for the separatists; but nationalism in Quebec remained a virulent force. The referendum and the impasse in 1982–1983 in getting Quebec's assent to a new Canadian constitution caused Washington to consider seriously the possibility that Quebec might one day be an independent country. On the economic side, the Reagan administration protested Ottawa's protectionist energy policies, which had been instituted in the 1970s by Prime Minister Pierre Trudeau's Liberal government, and it objected to restrictions on private U.S. investment in Canada, also imposed by Trudeau. In 1984 the Liberals lost their majority in the House of Commons to the Progressive-Conservatives, headed by Brian Mulroney, and relations between Ottawa and Washington improved measurably. President Reagan and Prime Minister Mulroney exchanged frequent official visits, and one result was their conclusion in 1987 of the Free Trade Agreement (FTA). This economic arrangement had been sought by Mulroney to shield Canadian exports to the United States from growing protectionist sentiment in Congress.

Canada: One Nation or Five?

The cliche that the 3,000–mile undefended transcontinental U.S.-Canadian border is a reflection of a unique relationship between two countries and contributes to the assumption that Canada will always be a united, prosperous, and friendly neighbor. This view masks the reality that in 1990 Canada faced a potential constitutional crisis that could one day result in a breakup of the confederation.

In 1982, when Canada adopted a new constitution that replaced the British North America Act of 1867 as its basic law, most Canadian and American political observers believed that this achievement would diminish resurgent Quebec nationalism and end the specter of political fragmentation that had been fostered by Quebec's Parti Quebecois during the 1970s. In 1990 those old fears were revived, first by the renewed growth of separatist sentiment in Quebec, as revealed in the provincial elections of September 1989, and subsequently by the failure of Canada's ten provinces to ratify the Meech Lake Accords by the deadline in June 1990. These amendments to the 1982 constitution were negotiated in 1987 by the premiers of Canada's ten provinces and the federal prime minister in an effort to accommodate Quebec's long-standing demand to be treated as a "distinct society" within the confederation. This was the price Quebec asked for accepting the 1982 constitution, which it had until then refused to ratify. Part of being treated as a distinct society, Quebec's provincial government insisted, was the right to override certain federal statutes with which it disagreed. This included the imposition of a French-only language law, which the Quebec Assembly enacted in 1988 over the strong protests of the province's English-speaking minority in Montreal. Quebec's unilateral action on this sensitive issue shocked people in other provinces and was a major factor in the ratification failure of the Meech Lake Accords.[1]

Until 1990, few Americans were aware of Canada's serious constitutional problem, largely because the U.S. media reported so little news from Canada. In January 1990, however, the *Wall Street Journal* published a commentary by David Frum, "Would Two Northern Neighbors Be Better Than One?" Frum called attention to the possibility that the Meech Lake Accords would not be ratified and that Quebec might yet decide to become independent.[2] Thereafter, U.S. media coverage of Canadian constitutional problems increased substantially as the countdown on the Meech Lake ratification progressed. (See below.)

Some years ago, on March 4, 1979, the *Washington Post* published in its Sunday Outlook section a remarkable article by staffer Joel Garreau, "The Nine Nations of North America." Garreau's theme created a mild sensation in Washington, and he later expanded the idea into a book with the same title. His argument was that instead of only three major North American countries—the

United States, Canada, and Mexico—the continent actually contains nine different "nations" that cut across the borders of these sovereign states: (1) New England includes the four Canadian Atlantic provinces (New Brunswick, Nova Scotia, Newfoundland, Prince Edward Island); (2) the Foundry comprises the industrial heartland of the United States plus the southeastern part of Ontario; (3) Quebec, Garreau asserted, is the only true "nation" corresponding to present geographic borders; (4) Dixie is America's traditional south except for northern Virginia and southern Florida; (5) the Islands add the southern tip of Florida to the Caribbean islands; (6) the Breadbasket is made up of the Middle West, southern Manitoba and Saskatchewan, and western Ontario; (7) the Empty Quarter comprises the U.S. Rocky Mountain states, interior Alaska, Alberta, and most of western and northern Canada; (8) Ecotopia is the Pacific coastal region from south of San Francisco through western Oregon and Washington, plus British Columbia and the Alaskan coast; (9) Mex-america takes in southern California, parts of New Mexico and Arizona, and nearly all of the Republic of Mexico.

Garreau's book described in detail the cultural, economic, and ethnic distinctions separating the nine regions. The book's jacket blurb summed up his thesis: "Forget the map. The people of North America are dividing into rival power blocs—with separate loyalties, interests and plans for the future." Understanding these regional differences across national boundaries, Garreau maintained, would help people in all three countries to appreciate the political and economic issues confronting their governments in Washington, Ottawa, and Mexico City. And, he added, because the borders of the nine nations divide some of the U.S. states—for example, Colorado, Connecticut, California, Florida, Virginia—the problems of governance there are exacerbated by ingrained regional differences.[3]

If Garreau is correct about the divisions within Canada, there are five rather distinct economic and political regions lying north of the U.S. border. From east to west, they are the Atlantic Provinces, Quebec, Ontario, Manitoba-Saskatchewan, and Alberta-British Columbia. Some think that Alberta, with its large oil reserves and other natural resources, is a separate entity, but its small population (2.4 million) makes it unlikely that this province could stand alone. If forced to choose, it probably would join British Columbia because its own economic well-being is mostly south and west, into the U.S. Pacific Northwest and the Pacific Rim countries.

Canada's Strategic Importance
to the United States

By almost any measure, Canada is the single most important country to the United States in terms of its basic national interests. The following assessment of the U.S. stake in Canada uses the four basic national interests outlined in Chapter 1.

Defense of Homeland. Canadian territory, air-space, and adjacent waters in the Pacific, Atlantic, and Arctic oceans are indispensable for the defense of the United States—for its strategic interests. President Franklin Roosevelt and Prime Minister Mackenzie King understood this reality in August 1940 when they met in Ogdensburg, New York, and signed a historic agreement pledging mutual support to Great Britain in its war against Nazi Germany. Canada was already engaged in that war, and Roosevelt knew the United States would eventually become involved. Two months earlier France had fallen to Hitler's armies. Roosevelt now realized that U.S. vital interests were at stake in assisting Britain to survive the Battle of Britain and prevent Germany from conquering all of Europe. After World War II, Canadian-American defense cooperation expanded, culminating in the North American Air Defense (NORAD) Agreement in 1958. Canadian and American military personnel jointly operated the NORAD command at Colorado Springs and the aerial warning stations in northern Canada. In addition, the U.S. military services used Canadian territory to test cruise missiles and defense equipment designed for use in a cold climate. Canada is a charter member of the North Atlantic Pact, and in 1989 it became a full member of the Organization of American States (OAS). Canada maintains a very small military force, however, because Canadians have come to assume that the United States will protect their territory regardless of their own military contribution. This attitude has led some to fear that Canada is becoming an American protectorate. Canadians are right, however, in believing that their country is so vital to the defense of the United States that if it were threatened by a hostile power, Washington would deploy whatever forces were required to prevent it from being occupied or intimidated. That fact reassures most Canadians, but many of them—particularly in Ontario—resent the reality that Canada is dependent for its security and economic well-being on its southern neighbor. A small minority thinks that neutralism and detachment would be a preferable foreign policy. The New Democratic Party, for example, advocates that Canada withdraw from NATO and NORAD and reduce its military forces even further. Most Canadians, however, reject that course and accept alliance with Washington as a vital interest for Canada.[4]

Economic Well-being.   Like defense, the economic relationship between the United States and Canada is vital for both countries. U.S. trade with Canada has for many years been larger than that with any other country, particularly after the two governments concluded the 1966 Auto Pact to move motor vehicles and parts across their borders without tariffs. U.S. trade with the province of Ontario alone is larger than with America's second largest trading partner, Japan. The United States is the major importer of Canada's vast mineral and oil resources. When the U.S.-Canada Free Trade Agreement, which took effect in 1989, was fully implemented by 1999, two-way trade would expand substantially.

American private investment in Canada, too, is larger than in any other country, totaling some $62 billion in 1988. During the 1970s and early 1980s, U.S. investment, particularly in energy-related industries, was a controversial issue in U.S.-Canadian relations when the Trudeau government enacted the Foreign Investment Review Act. This protectionist legislation was strongly criticized by the Nixon, Ford, and Carter administrations and was rescinded after the Progressive-Conservative Party, headed by Brian Mulroney, came to power in 1984 and adopted free-market policies. Some Canadians continue to oppose the massive U.S. ownership of businesses in their country, but they tend to forget the huge Canadian financial stake in the United States.

In November 1988 Canada held a crucial general election on whether it should ratify the U.S.-Canada Free Trade Agreement, which the Mulroney government had concluded with the Reagan administration. Opposition parties charged that the FTA was so fundamental to Canada's future independence that it should not be decided in the House of Commons, where the government held a comfortable majority, but by the voters in a general election. Mulroney's Conservative Party won the election, and Canada ratified the FTA in time for it to become effective on January 1, 1989.

Much of the opposition to the FTA came from Ontario, Canada's largest and most prosperous province. Its enactment meant that the enhancement of north-south trade between Canadian and American regions would reduce Canada's east-west continental trade, from which Ontario had historically benefitted. The irony in Ontario's opposition was that although this province had profited enormously from the 1966 Auto Pact, it was reluctant to take the next step and abolish trade barriers on all products.

By the end of 1990 the FTA was viewed in Canada as a mixed blessing because of many plant closings, a decline in some exports and a reduction in new U.S. investment. However, its long-term political and economic benefits led Washington and Ottawa in late 1990 to agree to enter negotiations with Mexico to enlarge the area, potentially creating a North American free-trade zone of nearly 400 million people.[5]

World Order. Canada's importance to the United States as a partner in building and preserving a favorable international security environment may not be as fundamental as are the close defense and economic relations; but the assistance of a cooperative Canada in NATO, in international economic policy, and in Western Hemisphere security is of great value to any administration in Washington. The presence of Canadian forces in West Germany gave added weight to North America's voice in defining NATO's future political and defense strategy.[6] Canada's membership in the Group of Seven (industrialized countries) contributed to North America's influence in international economic policy, and its contribution to numerous United Nations peacekeeping missions also enhances U.S. world-order interests. Canada's decision in 1989 to accept full membership in the Organization of American States added an important democratic voice to an organization that had not traditionally consisted of democratic governments. Canada has extensive contacts and substantial aid programs with the Commonwealth countries of the Caribbean, enjoys good relations with most Third World countries, and because of its close ties to Washington is seen as a country with some influence on American policy.

Canada did not support all of Washington's policies, however. For example, Ottawa maintained diplomatic ties and trade links with Cuba, even though the United States broke its own in 1961. Canada did not support U.S. aid for the Nicaraguan Contras during the 1980s, and it opposed American military involvement in Vietnam's civil war in the 1960s. Although Ottawa has traditionally favored diplomacy rather than force to settle international disputes, in December 1989 the Mulroney government supported President Bush's decision to use force against the Noriega dictatorship in Panama as a means to restore democratic government there. Like the United States and Britain, Canada strongly supported an international effort against Iraq's annexation of Kuwait in 1990.

Promotion of Values. Canada constitutes a major U.S. asset in promoting democracy and human rights abroad. Its parliamentary government is based on the Westminster model, and in 1982 it modified its constitution to incorporate a Charter of Rights and Freedoms—similar to the American Bill of Rights. Canada also enjoys a thriving free-market economy and has one of the world's highest standards of living. Since World War II it has absorbed millions of refugees and immigrants from Eastern Europe, Asia, and Latin America who have contributed to what Canadians call their model "multicultural" society. The United States benefits considerably from having a northern neighbor that shares its democratic values and promotes them abroad.

Fundamentally, then, Canada constitutes an overwhelmingly vital interest for the United States—in defense, economic, world-order, and promotion-of-values terms. If there were an imminent threat of attack on the United States from any part of the Northern Hemisphere, Canada would immediately become a war zone, and American and Canadian forces would defend this vast territory. Although most Americans do not fully appreciate the depth of the relationship, Canada occupies an essential position in the strategic thinking and foreign policy of the United States.[7]

"Continentalism" and Fear of the United States as Issues in Canadian Politics

A turning point in U.S.-Canadian relations and in Canadian politics took place in the parliamentary elections of November 21, 1988. Three key questions were decided in the hard-fought campaign. First, should Canada join in a free-trade association with the United States and thereby link itself more closely to its huge neighbor? Second, which political party, Progressive-Conservative or Liberal, would dominate Canadian politics into the 1990s? A third, less obvious issue was: would Quebec again abandon traditional support for the federal Liberal Party, as it did in 1984, and ensure that the Conservatives would stay in power in Ottawa for another five years?

Economic association with the United States, labeled

"continentalism" by its opponents, has long touched a sensitive nerve in Canadian politics. In 1911, for example, the government of Prime Minister Wilfrid Laurier concluded a "trade reciprocity agreement" with the William Taft administration in the United States. This was hailed by Canadian agricultural and mining interests as a great boost to the country's economic well-being. The Conservative Party, sensing strong nationalist doubts among many Canadians, decided to oppose the agreement. President Taft contributed to these doubts by stating publicly that Canadians were coming to a point in their foreign policy when they "must soon decide whether they are to regard themselves as isolated permanently from our markets by a perpetual wall, or whether we are to be commercial friends."

Speaker of the House of Representatives Champ Clark stirred up a political tumult in Canada with this imprudent comment on the agreement: "I am for it, because I hope to see the day when the American flag will float over every square foot of the British North American possessions clear to the north pole. . . . I do not have any doubt whatever that the day is not far distant when Great Britain will see all of her North American possessions become a part of this Republic. That is the way things are tending now."[8] As the storm broke in Canada, the embarrassed American president issued a statement that his government had no thought of political annexation or union of the two countries and that Canada would continue to remain an independent country. But the damage was done. Century-old Canadian fears of U.S. annexation, which subsided after Britain granted Canada its independence in 1867, had abruptly resurfaced some forty years later.

In Canada's general election on September 21, 1911, trade relations were the key issue. Opposition leader Robert Borden, who headed the Conservative Party, warned that the reciprocity agreement proposed by the government would lead to commercial union and to political annexation by the United States: "We must decide whether the spirit of Canadianism or of Continentalism shall prevail on the northern half of this continent." The election produced an astonishing reversal of political fortunes for Canada's political parties. Laurier's powerful Liberals were defeated by Borden's Conservatives, who captured a strong majority in the House of Commons. As a consequence, from 1911 until 1988 very few politicians were willing to suggest close trade relations with the United States. "Continentalism" was the slogan by

which Canadian nationalists attacked opponents who appeared
to be pro-American.

In October 1988, a month before a new general election was
scheduled, the leaders of Canada's three major political parties
held two (three-hour) television debates covering a range of issues. The second, telecast on October 25, produced a dramatic exchange between the Liberal Party's leader, John Turner, and the
Progressive-Conservative Party's leader and Prime Minister, Brian
Mulroney, on the issue of free trade with the United States. Their
exchange transformed what had been a dull campaign into an
emotion-charged national referendum on the government's plan
for ratification of the FTA. A third participant was Edward
Broadbent, leader of the New Democratic Party (NDP), who also
opposed the FTA but did not get involved in the sharp exchange
between Turner and Mulroney.

Because of the debate's importance to the election outcome
and to U.S.-Canadian relations, I cite a portion of that exchange.
In answer to a panelist's question, Turner asserted that Canada
had given away too much in the FTA and warned that thousands
of people in agriculture, energy, and business were in danger of
losing their jobs. Mulroney countered by citing an Economic
Council of Canada report predicting that 250,000 jobs would be
created. Turner charged that because the issue of government subsidies was left vague in the FTA, it gave the United States an opportunity to insist on its own definition of the term and thereby
threaten Canada's extensive social welfare programs. He asserted:
"I think the issues happen to be so important for the future of
Canada. I happen to believe you have sold us out." Mulroney re-
torted that his family had worked for 120 years to help build
Canada, and he challenged Turner's attack on his patriotism: "I
believe that in my own modest way I am nation-building because
I believe this benefits Canada, and I love Canada." Turner said
that Canada was built on infrastructure that resisted the continental pressure of the United States and charged that with one signa-
ture "you've reversed that, thrown us into the north-south
influence of the United States, and will reduce us . . . to a colony
of the United States because, when the economic levers go, the
political independence is sure to follow."[9]

The television debate changed the entire tone of the campaign
and stirred nationalist sentiments across Canada. The remaining
four weeks of the campaign produced an intense debate about the
future of Canada, somewhat similar to the one that had occurred

in 1911. In 1988, however, Liberals and Conservatives took opposite sides in the debate from that of their predecessors: in 1911 Liberals defended economic reciprocity and Conservatives opposed
it; in 1988 Liberals opposed free trade while Conservatives defended it. The outcome was also reversed in 1988: the proponents
of closer trade relations with the United States won the November election. Although John Turner and the Liberals gained some
support following the TV debate, they failed to cut into
Mulroney's strong support in Quebec and in western Canada.[10]

The 1988 General Election

The results of the November 21, 1988, elections gave the Conservatives 169 seats and 43 percent of the vote, and the Liberals 83
seats and 32 percent of the tally. The leftist NDP got 43 seats and
20 percent. Mulroney's majority in the House of Commons was
smaller than in the 1984 elections, but his Progressive-Conservatives nevertheless had achieved an impressive victory. The outcome vindicated his belief that when Canadian voters were
presented with all the facts about the benefits of the Free Trade
Agreement, they would support the government. Mulroney's continuing hold on his native Quebec was the single most important
factor in ensuring a Conservative victory. Had the Liberals swept
Quebec, as they did in the 1960s, 1970s, and early 1980s, they
would likely have received the needed margin to regain power in
1988, either as a majority government or in coalition with the NDP.
Mulroney's roots in Quebec and his fluency in French were important personal factors in his victory. Another was that Quebec
business interests favored free trade with the United States, and
the Liberals' opposition to the FTA hurt the party's chances in a
province where it had traditionally been strong. The 1988 election
also held serious implications for Canadian unity. For many years
Quebec had been known as a Liberal bastion in national elections,
particularly from 1968 to 1984, the Trudeau era. Whenever
Ontario's Liberals pooled their votes with those of Quebec's Liberals, the federal Liberal Party dominated national politics.
Quebec's support for free trade was galling to Ontario Liberals
because they had been willing historically to make large concessions to French Canada's desire to be accepted as an equal partner in the confederation. If Quebec now supported free trade,
many Ontario Liberals concluded, Quebec was no longer worthy
of their support on the "distinct society" issue.

A major reason why Quebec decided to give overwhelming support to the FTA and to Mulroney's Conservatives was summed up by a well-known Quebec nationalist and Conservative Party candidate, Lucien Bouchard. He accused Ontario Liberals of opposing free trade in order to protect their province's special trade relationship with the United States. He charged that Ontario's interests were at odds with those of Quebec, the Maritimes, and the Canadian West: "Ontario is the pipeline through which Canadian and American wealth are traded." He said that Ontario cautioned Quebec not to trade too heavily with the United States "because it is bad for our Canadian identity." Bouchard observed that in 1980, when the referendum on "sovereignty-association" (independence with economic links) was being debated in Quebec, Ontarians flocked there and urged voters not to vote "yes" to separation because separation would damage Quebec's economy by cutting it off from Canada. Quebec voters decided in 1980 not to separate from Canada, Bouchard said, but then Ontario began to admonish Quebec: "Hold it. You, in Quebec, just stay at home and just be an economic ghetto vis-a-vis the United States. We'll do the trading with them, and you'll get the equalization payments." That treatment for his province caused Bouchard to conclude that "Quebec is the one playing straight inside Confederation and Ontario has become the separatist force, the one that wants to go it alone."[11] His endorsement of Mulroney and the FTA in 1988 helped swing Quebec's large electoral vote to the Progressive-Conservatives.

The Meech Lake Constitutional Controversy

Quebec's role in the Canadian Confederation came to the fore in 1987 when the First Ministers—prime minister and ten provincial premiers—met at Meech Lake, a government retreat north of Ottawa. Their objective was to work out an agreement to bring Quebec into the 1982 constitution, which had been negotiated by the Trudeau government but rejected by Quebec, then governed by the separatist Parti Quebecois. So long as the PQ held power, there was no chance of ratification, but in 1985 it lost power to the Quebec Liberal Party, headed by Robert Bourassa. Prime Minister Brian Mulroney seized this opportunity to negotiate an agreement making Quebec a full partner in the new Confederation. In 1987 Bourassa and the nine other provincial premiers concluded the Meech Lake Accords, which guaranteed Quebec's special status within Canada. Quebec persistently argued that its "distinct society" status had been recognized in 1774 by Britain when Parliament passed the Quebec Act and formally incorporated French Canada into the Empire. Two centuries later Quebec was demanding that English Canada reaffirm Quebec's special rights in matters of language, immigration policy, and social security programs.

The Canadian parliament and all ten provinces had to ratify the Meech Lake agreement by June 1990 in order for it to become effective. All of them except New Brunswick and Manitoba did so in 1988–1989. But public opinion in western Canada and parts of Ontario was not pleased with the concessions granted to Quebec, especially after Bourassa ignored a Supreme Court ruling in December 1988 and enforced a law mandating that French would be the only official language in Quebec. Other provinces were obligated under federal law to recognize French and English as official languages, and federal government officials were required to be proficient in both languages. After December 1988 support for the Meech Lake Accords began to erode in English Canada, especially in Ontario, where it previously enjoyed wide support.[12]

The specter of Quebec's separation from Canada resurfaced in September 1989 during the provincial election campaign. The Parti Quebecois, under the leadership of Jacques Parizeau, argued that, unlike the case in 1980 when the province rejected sovereignty-association because of economic fears, in the 1990s an independent Quebec would be fully capable of sustaining a strong economy. Liberal Party leader Premier Robert Bourassa campaigned on the viewpoint that the Meech Lake agreement confirmed Quebec's ability to attain its objectives within the Confederation and argued that its economy would be stronger if it remained part of Canada. The Free Trade Agreement had already stimulated Quebec's economy, he argued, and the arrangement with the United States should not be jeopardized.

The provincial election returned Bourassa's Liberals to power, but with a reduced majority. The surprise was that the Parti Quebecois, running for the first time since 1973 on a straight independence platform rather than sovereignty-association, won 40 percent of the vote. That outcome shocked both Bourassa and English-speaking Canada because the PQ was thus entrenched as the only viable opposition party in Quebec, with prospects for regaining power when the electorate tired of the Liberals—perhaps as early as 1991. Bourassa for the first time began talking about the possibility that Quebec might have to separate from Canada if the Meech Lake Accords were not ratified by the deadline in June 1990. Western Canadians and an increasing number of Ontarians questioned whether it was worth further effort to persuade Quebec to remain in Canada. At the end of 1989, the previously avoided question of Canada's breakup was being seriously discussed in Ontario.

In November 1989 the First Ministers assembled in Ottawa to try to negotiate the disputes which had arisen over Meech Lake. Not only had Manitoba and New Brunswick not ratified, but Newfoundland's new premier, Clyde Wells, declared that his province's legislature would rescind its earlier endorsement unless the plan for Quebec's special status was watered down or all provinces were given similar rights. Wells and Mulroney engaged in heated debate on national TV and dramatized for Canadian viewers the intensity of the split between English-speaking Canada and French-speaking Quebec. The press reported that Wells received a huge amount of mail from all parts of Canada supporting his stand against Meech Lake.[13]

The principal debate in English-speaking Canada on Quebec's role in Confederation has always taken place in Ontario, Quebec's neighbor and a founding member of Confederation. Since 1867 Ontario has been in the forefront of efforts to accommodate Quebec's special status. The dilemma facing Ontario was analyzed by Professor Thomas Courchene in his Robarts Lecture at York University in 1988, "What Does Ontario Want?" Courchene speculated that Ontarians were in the process of redefining themselves: "More than a decade of wrestling with either Quebec's challenges or Quebec's aspirations has left English Canadians both weary and exasperated. . . . Moreover, as a result of all of this internal focus, Quebecers (or at least the Quebecois) have emerged with a new confidence and awareness of who they are in relation to themselves, to their province and to their country. . . . Ontarians emerged from this process more confused about who they are and more divided in terms of what they want."[14] Courchene did not predict the outcome of Canada's constitutional crisis, but he argued that the responsibility for resolving it lay as much with Ontario as with Quebec.

Early in June 1990 Prime Minister Mulroney made a last-minute effort to save the Meech Lake agreement by calling a special First Ministers' meeting designed to persuade Manitoba and

Newfoundland to ratify it.[15] The premiers of these two holdout
provinces agreed to put the issue to their legislatures, but a fili-
buster in the Manitoba House effectively blocked the vote before
the deadline for ratification passed. It was a severe personal defeat for Mulroney, and the country was in a mild state of shock.
Premier Bourassa announced that since French Canada had been
rejected by English-speaking Canada, Quebec would have to reconsider its options; in the meantime, it would deal only with the
federal government in Ottawa, he said, and would not attend future First Ministers' meetings on constitutional matters. Bourassa
set up a commission of representatives from many segments of
provincial society to study Quebec's options and asked for its report by March 1991. There was media speculation that the commission would probably recommend that unless Quebec were
granted larger concessions than those contained in the failed
Meech Lake compromise, it should unilaterally declare its independence and then negotiate an economic association with
Ontario, its principal trading partner. A recession in Canada could
slow the process, but Quebeckers at that point seemed intent on
having a sovereign state.

As the new debate on Quebec's future commenced, Eugene
Forsey, one of Canada's respected constitutional authorities and a
strong supporter of Canadian unity, wrote a commentary for the
Globe and Mail: "Can Canada Get By without Quebec? Absolutely."
He asserted that "there is no reason why a new political entity,
sans Quebec, need strike fear in our hearts—however much it is
entered upon unwillingly." He agreed that a change of this magnitude would be an immense challenge to Canada, but concluded,
"I have faith that Canadians, both English-speaking and French-
speaking (of whom there would still be over a million), would be
able to face the future united."[16]

On November 1, 1990, Prime Minister Brian Mulroney announced the creation of a "Citizens' Forum on Canada's Future"
under the leadership of Keith Spicer, a widely known expert on
the communications industry. Mulroney told the House of Commons that "Canada is running the risk of fracturing along the lin-
guistic and regional fault lines that have run deep throughout our
history." The Spicer commission would be charged, he said, with
canvassing the views of Canadians throughout the country and
reporting its findings in June 1991 (three months after the Quebec
commission set up by Premier Bourassa was due to report).
Mulroney left no doubt about the seriousness of Canada's consti-

tutional crisis: "The situation is urgent and I think that all members, irrespective of political party, recognize that the problem is serious." He continued: "It is time we all did some real soul-searching. The future of Canada depends upon the answer to some very simple but very important questions: Do we all still want to live together? What kind of country do we want? Do Canadians still have common values and hopes and interests? Can Quebec, as the only predominantly French-speaking province in Canada, find cultural security and respect for its identity with our federal system?" Mulroney addressed the alienation of western Canada and of the country's aboriginal population and asked: "Has our pride and our multiculturalism focused too much attention on our differences and begun to be a problem for a common Canadian identity?"[17]

Potential Fragmentation of Canada and the U.S. Response

At the beginning of 1990, before the failure of the Meech Lake compromise, Canadian public opinion appeared to favor additional efforts to persuade Quebec to accept the 1982 constitution, but the trend was negative. A Gallup poll published in January asked: "There has been quite a bit of talk recently about the possibility of the province of Quebec separating from the rest of Canada and becoming an independent country. Would you, yourself, be in favor of separation or opposed to it? " In Quebec, 39 percent said they favored separation, 1 percent gave it qualified support, and 15 percent were undecided. A similar poll taken six months earlier showed 34 percent in favor and 10 percent undecided. A bare majority, 52 percent, of all Canadians in January 1990 was opposed to Quebec's separation, compared with 61 percent just six months earlier.[18] One could conclude that Canadians were coming to accept the probability of separation. By September 1990, the polls showed that independence sentiment in Quebec had risen to an all-time high of 43 percent, and some polls showed it had risen to 60 percent when combined with "economic association."[19]

A fundamental question for the United States at the end of 1990 was how to respond to the prospect that two or more sovereign states could emerge on its northern border. The odds were about even that Quebec would declare its independence from Canada by the mid-1990s, after holding a new referendum on the question. If (many said "when") the Parti Quebeqois won the next election, probably in 1994, it would either move quickly to declare Quebec a sovereign state or hold another referendum before doing so. (See Chapter 8.)

Could U.S. national interests accommodate a sovereign Quebec? Probably yes, particularly if the new country facilitates U.S. investment and trade and accepts the many U.S. treaties with Canada as they affect Quebec's territory and airspace. This does not mean that dealing with sovereign Quebec would be easy, but the national interests of both countries, should Quebec choose independence, would likely be parallel in defense and economic matters while differing on many other international issues.

If Quebec becomes a sovereign state, with or without economic association with Canada, the four Atlantic provinces would be cut off from Canada and might begin to explore the possibility of some associated status with the United States, leading eventually to statehood. Washington would have some difficulty dealing with such requests because none of these provinces is economically viable without large transfer payments from Ottawa. Late in 1990 the premier of New Brunswick proposed an economic union with Nova Scotia and Prince Edward Island, but it is doubtful that the three could survive as an independent country. Newfoundland, the poorest of the four and with a history of pro-U.S. sentiment, is most likely to sound out Washington on the possibility of statehood. Or, the four provinces might consider merging in order to propose themselves as one U.S. state. Joining the United States would pose a particularly difficult dilemma for Nova Scotia, the original British colony in Canada, but as Garreau demonstrated in *The Nine Nations of North America*, the four eastern provinces are economically and culturally already a part of New England and have far more in common with Boston than with Toronto.[20]

If eastern Canada were to secede following Quebec's withdrawal from Confederation, would Ontario and the four western provinces be willing to build a new, internally more cohesive Canada? Their economies are strong; they possess vast natural resources; and together they form a contiguous area with excellent transportation links. The principal impediment to closer ties among them is political: western Canada has long felt alienated from Ontario because of the latter's traditional desire to accommodate Quebec, and also Toronto's protectionist economic attitude, which historically has worked against the economic interests of the West—particularly Alberta and British Columbia. If Ontario, following a separation of Quebec and the Atlantic provinces, were willing to alter its outlook, a new, more united and vigorous Canada could emerge and concentrate its energies on developing the West rather than subsidizing the East. This new Canada could be a stronger continental partner for the United States because it would be self-confident and probably more prosperous. Skeptics argue that Ontario is incapable of reorienting its outlook, that it would be more likely to concentrate on its own internal interests than to make the concessions required to build a more unified country in cooperation with the four western provinces. An alternative would be for the three prairie provinces— Manitoba, Saskatchewan, and Alberta—to form their own country and for British Columbia to go its own way.

A fragmented Canada would not be in the interest of the United States, however. Should Quebec decide to become independent, a united English-speaking Canada stretching westward from Quebec would be a far more preferable outcome. The national interests of the United States, then, would not necessarily be damaged if Canada became two sovereign entities, provided the separation was peaceful. A division of Canada into two countries would, of course, be painful for many Canadians, especially in Ontario. But with patience and understanding by the U.S. government and the American public, the transition would be manageable and should result in continuing strong relationships across our 3,000–mile transcontinental border.

U.S. Interests in Mexico and Central America

The countries south of the U.S. border clearly were not taken for granted by the American government or public in the 1980s. The reason is that with a few notable exceptions such as Mexico, Venezuela, and Costa Rica, most of the countries in Central and South America and the Caribbean were politically unstable or economically depressed, and some (El Salvador, Haiti, Colombia) were threatened with civil war. During the 1980s, countering a Communist-led insurgency in El Salvador was a top priority of the Reagan White House. Similarly, Reagan's decision to use force in November 1983 to oust a brutal Communist dictatorship in Grenada dramatized his determination to prevent that island from becoming a base for Cuban and Soviet military operations in the

Caribbean. Moreover, revelations made during congressional hearings into the Iran-Contra diversion in 1987 showed that the White House was deeply involved in covert actions to undermine the Marxist government in Nicaragua.

More recently, the U.S. invasion of Panama in December 1989 to depose its dictator and drug trafficker, General Manuel Noriega, underlined the sensitivity of U.S. relations with Latin America. Nearly all other countries in the Western Hemisphere deplored the U.S. intervention, even though they had little respect for the Noriega regime. Within a few months, however, this opposition dissipated as it became clear that the Panamanian people applauded President Bush's decision to help restore constitutional rule in their country. The intervention also demonstrated anew that Panama is a vital U.S. interest, even though the Panama Canal may no longer be militarily vital. Bush's action announced to all countries that the United States will not tolerate a hostile government that threatens the safety of Americans and the smooth operation of the canal. It also reinforced the view of most Americans that Central America and the Caribbean are areas of vital interest where the United States should not tolerate hostile regimes.

Soon after coming to office in January 1981, President Reagan decided to confront the revolutionary Sandinista regime in Nicaragua—politically, economically, and with covert military force. The U.S. government trained an army of more than 10,000 Nicaraguan resistance forces, known as Contras, for infiltration into Nicaragua. This clandestine operation was viewed by many leaders in Central and South America as the beginning of another phase in Yankee imperialism in the region. Reagan's large economic and military aid program to help El Salvador's newly established democratic government fight a Communist insurgency, heavily supported by Cuba and Nicaragua, heightened political tensions in Central America. Efforts by the Contadora Group, which included Mexico and Venezuela, to negotiate an end to the insurgencies in El Salvador and Nicaragua proved fruitless, and many blamed the Reagan administration for intransigence. The Iran-Contra affair in Washington in 1986–1987 ruined Reagan's chances of getting Congress to renew military aid for the Contras, and in 1989 the Democratic-controlled House and Senate persuaded the Bush administration to stop support for the Contras if the Sandinista government followed through on its pledge to hold democratic elections in February 1990.[21]

Mexico. Like Canada, Mexico constitutes a vital national interest for the United States in North America with regard to military security and, increasingly, economic well-being. Mexico's population of 95 million is more than three times that of Canada and is a vast market for U.S. exports as its economy continues to grow. Geography is a key to the U.S. defense interest: Mexico has a 2,000-mile American border, and several million of its citizens work legally or illegally in the United States. The country also occupies a staging area for illegal drug smuggling into the United States. If the U.S. defense-of-homeland interest is defined broadly, the border with Mexico clearly is vulnerable to invasion by millions of Mexico's poor people, international drug smugglers, and possibly terrorists. Given its large unemployment problem, the disastrous 1985 earthquake in Mexico City, and evidence of massive corruption in its government, Mexico might be considered a potentially unstable country. The sensitivity of the drug-trafficking issue in U.S.-Mexico relations was noted in the handling of an investigation into the assassination of a U.S. drug enforcement agent, Enrique Camarena, in 1985. The incident touched off a diplomatic row in April 1990 when one of the suspects in the killing was kidnapped in Mexico, transported to Texas, and there arrested by U.S. officials. President Salinas protested what he called an infringement on Mexico's sovereignty. The U.S. Justice Department denied that any Americans were involved in the kidnaping and suggested that high-ranking Mexican police officers had spirited the suspect out of the country. The Mexican government contradicted the U.S. version but decided to continue drug-enforcement cooperation with the U.S. government.[22]

In Mexico's federal elections of 1988, the Institutional Revolutionary Party (PRI) for the first time in sixty years encountered serious competition for the presidency. Its candidate, Carlos Salinas de Gortari, a forty-year-old economist, won with only 50.4 percent of the vote, compared with the 70 to 80 percent margins enjoyed by his predecessors. A *New York Times* Magazine's cover story by Mexico City bureau chief Larry Rohter observed: "Salinas comes to office not only with less internal support than any Mexican President in modern times, but also at a time when the institution of the presidency—traditionally the fount and repository of all power in the country—has been weakened or discredited, through corruption, incompetence, or other scandals, by each of his four immediate predecessors." Citing public demonstrations against the election results, Rohter continued: "These events not only shattered what still remained of the mythology surrounding the presidency, but also provided the strongest proof yet that Salinas, unlike any of his PRI predecessors, will have to govern on a basis of consensus and persuasion if further erosion is to be prevented."[23]

After his inauguration in December 1988, Salinas quickly put his mark on Mexican politics by cracking down on drug dealing and arresting the country's most powerful labor leader on corruption charges. Salinas and George Bush, who became U.S. president a month after Salinas's inauguration in Mexico City, continued the cordial relationship between the Mexican and American presidents that had blossomed during Ronald Reagan's presidency. Reagan established good personal ties with two Mexican presidents—Jose Lopez Portillo and Hurtado de la Madrid—during his eight-year tenure, in contrast with President Carter's inability to forge close relationships with the Mexican leaders. Just before leaving office, President de la Madrid, at Reagan's urging, instituted sweeping changes in the country's laws and regulations governing foreign trade and investment, in an effort to attract foreign capital and improve Mexico's international financial position. It was left to President Salinas, however, to implement the unpopular but essential structural changes in the Mexican economy.

Mexico's political and economic importance to the United States was underlined in 1982 by the Reagan administration's special steps to assist Mexico financially at a time when its economy was on the verge of bankruptcy because of a sharp drop in world oil prices. Again in 1989, when the Mexican economy was in serious difficulty because of massive foreign indebtedness, the United States took the lead in working out an arrangement, under provisions of the Brady Plan (named for U.S. Secretary of the Treasury Nicholas Brady), whereby banks would write off part of the Mexican debt in exchange for U.S. guarantees of new loans. In return, Mexico pledged to open its markets to foreign investment and reduce trade barriers. The *Christian Science Monitor* headlined its story "Historic Debt Deal Buys Breathing Room for Mexico."[24] The country's future economic stability could not be assured, however, without sustained U.S. government involvement with and pressure on international lending agencies and U.S. banks.

President Salinas continued the austerity program of his predecessor, and in 1990 Mexico's economy appeared to be improving slowly but steadily. Meanwhile, Washington persuaded Japan to lend Mexico large amounts of capital. In the 1990s Mexico was destined to occupy an almost unique position in terms of its priority for U.S. financial assistance—evidence of its status as a vital interest of the United States.

Whereas Mexico is a vital U.S. defense-of-homeland and economic interest, its role in U.S. world-order interests is at the major level because the Mexican government very often opposes Washington on controversial international issues—in the United Nations, in the Organization of American States, and in Third World forums. Unlike other Latin American countries, Mexico did not break diplomatic relations with Cuba in the early 1960s when the United States did so in response to Fidel Castro's new defense agreement with the Soviet Union. Mexico also recognized the legitimacy of El Salvador's Communist rebels in 1982 and strongly criticized U.S. aid to the Nicaraguan Contras as interference in the internal affairs of a Latin American state. Its condemnation of U.S. policy toward Nicaragua was muted in the mid-1980s when it became clear that Managua was supporting insurgencies in El Salvador, Guatemala, and Honduras and accepting large quantities of Soviet weapons. Critics in Mexico then charged that the de la Madrid government had toned down criticism of U.S. policy because of Washington's help in ameliorating Mexico's economic crisis in 1982.

President Bush had the opportunity in the 1990s to build a close, longer-term relationship with Mexico than previous American presidents had, for two reasons. First, Mexico, like Canada, understood that its economic well-being and national security depended on good relations with the United States. Neither Canada nor Mexico spent much of its national budget on defense, because they knew that Washington would protect them in case of an external threat. Second, the United States was the most important market for Mexico's exports, and Mexico desperately wanted to export even more of its products across the U.S. border.

Significant changes in Mexico's outlook on international trade, a free-market economy, and the role of government bureaucracy would have to be implemented, however, before the country was ready for free trade with its northern neighbors. Mexico refused to become a member of the General Agreement on Tariffs and Trade (GATT) until 1986 because it wanted to protect many inefficient domestic industries. President de la Madrid made the decision to put Mexico under the discipline of GATT as part of an agreement

with the United States and the International Monetary Fund to reduce government subsidies and protection of Mexican industries.

During 1989, in response to concerns about the potential formation of a restrictive European trading bloc in 1992, there was
speculation about the feasibility of establishing a North American
free-trade zone that would involve nearly 400 million Americans,
Canadians, and Mexicans. In the autumn of 1989 Mexican and
American trade officials began talks about lowering trade barriers. By March 1990 these discussions had proceeded to the point
where officials began to speak openly about negotiation of a free-
trade agreement that would also include Canada. The *Wall Street
Journal* headlined its story from Washington "U.S. and Mexico
Agree to Seek Free-Trade Pact; Bush Aides Confirm Talks; Result
Would be Market For All of North America."[25] In June 1990, Presidents Bush and Salinas, meeting in Washington, endorsed the goal
of a comprehensive free-trade agreement between the United
States and Mexico and directed their trade ministers to begin consultations and report at their next meeting in December 1990. Economically, a free-trade arrangement with Canada and the United
States would be attractive to Mexico. Politically, however, the historical antagonisms between Mexico and the United States
dwarfed the problems that the United States and Canada encountered when they negotiated their free-trade agreement.

Alan Riding, in a comprehensive book on U.S.-Mexico relations titled *Distant Neighbors*, observed: "Contiguity with the
United States has proved a permanent psychological trauma.
Mexico cannot come to terms with having lost half of its territory
to the United States, with Washington's frequent meddling in its
political affairs, and the U.S. hold on its economy and with growing cultural penetration by the American way of life." (In part, this
statement might have been applied also to Canada early in the
twentieth century, when nationalists there harbored deep fears
about being absorbed into the United States.) Riding observed,
however, that Mexico's "emotional nationalism is also tempered
by realism." Mexico knows it needs good relations with its powerful neighbor, he said, because "it cannot risk the economic and
political repercussions likely to flow from alienating Washington.
It knows that a stable and prosperous Mexico serves the United
States' best interests, but it also understands that its autonomy is
limited." He noted that in practice, Mexico's nationalism must be
"a controlled ritual, reduced largely to rhetoric and occasional dis-
plays of independence in foreign policy."[26]

Mexico's trade and diplomatic relations with Canada expanded markedly during the 1980s. The two countries established a Joint Ministerial Committee in 1971 to handle the bilateral relationship, and Canada soon became Mexico's fourth largest export market. The "Maquilladora" free-trade industries established in Mexico along the U.S. border provided employment to 300,000 Mexicans, but they were of concern to Canada because they could be serious competition for auto parts manufacturers, one of Ontario's principal industries. These free-trade border industries became part of the trilateral negotiation among the three North American countries to ensure that integration of their trade was accomplished in a politically acceptable manner. (See Chapter 8 on the 1992 NAFTA treaty among the U.S., Canada, and Mexico.)

While Canada made a historic choice on economic association with the United States in its November 1988 elections, Mexico showed reluctance at first to make a similar decision. This was so because its economy was not at the point where it could risk free trade with the United States and Canada and because the "psychological trauma" cited by Riding needed to be mitigated. The fact that Canadian business interests were willing to risk entering a free-market competition with American rivals gave Mexican business leaders confidence that they too could compete in a new, enlarged North American free-trade area, if their own government's policies were favorable. Implementing a Mexico-U.S.-Canada FTA over a ten- to fifteen-year period would ease the difficult transition and permit Mexico to adjust its economy to a North American free-trade standard. A similar time frame would be required to allay the worst fears of U.S. labor and some industries about the dangers to them of expanded free trade.

Central America. The United States reasserted its traditional interest in Central America during the 1980s, beginning with President Carter's 1980 decision to supply military and economic aid to El Salvador to help its democratically elected government defend itself against Communist insurgents aided by Nicaragua, Cuba, and the Soviet Union. In 1981 President Reagan directed the Central Intelligence Agency to build and arm a Nicaraguan resistance force in order to curb the flow of arms from Nicaragua to Salvadoran guerrillas and to destabilize the Sandinista regime. By the end of the decade, civil war in El Salvador had not ended, but a democratic government headed by President Alfredo Cristiani was in control of most parts of the country. Also in 1989 the Marxist government of Nicaragua, with a nearly bankrupt economy resulting from economic sanctions imposed by the United States as well as its own inept policies, decided to hold elections in 1990 in return for a U.S. pledge to stop aid to the Contras. The Soviet Union agreed as part of President Gorbachev's detente relationship with Washington to stop arms shipments to Nicaragua. This reversal of Soviet policy infuriated Cuba's Fidel Castro, who continued to urge revolution in Central America. President Bush decided to support the peace initiative of Costa Rica's President Oskar Arias to end all the insurgencies in Central America and to settle disputes through negotiations. Elections in Nicaragua were a key part of this plan.

The general elections of February 24, 1990, represented a stunning victory for the non-Communist parties and an equally stunning defeat for the Sandinista government. President Daniel Ortega and the Sandinista leadership campaigned with the advantages offered by their control of the army and police and large amounts of money. The opposition was led by Violeta Chamorro, widow of a respected newspaper editor who had been killed by the Somoza dictatorship in 1978. Her campaign was given some financial support by the United States, but she did not appear to have a chance of winning. Nevertheless, the opposition parties won a decisive victory, and Chamorro became president in April. Her political situation was precarious, however, because the Sandinistas continued to control the army and police and large segments of the labor movement. She negotiated with the Sandinista leaders to permit the Contras to return to Nicaragua and turn in their arms, in return for the demobilization of a large part of the Sandinista-controlled army. That process proceeded slowly during 1990.

This turnabout in the political situation in Nicaragua represented a victory for the peace process initiated earlier by five Central American presidents. It was also a foreign policy victory for the Bush administration, which had decided in 1989 to pursue a negotiated settlement rather than continued support for the Contras. Following President Chamorro's inauguration on April 25, 1990, the Washington Post observed: "Much of the hope that a lot of people in Nicaragua and around the world had for it at the time the Sandinistas took over was based on a misguided belief that the Sandinistas would establish a large new measure of political freedom and economic equity. That, to put it mildly, was not to be. Yesterday's inauguration of the Chamorro government provides a new—a second—chance."[27]

With Soviet and Cuban influence collapsing in Central America, the Bush administration could afford to treat the area as a regional problem rather than as an East-West power issue. Among the implications of the change from a U.S. strategic to a world-order interest in Central America was the beneficial effect it could have if the governments there took dramatic steps, especially land reform, to alleviate the serious economic and social problems that had long affected their populations and encouraged insurgencies. It was clear that the creation of a favorable political climate would require much greater economic aid from the United States, at a time when Washington was grappling with a huge budget deficit and the public's reluctance to pay higher taxes. But in the spring of 1990, Congress was disposed to grant additional economic aid to Nicaragua and Panama while it reduced military aid to El Salvador.

Early in 1989 a serious threat to U.S. defense and world-order interests throughout the Central American and Caribbean region developed in Panama. In May, military leader General Manuel Noriega—who had been the de facto political power there for eight years, following the death of General Omar Torrijos in 1981—overturned the results of a free national election and installed his own government. In November 1989 he had himself appointed head of state with dictatorial powers. During the 1970s and early 1980s Noriega had cooperated with the U.S. military command in Panama and with the CIA to combat Communist subversion in Central America. But in 1988 Noriega's dealings with international drug traffickers led to his indictment in the United States on drug charges. Several coups attempted by military officers failed to topple him. As Noriega grew increasingly hostile to the U.S. military presence in Panama, his troops began to harass U.S. service personnel stationed there under a treaty to protect the canal. In December 1989 President Bush ordered the 12,000 U.S. troops stationed in Panama, plus an additional 12,000 sent from the United States, to oust Noriega's dictatorship and restore democratic government to the country. After several days of fighting, most resistance stopped and Noriega eventually gave himself up to U.S. authorities. They then transported him to the United States to stand trial on drug charges.[28]

The Panamanian candidates who ostensibly had won the May 1989 elections were soon installed in office by U.S. authorities, and

in January 1990 U.S. troops began withdrawing. A new government, headed by President Guillermo Endara, abolished the
Panama Defense Force established by Noriega and created a new
police department. Polls showed that U.S. intervention was
widely supported by the American public and Congress and by
an overwhelming majority of the Panamanian people. David
Broder, columnist for the *Washington Post*, summed up the American reaction in the title of his commentary: "Panama: An Intervention That Made Sense."[29]

The reaction in Latin America was not positive, however. At a
news conference on January 5, 1990, President Bush acknowledged the diplomatic problem his intervention had created but
welcomed the public support of the Panamanians: "I am well
aware of how our friends south of our border, including my
friend, President Salinas [of Mexico], look at the use of American
force anywhere. . . . But given the history of the use of U.S. force, I
would be remiss if I didn't face up to the problem that we must
go forward diplomatically now to explain how this president
looks at the protection of American life, that we acted, in our view,
well within our rights. . . . I feel strongly about the protection of
American life, so we've got to get them to understand that this
isn't a shift away from what some had termed excessively timid
diplomacy." In response to a question about future use of U.S.
forces, the president said that Panama was a unique situation: "I
can't visualize another situation quite this unique." He welcomed
the public support of the Panamanians: "One thing that's helped
on this . . . is the way the Panamanian democracy is now starting
to move forward. The certification of the three people who had
been deprived of their right to hold office by the previous regime—that's been of enormous help. And then I think the other
thing is the reception, the public reception in Panama, for our action. It has been overwhelming, overwhelming."[30]

On January 1, 1990, in accordance with its treaty obligations,
the United States turned over the presidency of the Panama Canal Commission to a Panamanian and pledged its intention to relinquish control over all operations of the canal at the end of the
decade. The Noriega episode, however, raised the question of
whether the United States should withdraw completely from
Panama at the end of the century or remain there in a reduced security role, in agreement with the Panamanian government. In
anticipation of a full withdrawal in 1999, U.S. policy in the 1980s
supported the buildup of the Panama Defense Force to take on

the security responsibility. But this force soon became the means whereby General Noriega imposed his personal rule on Panama and turned the country into a haven for drug and arms smugglers. Following the U.S. intervention in December 1989, Washington encouraged President Endara to abolish the armed forces and create a police organization shorn of any responsibility for defending the country or the canal. If Panama continued to follow this course, it would be more difficult by 1999 for U.S. military forces to leave Panama because there would be insufficient security for the Panama Canal in the twenty-first century. The *Economist* put the question succinctly after quoting a Panamanian official who thought it would be good to find a new word for "colony": "In a fastidious world, perhaps he is right, but a colony is what Panama is, just as Puerto Rico is. There is little point in America pretending it is not a colonial power. Instead, it might concentrate on being a good colonialist in those parts of Latin America where that is what it is."[31]

U.S. Interests in the Caribbean and South American Countries

The island nations of the Caribbean are no less vital to U.S. defense and world-order interests than is Central America. Cuba, Jamaica, the Dominican Republic, Haiti, Puerto Rico (a U.S. territory), the Bahamas, and the small islands on the eastern approaches to the Caribbean are all strategically located on shipping lanes and air routes between North and South America as well as the South Atlantic. Most of them lie in the area that Joel Garreau, in *The Nine Nations of North America*, called "the Islands." They are mostly Spanish-speaking nations (exceptions are Jamaica, Haiti, the Bahamas) that have a strong affinity with south Florida, which has a large Hispanic population. They have, in one degree or another, developing economies under various styles of government: a functioning parliamentary system (Jamaica), a newly acquired constitutional system (Dominican Republic), a military-led regime (Haiti), a Communist dictatorship (Cuba), and various other forms of authoritarian government (the Bahamas, Grenada).

The United States has demonstrated a vital national interest in this area over thirty years: in the ill-fated Bay of Pigs invasion of Cuba, 1961; the Cuban Missile crisis, 1962; armed intervention in the Dominican Republic, 1965; the invasion of Grenada, 1983; support for the ouster of the Duvalier regime in Haiti, 1987; and charges of drug money laundering against the Bahamian government in 1988–1989. In addition, Puerto Rico accommodates important U.S. military facilities. Of all these states, only Cuba is hostile to the United States, a situation that many think will not change until Fidel Castro dies or is removed from power. Castro became increasingly isolated when Mikhail Gorbachev's government cut the annual Soviet subsidy to Cuba, causing great difficulty for its depressed economy. Tough U.S. economic sanctions have made it impossible for Cuba to export sugar and other products to its traditional market, the United States, and Cuba was denied the U.S. trade and investment that were offered to the rest of the Caribbean countries during the 1980s through President Reagan's Caribbean Basin Initiative (CBI). The security and economic well-being of the Caribbean area remained vital U.S. interests in 1990 and were certain to remain so into the future.

Venezuela and Colombia, on the South American continent, are also important—probably vital—national interests of the United States because of their strategic locations, economic links to North America, and relatively long tradition of democratic government. At the beginning of the 1990s, however, both countries had serious economic problems. Venezuela, like Mexico, overinvested during the 1970s when oil prices were high and then found itself burdened with huge debts after oil prices plummeted in the 1980s. Unlike Mexico, Venezuela has a relatively small population (20 million) and possesses vast mineral wealth. Its trade is heavily oriented northward to the United States and Canada, and its cultural attraction to Florida and other parts of the United States is pervasive. U.S. private investment in Venezuela is higher than in most Latin American countries because of the favorable investment climate there. In foreign policy Venezuela supports Latin American causes, as it did in Argentina's war with Britain in 1982, but is generally cooperative with the United States. When the Middle East crisis began in August 1990, Venezuela tacitly agreed to increase oil production to make up for the cutoff of Iraq's and Kuwait's oil to world markets.

Colombia too was a friendly, cooperative neighbor during the 1980s, but the powerful Medellin drug cartels and their assassination of public officials put a heavy strain on that country's democratic institutions and created serious problems in Bogota's relations with Washington. In 1989 President Virgilio Barco forged a close working relationship with the Bush administration to curb the power of the "drug lords" in his country; his efforts included the apprehension and killing of one of Colombia's most notorious drug leaders. The U.S. invasion of Panama temporarily suspended the two governments' efforts to coordinate military moves against drug exports from Colombia to the United States, but in early 1990 these operations were resumed. For example, Colombia hosted a drug summit at Cartagena on February 15 which brought together the presidents of Colombia, Peru, Bolivia, and the United States to work out a comprehensive anti-narcotics strategy. The four presidents agreed that international efforts to curb drug trafficking must deal with U.S. consumption of drugs as well as their production and shipment.

The United States provided Colombia with economic, military, and technical assistance in its effort to reduce the drug trade and find new sources of income for peasants whose livelihood depends on growing the raw material. These efforts were only partially successful, however. The Colombian government argued that the long-term solution to the drug problem lay in curbing demand in the United States—an argument dramatized in January 1990 with the arrest of Washington, D.C.'s flamboyant mayor, Marion Barry, on charges of repeated use of cocaine. His arrest and trial focused attention on the demand side of the drug problem and helped place the supply problem in Colombia, Peru, and Bolivia in better perspective. However, Barry's conviction in August 1990 on only one misdemeanor charge produced dismay in Colombia and reinforced a view that the United States was not truly serious about curbing cocaine use.

U.S. national interests in other major South American countries—Brazil, Argentina, and Chile—are important but not at the vital interest level. From a defense-of-homeland perspective, these countries' territory is not a significant strategic factor. Economically, all three nations have the potential to flourish and become good trading partners of the United States, but they had for many years been held back by authoritarian military regimes, protectionist policies, huge foreign debts, and high rates of inflation. In 1990 Brazil agreed to reduce protectionism. The Bush administration responded by eliminating it from the list of countries it had named "unfair traders" (under terms of the 1988 Trade Act) and dropped plans to impose economic sanctions. Argentina and Chile, as well as smaller South American countries, continued to emphasize free markets and encourage foreign investment, but debt and inflation continued to trouble their newly established democratic governments.

Among U.S. world-order interests, South America as a whole is very important, near-vital, to this country. This applies to maintenance of peace and security in the Western Hemisphere; cooperation in the Organization of American States when regional issues such as those in Grenada, Panama, and Nicaragua arise; and hemispheric solutions to such issues as drug trafficking, money laundering, and threats to the environment. On promotion of values, South America is of major interest to the United States, which desires to have democratic governments in power in Central and South America. Governments that promote human rights and democratic elections, it believes, are less likely than dictatorships to use military forces to threaten neighbors, and they tend to encourage free-market economies.

To emphasize the growing importance of South as well as Central American countries to the United States, President Bush announced in June 1990 a proposal that would cut part of the $12 billion debt these countries owe to the United States and suggested a $300 million annual fund to spur investment in Latin America. In addition, he proposed that Latin America explore with the United States and Canada a hemispheric free-trade zone to encourage trade and investment throughout North and South America.[32] The proposal met with an immediate favorable response from most Latin American counties. Political leaders as well as business groups showed new interest in the recently announced agreement between President Bush and Mexican President Salinas to negotiate a free-trade agreement between their two countries. But reaction in the United States, particularly in organized labor, was marked by skepticism.

The 1990s would see a strengthening of U.S. government ties with nations immediately south of the border because they directly affected all four of this country's basic national interests. Defense-of-homeland and world-order interests are affected at the vital level by economic and political instability in Central America and the Caribbean and would command larger U.S. resources. The economic interest was a major, not a vital one, although Mexico was approaching the vital economic level because of its oil reserves and its large market for U.S. exports. The United States also had a major, perhaps vital, interest in building democracy and human rights in all the Americas. President Bush, like Presidents Reagan and Carter, understood the great importance of promoting democracy and social justice in America's own "neighborhood" as a means to improve hemisphere security.

6
U.S. Interests and Policies in East Asia, 1990

East Asia is the principal region of the world where America's vital national interests were vastly expanded in the 1950s and 1960s. This resulted from a new Sino-Soviet security threat precipitated by the Chinese Communist Party's achievement of power in 1949 and Mao Zedong's conclusion of a defense alliance with Stalin in February 1950. It was natural, therefore, that the region should be given special scrutiny by U.S. policymakers in 1990 as the United States reordered its worldwide national security priorities to reflect the realities of a post–Cold War world. This did not suggest that U.S. interests and policies in East Asia would return to the pre-1950 period of detachment; rather it was an effort to find the proper balance between maintaining a favorable world order there in the 1990s and sharing the costs of doing so with Asia's newly vigorous economies.

Before the outbreak of the Korean War in June 1950, only Japan, the Philippines, Australia, New Zealand, and the U.S.-administered Trust Territories of the Pacific were judged by Washington to constitute America's vital interests in East Asia. The mainland, including China, Korea, and Southeast Asia, was of lower priority before the People's Republic of China emerged as a major power center in Asia, in alliance with the Soviet Union. In the 1970s, after Beijing moved away from Moscow and into better relations with the United States and Japan, China began to play a more constructive role in Asia. During the same thirty–year period other major changes occurred. Japan became an economic superpower, the Southeast Asian states threw off their colonial masters, and six of them formed the Association of Southeast Asian Nations (ASEAN), with emphasis on economic and political cooperation. ASEAN's original membership comprised Thailand, Malaysia, Singapore, Indonesia, and the Philippines; Brunei joined in the 1980s. Australia became a significant regional power with close ties to New Zealand and the island states of the South and Southwest Pacific. Taiwan and South Korea, two vulnerable and economically dependent states in 1950, emerged in the 1980s as economic powers, encountering fewer military threats from China and North Korea than had been true in the 1950s and 1960s. Most of the Pacific islands formerly under U.S. trusteeship became either territories of the United States or independent states in free association with it. In the Indian Ocean the United States Navy assumed a major role in Diego Garcia and the Persian Gulf region following the 1979 fall of the Shah's regime in Iran and the subsequent Soviet occupation of Afghanistan. India emerged in the 1980s as a major military and political power in Asia and sustained a rapidly expanding economy and a viable democratic political system. In 1989 the Soviet Union withdrew its occupation forces from Afghanistan; Iran ended its Gulf War with Iraq; and India and Pakistan established more friendly relations than had existed in the 1960s and 1970s. In sum, by 1990 the political, economic, and security relationships in East Asia and the Indian Ocean area had become significantly different from those of the previous forty years. (The 1990 Persian Gulf crisis is discussed in Chapter 8.)

In 1950 President Truman decided, following the North Korean invasion of South Korea, to confront the growing Soviet and Chinese military threat in East Asia with a major buildup of American power in the Pacific. He also concluded a series of bilateral and multilateral defense pacts with Asian states seeking protection from Communist pressure: Japan, South Korea, Taiwan, the Philippines, Australia, and New Zealand. Thailand was added in 1954. After Deng Xiaoping replaced Mao Zedong in 1976 and China requested Western help in modernizing its economy, the balance of power in East Asia gradually shifted and became more favorable to the United States and Japan. The significant economic changes in China and the profound political changes in the Soviet Union under Mikhail Gorbachev's leadership in the late 1980s called into question the necessity of some U.S. defense commitments in the region and the continued heavy emphasis on military forces and bases that had prevailed there since the 1950s.

The beginning of a reevaluation and retrenchment of U.S. military power was underlined in February 1990 during Defense Secretary Richard Cheney's discussions with leaders of South Korea, the Philippines, and Japan. He informed them of President

Bush's planned 10 percent reduction in U.S. forces in their countries while also emphasizing that the United States intended to remain a strong Pacific power. Although 10 percent represented a small reduction in the total of 120,000 U.S. troops then stationed in East Asia (excluding Guam), it nevertheless signaled to countries hosting U.S. forces that additional cuts would probably be forthcoming if Congress and the Bush administration concluded that the desirability of maintaining them was outweighed by a declining Soviet military threat to the region and an increased ability by East Asian states to provide a larger share of their own defenses.

By 1985 it appeared to some observers that America was overextended in East Asia in light of the greatly altered political situation in Northeast and Southeast Asia resulting from the political change in China. By 1990, retrenchment seemed a reasonable course because of profound changes within the Soviet Union, a significant reduction in tensions among the East Asian countries, and growing budgetary concerns in the United States. A major cautionary note in 1990, however, was the internal political situation in the People's Republic of China (PRC), whose leadership had crushed the liberal student movement in Beijing in June 1989. Congressional critics pressed for severe economic and political sanctions against the PRC government, but President Bush resisted these efforts. In January 1990, after the House of Representatives overrode his veto on legislation calling for such sanctions, the Senate upheld the president in a very close vote. The future composition of China's leadership and its effect on China's foreign policy, after the death of the aging Deng Xiaoping, was the major ambiguity in the international politics of East Asia.

An Emerging Economic and Security System

In the 1990s five Asian countries were likely to be key players in the international relations of East Asia: Japan, China, India, Indonesia, and Australia. Each of the five had the population base, resources, military capability, and internal political cohesion to act with some independence in relations with other states. They clearly influenced the security of their smaller neighbors in Northeast Asia, Southeast Asia, the Indian Ocean region, and the Southwest Pacific. In addition, Japan's economic power was felt in East Asia, and its growing military strength stimulated concern among the countries that Japan had conquered during World War II.

China, with one billion-plus people and a large land mass, affected the security of many states in East and South Asia and the Soviet Union. India exercised increasing influence in Southeast Asia as well as the Indian Ocean area because of its large population, its rapidly growing economy, and its ability to project military and economic power beyond its immediate geographic location. Indonesia, given its size, strategic location, and large natural resources, was potentially a key player in East Asian security relationships, but some observers argued that it had not developed the industrial base and economic infrastructure to sustain a power role there. Australia, occupying a highly strategic location in the Southwest Pacific and also bordering on the Indian Ocean, had all the ingredients of major power status except for the small size of its population—about 17 million. It possessed a strong modern economy, vast natural resources, and powerful, if small, military forces capable of deployment well beyond its immediate vicinity.

Mainland Southeast Asia could have become a power vacuum because no single state there had the economic and political power or military force in 1990 to dominate the actions of its neighbors. A united Vietnam, under Hanoi's iron control since 1975, may have had pretensions to the leadership role on the mainland and in the South China Sea (its occupation of Kampuchea—Cambodia—in 1978 may have been a part of that design). However, if that was Hanoi's intention, the next fifteen years demonstrated that Vietnam could not expand its area of influence so long as China, the U.S.S.R., and Thailand were prepared to resist such pressure. Vietnam's withdrawal from Kampuchea in 1989 underlined this reality. The political solidarity of the ASEAN states contributed significantly to the outcome, even though an internal political settlement in Kampuchea remained elusive.

How would the five major players in East Asia interact in the 1990s? What conflicts, if any, were likely to arise from their competition for markets, political influence, and military advantage? A brief description of the foreign policies of these five powers in 1990 will lead to an elaboration of their interactions in four areas: Northeast Asia, Southeast Asia, India, and the Southwest Pacific (Australia, New Zealand, Papua-New Guinea, and the smaller South Pacific island states).

Japan. Japan emerged in the 1980s as the world's second largest economy after the United States, and by 1990 it had become an economic superpower in international relations. Although Japan spent 1 percent of its gross national product on defense, compared with the American level of 5–6 percent and Britain's nearly 5 percent, Japan's defense budget grew rapidly as its GNP increased. In 1990 its military budget was the world's third largest, smaller only than those of the Soviet Union and the United States. Although officials in Japan's defense establishment speculated about building an aircraft carrier to underscore the country's growing interests in Asia, the Japanese government showed little inclination to expand its 1,000–mile defense zone into the Pacific or to replace the United States as the principal guarantor of international security in Northeast Asia and the South China Sea. This was so even though the Japanese economy was vitally dependent on the unimpeded transit of oil from the Middle East through the Malacca Strait, the South China Sea, and the western Pacific approaches to the Japanese home islands.

In 1990, Japan closely monitored the changing foreign policy mood in the United States to assess whether Congress and the president would continue to support the U.S. commitment to guarantee regional security in the Western Pacific, particularly in Northeast Asia. If Washington provided reassurance, Japan's attitude toward its own defense and security capability would continue to be confident. Conversely, if the United States substantially reduced its security role in Southeast Asia, Japan might increase its own security presence there in order to protect its large economic stake. Tokyo's calculations would take account of ASEAN's success in maintaining peace and stability in that important region and ASEAN's receptivity to a limited Japanese naval presence. Conversely, Japan might avoid involvement there.

China.   China took a considerable step backward on the road to modernization in June 1989 when its army crushed the student-led democracy movement in Tiananmen Square in Beijing. For more than ten years before that sobering episode the Chinese economy had expanded rapidly; and foreign investment was assuming potentially major proportions as many countries and investors became involved in what promised to be a large market for exports and a source of cheap foreign labor for new industries. This period in China's history was stalemated by the decision of its Communist leaders to retain tight political control, even though their actions stalled economic development. After June 1989 the country was an uncertain factor in Asian politics and caused the other Asian and Pacific powers to reassess their relations with Beijing.

At the beginning of 1990 it was difficult to predict the outcome of the internal struggle for power that would result after the death of Deng Xiaoping, and the resulting foreign policy orientation of China. If the emerging leadership adopted an isolationist policy and relied on military power to maintain tight internal security, China could become a source of apprehension and insecurity for all Asian countries, as it was in the 1950s and 1960s. Conversely, if the new leadership resumed the policy of welcoming foreign investment and gradually adopted liberal internal policies, China's neighbors would be reassured and respond favorably to Beijing's desire for expanded economic and political relations. Whatever the outcome of the internal political struggle, this huge country would continue to exert a profound influence on the politics and security relationships of East Asia, South Asia, and the Soviet Union. The United States could have some influence on the way China viewed its external environment in the 1990s, but it was doubtful whether the United States or any other country would significantly influence the way China managed its emerging struggle for political power among competing groups in Chinese society.

India.   Although not an East Asian country, India was destined to have an increasing impact on the region in the 1990s for two reasons: the U.S. and Soviet navies would play a smaller role in the Indian Ocean area as the Cold War receded and both powers sought ways to reduce defense expenditures; and India apparently thought that it had a destiny to dominate the Indian Ocean region and perhaps the sea approaches to it in Southeast Asia. Historically, India was involved in Southeast Asia before the Europeans invaded in the sixteenth and seventeenth centuries, and it had strong ethnic ties with minorities in many of those countries. In addition, India was building a powerful navy and air force with the potential for operations beyond its South Asian defense area. In March 1990 New Delhi announced a 21 percent increase in defense expenditures, justifying it as a response to increased tensions along its border with Pakistan. This military buildup, particularly in a more powerful Indian navy, caused real concern in Malaysia, Singapore, Indonesia, and Australia, all of which harbored suspicions that India would soon possess the nuclear capability to become the major power in the Indian Ocean region.

India's interest in becoming heir to Britain's dominant position in the Indian Ocean increased following the United Kingdom's withdrawal from "East of Suez" in 1971. Unlike China, which had internal political problems resulting from the leadership's instituting widespread economic reforms, India possessed a viable, democratically elected government based on the British parliamentary model and a robust economy. Despite separatist pressures in parts of the country and constant revelations of corruption among government leaders, India, like Japan, developed an orderly means of transferring political power from one major group to another through the electoral process. Still, China, Japan, Australia, and some ASEAN countries had concerns about what might occur if a power vacuum developed in the Indian Ocean area as a result of U.S. and Soviet withdrawals. A continuing, if lower, U.S. naval presence there would suit the interests of most East Asian states. Pakistan, a non-East Asian state, probably had the most reason to be apprehensive about the growing power and ambition of India. The possibility of war between them could not be discounted. The United States, for its part, had an important, although not vital, interest in the continued viability of Pakistan and would bring strong pressure to bear on New Dehli if it were to initiate hostilities against its neighbor.

Indonesia.   During the first sixteen years after Indonesia's independence from the Netherlands in 1949, Jakarta exhibited the nationalist, expansionist tendencies that many colonial states showed following their successful revolutions in the 1950s and 1960s. Under the charismatic leadership of President Sukarno, Indonesia took control of West New Guinea (West Irian) through military confrontation with the Dutch, who claimed a historic legal right to hold the area. In 1963 Sukarno launched another armed confrontation against Malaysia, which included Singapore and the North Borneo provinces of Sabah and Sarawak. This effort failed, largely because Britain, Australia, and New Zealand joined in a Commonwealth campaign to protect Malaysia against Indonesian incursions. Sukarno also moved Indonesia's policy into alignment with those of the People's Republic of China and North Vietnam, in the expectation that the United States would not remain in Southeast Asia and that Jakarta could then become the dominant power in the offshore part of that region. His ambition brought on a political crisis in the summer of 1965, resulting, with Sukarno's complicity, in an abortive coup on October 1 by the Indonesian Communist Party (PKI). Thereafter, the army took effective control of the country, and its leader, General Suharto (who was not targeted in the Communist-instigated assassination of the army's top command), became president in 1966.

After the 1965 coup attempt and Sukarno's subsequent removal from power, Indonesia was a "good neighbor" to the smaller Southeast Asian states and a leading participant in the development of ASEAN, especially its effort to contain a victorious Vietnam following the withdrawal of U.S. influence from Indochina in 1975. Jakarta was strongly criticized abroad for its annexation in 1975 of Portuguese East Timor, which it claimed posed a security threat after Portugal suddenly decided that year to abandon its colony. The other ASEAN countries and Australia did not condemn the Indonesian action, thereby accepting the reality that East Timor could have posed a serious political problem for ASEAN unity.[1]

Despite large natural resources, a huge population (180 million in 1990), and an effective army, Indonesia had not yet achieved the economic advancement exhibited by its ASEAN partners—Singapore, Malaysia, and Thailand—or by South Korea and Taiwan. The geography of the country—great distances between its many islands and overpopulation on Java—was a major factor slowing its development as an economic power. And a fundamental problem for Indonesia, as for China, was the authoritarian nature of its government, inaugurated in 1949. Moreover, although the army-backed regime brought peace and order to a country that had been plagued by deep conflicts and occasional bloodshed between warring factions, a major characteristic of the long Suharto regime was massive corruption.

When President Suharto eventually decided to step down, the issue of succession would deeply concern Indonesians and their neighbors. If the army exerted its obvious political power to install another military leader as head of state, economic and political development would be further inhibited. Indonesia had the potential of being a major power in Asia, but it clearly required a restructured political system and a more open economy to take full advantage of its opportunities.[2]

Australia and New Zealand.   Australia normally would not qualify as a major power because of its small population (17 million in 1990) and the large, sparsely inhabited parts of its continent. The long and relatively unguarded coastline makes

Australia one of the most exposed countries in the Southwest Pacific to incursions by sea, a theme underlined in a 1990 book, *A Coast Too Long,* by Australian defense expert Ross Babbage. Still, Australia had the advantage over other East Asian states of being located at a great distance from the Asian mainland and having thus been removed from the great power rivalries and confrontations of the post–World War II period. Except for Indonesia's annexation of West Irian from the Netherlands in the 1950s, Australia has had no major threat to its own territory since the Japanese bombing of Darwin during World War II. However, it has long felt a vital interest in helping to protect the security of other parts of East Asia, particularly Malaysia, Singapore, and Papua-New Guinea.

Because of its small population and vast territory, Australia allied itself closely to Great Britain before World War II and afterward to the United States. The ANZUS alliance in 1951 was a manifestation of Canberra's swing away from a long dependence on Britain and an emergent dependence on the United States for security against Soviet and Chinese expansionism. After the U.S. withdrawal from Vietnam and President Nixon's enunciation of the Guam Doctrine in 1969, however, Australia began to distance itself from heavy dependence on the U.S. security shield and adopted a policy of "self-reliance" in defense. It built a relatively large navy and air force and concentrated its efforts primarily on defense-of-homeland interests rather than on world-order interests in Northeast and Southeast Asia.

Until 1985 New Zealand was a strong partner of Australia in its appraisal of events in East Asia and the Pacific. Wellington participated fully with Canberra in ANZUS and in Commonwealth efforts to protect Malaysia and Singapore against Indonesia in the 1960s. However, the anti-nuclear movement in New Zealand exerted a decisive influence on the Labour Party when it came to power in 1985 and persuaded Prime Minister David Lange to prohibit ships of the U.S. Navy from visiting New Zealand unless their captains verified that there were no nuclear weapons on board. This challenge to the U.S. policy of neither confirming nor denying the kinds of weapons carried by Navy ships caused Washington to suspend its ANZUS relationship with New Zealand in 1986. As there was little reason to think that either Washington or Wellington would change its position on this issue, Australia was in the somewhat awkward position of working separately with New Zealand in security affairs and, increasingly, having to bear a heavier financial and defense burden than before. The election of a conservative government in New Zealand in October 1990 was unlikely to change that country's antinuclear stance, but could make it easier for Wellington to establish better working relations with Washington.

Regional Opportunities and Insecurities

The winding down of the Cold War during 1989 and 1990 had an unsettling effect on the international outlook of many countries in East Asia. Three key issues had large implications for the region. First, did an end to the U.S.-Soviet rivalry for world supremacy mean that the United States would withdraw its security shield from East Asia and focus its world-order priorities on Europe and North America? Second, if the United States took a more detached view of security issues in East Asia in the 1990s, would local antagonisms and rivalries become more dangerous and lead to instability and armed conflict in the region? Third, if the U.S. security umbrella were greatly reduced, if not withdrawn, would some other major power—China or Japan—be encouraged or obliged to play a larger security role in Southeast Asia in order to maintain stability in an area where its economic and world-order interests may border on vital? With these considerations in mind, we will first consider the Asian political and security outlook in 1990 and then assess U.S. interests and policies in the region.

Northeast Asia. The end of the Cold War between Moscow and Washington probably affected the security of Northeast Asia more than other parts of the region because three major powers— the U.S.S.R., China, and Japan—share borders. The Korean War was fought in that sector of East Asia, and American troops still remained there forty years later in order to provide security for Japan and South Korea and to dissuade the Soviet Union and China from embarking on other adventures there. China's altered foreign policy in the 1970s and its rapprochement with the United States and Japan helped reduce tensions in Northeast and Southeast Asia. The Soviet Union's change of policy in the late 1980s reduced tensions further, so that by 1990 the principal security issue was how North Korea could be persuaded to abandon its quest to unite the whole Korean peninsula under Communist control. The expected retirement of North Korea's aging president, Kim Il-Sung, could enable younger, more pragmatic leaders to emerge and negotiate an accommodation with South Korea that would benefit both. In addition, South Korea was both economically and militarily stronger than at any time in four decades and had a greater capability, with the help of its neighbors, to defend its territorial integrity until such time as the peninsula could be united through negotiation. The process of detente between North and South Korea was considerably enhanced in 1990 by the Soviet Union's decision to open diplomatic relations with South Korea and the subsequent meetings between officials of the two Koreas (see Chapter 8).

Japan's relations with the Soviet Union in the era of detente and *perestroika* continued to be of concern. Soviet military power largely receded from the Indian Ocean and Southeast Asia (Vietnam) in 1989–1990, but Soviet power in Siberia remained formidable, even though President Gorbachev exhibited no inclination to use it in a belligerent manner. The new, more cooperative Soviet posture opened for Japan the possibility of reaching an accommodation with Moscow, including a return of the Kurile Islands, which were given to the Soviet Union at the Yalta Summit in 1945. Fundamentally, however, the U.S.-Japan Security Treaty of 1951 and subsequent renewals—the underpinning of postwar Japanese foreign policy—would have to be reviewed if the Soviet Union posed a major threat to Japan in the 1990s.

This new reality was hinted at by Takashi Inoguchi of Tokyo University, a leading Japanese authority on Japan's foreign policy, in a lecture at the Australian National University (ANU) in early 1990. In his view, reduction of tension between Japan and the Soviet Union would have to take place if Japan were to assume responsibility for its own territorial defense. "Japan's Self Defence Force should not aim at defending itself against a totally antagonistic Soviet Union," he said, because that could force Japan to spend too much on defense and result in its neighbors reacting negatively. Inoguchi thought that "some form of limited detente with the Soviet Union on such matters as economic, technological, cultural and academic cooperation" would take place before President Mikhail Gorbachev visited Japan in 1991.[3]

Another imponderable was China. As that country sought economic modernization under Deng Xiaoping's leadership between 1976 and 1989, its relations with the United States, Japan, and the countries of Southeast Asia (except for Vietnam) improved. China also opened informal talks with South Korea and served as a restraining influence on North Korea. Although

Beijing tried to follow a cautious foreign policy after the June 4, 1989, suppression of the student movement in Tiananmen Square, the United States, Japan, and other countries halted new investments in China and questioned whether the People's Republic had the ability to continue modernizing its economy while refusing to permit any political reforms. President Bush argued with a reluctant Congress in the autumn of 1989 that China's strategic importance for the United States was such that it would be unwise to impose heavy sanctions and risk nearly two decades of progress in U.S.-China relations and China's improving relations with its Asian neighbors. China's cooperation with the United States at the United Nations in the fall of 1990 regarding sanctions against Iraq suggested that President Bush's policy was a prudent choice. (See Chapter 8.)

In 1990 it was difficult to predict the outcome of the power struggle that might occur when Deng Xiaoping died, but it was unlikely that China, in the near future at least, would again pose the serious security threat to its neighbors that it did in the 1950s when it was allied with the Soviet Union. There might be difficulty over Taiwan, which was officially recognized by the United States and others as a part of China but many of whose citizens felt they had earned the right to be independent. In the 1990s the Taiwan independence issue would have to be addressed by the United States if Taiwan's leaders bowed to public pressure and pressed for independence. Washington reserved the right to prevent Taiwan from being forced to integrate into China. (See Chapter 9 for a fuller discussion of this issue.)

Southeast Asia.   Southeast Asia is potentially the most unstable part of East Asia, and many of the states there feel the need of external protection. Before 1971 the United States and Great Britain provided the security umbrella for the region, but after the British withdrew from Malaysia and Singapore in that year and the United States departed Vietnam in 1975, Soviet influence increased in Indochina. Moscow was provided base facilities by Vietnam at Cam Ranh Bay, a large naval installation built by the United States in the 1960s. In 1989, however, the U.S.S.R. largely withdrew its forces from Vietnam. The United States, with its bases in the Philippines, was once again the sole outside power to have forces in Southeast Asia. China increased its role in the region in the 1980s by supplying arms to rebel forces fighting the Vietnamese occupation in Kampuchea. Indonesia, which in the early 1960s had been a threat to several of its neighbors, remained quiescent in the 1970s and 1980s under the leadership of President Suharto. The United States continued economic and military assistance to the ASEAN states and provided political support in the United Nations for ASEAN's position on Kampuchea. By 1990 most of the states of Southeast Asia had concluded that a U.S. military presence in the region was important to their security.

A fundamental issue for the countries of Southeast Asia in 1990 was how their security would be affected by a U.S. military withdrawal from the Philippines, either voluntarily because of cost, or because of a refusal by the Philippine government to renew its bases agreement, which expired in 1991. One might argue that no Philippine government, with the exception of a Communist regime, would be willing to risk the economic and political costs of such a withdrawal, even though nationalism was a potent force in the Philippines. Filipino elites did not appear so shortsighted as to risk a cutoff of U.S. aid and the major loss of income the country realized from the bases and the 20,000 Americans stationed there. Some, however, thought the era of American neocolonialism in the Philippines should end. The Philippines, in this view, would be a better, more democratic ally if the bases issue were removed. Furthermore, with the Soviet threat diminished and no other large security issues on the horizon, some argued that it was safe for the United States to withdraw.

A problem with the "withdrawal is inevitable" view was that it took too little account of the potential impact on the rest of Southeast Asia, Australia, and Japan. The relative peace and security that prevailed among member states of ASEAN since its formation in 1967 may be attributed in some measure to the presence of the United States as a major power in the region, even after its humiliating withdrawal from Vietnam. Although Thailand seriously questioned the U.S. commitment in the post-1975 period, it was reassured by the strong U.S. backing for ASEAN's resistance to Vietnam's invasion of Kampuchea in 1978 and the continued U.S. military assistance program to the Thai armed forces. Singapore too believed that a U.S. military presence was essential not only to prevent Soviet encroachments, but to deter Indonesia from reverting to a Sukarno-style adventurist foreign policy. Indonesia's annexation of East Timor in 1975 was a worrisome development to its neighbors, but the Jakarta government played a constructive role in the ASEAN relationship. If the U.S. presence in the Philippines were removed, all the states in Southeast Asia might feel less secure.[4]

Indian Ocean. Although not geographically part of East Asia, the Indian Ocean is vitally important to Japan because of that country's heavy dependence on Middle East oil, which is shipped through the Indian Ocean from the Persian Gulf. It is also important to the ASEAN states because of heavy commerce passing to and from the South China Sea through the Strait of Malacca and Sunda Strait, and to Australia, which has a long exposed western coastline on the Indian Ocean. Until 1970 Great Britain, particularly the Royal Navy, exercised the general peacekeeping role in the region. After Britain withdrew from Singapore and other Indian Ocean bases in 1970, this vast ocean area was viewed by some as a power vacuum. India on various occasions indicated that the superpowers should refrain from trying to replace the British, the implication among other interested states being that India itself intended to play the major power role there, even though at the time it did not have the military capability to do so. During the 1970s the United States established a small presence on the island of Diego Garcia, leased from Great Britain, to counter a modest rise in Soviet naval activity in the area.

Following the Arab oil embargo of 1973–1974, the Iranian revolution in 1978–1979, and the Soviet invasion of Afghanistan in 1979, the United States greatly expanded its military presence and capability in the Indian Ocean and even established the Central Military Command for the region, capable of bringing military power to bear on Iran and the Soviet Union in case of hostilities in the Persian Gulf. In his State of the Union address in January 1980, President Jimmy Carter declared the Gulf area to be a U.S. "vital interest" and said he would use force if necessary to protect that interest. Expansion of the American military presence there occurred in 1987 when President Reagan dispatched thirty-three warships to the Gulf to prevent Iran from interfering with commercial shipping and to pressure its government to end its eight-year war with Iraq. Following the cessation of that war and the subsequent death of Iran's Ayatollah Khomeini, most U.S. ships were withdrawn. When a new detente relationship was established between Moscow and Washington in 1988–1989, particularly after Moscow withdrew its troops from Afghanistan in February 1989, the Indian Ocean became a quieter area in international relations. The United States thereafter shifted its attention from the Persian Gulf to Western Europe and the Caribbean area.[5] In 1990 the Iraq-Kuwait crisis abruptly changed U.S. priorities in the Persian Gulf (see Chapter 8).

The question for the Southeast Asian countries, Australia, and Japan was what would happen to security in the Indian Ocean area in the 1990s if the superpowers disengaged and the United States decided it had a higher priority for its military resources elsewhere. Many observers pointed to the buildup of India's navy and air force as an indication that New Delhi intended to exert increasing influence there and would eventually have the capability to project its power into most parts of the region. India was increasingly self-reliant in the manufacture of military equipment, although it continued to buy major arms from the Soviet Union and Great Britain. In sum, India was acquiring the military capability, including possession of aircraft carriers, to exercise the primary security role in what many Indians believed should be an Indian-dominated ocean devoid of superpower challenge.[6]

A.D. Gordon, of the Australian National University's Strategic and Defence Studies Centre, wrote in 1989 of India's intentions: "Given the likelihood of continuing instability in the South Asian neighborhood and given that it is likely to be some time before India develops fully its naval capability, India may not be able to project power with confidence throughout the Indian Ocean region until towards the end of the 1990s or even beyond." The issue is further complicated, he said, by the role of the superpowers, especially the United States. Should relations between the U.S. and the U.S.S.R. continue to improve, however, Washington may increasingly be content to leave some of its lesser interests in the Indian Ocean to a regional power such as India. "Whether this occurs or not, the comparative power of India in relation to the United States in the Indian Ocean is likely to continue to grow and the regional power balance to change. Some regional countries may react by building up their own armed forces."[7]

Southwest Pacific. By far the most important country in the Southwest Pacific area in 1990 was Australia because of its location and size, its modern and dynamic economy, and its significant military force. Even though, as noted earlier, Australia has a small population by comparison with most major East Asian states, it nevertheless dwarfs those of other countries in the Southwest Pacific. Were it not for the proximity of Indonesia with its nearly 200 million people, Australia would be the undisputed power in the region. The next most influential country there is New Zealand, which exercises considerable influence among the small island states of the South Pacific. But its isolation, its small population (3.2 million), its modest military forces, and its neoisolationist foreign policy make New Zealand a peripheral player in the power politics of East Asia. Unlike Australia, which maintained close ties with the United States in the ANZUS relationship during the 1980s while assuming a more self-reliant defense posture, New Zealand not only broke its previous close working relationship with Washington in 1985 but also let its defense forces run down. For all practical purposes, therefore, New Zealand became a protectorate of Australia. For reasons of its own national interest, Canberra continued to maintain close defense ties with Wellington, even though the Washington-Wellington defense link was ended. The Bush administration took steps early in 1990 to improve diplomatic ties with New Zealand by renewing talks between foreign ministers, but there appeared little possibility that New Zealand would reverse its strong antinuclear stance, even under a new government: in February 1990 the opposition National Party declared that it would not change the antinuclear law if it won the elections scheduled for October, a promise it kept after it won and formed a new government.

Australia's economy during the 1980s moved toward larger trade with Japan, South Korea, and Taiwan and less with Europe and North America. It also encouraged larger Japanese investments in Australia.[8] In national security affairs, the Labor government continued and reinforced the policy of self-reliance that it had begun in the mid-1970s as a result of uncertainty about U.S. intentions. Following the withdrawal of American forces from Vietnam and the retrenchment of U.S. policy in the Pacific, many Australian leaders questioned whether the ANZUS commitment was as firm a defense against a regional threat, particularly in New Guinea, as they had previously assumed.[9]

Australia's assessment of its defense and world-order interests into the 1990s was contained in a White Paper, issued by Minister of Defense Kim Beazley in 1987, whose opening chapter set out Australia's security interests: "This Government's policy of defence self-reliance gives priority to the ability to defend ourselves with our own resources. Australia must have the military capability to prevent an enemy from attacking us successfully in our sea and air approaches, gaining a foothold on our territory, or extracting political concessions from us through the use of military force. These are uniquely Australian interests and Australia must have the independent military capability to defend them." Defense self-reliance would be pursued within a framework of alliances and agreements, he said, the most significant of these being with the United States and New Zealand. Australia also had important arrangements, the report continued, in Papua-New Guinea and with the United Kingdom, New Zealand, Malaysia, and Singapore in the "Five Power Defence Arrangements" for the Malacca Strait area.[10]

Perhaps the most sensitive among Australia's national security interests is its relationship with Indonesia. Part of the concern is geography (Indonesia dominates the northern approaches to the Australian continent), disparity in population, and history (the confrontation in North Borneo in the 1960s over Malaysia's security). Once the Sukarno era's adventurism ended in 1966, however, relations between the two countries improved. They were set back briefly in 1975 when Indonesia intervened to stop a civil war in East Timor and then annexed the territory after Portugal withdrew. Relations became strained again in 1985 following publication in a Sydney newspaper of an article that was critical of corruption within President Suharto's family. Indonesia reacted negatively by cutting off exchanges, including military visits, and imposing new visa requirements. Normal relations, including military exchanges, were restored in 1990, but the 1985 episode reminded Australians that their northern neighbor was not a democratic country that understood freedom of the press.[11]

In addition, Indonesia has a long border with independent Papua-New Guinea, which until 1975 was under Australian administration and which Canberra is obliged to assist if it is attacked. This border was generally quiet in 1990, but dissident West Irians who oppose Indonesian rule sometimes crossed the border, and Indonesian security forces occasionally gave hot pursuit. With good relations between Canberra and Jakarta, these problems were manageable. But when relations were strained, the danger existed that border incidents and other disputes would assume crisis proportions. Australians were therefore insecure in relations with their "colossus to the north" and sought reassurance that the United States would honor the ANZUS commitment to defend them in case of attack.

In December 1989 Minister of Foreign Affairs and Trade Gareth Evans published a document that outlined his government's view of Australia's regional security in the 1990s. Evans's statement complemented and went beyond the Defense White Paper of 1987 to look also at nondefense aspects of Australia's security in Southeast Asia and the southern Pacific, particularly trade, aid, and cultural exchanges. He was optimistic about Australia's security prospects but cautioned that they could not be entirely assured for the future because of the significant changes taking place in the international environment: "The dominant external power in the region, the United States, seems likely over time to reduce its strategic involvement in the region, and in relative terms, other major external powers may play a great role." Evans said there were many elements to this process of major change, which might not necessarily be peaceful. Although the government assumed, he wrote, that in the next ten years and beyond states either in the region or outside it would not use military power and influence to achieve goals that were contrary to Australia's security interests, "for Australia, the essential fact is that we will be dealing with a more fluid and complex region, and that in doing so we will be required to be much more the master of our own fate than we have been prepared to accept until recently." Evans reflected on the growing uncertainty within Australia of the new shape of both security and economic relationships in East Asia following the end of the Cold War and the reevaluation of national interests in the United States, Japan, China, and other Asian countries. Australia was positioning itself, he said, to adjust to a new international environment in which "self-reliance" would be the hallmark of its foreign and defense policies.[12]

Australia held a general election on March 24, 1990, to decide whether the Labor Party headed by Prime Minister Bob Hawke—in power since 1983—should continue to lead the government or turn over power to the Liberal-National coalition. Foreign and defense policy played little part in the month-long debate leading up to the election because there was general agreement among the major parties on Australia's national interests and foreign policy objectives. One disagreement did arise over the Hawke government's plan to permit Japanese interests to build a high-tech city that critics said would give many Japanese a separate enclave within Australia. Strong support for the ANZUS defense relationship with the United States, self-reliance in regional security, and close economic relations with Northeast Asia and North America seemed to be accepted by a large majority of Australians. The election outcome returned the Labor government to power with a

smaller majority and assured three more years of continuity in
Australian foreign policy.

U.S. Priorities in East Asia in the 1990s

In view of the apparently receding Soviet military threat in Asia
and the preoccupation of China with its impending leadership
transition, the United States had a unique opportunity in 1990 to
step back and reassess its national interests in East Asia and establish new priorities for U.S. policy. The questions it needed to
address were, first, what were U.S. vital interests in the area, and
second, which interests were major, requiring considerable attention in the new decade, even though they were no longer vital to
the security of the United States?

U.S. economic interests in Northeast Asia clearly had risen
since the early 1980s, especially in Japan, where both U.S. trade
and investment had grown enormously. As Japan also had large
and growing economic links with nearly all the East Asian countries, the United States would experience a significant economic
loss were the Japanese economy or government policy to turn
against America. Still, the U.S. government needed to continue
pressing the Japanese broadly to take measures to reduce the immense trade imbalance between the two countries. The United
States clearly had a high stake—a vital interest—in the stability of
the Japanese economy and in the nation's political orientation. In
sum, it was essential for Washington and Tokyo to ensure the continuation of a close bilateral relationship.

China continued to be of strategic importance to the United
States, but the PRC remained a major, not a vital, U.S. interest be-
cause its economy was "on hold" until Beijing's leadership sorted
out the internal political orientation of the country in the 1990s.
Southeast Asia remained a major interest of the United States, and
Washington continued to devote diplomatic effort and provided
military equipment to the countries there to help them defend
themselves. The same was true for the Indian Ocean area, where
India clearly was emerging as the principal power. The Indian
Ocean is not a vital U.S. world-order interest, but it would con-
tinue to be a key transit area for U.S. ships headed for the Persian
Gulf.

Finally the U.S. interest in the Southwest Pacific was growing, suggesting that Australia would remain a key ally in the 1990s
and that its role as leading power in the southern Pacific region

would command even greater importance. Australia and New Zealand were expecting to work out their relations so that the break between Washington and Wellington in security matters did not diminish New Zealand's important contribution to regional security. A closer U.S. world-order relationship with Australia clearly suggested a firmer economic relationship as well, including special trade arrangements for the import of Australian agricultural products into the United States. Washington needed to appreciate—as it apparently did not in the 1980s—that Australia's export economy can be vitally affected by small changes in U.S. trade policy, particularly on grain and beef exports.

Although not generally considered to be part of the Southwest Pacific, the Republic of the Philippines is an offshore country—like Australia—and a near vital U.S. interest so long as its government reciprocates that interest. The Philippines needed to be realistic about the fact that U.S. interests in the Indian Ocean and Southeast Asia would probably decline in the 1990s and that the need for U.S. bases in the Philippines was declining. Therefore, a new and more equitable relationship needed to be built between Washington and Manila whereby the psychology of the 1970s and 1980s would give way to a better appreciation of the national interests of both countries.[13]

Policy Options for the Post–Cold War Period

The United States had two distinct but related policy options that could be adopted to support its changing national interests in a new and less threatening East Asian environment: a modified status quo posture and partial withdrawal.

1. Modified Status Quo.   This posture was the one the Bush administration appeared to adopt in 1990 and seemed likely to continue for some years. Essentially, it meant that the United States would maintain substantial military forces in Japan and South Korea; major military assistance programs in Thailand, Indonesia, and the Philippines; regular ship visits to Singapore and into the Indian Ocean; and close cooperation with Australia in intelligence and nuclear-test monitoring through the joint facilities at Alice Springs and Nurrungar.

Secretary of Defense Dick Cheney, during a visit to the area in February 1990, underscored the administration's decision to maintain a policy of relative status quo in East Asia. Although an-

nouncing a 10 percent reduction in U.S. forces in Korea, Japan, and
the Philippines over three years, he reaffirmed the U.S. government's determination to remain a Pacific power and to play a
major political role in East Asia. In an address to the Japan National Press Club on February 23, 1990, Cheney asserted: "The
past year's events do not justify dismantling the security structures that have served us so well in the postwar era. What's more,
the national interest that led the U.S. to pursue common policies
with its Asian friends and allies have never been merely responses
to the Soviet Union. We would want to be engaged in the Asian-
Pacific region even if the Soviet Union were not." The defense secretary emphatically assured his audience that the United States
would not withdraw from the region:

> If I had one and only one message to leave with you to-
> day, it would be this: the United States intends to remain
> involved in Asia. We will do so because we believe that
> our security presence helps contribute to peace, demo-
> cratic development, economic growth, and free interna-
> tional commerce. All of that is in the U.S. national interest.
> It is in the interest of our friends in the region. And it is in
> the interest of freedom loving people everywhere. If we
> were to withdraw our forward deployed forces from the
> Asia-Pacific region, a vacuum would quickly develop.
> There almost surely would be a series of destabilizing re-
> gional arms races, an increase in regional tensions, and
> possibly conflict.[14]

One might question Cheney's claim that U.S. security policies
in Asia were not just responses to the Soviet Union, because the
United States followed a somewhat detached policy toward the
mainland from 1947 until the outbreak of war in Korea, which was
instigated with Stalin's approval. Thereafter, a fundamental
change in U.S. policy on Asia occurred, including the conclusion
of many alliances with regional states. Nevertheless, Cheney's
strong reaffirmation of post-1950 U.S. policy suggested that President Bush would take a wait-and-see posture. In the meantime,
only modest reductions in force levels, elimination of marginal
facilities, and some cutbacks in military assistance programs
would be implemented. The status quo option also included pressure on Asian allies to pay more of the costs of maintaining U.S.
forces in the region. Cheney did not specifically request such aid

in his Tokyo address, but in answer to a question from a Japanese reporter he said: "We would like as much support as we can get from Japan. I would note that Japan has significantly increased in recent years its host nation support for U.S. forces. We think that is a very positive trend and we will continue to work with our Japanese allies to expand that level of support."[15] Washington also negotiated a larger financial contribution from South Korea for the U.S. troops based there.

2. Partial Withdrawal and Retrenchment. Under this option the United States would withdraw significant portions of its military forces in East Asia, substantially reduce military assistance programs, and phase out some major military bases and facilities. The plan could include withdrawing most of the 37,000 U.S. troops from Korea and most of the Marines from Okinawa, closing some Air Force facilities in Japan, and phasing out Clark Air Base and several smaller facilities in the Philippines. The United States would maintain a naval presence at Yokosuka, Japan, and, if agreement with Manila was reached, at Subic Bay in the Philippines. These might also include a small naval presence in the Malacca Strait region, perhaps in Singapore, if this had the support of the ASEAN states. The United States would also continue good military relationships with the Thai and Indonesian armed forces, but would not engage in joint military exercises.

Under option 2 the United States would forge close links with Australia's defense forces and encourage Canberra to maintain close working relationships with New Zealand's armed forces. On the political side, this option would place heavier emphasis on diplomacy, economic aid, and trade policy, instead of military moves, as the means to exert continuing U.S. influence in the area. It suggested a continuing close economic relationship between Washington and the region's major trading states. In this connection the first ministerial meeting held by APEC (Asia Pacific Economic Cooperation) in Canberra in November 1989 was a favorable development. It brought together twenty-six ministers from twelve countries: the six ASEAN nations, Japan, South Korea, Australia, New Zealand, Canada, and the United States. The group agreed to hold a second meeting in Singapore later in 1990 and a third in Seoul in 1991.[16]

United States trade relations with Japan would likely be strained under this option but would improve later as both countries came to understand what internal changes needed to be made to ensure continuing good economic and political relations. The partial withdrawal option assumed that U.S. negotiations with the Philippines for the renewal of the naval base at Subic Bay would be successful. However, if the Philippine government decided not to renew the agreement in 1991, a fundamental reassessment of U.S. interests and policies in the Western Pacific might well result. Option 2 was contingent on continuing Soviet force reductions, cuts in Soviet defense budgets, and the conclusion of major nuclear arms control agreements between Washington and Moscow. The option also depended on the continuance of moderate Chinese policies toward its neighbors in East Asia.

The problem for the United States in East Asia in 1990 was how to achieve a reduction in forces and defense costs without raising in the countries of the region the fear that it planned to withdraw. Moving from a forty-year-old policy of considering everything in the region to be vital in the struggle with Moscow to a new era in which the regional threat was greatly diminished meant convincing countries in the region, both large and small, that Washington could retain a major interest and role without maintaining a large military reserve there. This was a task that Secretary of Defense Cheney initiated in his Tokyo speech in February 1990. His efforts would have to be reinforced in the remainder of the 1990s if the U.S. government expected to be successful in reassuring its friends and allies in East Asia that the United States would remain a powerful player and a faithful ally.

7
U.S. Interests and Policies in Europe and the U.S.S.R., 1990

For more than forty years following World War II, Europe was the major battleground in a global struggle for preeminence between the Soviet Union and the United States. This confrontation engaged most of the countries in Europe, which were arrayed against one another in the Warsaw Pact and the North Atlantic Treaty Organization. Despite interludes of detente in the late 1950s and early 1970s, the struggle for control of Europe—particularly Germany—dominated international politics for nearly half a century and at times brought the world dangerously close to a third world war.

On June 4, 1990, during an official visit to the United States, Soviet President Mikhail Gorbachev told an audience at Stanford University: "The cold war is now behind us. Let us not wrangle over who won it."[1] Gorbachev was voicing a reality that most Western Europeans had accepted several years earlier and Americans were gradually acknowledging: the U.S.S.R. had abandoned its goal of communizing Western Europe and bringing a united Germany into the Soviet sphere of influence. Events during the spring and summer of 1990 confirmed the fact. Moscow accepted decisions of the newly elected East German legislature and West Germany's Bundestag that political unification would take place in 1990, and it acquiesced in the idea that a united Germany would be associated with NATO. Both of these events occurred on October 3, when the two German states formally merged. The future of 360,000 Soviet troops stationed in East Germany was finally resolved, and Moscow agreed to their gradual withdrawal over four years in return for large economic aid from a united Germany.

Europe would continue to dominate international politics in the 1990s because of three realities: (1) the economic and political power of a united, resurgent Germany and its growing influence in the European Community; (2) the economic weakness of the Soviet Union and the Eastern European states; and (3) the massive nuclear and conventional war capability remaining at Moscow's disposal. Consequently, Europe would receive a high regional priority among U.S. world-order and defense-of-homeland interests in the 1990s, and continue to command major attention from the president and Congress.

Using the national interest framework outlined in Chapter 1, this chapter looks at the implications for U.S. interests of the momentous changes that took place in Europe during 1989 and 1990 and how the United States, the Soviet Union, Germany, Britain, and France viewed the security implications of a new Germany comprising nearly 80 million people. It assesses the U.S. economic interest in the projected integrated European economy (European Union) after 1992, examines the new definition of Soviet national interests enunciated by the Gorbachev leadership, addresses the emerging national interests of a united Germany, and briefly summarizes British and French interests in Europe.

United States Interests in Europe

Defense of Homeland.   In 1949 the United States declared that Western Europe constituted a vital defense-of-homeland interest. It did so by adhering to the North Atlantic Pact, which pledged that an attack on any member would be viewed as an attack on the United States and thus call for the use of American military force. For forty years that pledge was reinforced by the buildup of U.S. air, ground, and naval forces in Europe and the Mediterranean and by the assignment of an American as supreme commander of NATO forces in Europe. Every president from Harry Truman to George Bush pledged that the United States would go to war to defend the NATO countries of Europe against a Soviet attack. The presence of American conventional and nuclear power in Europe and the Mediterranean, reinforced in 1983 by the deployment of Pershing II and cruise missiles in several NATO countries, bolstered the 1949 U.S. commitment that defense of Western Europe was synonymous with defense of North America.

A fundamental issue for American strategic planners and political leaders in 1990 was whether continental Western Europe remained a vital defense-of-homeland interest for the United States in light of the profound changes that had occurred in Europe's political, economic, and military status since the 1960s. This did not suggest that Europe was no longer vital to the United States but rather that its importance in the 1990s would shift from the defense-of-homeland to the world-order category of interest. Western Europe now had the economic and military capability to defend its own territory against a diminished Soviet conventional war threat, and it was therefore not necessary for Washington to maintain large ground forces there to deter a Soviet attack. Nevertheless, the United States needed to maintain strategic forces in the North Atlantic region as a deterrent to a Soviet nuclear attack on Europe or North America. A modest U.S. conventional force in support of NATO commitments would be needed on the continent in the 1990s for world-order reasons. To the extent that NATO countries on the periphery of Europe—Britain, Iceland, Portugal, and perhaps Italy—were prepared to accommodate U.S. strategic forces in the 1990s, their territory would remain in the vital defense-of-homeland category because of their vulnerability to nuclear blackmail, from the Soviet Union or other sources. For that reason, these countries might require a special defense relationship with the United States.

In sum, the end of the Cold War, the emerging economic and political power of the European Union, and the need for the United States to reduce defense expenditures as the Soviet threat in Europe declined suggested a reevaluation of the U.S. defense-of-homeland interest in Europe, including the stationing of nuclear weapons, and a larger priority for U.S. economic and world-order interests.[2]

Economic Well-being.   Unlike the late 1940s and early 1950s, when the United States had a vital economic interest in rehabilitating Western European countries and forging an alliance against the Soviet Union, America was witnessing in 1990 the emergence of an economically powerful Europe moving toward economic and political union. Before the end of the 1990s additional European countries would be added to the 335 million people living in the existing EC area and thus make Europe the world's largest economic bloc. In 1990 it was too soon to know whether Europe would tend toward protectionist policies and be in competition with the United States and Canada, or whether it would adopt relatively free trade policies and avoid commercial wars. The Uruguay Round of trade negotiations under the General Agreement on Tariffs and Trade (GATT), scheduled for completion in 1990, was a test of European and American wills to pursue free trade policies, especially in agricultural products.[3]

For the United States it was a vital economic interest that Europe be an open trading system welcoming the free flow of trade and investment between Europe, North America, and East Asia. It also had an important interest in encouraging Europe to invest its financial resources not only in Eastern Europe, but also in Latin American and African countries which desperately needed foreign capital to spur their economies. The leading European economy in 1990, in terms of trade and investment capability, was West Germany's. With the addition of the 16 million East Germans who were incorporated into West Germany on October 3, 1990, creating an integrated market of 77 million people, Germany became the most powerful economic entity in Europe and would be the principal focus of U.S. economic and world-order interests in the 1990s.

In sum, the United States had a vital economic interest in an open, prosperous European Union to which it could export without restrictions and from which it could import investment capital to help it cope with the massive international indebtedness America had incurred in the 1980s.

Favorable World Order.   A serious question for U.S. policymakers in the 1990s was how much U.S. military strength should be retained in Europe in order to (1) ensure that the Soviet Union carried out the arms reduction policies initiated by President Gorbachev in 1989–1990, (2) reassure the Europeans that a united and resurgent Germany would not become a security threat, and (3) preserve enough American influence to help organize a politically united and cooperative Europe. These objectives had to do with the future balance of power in Europe, with the EC's international economic policies, and with the anxieties displayed by many Europeans over the possibility of a fourth German Reich. Although related, these were not defense-of-homeland interests for the United States. In the absence of a renewed Soviet military threat, the interest did not require a large U.S. military force in Europe. It did, however, call for a sufficient diplomatic, economic, and military presence to give the United States influence in decisions about Europe's political future, including the size and organization of its military forces. In 1990 some defense experts in Washington calculated that a reduction of American military personnel to 100,000 by 1995 would be a reasonable level to protect U.S. interests. Most Americans believed that maintaining a U.S. presence in Europe was in the country's continuing interest because they had been called upon three times since 1914 to send troops to prevent the continent from being dominated by one great power—Germany—in two world wars, and the Soviet Union during the Cold War. Although emergence of the European Community in the 1980s greatly mitigated the old nationalist antagonisms that had led to two world wars, and although the Soviet threat had greatly diminished, the United States nevertheless continued to have a vital stake in a peaceful and democratic Europe.

The task for the United States in the 1990s was to avoid becoming irrelevant to the future of Europe. At first glance, this appeared a small problem because Europe needed a stabilizing American presence to balance the continuing military power of the Soviet Union, even given the withdrawal of most Soviet troops from Eastern Europe and Germany. Some Soviet troops would remain in the eastern part of Germany until 1994 as part of an agreement reached with Germany and NATO. After Poland pressed for assurance as to Germany's intentions regarding the territories east of the Oder and Neisse rivers, which it had lost to Poland after World War II, Germany decided in November 1990 to conclude a formal peace treaty with Poland guaranteeing their current border. This served to reassure the Poles on future relations with Germany.

A second, less articulated, reason Europeans wanted a U.S. military presence was to ensure against a resurgence of German nationalism and military adventurism. The unease with which West Germany's NATO partners, as well as the Eastern European states, viewed German Chancellor Kohl's successful efforts in 1990 to integrate the East and West German economies and unify the country suggested their need for an American military presence on the continent in the 1990s. Although most Europeans conceded that the German people had experienced forty-five years of democracy and the rise to maturity of a new generation since 1945, many nevertheless needed reassurance that a united Germany would not try again to dominate them.

The nature and size of the American force to be based on the continent was the subject of continuing negotiations in 1990 within NATO and at the Conventional Forces Europe (CFE) talks in Vienna. These negotiations led to an agreement to limit NATO and Warsaw Pact armaments, which was signed in Paris in November. Another agreement on the size of all armed forces in Europe was expected to be concluded in 1991. A second issue was nuclear weapons. For example, would a unified and fully sovereign Germany ask for the withdrawal of all American nuclear weapons from its soil, including tactical ones? German public opinion, unlike French and Italian opinion, was strongly anti-nuclear. An opinion poll conducted in June 1990 found that 54 percent of West Germans thought all such weapons should be removed from German soil, and 42 percent insisted that this should be done even if it meant the withdrawal of U.S. forces from Germany.[4] The nuclear issue could, unless handled with great care, cause a rupture in the U.S.-German relationship and play into the hands of American critics who thought U.S. forces should be completely withdrawn from Europe as a budget-saving measure. The issue was so sensitive in 1990 that the Western allies agreed prior to the NATO summit in July not to have their leaders discuss a "no first use" strategy. Officials feared that opening this issue at the summit could lead to a divisive debate about keeping any nuclear weapons in Germany.[5]

Except for NATO, the United States had no institutional means by which it could exert a key voice in European security affairs. It was not a member of the European Community (although it did have observer status); it was not part of the smaller Western European Union, which was overshadowed by NATO in the 1950s; and it probably would not be accepted into a new European Defense Community (EDC), should one be set up, because of traditional French objections. [6] Although the United States was signatory to the 1975 Helsinki Accords, which brought into being the Conference on Security and Cooperation in Europe (CSCE), the Bush administration in 1990 did not accept the loosely defined organization as an alternative to NATO. If the United States expected to have a large voice in the political and security affairs of Europe in the 1990s, NATO was the only vehicle through which it could effectively do so.

President Bush addressed the issue of America's future security role in Europe in his commencement address at Oklahoma State University on May 4, 1990. He cautioned that because no one could predict the course of Soviet policy or the longevity of the

Gorbachev leadership, the United States should retain sizable forces—conventional and nuclear—in Europe for the foreseeable future. Bush saw a useful place for the CSCE in the political and social spheres of relations among European states, but he opposed giving it a role in security matters—as West German leaders had advocated. The defense role should be the responsibility of NATO, the president asserted: "My European colleagues want the United States to be a part of Europe's future. I believe they are right. The United States should remain a European power in the broadest sense, politically, militarily, and economically. And as part of our global responsibilities, the foundation for America's engagement in Europe has been, and will continue to be, NATO."[7]

A few weeks later Secretary of Defense Cheney proposed to NATO's defense ministers at a meeting in Brussels that NATO revamp its military structure and consider a new concept that would combine the national forces of members into multinational corps units—a measure that might ease opposition to American troops on the continent. He cited as an example the creation of an army corps that would include British, German, and U.S. forces. Cheney's proposal was part of the Bush administration's effort to start discussions on a revamped NATO military structure.[8]

France, however, would have to reverse its foreign policy in order to participate in a revised military arrangement because Charles de Gaulle took his nation out of NATO's military structure in 1966, and no succeeding French government had shown interest in altering his decision. That policy might change if France were accorded a larger role and if the dominant position of the U.S. were reduced.

Promotion of Values.   In the post–World War II period, the United States placed heavy emphasis on building democratic institutions in Europe and on fighting Moscow-sponsored Communist ideology worldwide. This policy succeeded remarkably, as events in Eastern Europe in 1989–1990 demonstrated and as functioning democracies in West Germany, Italy, and Spain—three previously fascist states—attested. It was a major national interest of the United States to support democracy not only in Western but also in Eastern Europe and the Soviet Union after the Communist Party's monopoly of power had been broken. Another aspect of the U.S. ideological interest was the promotion of free trade and the free-market system in Europe because these could improve standards of living and also because free political and economic institutions were consistent with America's two-hundred-year-old value system. The U.S. government had reason in 1990 to be proud of its record of restoring strong democratic governments to Western Europe after World War II and of encouraging free elections in Eastern Europe.[9]

The Soviet Union's Interests in Europe

For forty years after World War II—from 1945 to 1985—the Soviet Union's vital interests in Europe were to create a buffer zone of client states in Eastern Europe in order to prevent another invasion of its territory, rebuild its war-torn economy, match the United States as a military power, gain control of West Germany's economic base and add it to the Soviet empire, and promote the Marxist-Leninist ideology in Western Europe. By 1985 the Kremlin had reached only one of these objectives: the building of massive military power. Its Warsaw Pact allies were unreliable; Moscow's economy was stagnating; West Germany had strengthened its democratic institutions and ties with NATO; and Communism in Western Europe was in disrepute.

In 1985 the Soviet Politburo brought to power a younger, pragmatic leader who understood the dangerous internal situation the Soviet Union faced and was willing to revise the country's interests to fit the new realities. After five years as head of the Communist Party and one year as president of a vast governmental structure, Mikhail Gorbachev had not solved the country's internal economic and political crisis. Yet, he had reduced the perceived external danger to Soviet security and had begun a program of reducing the enormous Soviet military budget and the expensive aid programs to allies such as Cuba, Syria, and Ethiopia. He also extricated 120,000 Soviet troops from a costly and inconclusive occupation of Afghanistan.

In 1990 the principal foreign policy and national security problems Gorbachev faced were in Europe, not just in Eastern Europe and the Baltic states but, more importantly, in a reunited Germany linked to NATO. A fundamental question for the Soviet leadership was how to redefine Soviet economic and ideological interests while causing the least amount of damage to vital security interests.

Defense of Homeland. Although the Soviet Union was concerned about the security of its western borders, it no longer be-

lieved that the best way to ensure the cooperation of its neighbors
in Eastern Europe was to maintain Communist regimes there.
Unlike Stalin, Khruschev, and Brezhnev, Gorbachev considered
the massive military power accumulated by the Soviet Union in
the past thirty years an adequate guarantee against attack by any
combination of European powers in the foreseeable future. If the
deterrent power of Soviet conventional and nuclear forces was
successful, he calculated, tightly controlled client states were no
longer required. The Eastern European countries should then be
free to choose their own economic and political course—so long
as their choices posed no security threat to the Soviet Union. These
considerations could eventually apply to the three Baltic states as
well, even though Gorbachev insisted in the spring of 1990 that
their moves toward independence must be in accordance with
constitutional procedures, requiring negotiations over a period of
several years. Eventually, the status of the countries that comprised Moscow's East European security buffer, he calculated,
would resemble that of Finland after World War II—independence
with a foreign policy acceptable to Moscow.[10]

The exception to Gorbachev's view of the Soviet defense-of-
homeland interest in Europe was East Germany. Once a loyal,
relatively prosperous ally and (until 1989) host to more than
400,000 Soviet troops, the German Democratic Republic (GDR)
was effectively removed from the Soviet security and economic
zone by its merger with West Germany on October 3, 1990. The
dismantling of the Berlin Wall in November 1989 shattered whatever plans Gorbachev had of managing a gradual unification of
East and West Germany and of negotiating an international agreement on neutralization of the new German state. In early 1990
Moscow moved away from this objective and tried to bargain for
German membership in both NATO and the Warsaw Pact.
Gorbachev was reluctant to accept the Western plan that a united
Germany should continue to be tied only to NATO. Soviet Foreign Minister Eduard Shevardnadze proposed in June the withdrawal of all foreign troops from both parts of Germany and
conclusion of an international agreement to restrict the size of the
unified country's armed forces. But this proposal was rejected by
the United States and other participants in the so-called "two-
plus-four talks" held by a six-nation group (the United States, the
Soviet Union, Britain, France, and the two German states). The
New York Times reported from Berlin that behind Shevardnadze's
proposal lay a basic Soviet objective: a continuing insistence that

the wartime Allies set a transitional period following German political unification during which they would retain some residual
rights in Germany. Shevardnadze also sought to include substantive security issues in this agreement, such as the size of the all-
German army, the alliance(s) to which Germany would belong,
and the withdrawal of foreign troops. The apparent Soviet concern, the *Times* reported, was that "without these conditions, Moscow would lose any leverage over a united Germany."[11]

President Gorbachev asked for American understanding of
Soviet defense-of-homeland concerns when visiting Washington
for a summit meeting with President Bush in May-June 1990. At a
joint press conference on June 3, following several days of discussions about European security and other issues of mutual concern,
Gorbachev was asked whether his objections to a united Germany
within NATO were mainly "psychological," whether it would be
"a humiliating admission . . . that you've lost the Cold War."
Gorbachev's reply is quoted at some length because it reflects his
concerns about the Soviet Union's defense interest following
Germany's reunification:

> While applauding the Germans' desire to be united, we
> must, at the same time, think about ways of preserving
> the balance that has been emerging and taking shape for
> decades. And here is the central point: If we were to adopt
> only one point of view, then I think that it would not be
> complete. For it gives rise to concerns, and if that is the
> case, then we—if there were no other way out, but I be-
> lieve that such a way out will be found to mutual satis-
> faction. But if this were the only option—and some would
> like to impose it on us and say that we reject this—then
> we should go back and see where we are. What's happen-
> ing to our security? What should we be doing with our
> armed forces, which we are both reforming and reducing.
> What should we do about Vienna, how should we behave
> there? All these are matters of strategic importance, for
> everything happening in Europe is really the highest level
> of strategy. . . . As to the second part, is it a question of
> pride. Well, I'd say that the problem is not pride, really, if
> today I have to remind you once again that we lost 27
> million people in the fronts, in partisan detachments, 27
> million people during World War II. And 18 million
> people were wounded and maimed. Then I think it's not

a matter of pride but of justice, supreme justice, for these sacrifices of our people enable us to raise these matters with all nations, and we have a moral right to do so, so that everything that was obtained at such tremendous cost, that so many sacrifices would not spell new perils.[12]

The Soviet leader thus said publicly, on worldwide television, that for historical security reasons the Soviet Union could not agree to be pushed out of Europe and permit a united former enemy to join the opposition camp—NATO. The implications of his remarks for continuation of East-West negotiations on future European security were sobering. One could argue in June 1990 that Moscow had no real alternative to agreeing to withdraw from East Germany once unification took place, but it was also possible to argue that Gorbachev, or a successor, would insist that, in the absence of a negotiated settlement, some Soviet troops could remain in Germany. A month later Chancellor Kohl and President Gorbachev reached an agreement that permitted Soviet troops to stay in Germany until 1994.

Economic Well-being. The Soviet view of its economic well-being interest changed sharply after Gorbachev's introduction of *perestroika* into the Soviet economy in 1987. No longer did Moscow intend to rely on its own resources and those of the Council for Mutual Economic Assistance (COMECON) countries to insulate the Soviet economy from Western capitalist influences. *Perestroika* had not proceeded very far by 1990, and Gorbachev understood that he would need considerable economic assistance from the West in order to make it work. Soviet diplomacy in 1989–1990 therefore put heavy emphasis on persuading European Community member states, particularly West Germany, to provide long-term credits to support trade and investment in the U.S.S.R. Gorbachev also tried to convince the United States to grant the Soviet Union most-favored-nation (MFN) trading status, a concession that Congress had denied in 1974 when it attached conditions regarding Soviet emigration policies to legislation proposed by President Nixon. When Gorbachev met with President Bush in Washington in May and June 1990, he asked again for MFN treatment and cited the large number of Soviet Jews who had recently been allowed to emigrate to Israel. Congress seemed unwilling to make the concession so long as Moscow had not resolved the Lithuanian independence issue, but Bush decided during the summit to sign an agreement with Gorbachev making expansion of trade between the countries easier—although not on concessionary terms. The West German government decided a few weeks later to go further and guarantee a bank credit of five billion German marks (about $3 billion) to help bolster Gorbachev's economic reform program.

Chancellor Helmut Kohl and French President Francois Mitterrand rejected President Bush's view that economic aid to assist Gorbachev's reforms should be tied to arms reductions. The German and French governments believed they could persuade Gorbachev to accept German reunification within NATO by offering economic incentives, an opinion not then shared in Washington.[13] The European Community, under prodding by Kohl and Mitterrand, agreed in principle late in June to provide Moscow economic assistance but stopped short of identifying specific programs or a price tag. The agreement among the twelve EC members represented a compromise between the French-West German position and that of Britain, which opposed large financial assistance to Gorbachev. President Bush stated in a news conference a few days later that although he would not oppose European assistance to Moscow, the United States would not give such aid until the Soviet economy was reorganized and after defense expenditures and foreign military assistance had been substantially reduced.[14]

It is unclear whether obtaining large amounts of Western economic aid represented a major or a vital interest for Soviet leaders in 1990. Such aid would help Gorbachev to cope with rising demands from Soviet citizens for more consumer goods, but it might also lead to greater tensions between reformers and the Communist bureaucracy over the pace of change to a market economy. Although the conditions in Moscow in 1990 were different from those in Beijing in the spring of 1989, Gorbachev's dilemma resembled that of Deng Xiaoping a year earlier: a choice between the effects of greater exposure to Western trade and free-market ideas, and the need for internal political stability to avoid chaos and perhaps civil war. Although the Soviet Union was a more open society than China, tensions between entrenched bureaucrats and the rising expectations of a frustrated public were similar in the two countries.

Favorable World Order.   Gorbachev also changed rather significantly the Soviet Union's view of its world-order interests. The withdrawal of Soviet troops from Afghanistan and the large reduction in Soviet aid to Cuba,. Nicaragua, Ethiopia, Vietnam, Syria, and Angola altered regional security relationships in significant ways. South Africa was persuaded to give independence to Namibia; Nicaragua ousted the Sandinista government in free elections; Vietnam withdrew its troops from Cambodia; South Yemen merged with the nonsocialist state of Yemen; and the prospects for an end to civil war in Afghanistan improved. Furthermore, after thirty years of alienation in Sino-Soviet relations, Gorbachev visited Beijing in 1989 and improved the ties between the world's two largest Communist states. In December 1989 *Time Magazine* named Gorbachev its "Man of the Decade" for his contributions to peace.

In the 1990s, Soviet world-order interests seemed likely to center on Europe and, like its defense-of-homeland interest, to continue to be viewed as vital. The countries of Western Europe, including the Scandinavian states, Greece, and Turkey, were key concerns of Moscow in 1990 and would be the objects of some pressure to accommodate Gorbachev's call for an "all European home," without the American military presence. From Moscow's standpoint, a united Germany, free of the NATO relationship with Washington and cooperating with Moscow to influence the politics of Europe and the Near East would have been an ideal outcome of the debate over German reunification. At the Washington summit in June 1990, President Bush argued that a united Germany tied to NATO would be a better guarantee of Soviet security than a neutral and armed Germany possibly trying to establish a fourth Reich. But Gorbachev was not yet willing to give up completely on the Soviet Union's forty-five-year-old design of combining the power of Germany with that of the Soviet Union and creating the "heartland" combination that he hoped would dominate Europe and the Middle East. Whereas Stalin had sought to make Germany a Communist satellite in the Soviet empire, Gorbachev's view of the U.S.S.R.'s world-order interests in the twenty-first century would be well served by reaching a state-to-state understanding with Germany regarding Europe. Barring that, Soviet leaders may have calculated that, because of growing disenchantment among many Europeans over the size and nature of American forces based on the continent, they could influence opinion in Britain, Germany, Spain, Italy, Portugal, and Iceland with the argument that there was no further need for an American military presence because the Cold War was over. Destroying the NATO linkage between Western Europe and North America may have been a declining Soviet ambition, but it remained a continuing world-order interest for the 1990s.[15]

Promotion of Values. Marxism proved to be a bankrupt economic and political system, and Gorbachev understood that his country could not remain viable unless it abandoned this rigid system. Consequently, Communist regimes and parties around the world lost their anchor, although some—such as Cuba and North Korea—apparently believed they could go on without Moscow. Still, abandoning Marxist economics did not mean that Moscow had given up its interest in promoting its own ideas about how societies should be ordered. The basic Russian tradition of government control of political activity predated the Bolshevik Revolution and remained an important part of Russian culture. This authoritarian heritage was not compatible with the liberal political traditions of many Western countries and remained in ideological competition with the values of the West. Nevertheless, as long as Gorbachev pursued *perestroika* at home and detente abroad, Moscow's ideological interest would have a lower priority than economic and world-order interests. At the end of 1990, however, Gorbachev's liberalizing policies were under severe attack within the Soviet Communist Party.

Germany's National Interests and Policies

Few experts in 1990 doubted that a united Germany would become the strongest economic and political state in Europe and probably lead the European Community (soon to become the European Union) in the twenty-first century. It was therefore crucial to an appreciation of U.S.-Europe relations, and U.S.-Soviet relations, to understand what were likely to be the new Germany's national interests. This was a formidable task because Germany— unlike the Soviet Union, France, Britain, and the United States— did not have national interests similar to those it had held from 1933 to 1945, when the Nazi regime was finally crushed. To understand future German interests one needed to look at (1) Germany's history after it was first united in 1871; (2) the impact of defeat in two European wars; (3) the effects of West Germany's forty-five years of training in democracy under the tutelage of Britain, France, and the United States; and (4) the environment in which a united Germany found itself in 1990, including the embracing European Community and the ebbing Soviet influence in Europe. On the basis of these factors and an analysis of major speeches by Chancellor Kohl and Foreign Minister Genscher in the spring of 1990, Germany's basic interests for the 1990s could be assessed as follows.

Defense of Homeland. From Germany's perspective another European war—nuclear or conventional—would destroy its homeland and most of its population. Thus, avoidance of war was a vital defense-of-homeland interest. For those who believed that Germany should be a neutral, even pacifist, country in order not to antagonize any foreign power, it was a survival interest. The events of 1983–1984, when West Germany had to make the agonizing decision whether to permit the introduction of U.S. Pershing II nuclear missiles on German soil, had a profound effect on German public opinion. The antinuclear movement, which expanded in those years, continued to influence the Kohl government and led to its demand in April 1989 that the United States not modernize its short-range Lance missiles, even though NATO had recommended doing so after Washington and Moscow agreed to remove their medium-range missiles from Europe.[16]

A new factor influencing Germany's view of its defense-of-homeland interest was the absence of a Soviet military threat. The dismantling of the Berlin Wall was viewed as proof that Soviet forces no longer posed a threat to Germans; the reduction of Russian troops in East Germany in 1989–1990 reinforced that view. German leaders therefore had the task of persuading public opinion that a united Germany would need NATO's continued protection and that Germany required a credible defense force of its own.[17] One result of growing public confidence about security matters was the possibility of serious opposition to the whole idea of foreign troops on German soil. Germans were well aware of France's decision in 1966 to withdraw from the NATO military structure and ask foreign troops to leave; yet France remained part of the North Atlantic Alliance. Citing France as a model, Soviet Foreign Minister Shevardnadze suggested to German officials on several occasions that foreign forces should be withdrawn from both East and West Germany as part of a European settlement. Although the proposal was rejected by the Bonn government and NATO, Moscow understood that this idea would find sympathetic ears in both parts of Germany. It could become increasingly difficult for any German government to argue persuasively that foreign troops should remain in Germany for defense-of-homeland reasons after the Soviet Union withdrew all of its forces from Germany in 1994.

Economic Well-being. Germany's economic well-being in 1990 was vitally tied to the European Community's plan for an all-European market and Germany's ability to trade freely with the rest of the world, especially the United States. Like Japan, West Germany had developed a highly productive and expanding economy overshadowing that of most competitors. Bonn's monetary policy kept inflation low and savings high, and the economy appeared capable of absorbing 16 million East Germans without serious disruption. A unified Germany positioned itself to lend large sums of money to Eastern European countries and the Soviet Union, thereby providing the German government with considerable political leverage in dealing with Poland, Czechoslovakia, Hungary, and Romania.

Chancellor Kohl summed up Germany's international economic interest in an address to the American Council on Germany in New York on June 5, 1990: "A united Germany will be an economically sound and socially stable country. The unanimous opinion of international economic organizations is that German unification will significantly boost world economic growth. The huge pent-up demand in the GDR and in the reformist countries of central, eastern, and southeastern Europe affords substantial market opportunities for everyone." He went on to address the importance to Germany's future of the coming economic union of the European Community: "A united Germany will take part in 1992 when the large single market with 336 million people is completed. A united Germany will, together with France, be a driving force behind European unification. Before the end of this year, two parallel intergovernmental conferences will be started to lay the contractual foundation not only for economic and monetary union, but also for political union."[18]

Favorable World Order. It is in the area of Germany's wider political objectives in Europe that most of the ambiguity about its national interests persisted in 1990. Differences in emphasis existed between Chancellor Kohl, leader of West Germany's large Christian Democratic Party, and Foreign Minister Genscher, head of the small Free Democratic Party. These subtle differences could have a significant bearing on how the united Germany assessed its larger European interests in the 1990s, particularly if the two parties remained in a coalition government. A careful reading of the major foreign policy speeches they delivered in 1990 suggests that Kohl favored basing Germany's political and security interests on continued close association with the North Atlantic Alliance and the European Community, whereas Genscher wanted to go beyond these two organizations to build a new political and security framework that included Eastern European countries and the Soviet Union. Genscher referred repeatedly in his speeches to the idea of a "common European home" in which Germany would play a major role. He was more willing than Kohl to accommodate Moscow's interests, especially the views of Gorbachev. This apparent difference may have been only a matter of tactics between the two parties. But it could also reflect a significant difference in outlook between Genscher, who was born in East Germany and had long expressed interest in an East-West accommo- dation, and Kohl, who was a product of West Germany who represented a more conservative, more skeptical view of Soviet intentions and Gorbachev's ability to change Soviet society. Excerpts from their speeches in April, May, and June 1990 are instructive.

In a speech titled "The Future of a European Germany," Genscher told the American Society of Newspaper Editors in New York in April that "We wish to dominate no one. Our aim, as Thomas Mann wrote as early as 1952, is to create not a German Europe but a European Germany. Both German states are therefore called upon to provide not only a German but a European answer as they pursue national unity. That answer must dovetail with the future architecture of Europe." Genscher said that Germany's history and geographical position, "gives the Germans the chance to become the motor of the process ending the division of Europe." He wanted a united Germany to be a member of NATO within the context of the European Community and in the CSCE process. He then added: "We want it as a contribution to the development of a partnership between West and East based on stability, to the construction of the common European home, and to the establishment of the peaceful order spanning the whole of Europe."[19]

In May 1990 Genscher reiterated his call for an all-European security system in an address to the Bundestag:

> We believe that in the Europe of the future, whose contours are now becoming visible, the Soviet Union should play an important and constructive role. Europe does not

end at Poland's eastern border. In line with the Soviet Union's greater openness towards the West, we must open up to the East. Foreign Minister Shevardnadze made clear the Soviet Union's determination to participate actively in the Europe of the future. It lies in our own interest that President Gorbachev's policies at home and abroad prove successful. The problems of the Soviet Union have to be solved there, but a confidence-building policy and solidarity on the part of the West can also generate confidence in the Soviet Union and promote progress. . . . The central importance of German-Soviet relations will not come fully to bear until after German unification.[20]

On May 26, 1990, addressing an audience at Georgetown University in Washington, Genscher assured his audience that "a united Germany will remain a decisive advocate of the close bonds between Europe and America and will remain a member of NATO." But he went on to say that since Presidents Bush and Gorbachev had stated that they no longer perceived each other's country as a threat, it was time to restructure NATO: "This will have an effect on strategy, organization and arms. The political significance of our alliance must be enhanced, and cooperative security structures must be created for the whole of Europe."[21]

Chancellor Kohl's speeches also reflected optimism, but his emphasis was less on building a common European "home," particularly on accommodating the Soviet Union, and more on the importance of the transatlantic partnership. In his commencement speech at Harvard University on June 7, 1990, the chancellor cited Secretary of State George Marshall's address there forty-three years earlier, in which he proposed what came to be called the Marshall Plan for European economic recovery from World War II. Kohl said that by virtue of America's postwar assistance, the Europeans were in a position in the 1990s to perform a major part of the necessary reconstruction work in Eastern Europe through their own efforts. But, he added, "we need continued partnership with our American friends." The drive toward European unification had made "a decisive contribution to the change of outlook" in Eastern Europe, and "the hopes of the people and nations there are based on what has been achieved in Western Europe." As to the security of Europe, he continued,

it is more essential than ever for the Americans and Europeans to achieve the greatest convergence possible on important issues of foreign policy. This applies to aspects of East-West relations and to subjects that move up the agenda for the future. The Atlantic separates us only in a geographical sense. Even more than in the past we now have the opportunity to devote our combined energies to new goals. Transatlantic relations are today denser than ever. America will continue to have a firm position in Europe. It has a triple anchorage there: via Atlantic Alliance, via increasing cooperation between the United States and the European Community and via American's active role in the CSCE process.

Regarding the future of NATO, Kohl echoed Genscher's view that the Atlantic Alliance would remain but in a changed form. He differed somewhat with Genscher on the need for a new European security system: "Although we are emerging from the shadow of the East-West conflict and are making progress in the field of disarmament, who can rule out risks in the future? Therefore, vigilance is the price of our common freedom, as NATO's motto points out."[22]

Kohl and Genscher both voiced support for NATO and wanted the United States to be fully involved in the future of Europe. But Genscher appeared to place greater emphasis on reaching accommodation with Moscow as a priority of Germany's world-order interest. Kohl's stress, however, was on maintaining a strong Atlantic alliance as the primary ingredient in Germany's long-term security interests and on helping to build an enlarged and dynamic European system.

Promotion of Values.   The remarks of the two German leaders conveyed an impression that a united Germany saw its ideological interest to be centered on creating a united Europe free of the historical antagonisms that had plagued the continent for hundreds of years and produced two devastating wars in the twentieth century. Genscher seemed intrigued with the dream of a united Europe from the Urals to the Atlantic, an idea French President Charles de Gaulle had expressed a generation earlier and Mikhail Gorbachev had stated as his objective. The extent to which Germany would adopt such an objective as a promotion-of-values interest remained to be seen.

An insightful glimpse into united Germany's thinking regarding Europe was provided by Chancellor Kohl in an interview with *Time Magazine* in June 1990. Asked how the world would change in the next decade, Kohl said: "We will reduce the East-West confrontation further. We will make a lot of progress on the road to disarmament and detente. We will still need weapons and soldiers by the year 2000 because even then we will not have freedom for nothing. I am against a disarmament policy that takes announcements as deeds. You must be sure you get something in exchange for your concessions." Responding to a question about Europe's new role in the world, Kohl replied:

> The North-South conflict will become far more dangerous than it is today. I foresee three very important economic regions developing by the year 2000: the U.S. and Canada, perhaps on the road to an association with Mexico; the Far East; and Europe—the European Community, which will continue to grow into a political union, beyond economic union. Europe, of course, is not the E.C. alone. The E.C. is just a torso. A wider network will be constructed with other European countries, not necessarily by making them members but perhaps through association treaties. The Soviet Union too is going to seek its place in this emerging Europe, at least economically. For the Germans, this is essential. Geographically, our location offers great advantages, but there are also disadvantages. For a long time our central location has been more of a scourge and a danger for us. Now it may be our big chance; perhaps we can be the bridge. But we can be that bridge only if what supports it in the West is very strong. That brings me back to NATO and Europe. I am convinced that this is going to be the decade of the Europeans.

When asked, "How important will the U.S. be in Europe's future?" the chancellor replied: "Very important. For me, Europe would risk a part of its future if it did not include the Americans. We need them not only for military security, as important as that is, but in every possible way-in the economic field, in the cultural field. For the future of Germans in the 21st century, it is of existential importance that our policy rest on two secure pillars; the German-American pillar and the German-French pillar. It is not a matter of either-or, but one of as-well-as. And that does not mean we are diminishing other partners."[23]

In sum, it seemed clear that Chancellor Helmut Kohl, the "hero" of German reunification in 1990, was committed to NATO and a continuing U.S. presence in Europe. But he also saw a great opportunity for a united Germany to lead the continent toward economic and political union and to persuade the Soviet Union that it too should join the new Europe.[24]

The National Interests of Britain and France in Europe

Britain and France, two of America's wartime allies who defeated Nazi Germany and in 1990 participated in the two-plus-four talks on German unification, had more predictable national interests in Europe than did Germany and the Soviet Union. A brief description of their interests follows.

Great Britain.   Britain remained ambivalent about joining fully in a united Europe, even though it had benefited from participation in the European Community. This hesitancy reflected the traditional British desire to retain special relationships outside the continent, notably with the United States and the Commonwealth. By joining the EC in the 1970s for what it thought were vital economic reasons, Britain reduced its links with the Commonwealth and loosened its political and economic ties with the United States. In the 1980s Prime Minister Thatcher followed an independent viewpoint in the EC on monetary and political union, seeing the French-German drive for European political union as premature. Many members of her Conservative Party disagreed with her European policy and forced her resignation in November 1990. The new party leader, John Major, replaced her as prime minister shortly thereafter. In defense-of-homeland terms, Britain maintained an independent, nuclear-capable submarine force. It also retained a sizable surface navy and air force, although the Falkland Islands War in 1982 revealed inadequacies in both. The British government greatly valued its special defense relationship with the United States and provided it with important nuclear-capable bases. In 1986 Britain alone among the NATO countries permitted the United States to use its territory to launch an air strike against Libya.

The British government believed in 1990 that NATO forces should remain in Germany to ensure the withdrawal of Soviet troops and to help reassure Europeans that a united Germany was tied firmly to the West and would reject nonalignment in foreign policy. Although Thatcher shared some values with the Kohl government in Germany, she and many of her compatriots worried about future German foreign policy, particularly if the Social Democratic Party there should form a government and ask Britain and America to withdraw their forces. Even more sobering to the British would be the election of a German government that sought to reach accommodation with the Soviet Union at the expense of relations with NATO. For these and other reasons, Britain had a vital world-order interest in keeping the United States involved on the continent as well as in the British Isles.

Prime Minister Thatcher stated Britain's national interest regarding Europe during a speech in Cambridge, England, in March 1990: "No one must feel threatened, humiliated or resentful. Above all, we must ensure that a Germany rooted in NATO and the European Community, content within its borders, and democratic in its government, strengthens the security and the stability of Europe as a whole." Although she regarded some military force reductions as desirable, she insisted that Britain, France, and the United States needed to keep sizable forces on the continent for the foreseeable future.[25]

France.   The French government made a commitment early in the postwar period to reach political accommodation with the Federal Republic of Germany in order to build a more united, peaceful and prosperous Europe. Through the Schuman Plan, the Common Market, and the European Community, France's national interests in Europe were closely linked with those of Germany. Although a charter member of the North Atlantic Pact, France saw no need of NATO forces on its territory. Like Britain, it had built an independent nuclear deterrent for defense-of-homeland reasons. France welcomed Soviet participation in security arrangements for a post–Cold War Europe and, like Germany, was prepared to give substantial financial assistance to the Gorbachev government. Unlike Britain and Germany, however, France was not persuaded that a politically united Europe needed a long-term American military presence. French opinion remained attached to the de Gaulle idea of an independent Europe having superpower status and dealing as an equal with the United States and the Soviet Union. Some French leaders worried that Germany, not France, would become the leading power in Europe, but President Mitterrand concluded that French interests were best served by a united Europe in which France and Germany shared the leadership role, with Britain being a junior partner.

One complication, from France's point of view, was that the European Commission, located in Brussels and headed by Jacques Delors (a French national), seemed prepared in 1990 to give more support to Helmut Kohl's rapid drive for German reunification than did President Mitterrand. The *Economist* reported one West German official as saying, "Here in Bonn we know we have two friends, Jacques Delors and George Bush. They are the ones who understood what we wanted." In addition, Kohl's idea of an integrated Europe was closer to Delors's vision of the European Community's role, whereas Mitterrand appeared at times to be closer to sharing the British view of maintaining national sovereignty on key EC issues.[26]

France, like Britain, nourished its world-order interests outside Europe—in the French-speaking African countries, the Middle East, and Southeast Asia. Unlike Germany and Britain, however, France did not have a strong antinuclear movement and it therefore encountered little difficulty in justifying to its public large defense spending and nuclear testing in the Pacific. In fact, France even considered raising its defense budget in 1990 while other European countries were cutting theirs.[27] Although the French government believed in 1990 that some American forces should remain in Europe for the time being, Paris had not softened its stand against even modest American units located in France.

U.S. Policy toward Europe

In July 1990 the United States needed to make fundamental decisions about its future European policy. President Bush had stated unequivocally in May that the United States would remain a power in Europe and that he saw NATO as the key organization for providing military security and political stability on the continent. Many Europeans, however, were beginning to wonder why it was necessary to have an American military presence if the Kremlin was gradually withdrawing its forces. In particular, there was strong opposition in Germany and the Benelux countries to the stationing of nuclear weapons, whether tactical or air-launched, on their soil. Although pro-NATO and pro-defense governments were in power in Germany and Britain and the French government supported strong defense, opposition parties in Ger-

many and Britain were not strongly pro-NATO, and many German Social Democrats probably favored a nuclear-free central
Europe. How would an American president and an economy-
minded Congress react to calls from a German government for
withdrawal of all U.S. nuclear weapons but continued stationing
of U.S. forces?

Jeane Kirkpatrick, former U.S. Representative to the United
Nations and a professor at Georgetown University, wrote in the
Washington Post in June 1990 that the United States should map
out a strategy for Europe because "time and the opportunity to
influence events are slipping away." She observed that Germany,
France, the U.S.S.R., and Britain had clearly stated their objectives
for the new Europe: "Germany wants unification at almost any
price. The Soviet Union wants NATO dismantled. France wants a
strong Europe. Britain wants a strong Atlantic Alliance. . . . Each
country also desires to strengthen the institution in which it is, or
hopes to be, strongest. France seeks to strengthen the EC;
Gorbachev wants an all-European forum (CSCE); Britain values
NATO, and Germany will settle for any terms necessary for reunification." She then asked, "And the United States? What do we
think, and what do we want?"[28] In mid-1990 Kirkpatrick was one
of many foreign policy experts, on both the left and the right of the
political spectrum, urging Bush to lay out a strategy for Europe, not
just a "wish list" whose top priority was preservation of NATO.

A few American commentators on foreign policy were not
convinced, however, that it was in the U.S. or Europe's interest to
retain NATO and keep an American presence in Europe. Ronald
Steel, sometimes accused of being a neoisolationist, questioned
whether NATO served any essential purpose after the Cold War
had ended. Writing in the *New York Times*, Steel asked, "What
place will there be for the U.S. in a Europe whose armed forces it
can no longer control, whose economy is bigger than its and
whose citizens no longer feel dependent on an American protec-
tor—a Europe that is reaching out to embrace, even swallow, the
Soviet Union in its economic net? Clearly something far less important than it has been." Steel predicted that "in or out of NATO,
Germany will be the major actor in tomorrow's Europe. The Europe of the two superpower blocs will give way to a European
entity . . . in which Brussels or Berlin will carry more weight than
Washington."[29]

In 1990 the United States had four distinct policy alternatives
it could pursue in Europe: (1) a "wait and see" stance in relation

to NATO and the Soviet Union; (2) active engagement in promoting change in Europe; (3) gradual disengagement, including a substantial withdrawal of U.S. forces; and (4) full military withdrawal and political detachment.

1. Wait and See. This policy was followed by President Bush during his first year in office. He changed course at the Malta summit in December 1989, largely as a result of the remarkable events in Germany, and moved toward option 2. Option 1 still had proponents in conservative and some military circles, however. It was based on the premise that Gorbachev might not survive the battles between hard-liners and reformers in the Soviet government because his reforms would not bear fruit soon enough to ease the frustration of Soviet consumers and the ethnic turmoil afflicting some Soviet republics. Those who favored the wait-and-see policy thought the United States should not withdraw significant forces from Europe or give up nuclear weapons that might be required should a new, hard-line leadership take over in Moscow and abandon Gorbachev's policies. They agreed that the changes instituted by Gorbachev were probably irreversible; what had not changed, they claimed, was the massive military power and arms-making capacity of the Soviet system. Therefore, they concluded the West must keep up its guard and not be swept away by euphoria over the dismantling of the Berlin Wall, German unification, and the election of non-Communists to power in Eastern Europe. Secretary of Defense Cheney was an advocate of this cautious viewpoint.

2. Active Engagement in Promoting Change. This option, pursued with vigor by the Bush administration in 1990, had the United States taking an active leadership role in moving both Eastern and Western Europe toward a peaceful, cooperative era, with NATO as the cornerstone of the U.S. role. This policy accepted German unification, envisioned German leadership of the EC as inevitable, and foresaw a U.S.-German partnership to ensure the continued central role of NATO in political dealings with the Soviet Union and Eastern Europe. It accepted the possibility that Gorbachev would not survive politically in Moscow, but it was confident that a successor Soviet leadership would need economic assistance from the West and political reassurance that NATO would not take advantage of Soviet weakness. Underlying this strategy was an assumption that "the West won the Cold

War" but would need the continued active participation of the United States to organize the new Europe. Chancellor Helmut Kohl of Germany strongly supported this view.[30]

3. Gradual Disengagement. This strategy started from the premise that the Cold War was over, that it would not be resumed no matter who succeeded Gorbachev, and that the United States had no compelling need to maintain large forces in Europe or to be the leader in creating a new Europe of the 1990s. Those who supported this view thought that U.S. economic well-being should take precedence over its world-order interests in Europe and that the cost of a U.S. military presence there was too high. Democratic leaders in Congress tended to take this view, with Senator Sam Nunn of Georgia on the moderate side and Representative Pat Schroeder of Colorado on the liberal side of the disengagement view. Among European leaders, Francois Mitterrand favored the gradual withdrawal of the United States from Europe, although he wanted a continued U.S. strategic guarantee against a renewed Soviet threat. The Bush administration, however, rejected this option as contrary to U.S. long-term interests in Europe.

4. Political and Military Detachment. This option was not a likely strategy for the United States because it would be a new form of isolationism and interpreted as extremely risky. Its proponents assumed that the Soviet Union had lost its will to threaten Europe, that the European Community would create a powerful trade bloc competing vigorously with the United States for world markets, and that the United States should instead build a North American and eventually a Western Hemisphere free-trade zone to compete with Europe and Japan. These neoisolationists thought the United States had carried Europe's security burden long enough and that a resurgent Europe was becoming an economic threat to U.S. interests.

President Mikhail Gorbachev quietly subscribed to this view because he thought Europe would be more cooperative with the Soviet Union without the North Atlantic partnership. Leftists in Western Europe also supported it, believing their countries would be safer without an American military presence. Their counterparts in the United States included not only antidefense liberals but also conservatives who thought the United States was bankrupting itself by acting as "the world's policeman." (The 1992 presidential candidate Ross Perot espoused this viewpoint.)

To anyone who assumed that the United States had a continuing vital world-order interest and a vital economic interest in Europe, it was obvious that option 4 did not serve those interests, and that option 1 would work at cross-purposes with them because of the changed European economic and political environment. The only realistic alternatives that would serve U.S. vital interests in the 1990s were options 2 and 3, but the differences between them were significant.

Under option 2, active engagement, the United States would be heavily involved diplomatically in shaping European political and security relations, particularly as they affected the Soviet Union. Regular summit meetings between U.S. and Soviet presidents would assist Washington in persuading Moscow to continue moderate policies in Eastern Europe and sustained efforts to liberalize its society (these would include permitting independence for the Baltic states). This strategy entailed the basing of sizable U.S. forces in Europe (50,000–75,000), armed with tactical nuclear as well as conventional weapons. It also supported a larger leadership role for Germany in Europe. On the economic side, the policy suggested pressure on the European Community to resist protectionist policies, particularly discrimination against American agricultural products and U.S. companies. In addition, it promoted democratic values in Eastern Europe and the Soviet Union, on the assumption that free societies offered greater hope for peace than closed ones.

President Bush seemed wedded to option 2 because it coincided with his view of U.S. interests and was compatible with his leadership style. The United States was likely to pursue this strategy so long as Bush remained in the White House. The strategy might be upset by a serious economic decline or a social upheaval in the United States, neither of which seemed likely in 1990. Otherwise, U.S. policy toward Europe and the Soviet Union would see active U.S. participation in NATO in pursuit of security for a new, revitalized Europe.

Option 3, gradual disengagement, might occur later in the decade, not because of great changes in the world or in the United States but because the American public and Congress concluded that it was prudent for the United States to leave European security to the Europeans. Such a strategy assumed that the Soviet Union would not disintegrate politically, that it would continue to pursue a non-threatening foreign policy in Europe, and that its troops would all withdraw to the Soviet Union. It also assumed that the European Community would successfully integrate the economies of its membership and gradually accommodate those of new members in Eastern Europe. And it was based on the expectation that a united Germany would be a positive force in the new Europe, politically and economically. Those were large assumptions. Yet the positive momentum evident in 1990 could well generate that kind of Europe by the mid-1990s and cause most Americans to conclude that, having successfully completed a half-century of tutoring Europe, it was time to disengage.

Events in the Persian Gulf in the latter part of 1990 had a significant impact on NATO relationships because of uncertainty in France and Germany about their military participation in a potential war against Iraq (see Chapter 8). Britain sent 35,000 troops to the Gulf and strongly supported President Bush's decision to confront Iraq's aggression against Kuwait. France eventually sent 10,000 troops but insisted they were for the protection of Saudi Arabia, not the liberation of Kuwait. Germany did not send any forces, citing constitutional restrictions on the use of German troops outside the NATO area. Bonn did, however, provide financial aid to Turkey and Egypt to help cover their losses from the economic sanctions imposed on Iraq by the United Nations. The peace movement mounted demonstrations in major European cities, and the United States was widely criticized for preparing for war against Iraq. The Gulf crisis also affected NATO relationships in that Britain began to replace Germany as the United States' closest European ally, while France was seen as promoting an accommodation with Iraq's President Saddam Hussein that served France's national interests. These differences among the four principal NATO allies, on an issue of great importance to them all, was a poor omen for future cooperation on European security problems.

8
Post–Cold War Challenges to U.S. Interests, 1991–1995

In the spring and early summer of 1990 the United States re-emerged as the preeminent world power. The Soviet Union, which had been a serious competitor for international influence for more than forty years, decided to give up the race and concentrate its energies on rebuilding a failing economy. George Bush basked in the success of three summit meetings within six weeks: with Mikhail Gorbachev; with leaders of the Group of Seven industrialized countries (Britain, France, West Germany, Italy, Japan, Canada, the United States); and with the sixteen NATO heads of government, who had stood together against Moscow's pressure during the Cold War period. These meetings produced notable achievements for American foreign policy and enhanced the international reputations of President Bush and Secretary of State James Baker. U.S. political and economic interests were significantly advanced by an agreement on the phased withdrawal of Soviet forces from Eastern Europe, a unified Germany tied to NATO, an enhanced political role for the Atlantic Alliance, caution regarding large financial assistance to the Soviet Union and China, and support for the Uruguay Round of tariff reductions under the GATT framework. A historian would have to look back to the end of World War II to find a time when the danger of general war seemed so remote and the prestige of the United States was so high.

This mood of optimism came to an abrupt halt on August 2, 1990, when the Middle East exploded in another crisis as a result of Iraq's invasion and annexation of Kuwait. The quick movement of the Iraqi army to the border of Saudi Arabia caused the Bush administration to conclude that President Saddam Hussein intended to invade that country and the United Arab Emirates. The Iraqi dictator, who commanded an experienced army of nearly

1 million, appeared determined to use this formidable force to intimidate the region's oil-producing states into employing oil as a weapon against the industrialized countries and make Baghdad the center of a united Arab world.

Iraq's "blitzkrieg," as President Bush characterized it, shocked the world and brought condemnation from the United Nations and the Arab League. The action also resulted in the imposition of international sanctions and the virtual blockade of Iraq. Further, it became starkly clear to Western Europe, Japan, the United States, and many other countries that they faced a dangerous threat to their economic well-being if the industrialized world could be held hostage to Iraq's control of Kuwait's large oil reserves. For Kuwait this was a survival threat. To Saudi Arabia, the United Arab Emirates, Syria, and Jordan, Iraq's military move into Kuwait presented a dangerous security threat to their homelands.

For the United States, particularly George Bush, Iraq's invasion of Kuwait presented so serious an economic and world-order threat that it could not be negotiated, suggesting that the situation had reached the "intolerable" level at which policy-makers believe strong action, including the use of military force, must be taken to protect vital national interests. The Bush administration's response to the Persian Gulf crisis in 1990 is a prime example of how the conceptual framework for defining vital interests, as outlined in Chapter 1, may be used as a planning tool in crisis situations.

U.S. National Interests in the Middle East

The United States has had significant national interests in the Middle East since World War II, particularly in the Persian Gulf area because of its huge deposits of cheap crude oil. Until 1970 Washington was able to rely on Great Britain to defend its interests in the Gulf and the Indian Ocean area, but in that year Britain decided, for budgetary reasons, to withdraw its military presence, leaving a potential power vacuum in the region. At the urging of President Richard Nixon, the Shah of Iran agreed to fill the security role in the Persian Gulf relinquished by Britain, and in return was provided with large amounts of sophisticated U.S. military equipment. When the Shah was overthrown by an Islamic revolution in 1979, the United States faced a serious dilemma: whether to enlarge its own power and influence in the Gulf or to permit revolutionary Iran, Iraq, or possibly the Soviet Union to do so. President

Carter's enunciation of the Carter Doctrine,[1] following Moscow's invasion of Afghanistan, was a signal that the United States had a vital interest in the Gulf even though at that time it had very little means of defending it. When Ronald Reagan became president in 1981, his administration quickly made agreements with Saudi Arabia and other Gulf states, as well as Egypt and Israel, to build their defenses against a potential Soviet military move into the area. They were also directed against Iran's efforts to disrupt oil shipments during the Iran-Iraq War, which Iraq had launched in September 1980. Washington was mindful that Moscow had been Iraq's major arms supplier for nearly twenty years.

The crucial issue for the Reagan administration to decide was this: Is the entire Persian Gulf region with its vast oil reserves a vital national interest, or is only Saudi Arabia vital to the United States? Both Democratic and Republican administrations over the years had determined that protecting Saudi Arabia, the Gulf's largest oil producer and possessor of the world's greatest reserve of crude oil, was crucial to U.S. economic well-being. However, an additional question was whether the other Gulf states—Iran, Iraq, Kuwait, the Emirates—were also vital interests and should be defended with American military power. Reagan's decision to convoy Kuwaiti ships in the Gulf during 1987–1988 showed a heightened interest in Kuwait but did not explicitly answer this key question: Is Kuwait a vital interest?

Another important U.S. interest in the Middle East since World War II has been the safety of Israel. All U.S. presidents beginning with Harry Truman have stated that preservation of Israel as a sovereign state is a vital U.S. interest, even though no treaty similar to the North Atlantic or the Rio pacts was concluded. As the Cold War deepened in the late 1970s and 1980s, Israel and the United States forged a strategic partnership to counter Moscow's efforts to expand its influence among the Arab countries. This relationship began to wane following Israel's disastrous invasion of Lebanon in 1982, its unwillingness to grant self-rule to the 1.7 million Palestinians living in the Occupied Territories (as envisaged in the 1979 Camp David Accords), and its involvement in the Iran-Contra scandal in 1986–1987.

A fundamental foreign policy issue for Presidents Carter, Reagan, and Bush was whether the American interest in Israel's security was so large that it should overshadow U.S. relations with the Arab countries, particularly the oil-rich Persian Gulf states. So long as the Cold War had the highest priority in

Washington's view of U.S. world-order interests, Israel's strategic importance often proved more significant than U.S. relations with the Arab countries. The exception was Egypt, which made peace with Israel in 1979 and thereafter worked closely with Washington to build its defenses and its economy. Just as the new detente relationship between Washington and Moscow emerged in the late 1980s, however, security in the Gulf was threatened by Revolutionary Iran. President Reagan decided to use the U.S. Navy to prevent Tehran from interfering with the flow of oil from the Persian Gulf, and this limited naval operation in 1987–1988 was successful in keeping the Gulf open to shipping and in helping to end the eight-year-old Iran-Iraq War. It also restored the confidence of Saudi Arabia and other Gulf states that the United States would not abandon its security role in the area.[2] For Israel, however, the end of the Iran-Iraq war was no cause for rejoicing: its archenemy Iraq had emerged from that struggle with a large, battle-hardened army and a self-confidence that permitted Saddam Hussein to become an even greater threat to Israel.

A third long-term U.S. interest in the Middle East has been the security of Turkey. Since 1947, when President Truman decided to provide that country with military assistance in order to counter Stalin's pressure, Turkey has been a valuable ally, first bilaterally and then in NATO and the Central Treaty Organization. Turkey became even more important after 1979 when the United States was ousted from its military bases in Iran. The U.S. Air Force maintains strategic air bases in Turkey, and that country's armed forces receive much of their equipment from the United States. Turkey controls a major Iraqi oil pipeline across its territory to the Mediterranean, which it cut in August 1990 as part of the UN sanctions against Iraq. Because of its highly strategic location bordering the Soviet Union, Iran, and Iraq, Turkey is a pivotal country in any U.S. military intervention in the Middle East area.

The Persian Gulf War, 1990–1991

In August 1990, when President Bush ordered the deployment of over 200,000 forces to Saudi Arabia and adjacent waters, U.S. national interests in the Persian Gulf could be defined generally as follows.

Defense of Homeland. The territory, population, and constitutional system of the United States were not threatened by the

Persian Gulf crisis. There was no threat of a U.S.-Soviet confrontation because the Soviet Union concurred with the United Nations condemnation of Iraq's invasion of Kuwait. It, too, called on Saddam Hussein to withdraw. The detention by Iraq of several thousand American citizens, however, posed the specter of another hostage crisis even more dangerous than the one Iran had precipitated eleven years earlier. The hostages were later released, but the issue remained a major defense-of-homeland interest.

Economic Well-being. Persian Gulf oil became a vital economic interest to the United States in the 1970s—even though this country is less dependent on world oil than are most other industrialized countries—because American consumption of foreign oil rose substantially during the decade and because Saudi Arabia emerged as this country's largest supplier of crude oil. A major reason for the expanding U.S. consumption in the 1980s was price: as the cost of a barrel of crude dropped to $12–14 in the mid-1980s, consumption went up and domestic production and exploration for new sources declined. Imports then increased because exploring for additional oil in the United States and Canada was too expensive at those prices. When OPEC raised its price above $20 a barrel in July 1990, this was a signal that the United States was again heavily dependent on imported oil and would be obliged to pay substantially higher prices. In sum, the United States had become overly dependent on the willingness of Saudi Arabia, Kuwait, and other Gulf states to produce large quantities of oil in order to keep the price low. Iraq's attack on Kuwait and the subsequent embargo of its oil exports pushed the world price of oil to nearly $40 a barrel.

Favorable World Order. It is debatable whether the Persian Gulf constitutes a vital U.S. interest for regional balance-of-power reasons. A reasonable case could be made that, except for a Soviet military threat to the region, the United States has no historical interest there that could justify the need to send an army to defend it, unlike the case in Western Europe, the Caribbean Basin, and the Western Pacific. Nevertheless, Gulf oil is so crucial to Japan, Western Europe, and other allies that it became a derivative U.S. vital interest. Were the United States not the leader of a worldwide system of alliances with other countries, an argument might be made that it should not be the primary country to confront a Persian Gulf aggressor such as Iraq. But this was not the

reality of the 1990s, and the United States was therefore obliged
to lead. Another world-order interest at stake for the United States
was respect for international law. In August 1990 the United Nations branded Iraq an aggressor against Kuwait, and the United
States decided to uphold the principle of collective security em-
bodied in the UN Charter. Whether Washington was obliged as
well to provide most of the forces to protect Saudi Arabia and oust
Iraq from Kuwait was a different issue.

Promotion of Values. Although democracy and human
rights are not important values in Middle Eastern countries, an
attack by one Arab state on another is viewed by Arabs as deplorable and accounted for the support that UN sanctions on Iraq received from most Arab countries. That fact put the U.S. promotion-
of-values interest at the major level.

In sum, two vital interests of the United States, economic well-
being and world order, were at stake in the Persian Gulf in 1990.
The other two, defense of homeland and promotion of values,
were at the major level. By the criteria set out in Chapter 1, that
assessment of basic interests suggested that the situation was at
the "intolerable" stage for the United States in its relations with
Iraq and that Washington would probably use military force to
defend its vital interests in the Persian Gulf.

If one looks at the criteria listed in Table 4 (Chapter 1) for deciding whether a vital U.S. interest is at stake, a calculation of the
values and cost/risk factors suggests that the basis for a vital U.S.
interest was strong but not overwhelming, particularly in terms
of the potential costs of a military intervention. Looking first at
the value factors, a dispassionate observer would conclude that
three of them (proximity of the danger, sentimental attachment,
type of government aided) had a low value; four (nature of the
threat, effect on balance of power, national prestige at stake, and
support of key allies) had a relatively high value; and one (economic stake) had a very high value. On the cost/risk side, the results appeared to be less certain. For example, the economic costs
of hostilities and estimated casualties were not fully predictable
when President Bush decided to send ground forces as well as air
and naval units to the Middle East. The risk of an enlarged conflict seemed to be small because neither the Soviet Union nor any
other major power was likely to join Iraq. The cost of a protracted
conflict depended on how large a force the United States sent and
the anticipated type of combat. The likelihood of defeat seemed

remote, but the possibility of stalemate could not be ruled out if Iraq managed to survive the economic blockade imposed by the United Nations. International reaction to U.S. armed intervention could turn negative if Washington refused to give economic sanctions time to work before using force to oust Iraqi troops from Kuwait. U.S. public and congressional opposition to armed intervention would depend on the magnitude and duration of the conflict, the number of casualties, the fate of Americans held hostage by Iraq, and United Nations support for the use of force. In short, while President Bush found more factors in his favor in dealing with this crisis than President Johnson had when he decided to send troops to Vietnam, Bush's decision in November to deploy more than 400,000 troops to the Persian Gulf carried substantial risks and made his assessment of "vital interest" in this case a qualified one.

As to the instruments of policy outlined in Table 5 (Chapter l), it seems clear in retrospect that President Bush was prepared to use all eleven of the political/economic instruments and many of the political/military ones as well. For example, he strongly supported the UN Security Council's decision to declare a trade embargo and economic sanctions against Iraq, and he persuaded Turkey and Saudi Arabia to close Iraq's oil pipelines through their countries. He increased military assistance to Turkey, Saudi Arabia, and Egypt, helped provide economic compensation to Turkey for revenues lost by its boycott of Iraqi trade, and forgave a large portion of Egypt's debt for military assistance provided by the United States. The administration also apparently launched a covert action campaign to destabilize Saddam Hussein's regime. Among the military instruments, President Bush used a massive show of military strength, increased surveillance of Iraq's military movements, a blockade of Iraq's shipping, the mobilization of military reserve units, and the threat of retaliation with weapons of massive destruction if Iraq first employed them in combat. The president did not, however, break diplomatic relations with Iraq or initiate combat operations. The early buildup of U.S. and other forces in Saudi Arabia was designed primarily to protect that country against an Iraqi invasion. Nevertheless, Bush's public statements in August and his deployment of combat-ready U.S. forces, including more than 50,000 Marines, suggested that the White House was preparing for major hostilities and that these might not be confined to defensive operations if Iraq refused to withdraw from Kuwait and free all foreign hostages. An unan-

Table 7. The Persian Gulf Crisis, 1990–1991

Basic interest	Intensity of interest			
	Survival	Vital	Major	Peripheral
Defense of homeland	Kuwait	Saudi Arabia Iraq Turkey Jordan Syria Israel	U.S. Britain France Iran Egypt	U.S.S.R. Japan
Economic well-being	Kuwait	U.S. France Japan Turkey Saudi Arabia Jordan Iraq	U.S.S.R. Britain Iran Egypt Israel Syria	
Favorable world order		U.S. Britain France Egypt Iraq Saudi Arabia Israel Syria	U.S.S.R. Jordan Iran Japan Turkey	Kuwait
Promotion of values		Saudi Arabia Egypt Iraq Syria Kuwait Jordan	U.S. U.S.S.R. Britain France Japan	Iran Israel Turkey

nounced goal in August seemed to be the eventual removal of Saddam Hussein from power.

Given the information available in August and September 1990 about the policies of major countries involved in the Iraq-Saudi crisis, it is possible to calculate on the national interest matrix (Table 7) the comparative interests at the time of the fourteen most interested countries. This analysis suggests that war was probable because so many of them had vital interests at stake. For the United States, economic and world-order interests were affected at the vital level, and defense-of-homeland and promotion-of-values interests at the major level. Saudi Arabia had all four of its basic interests at the vital level, and Egypt had a vital world-order and values interest at stake. As the crisis unfolded, it became clear that Western European countries also had vital interests and, led by Britain and France, began to take active roles by sending military forces to the Gulf. Moscow's interests, however, remained at the major level. Diplomatic efforts were made at the United Nations and among the Arab countries to negotiate a political solution to the crisis before hostilities were launched. But when Iraq began rounding up citizens of the United States and other countries and holding them as hostages, the prospects for war increased.

President Bush said several times that U.S. forces would be in the Middle East for as long as it took to accomplish their mission, and Secretary of Defense Cheney suggested that it could be a long-term commitment of forces. On August 15, in remarks to Defense Department employees at the Pentagon, the president stated that his reasons for sending troops to Saudi Arabia had to do with "access to energy resources that are key, not just to the functioning of this country, but the entire world." He elaborated: "Our jobs, our way of life, our own freedom and the freedom of friendly countries around the world would all suffer if control of the world's greatest oil reserves fell into the hands of Saddam Hussein." He added: "Our action in the gulf is about fighting aggression and preserving the sovereignty of nations. It is about keeping our word and standing by old friends. It is about our own national security interests and ensuring the peace and stability of the world."[3] This was a clear presidential assessment of a vital national interest at stake in the Persian Gulf.

President Bush formally laid out his appraisal of U.S. interests in the Gulf in an address to a joint session of Congress on September 11, 1990. As was noted in Chapter 4 when discussing President Reagan's appeal to a joint session concerning U.S. interests at stake in Central America, such personal appeals for support are rare, and they highlight the crucial nature of the decisions facing the government. President Bush listed four objectives of U.S. policy in the Gulf crisis: (1) Iraq must withdraw immediately and completely from Kuwait; (2) Kuwait's legitimate government must be restored; (3) the security and stability of the Gulf must be assured; and (4) American citizens living abroad must be protected. He said that these objectives were not America's alone but had been endorsed five times in as many weeks by the United

Nations Security Council. Noting that he and Soviet President Gorbachev agreed on the nature of Iraq's threat to its neighbors, Bush quoted from a joint communique issued following their just-concluded meeting in Helsinki: "We are united in the belief that Iraq's aggression must not be tolerated. No peaceful international order is possible if larger states can devour their smaller neighbors." The president then outlined his view of U.S. national interests in the Gulf: "Vital issues of principle are at stake. Saddam Hussein is literally trying to wipe a country off the face of the earth. . . . Vital economic interests are at risk as well. Iraq itself controls some 10 percent of the world's proven oil reserves. Iraq plus Kuwait controls twice that. An Iraq permitted to swallow Kuwait would have the economic and military power, as well as the arrogance, to intimidate and coerce its neighbors—neighbors who control the lion's share of the world's remaining oil reserves. We cannot permit a resource so vital to be dominated by one so ruthless. And we won't." Seeking to reassure doubting Middle East allies who remembered the humiliating circumstances under which President Reagan withdrew American Marines from Lebanon in 1984, Bush made this pledge: "Recent events have surely proven that there is no substitute for American leadership. In the face of tyranny, let no one doubt American credibility and reliability. Let no one doubt our staying power. We will stand by our friends. One way or another, the leader of Iraq must learn this fundamental truth."

Finally, the president appealed to Congress to share his assessment of the vital nature of U.S. national interests in this crisis: "I am hopeful, in fact I am confident, the Congress will do what it should, and we in the executive branch will do our part. In the final analysis, our ability to meet our responsibilities abroad depends upon political will and consensus at home. This is never easy in democracies—where we govern only with the consent of the governed. And although free people in a free society are bound to have their differences, Americans traditionally come together in times of adversity and challenge. . . . If old adversaries like the Soviet Union and the United States can work in common cause, then surely we who are so fortunate to be in this great chamber—Democrats, Republicans, liberals, conservatives—can come together to fulfill our responsibilities here."[4]

In an earlier time—for example, in April 1917 or in December 1941, when Presidents Woodrow Wilson and Franklin Roosevelt appeared before similar gatherings of senators and congressmen—the president would have asked Congress for a declaration of war. George Bush did not do that, but he clearly laid the groundwork for a later request for a congressional resolution endorsing the use of force against Iraq. The president also needed the United Nations' endorsement for the use of force in the Gulf, and he wanted to show that America's allies were sharing the burden of driving Iraq out of Kuwait if sanctions and international political pressure failed. (He received UN endorsement of the use of force in a 12–2 Security Council vote on November 29.) The September 11 address to Congress thus committed the personal credibility of George Bush to a successful outcome of the confrontation with Iraq. In fact, his presidency as well as U.S. national interests were vitally affected by the Persian Gulf crisis.

In January 1991 President Bush launched a military assault known as "Desert Storm" on Iraq after concluding that economic sanctions and political pressure would not force Saddam Hussein to evacuate his forces from Kuwait within a reasonable length of time. He had named General Norman Schwarzkopf to lead the Coalition's force of half a million troops, nearly 400,000 of them Americans. The UN Security Council had set January 15 as the deadline for Iraq to withdraw its forces, but Mr. Bush wisely decided that he needed formal congressional approval before launching a military operation of such magnitude. Both the Senate and House of Representatives debated his plan for three days before a national television audience. The major issue between the Republicans, who supported the president, and most Democrats who opposed military action was whether the president was moving too quickly to use force, whether it would not be better to give the economic and political sanctions more time to work. On January 12 Congress gave the president authority to carry out the UN mandate, with the Senate voting in favor by 52 to 47 and the House approving by 250 to 183. Although the Senate vote was not a resounding show of support, Congress had nevertheless fulfilled its constitutional responsibility to decide whether to authorize the president to wage war. Opinion polls showed that most Americans supported the president, and after he launched the aerial war on January 16 public support for the war rose to nearly 80 percent. The air strikes, including cruise missiles, continued for five weeks while Moscow and several Arab governments tried to persuade Iraq to withdraw from Kuwait. When these efforts proved fruitless, President Bush on February 23 ordered a massive land attack. The results were astonishing: by February 28, Iraqi troops were defeated and fleeing from Kuwait. The Coalition forces were in position to capture Baghdad within a few days, but after conferring with other government leaders and his military commanders, the president ordered a cease-fire. Only 79 Americans were killed in action. Another 212 had been wounded and 45 were missing. Bush ended the war sooner than some critics thought prudent, but he did so because the mission, the liberation of Kuwait, had been achieved and Iraq's army had suffered huge losses. Some said he should have sent the victorious forces on to Baghdad and forced Saddam Hussein from power. However, the president had not been given authority, either by the United Nations or Congress, to occupy Iraq and install a new government. Kuwait had been liberated, Saddam Hussein's vaunted army had been crushed, and George Bush was not willing to suffer the potentially large number of American casualties that an assault on Baghdad would entail. He may also have been persuaded that Gorbachev's reluctance to approve military action would turn him into an opponent if the U.S. objective was suddenly changed to the removal of the Iraqi regime. In a televised address on February 28, the president asserted: "Kuwait is liberated. Iraq's army is defeated. Our military objectives are met. Kuwait is once more in the hands of Kuwaitis, in control of their own destiny. . . . This is not a time of euphoria, certainly not a time to gloat. But it is a time of pride, pride in our troops, pride in the friends who stood with us in the crisis, pride in our nation and the people whose strength and resolve made victory quick, decisive, and just."[5]

The Gulf War initially brought the U.S.-led coalition that included European and Arab countries closer together than they had been during the five months of planning. It also opened the possibility of organizing an international conference to deal with the vexing Palestinian homeland issue. This was now feasible because Israel's avoidance of involvement in the military action against Iraq won praise from Arab as well as European leaders. Even though Germany, a principal NATO member, declined on constitutional grounds to send its forces to the Gulf, it nevertheless agreed to pay a substantial sum of money to the United States to support the latter's large military contribution. Turkey, another key NATO member, declined to send troops but did authorize the United States to use its territory in the bombing of Iraq, an action that was not popular in Turkey. Saudi Arabia provided the Coalition forces with both bases and significant financial assistance, and it subsequently agreed to the stationing of U.S. air units on its soil in order to provide future security to the Persian Gulf region. President Bush and General Schwarzkopf were hailed for achieving a great victory, and the president's poll ratings reached 90 percent. He seemed assured of reelection in 1992.

George Bush and his national security adviser, Brent Scowcroft, wrote in their 1998 joint memoir that the Gulf War had a major impact on international relations: "The United States had recognized and shouldered its peculiar responsibility for leadership in tackling international challenges, and won wide acceptance for this role around the globe. American political credibility and influence had skyrocketed. We stood almost alone on the world stage in the Gulf Crisis, with the Soviets at best in sometimes reluctant support. Our military reputation grew as well. . . . The result was that we emerged from the Gulf conflict into a very different world from that prior to the attack on Kuwait."[6]

A less favorable outcome of the war was the plight of the Kurdish minority population in northern Iraq. After the defeat of the Iraqi army, the Kurds started a rebellion against Iraq's rule and expected support from the United States and other governments. However, Saddam Hussein organized his remaining troops and launched a brutal campaign to crush the Kurds. After photos of the refugees appeared on world television, public and congressional reaction led the president to initiate bombing of Iraqi troops in northern Iraq and to impose a no-fly zone there. However, these measures had only limited effect on Baghdad's ability to crush the resistance. The Kurds' rebellion provided ammunition to Bush's critics, who asserted that he should have ousted the Iraqi regime before halting the Gulf War. The issue detracted from the public euphoria over the war's end.

Emergence of Boris Yeltsin and Russia

The political situation within the Soviet Union, especially the authority of President Gorbachev, deteriorated markedly in late 1990 under pressure from hard-line Communist Party leaders and top military commanders. Much dissatisfaction had arisen among these conservatives over the large concessions that Gorbachev and Foreign Minister Eduard Shevardnadze had made to NATO regarding the reunification of Germany, the withdrawal of Soviet troops from Germany, and the dismantling of the Warsaw Pact. Moreover, the Red Army's military leaders were alarmed at large troop reductions that Gorbachev had proposed to help deal with the country's serious economic problems. In addition, Gorbachev's reluctance to support Iraq, Moscow's longtime ally, during the U.S.-led buildup in the Persian Gulf caused disaffection among old-guard party leaders and senior military officers. To placate these critics, Gorbachev in late 1990 replaced his moderate defense minister and interior minister with hard-liners. He was under growing pressure also to modify his economic reform policies and adopt conservative, even reactionary, measures to prevent the potential disintegration of the U.S.S.R. Because of Gorbachev's shift in policy, Shevardnadze resigned as foreign minister in December 1990 and warned that the U.S.S.R. was headed for "dictatorship." A month later Soviet troops in Latvia and Lithuania were ordered to take control and prevent these Baltic republics from moving toward independence. The political fallout from Moscow's use of force in the Baltics was intense and generated deep concern in the United States and Europe. After all, it was argued, if the Kremlin was willing to use force against Lithuania and Latvia to prevent their departure from the Soviet Union, what were the implications for Poland, Czechoslovakia, and Hungary, which had recently ousted Communist governments and replaced them with democratic ones? Moreover, if Moscow was shifting its policy only seven months after Gorbachev said the Cold War was over, how seriously would U.S.-Soviet relations be affected?

Moscow's military intervention in the Baltic republics temporarily stabilized the political situation there, and by spring Gorbachev seemed to have persuaded his Kremlin adversaries to hold off on further actions to enable him to negotiate with Washington and European governments for economic aid. He won approval for the Strategic Arms Reduction Treaty (START) with the United States, which had been initiated by the Reagan administration. It was now a litmus test in Washington of whether Moscow was serious about establishing a peaceful relationship with the United States and Europe. In July 1991 Bush and Gorbachev signed the historic treaty in Moscow, and this was viewed as a high-water mark in the superpowers' effort to end the threat of nuclear war. Brent Scowcroft recalled the positive mood of the presidential party as it left for home on August 1: "It had been a satisfying set of talks. . . . Gorbachev seemed upbeat, almost exuberant about his prospects for dealing with his domestic problems. The black cloud over the Baltics marred the proceedings, but we had established a good process and rapport for our bilateral summit dialogues and there seemed, on the whole, reason to see the glass as half full."[7]

The euphoria abruptly ended two and a half weeks later, on August 18, when a coup d'etat was staged in Moscow by military and KGB chiefs and Communist Party conservatives while Gorbachev was vacationing in the Crimea. For a few days the possibility loomed that the reactionary forces would gain control of the government, abandon Gorbachev's liberal reforms, and reverse the cooperative foreign policy that Moscow had adopted toward the United States. While Gorbachev and his wife were held captive at their vacation home, opposition to the coup plotters mounted in Moscow. Boris Yeltsin, the popularly elected president of the Russian republic, stood in front of the parliament building and urged Moscow citizens to gather in the square and save their democratic government. Meanwhile, Gorbachev steadfastly refused to bow to the coup leaders' demands that he resign, and after three days the crisis was over. The unwillingness of Russian tank units to fire on the pro-democracy demonstrators gathered around Yeltsin was a major factor in the coup's failure.

President Bush had been aware that Boris Yeltsin was competing with Gorbachev for recognition as a major political leader in the Soviet Union. As the elected president of Russia, the U.S.S.R.'s largest republic, Yeltsin was building ties with leaders of the other republics while Gorbachev shifted his policy in the fall of 1990. Yeltsin was opposed to the military crackdown in Lithuania and Latvia and voiced support for their desire for autonomy from Moscow. President Bush was skeptical when he received Yeltsin at the White House on June 20, just two months before the coup attempt in Moscow: "With all the well-publicized rivalry and difficulties between Yeltsin and Gorbachev over the past few months," he recorded in his diary, "I was greatly relieved and surprised when instead he sang [Gorbachev's] praises. I was impressed by him. . . . He was engaging and fascinating, and his infectious laugh made him easy to like."[8]

Even though Gorbachev survived efforts by the conservatives to remove him from office, his authority was severely challenged in the next few months while Yetlsin's influence steadily increased. Meanwhile, fifteen Soviet republics, including Russia, began discussions on dissolution of the Soviet Union and its replacement with a loose association of independent states. Ukraine, Belorussia, and Moldovia voted for independence soon after the coup against Gorbachev failed. And the three Baltic states also declared their independence. Finally, the Communist Party of the U.S.S.R., which had dominated the country since 1917, was disbanded and its property turned over to parliament. In desperation a weakened Mikhail Gorbachev proposed a new economic association among the republics, but his efforts were rebuffed. In a December 1 referendum the Ukrainian people voted, by 90 percent, for independence. The next day the United States signaled that it would grant recognition. A week later Russian President Yeltsin met with the presidents of Ukraine and Belorussia at Brest, where they announced the dissolution of the Soviet Union and its replacement with the Commonwealth of Independent States (CIS). This was a loose confederation of sovereign states that would coordinate foreign and military policy and adopt a customs union. The Brest Declaration formally marked the end of the U.S.S.R. and the dismantling of all its institutions in Moscow and elsewhere. It also marked the end of Gorbachev's role as the head of a state. Yeltsin now emerged as leader of the largest successor state, Russia.

Secretary of State James Baker spoke of the imminent demise of the Soviet Union in an address at Princeton University on December 12. He paid homage to George Kennan, a noted Princeton historian who was present and widely regarded as "the father of containment" toward the Soviet Union after World War II. Baker said that the state founded by Lenin and Stalin was gone and, "as a consequence of Soviet collapse, we live in a new world. We must take advantage of this new Russian Revolution, set in motion with the defeat of the August coup." Flying to Moscow a few days later, however, Baker worried about "whether it would be possible to find any solid footing in a country dissolving into chaos."[9]

On Christmas Day 1991, the red flag with hammer and sickle was lowered from the Kremlin Wall for the last time. The Soviet Union had gone out of existence without a war or revolution or other violence. Mikhail Gorbachev, who had helped to end forty years of Cold War confrontation with the West and had tried to reform the Soviet system, no longer had a job. American and European observers pondered for months why this momentous series of events had occurred so rapidly.

Michael Mandelbaum, a specialist on American foreign policy at Johns Hopkins University, offered this view: "How did it happen that a mighty imperial state, troubled but stable only a few years before, had come to the brink of collapse in 1991? Who and what were responsible?" His short answer: "The chief architect of the Soviet collapse was Mikhail Gorbachev himself." Mandel-baum contended that: "His aim had been to strengthen the political and economic systems that he inherited, to strip away their Stalinist accretions and make the Soviet Union a modern dynamic state. Instead he had fatally weakened it.[10]

Robert Gates, director of the Central Intelligence Agency in 1991, came to a similar conclusion based on the vast amount of intelligence material available in the U.S. government: "The collapse of the Soviet Union was not inevitable in 1991, but was precipitated by Mikhail Gorbachev, a leader who set out to save the Soviet Union and who, instead, destroyed it." Gates postulated that "His tenure as the Soviet leader was the embodiment of the law of unintended consequences. He did not intend to weaken then dismantle the Soviet Communist Party. He did not intend for Eastern Europe to become independent of the Soviet Union. He did not set out to unify Germany and then to allow it to remain in NATO. He did not intend to preside over the disintegration of the Soviet Union. And yet his policies and actions, intended to correct the economic and political mistakes of his predecessors and give new life to a reformed Soviet Union, surely sealed its fate and accelerated its doom."[11]

Gates also addressed the question of why there was no celebrating in the United States over the Soviet Union's demise: "Because in December 1991 there was no agreement in Washington that the United States had, in fact, helped push the USSR into an early grave, there was no sense of victory. Because the Cold War itself had been waged in shades of gray, there was little definition or sharpness to its conclusion." The former CIA director concluded: "And so the greatest of American triumphs—a triumph of constancy of purpose and commitment sustained over four decades at staggering cost—became a peculiarly joyless victory. We had won the Cold War, but there would be no parade."[12]

George Bush recalled in his memoirs that he had "a tremendous charge" as he watched the final breakup of the Soviet Union and considered himself "extraordinarily lucky" to have been president during the closing years of the Cold War. Gorbachev, Shevardnadze, and the others played key roles, he said, because without them "the Cold War would have dragged on and the fear of impending nuclear war would still be with us."[13]

Boris Yeltsin, the first elected president of Russia, took over the leadership mantle of the new power in Eastern Europe in 1992 and became custodian, along with leaders of Ukraine, of a major arsenal of nuclear weapons. For all their economic and political weakness, these independent states constituted a potentially serious nuclear threat that American and European leaders could not ignore. Yeltsin felt a similar urgency about the nuclear issue. Within a month of becoming head of the new state of Russia, he told Secretary of State James Baker in Moscow that he had established command and control over all strategic missiles in the four ex-Soviet republics possessing them and that a phone link would soon be established among their leaders.

Yeltsin and Bush met in February 1992 at a series of meetings at Camp David, Maryland, during which the issues that had divided Washington and Moscow over the years were discussed in depth. Yeltsin was eager to make an announcement to the world that the two countries were now allies, but Bush was not prepared to go that far. The Russian's proposal about ICBM targeting was accepted, however, including his assurance that weapons in the hands of the three other former Soviet republics would either be destroyed or delivered to Russia for safekeeping. No announcement was made about re-targeting of missiles, but this largely symbolic strategic shift took place over the next few months. Reporting on this first summit meeting between the two leaders, Secretary Baker observed, "For the first time, the elected leader of a democratic and independent Russia had sat down with an American president," and together they had laid out a course of future cooperation.[14]

During President Bush's final year in office, the United States and Russia continued to negotiate on arms limitation, relations with the other newly independent republics, especially Ukraine, and plans to assist Russia to inaugurate free market reforms. Bush could now bask in the success of two major objectives of his administration: (1) reestablishing a favorable balance of power in the Persian Gulf after the area's security was threatened by Iraq and (2) steering the United States and Western Europe through a dangerous transition period in relations with the bankrupt Soviet Union and the emerging Russia headed by Boris Yeltsin. Both objectives were vital interests for the United States, and the Bush administration was successful in achieving them. Another vital interest, cooperative relations with China, proved more difficult to manage. It was to Bush's credit that, despite strong congressional opposition, he kept open the lines of communication after the Tiananmen Square episode. In the Middle East, another vital interest had been bolstered when Secretary of State Baker brought together in Madrid all the parties to the Arab-Israeli disputes and laid the groundwork for the subsequent Oslo peace process between Israel and the Palestinian Liberation Organization. However, the fact that Saddam Hussein remained in power in Baghdad, and continued to run a ruthless Iraqi police state, tarnished George Bush's image as victor in the Persian Gulf War.

During the 1992 presidential election campaign, the Democrats, who were led by Governor Bill Clinton, gained support from undecided voters with the claim that Mr. Bush was too absorbed in foreign affairs and paid insufficient attention to the nation's domestic needs, including a lagging economy. In reality, the public appeared to be weary of burdens of the Cold War and international politics and was more concerned about unemployment, poverty, welfare reform, illegal drugs, and rampant crime. In sum, many voters thought it was time for a change.

When the Clinton administration took office in January 1993, it built on the foundation of close relations that Bush had established with Boris Yeltsin's reformist government. The new president chose as his secretary of state Warren Christopher, a respected international negotiator who had been President Jimmy Carter's deputy secretary of state. Clinton selected as the new deputy secretary of state a personal friend and an expert on Russia, Strobe Talbot. This team quickly established a good working relationship with Yeltsin and Foreign Minister Kosyrev.

As reforms in Russia's economy began to slow during 1993, Yeltsin came into sharp conflict with leaders of the old Congress of People's Deputies, a leftover Soviet-era legislature that had survived the 1991 demise of the U.S.S.R. American critics warned that Washington had put too much faith in Boris Yeltsin's leadership, to the exclusion of clearly defined U.S. objectives in the new Russia. Such criticism mounted after Yeltsin used military forces in October 1993 to bomb the parliament building and compel recalcitrant deputies to resign and make way for a new, popularly elected Russian assembly. Dimitri Simes, an expert on Russia at the Carnegie Endowment for International Peace, criticized the administration for a "blanket endorsement" of Yeltsin's action against parliament and called attention to the danger of "dealing with the emergence of a Russian strongman who has consolidated and increased his power through a gun barrel and, in the process, become indebted . . . to the military and security services."[15]

By 1995 the sweeping economic reforms recommended to

Yeltsin by western economists and the IMF had not been implemented, with the result that economic hardship and public dissatisfaction were widespread. Unemployment was a serious
problem, many pensioners were not receiving their payments, and
violent crime, which had not been tolerated under the Soviet regime, grew rapidly and was undermining public safety. Yeltsin increasingly ruled by decree whenever the new Duma failed to
accept his policies. Compounding the serious state of affairs was
Moscow's determination in 1994 to crush a rebellion in its southern province of Chechnya. The invasion of this Muslim-populated
territory was so poorly managed that it resulted in large casualties on both sides. Yeltsin's unpopular war to crush the insurgency
continued without resolution through 1995 and was seen by many
as a humiliation for the once-vaunted Russian military.

In May 1995 President Clinton made his first visit to Moscow,
to commemorate the fiftieth anniversary of the end of World
War II and Russia's victory over Nazi Germany. He and Yeltsin
discussed a range of issues that divided their countries, including
expansion of NATO, security of nuclear weapons, economic relations, and the civil war in Chechnya. Their joint news conference
on May 10 suggested that, even though a good personal relationship had developed between them, serious differences on key
questions were not resolved.

Yeltsin stated in his opening remarks that "we better understand the interests and concerns of each other, and yet we still
don't have answers to a number of questions. Our positions even
remain unchanged." On Chechnya he asserted: "Of course we discussed the Chechen issue. This is an internal matter for Russia,
but I also believe it does have an international aspect."President
Clinton addressed the NATO issue, saying that "while there was
not an agreement between us on the details on the question of the
expansion of NATO, Russia did agree to enter into the Partnership for Peace. And I committed myself . . . to encourage the beginning of the NATO-Russia dialogue, which I think is very
important. There must be a special relationship between NATO
and Russia." Regarding Chechnya, Clinton said "what I have
urged President Yeltsin to do is to try to make a permanent cease-
fire, to try to move rapidly with the cooperation of the OSCE [Or-
ganization of Security and Cooperation Europe] to get a
democratic government there and to bring this to a speedy resolution, because I do believe it is something that is very troubling
to the world, particularly in the dimensions of civilian casualties."

Clinton announced two major aid packages to Russia "to support the conversion to a market economy" and to assist in developing the institutions necessary to make this successful. Mr. Clinton also commended the progress that Ukraine had made during the year, saying he would continue to support its reform program. At the end of their lengthy press conference, Yeltsin asserted that the world was a safer place than it had been and that the two powers should avoid making implied threats which could harm the relationship. "We have seen more progress," he said, "on thorny difficulties, complex matters, than most experts predicted. As a result, the people of the United States, the people of Russia, and the people of the world are safer today than they were two years ago and than they were before this last meeting between us occurred. That is the fundamental story. We will have differences. They will have consequences. But we should stay away from big words like threats when we're managing matters which can be manage⟶a relationship that is quite good for the world, and that has made us all safer."[16]

The economic and political situation within Russia continued to deteriorate during 1995. This played into the hands of the Communist Party and several nationalist parties, which demanded a return to central economic control and the reestablishment of Russian supremacy over the former Soviet republics. The opposition charged that Gorbachev and Yeltsin had acquiesced in the decline of Russia's world prestige, and they blamed the United States for deliberately undermining Russia's economy in order to enhance its own domination in world affairs. A consequence of popular discontent with Yeltsin's policies was that in national elections for the Russian Duma in December 1995 the Communists won a plurality of the seats and nationalist parties also gained. Yeltsin now appeared in danger of losing in the presidential elections scheduled for June 1996, and of being replaced by the Communist leader, Gennady Zyuganov.

For the United States, the political trend in Russia at the end of 1995 was ominous. Yeltsin may not have been an ideal choice for a democratic leader, Clinton administration supporters argued, but the alternative of a Russia ruled by Communists and nationalists was far worse. The specter of dealing with a nationalist Russia that had reversed cooperation with the West, reinstituted a state-controlled economy, and rebuilt Russia's armed forces and nuclear arsenal was something that no U.S. policymaker wanted to contemplate. As a result, President Clinton continued to give Yeltsin general support while criticizing Russia's prolonged offensive against Chechnya.

Managing U.S.-China Relations Following Tiananmen Square

A few months after George Bush became president in 1989 events in China stunned the United States and the world. The Chinese leadership's decision to use the People's Liberation Army (PLA) to break up a massive student-led pro-democracy demonstration in Tiananmen Square in June, resulting in hundreds of demonstrators being killed and thousands wounded, was reached after nearly six weeks of indecision in the politburo over how to deal with what looked like a challenge to the regime itself. China's paramount leader, Deng Xiaoping, and the hard-liners eventually prevailed over the government's moderate reformers, and unarmed soldiers were deployed on June 2 to clear Tiananmen Square. However, they were ineffective and were driven off by thousands of demonstrators. Troops from the provinces were then called in and on June 4 they moved into Tiananmen and fired on the demonstrators. Scenes of massive violence and bloodshed were immediately televised around the world and soon produced international outrage over what was quickly labeled the Chinese government's "massacre" of pro-democracy forces.

President Bush recalled later that he was stunned by the violence but said he wanted "a measured response, one aimed at those who had pushed for and implemented the use of force: the hard-liners and the Army. I didn't want to punish the Chinese people," he said, "for the act of their government." Believing that contacts with the United States had helped the Chinese people in their quest for more freedom, the president decided quickly not to cut commercial relations but instead to suspend military sales and contacts between U.S. and Chinese military officials. "What I certainly did not want to do," Bush said, "was completely break the relationship we had worked so hard to build since 1972. We had to remain involved, engaged with the Chinese government, if we were to have any influence or leverage to work for restraint and cooperation, let alone for human rights and democracy."[17] In effect, the president thought China was too vital a world-order interest of the United States to allow relations to be broken even though a serious human rights violation (promotion of values issue) had occurred.

Bush had earlier met Deng Xiaoping and other top PRC (People's Republic of China) leaders in Beijing, in February 1989, following his attendance at the funeral in Tokyo of Japanese Emperor Hirohito. He now felt that if he could communicate quickly with Deng, following the Tiananmen Square tragedy, he might influence the U.S.-China relationship before things became so tense that a diplomatic break would occur. Deng responded favorably to his proposal to send National Security Adviser Brent Scowcroft to Beijing to hear the leadership's point of view as well as to convey the president's views. Scowcroft met with Deng in the Great Hall of the People on July 2. He later reported that Deng launched into a long monologue in which he suggested that the United States had promoted the protests in Tiananmen Square against his government. Quoting Deng, the American emissary wrote: "We have been feeling since the onset of these events more than two months ago that the various aspects of U.S. foreign policy have actually cornered China. That's the feeling of us here . . . because the aim of the counterrevolutionary rebellion was to overthrow the People's Republic of China and our socialist system. If they should succeed in obtaining that aim, the world would be a different one. To be frank, this could even lead to war."[18]

Scowcorft responded by talking about the progress in U.S.-Chinese relations that had occurred since President Nixon's first visit to China in 1972, especially after Deng had taken over government authority following the death of Mao Zedong. He noted the economic and strategic nature of the relationship, which he said had benefited both countries. Then, referring to "events at Tiananmen Square," he presented the U.S. view: "What the American people perceived in the demonstrations they saw—rightly or wrongly—was an expression of values which represent their most cherished beliefs, stemming from the American Revolution. . . . Our whole national experience, beginning with our revolution, has been a struggle to expand the boundaries of freedom as we define that term." He pointed out that President Bush was trying to "manage events in a way which will assure a healthy relationship over time," but that it had not been easy because of the Chinese actions on June 4. He cited the resolution passed by the House of Representatives by a vote of 418–0 to impose stiff sanctions on China. He did not propose any steps that China might take to make it easier for the president to withstand strong pressure from Congress. Subsequently, the envoy met with

Premier Li Peng, who asserted that the United States did not have a clear picture of what had happened on June 4, that much of the information abroad was only "rumors." He insisted, Scowcroft wrote, that the death toll given in the West was wrong; the actual number killed was "310 or so," and that the number included members of the PLA. "Only 36 Beijing students had died," Li insisted. In his appraisal of the China visit, Scowcroft observed: "It had been, from my perspective, a most useful trip. We had conveyed the message on behalf of the President of the gravity, for the United States, of what the Chinese had done, but also underscored for them beneath all the turmoil and torment, how important the President thought the relationship was to the national interests of the United States. In recent years we have been told several times by Chinese from different walks of life how crucial that trip and that gesture were to the Chinese, both in the regime and to those who had supported the demonstrations."[19]

In November both houses of Congress voted by overwhelming majorities to enact stiffer sanctions than the president had imposed in June. Bush vetoed this legislation, but sentiment was so strong against China that Congress tried to override his veto. In January 1990 the House of Representatives voted 390–25 to override, but the Senate upheld the veto by 62–37. Although Bush's policy of keeping open U.S. ties with China was not reversed, everyone recognized that restoring good U.S.-China relations would take much effort on both sides. This issue dominated executive-legislative branch relations over China throughout the Bush presidency. In his memoirs the president lamented the politics involved: "The Democratic leadership in the Senate fought me tooth and nail on MFN [normal trade relations] for China. . . . The great irony is that when President Clinton—a relentless critic of our China policy in the 1992 campaign—proposed continuing MFN for China in his first term, the Democratic leadership reversed themselves 100 percent and supported him."[20]

A major reason that Bush needed to avoid a rupture in his ongoing dialogue with China was Beijing's permanent seat on the United Nations Security Council. This gave it a veto over Council resolutions, including approval on the use of armed force. This became crucial during the fall of 1990 when the United States needed UN authorization for its plan to send forces to the Persian Gulf to dislodge Iraq from Kuwait. Secretary of State James Baker lobbied Foreign Minister Qian Qichen to vote for the resolution, but he was told that China opposed the use of force in the Persian

Gulf and that economic sanctions should be given time to work. Qian suggested, however, that China might be willing to abstain on the Council's vote if he were given an invitation to visit Washington, particularly if a meeting with President Bush could be arranged. In the Security Council on November 29, twelve members voted in favor of using force if Saddam Hussein did not withdraw his forces from Kuwait. Two members, Cuba and Yemen, voted against, and China abstained. Foreign Minister Qian was then invited to Washington to meet with Secretary Baker. However, upon learning that the desired visit with President Bush was not planned, the Chinese official threatened to cancel his trip. "For all our problems with the Chinese," Baker recalled, "we didn't want to isolate them further." George Bush agreed that it was "a small price to pay for avoiding a veto." But Baker also observed that Qian did not get what he and his government really wanted, a presidential visit to Beijing and a commitment to press for the removal of economic sanctions. That would have won a Chinese "yes" vote on the UN resolution, Baker said, but it was not worth the "terrible cost to principle."[21]

During President Clinton's first two years in office his administration quietly continued the engagement policy with China adopted by Bush, despite his heavy emphasis on human rights issues during the 1992 election campaign. However, Congress continued to strongly criticize China, not only for human rights violations but for its military sales to Iraq and Iran and its military exercises in the Taiwan Strait. A vocal group of congressmen and senators pressed the president to upgrade U.S. relations with Taiwan, even though American policy since Richard Nixon had been that Taiwan was a part of China, not a separate state as some Taiwanese claimed.

Relations between Washington and Beijing became severely strained in the spring of 1995 when the White House, under pressure from Congress, overruled the State Department and offered a visa to Taiwan's president, Lee Teng-hui, to visit the United States. Lee had an invitation from Cornell University, his alma mater, to attend a reunion of his class. But in accordance with a long-held understanding between Washington and Beijing, a State Department spokesman said that granting Taiwan's president a visa would violate U.S. policy. Secretary of State Warren Christopher had personally assured Foreign Minister Qian that the visa would be denied. When the White House nevertheless announced that Lee would get a visa, both Christopher and Qian were humiliated. In a show of displeasure, China recalled its ambassador and Chinese hard-liners, particularly in the PLA, accused Washington of pursuing a policy of "containment" toward China. Although Chinese President Jiang Zemin initially adopted a relatively mild response to the U.S. action, his military chiefs apparently exerted pressure in the politburo and persuaded Jiang to take a tough attitude toward Washington.

President Clinton was asked by a reporter at a White House news conference in August why he had given a visa to Taiwan's president, in view of his earlier statements that he would adhere to a one-China policy. Clinton replied that he would continue to adhere to the one-China policy and added: "We are going to do everything we can to make sure that our policy is clearly understood in China and in Taiwan. I made the decision personally to permit President Lee from Taiwan to come into this country not as the head of state, not as the head of a government that we had recognized, but because he wanted to come. . . . It was not an abrogation of our one-China policy in any way."[22]

What is not clear is whether Clinton realized when he overruled the State Department what a storm of protest he would cause in China and the potential harm it could do to U.S.-China relations. He seemed to be motivated primarily by views of the liberal wing of the Democratic Party, which held that human rights (promotion of values) was at least as important to U.S. national interests and foreign policy as economic considerations and world order issues. This was an example of how the president alone can decide the level of a national interest when there are strong competing domestic constituencies pressing him on a specific issue.

Kenneth Lieberthal, a China expert at the University of Michigan, warned at the end of 1995 that "Sino-American relations are in danger." He worried that miscommunication between Taipei and Beijing might produce political initiatives by Taiwan that would trigger a military response from China. "While America is not rigidly bound by the Taiwan Relations Act to protect Taiwan at all costs," he wrote, "political pressure in Washington to move in that direction would be strong" if a new political crisis resulted from further repression on the mainland. Lieberthal was concerned that America and China would "stumble along in a manageable relationship" but that, "in the absence of realistic strategies on either side, the chances that they will stumble into mutual hostility are growing unacceptably high."[23]

Japan, and the North Korean Nuclear Threat

Japan in the early 1990s failed to live up to expectations in Washington that it would accept a more active role in security as well as in economic relations with countries in Northeast and Southeast Asia. On the economic side, Japan's economy went into deep recession early in the decade and caused its government to be even less willing than before to move away from the quasi-protectionist trade policies that Japan had pursued for twenty years. In addition, Japanese politics entered a period of instability after the Liberal Democratic Party (LDP) for the first time lost its majority in parliament. Thereafter, a succession of governments was not receptive to U.S. urgings that they assume a larger defense role in East Asia or make the structural changes in their financial institutions that would lift Japan out of recession. Although Japan had begun to participate in several UN peacekeeping missions, in Cambodia and Africa, these units were all noncombat personnel.

Of particular regret to the Bush administration was Tokyo's refusal to send any of its forces to the Persian Gulf in 1990 to assist the United States and its allies in the UN-sanctioned drive to force Iraq's withdrawal from Kuwait. Japan's action caused embarrassment in foreign policy circles in Japan, and U.S. pressure resulted in the government's eventual agreement to pay the huge sum of $13 billion as its contribution to the war effort. Despite the urgings of political leaders such as Ichiro Ozawa, an outspoken, defense-minded critic in parliament, the government continued to pursue its long-established policy of relying on the United States for defense while choosing to build Japan's economic power as the means to increase its international influence. Tokyo's policy was not swayed by the reality that Persian Gulf oil was far more vital to Japan's economy than it was to the economic well-being of the United States.[24]

Overshadowing both American and Japanese security concerns in Northeast Asia was North Korea's pursuit of a nuclear weapons capability that could threaten the security of South Korea, Japan, and potentially the United States. This threat engaged the Bush administration in urgent discussions with Japan, China, and South Korea in an effort to find a way to dissuade the Communist Pyongyang regime from following a dangerous policy that could result in war. Because of the American forces' impressive use of cruise missiles during the Persian Gulf War, Secretary of

State James Baker believed that "we enjoyed significant credibility with a country with whom we had no diplomatic relations." But, he warned, North Korea's nuclear, chemical, and biological programs were far more advanced than Washington had imagined and aerial surveillance of the Yongbyon nuclear complex consequently needed to be intensified. He wrote later that "while the situation never reached the point of our actively considering a military strike against North Korea's nuclear facilities, the Pentagon nonetheless refined existing contingency plans for such an attack using cruise missiles, whose performance had been so impressive in the Gulf."[25]

In October 1991 President Bush announced that the United States would withdraw unconditionally all of its nuclear weapons from South Korea. This action would wipe out North Korea's major argument for pursuing its own nuclear program. Within a month North and South Korea began holding discussions on normalizing their relations. They also signed agreements pledging peaceful coexistence and confirming that the Korean peninsula should be free of nuclear weapons. As a result of these moves, senior American and North Korean officials met for the first time in forty years, in January 1992, at the United Nations. On this occasion the United States warned of severe sanctions against the North if it did not permit international inspections of its nuclear facilities, to ensure they were for peaceful purposes only.

By the time the Clinton administration took office in January 1993, it was clear from all the intelligence data available that North Korea was camouflaging its nuclear arms program. The new president was thus faced with the choice of persuading an international coalition to impose tight sanctions on the Pyongyang regime, including cutting off private Japanese funds going to people in the North, or threatening to use air strikes to destroy the nuclear plants at Yongbyon. Predictably, China and Russia were strongly opposed to using force. Japan and South Korea wanted more time to negotiate, believing that the threat of severe sanctions would bring the desired result. South Korea had in 1993 elected its first civilian president in thirty-two years, Kim Young Sam, and he was more inclined than his predecessors to build bridges to the North if at all possible. Many observers accepted the view that the rigidly controlled Communist state, ruled by the aging Kim Il-Sung, who had held power since 1945, wanted to acquire nuclear weapons in order to extract economic and political concessions from Japan and the United States. One of these was

Pyongyang's demand that the United States withdraw its 38,000 troops then protecting South Korea. Another was for a large amount of economic aid to replace the assistance that had been cut off after the Soviet Union collapsed.

The Clinton administration moved in early 1994 to obtain a resolution in the United Nations Security Council imposing tough sanctions against North Korea for continuing to refuse international inspection of its nuclear sites. In June former president Jimmy Carter notified President Clinton that he had received an invitation from North Korea's leadership to visit their country and talk about ways to deal with the mounting crisis. Ignoring strong objections from the State Department, Clinton permitted Carter to make the trip after being briefed on U.S. policy. Clinton also made it clear that the ex-president was not representing the U.S. government. Carter then spent several days in Pyongyang conferring with Kim Il-Sung and reached a tentative understanding with him that North Korea would suspend its nuclear program and allow inspectors to look at the Yongbyon facility; in return, the United States would drop its efforts to obtain a UN sanctions agreement. At a press conference announcing the freeze on North Korea's nuclear program while talks continued, Clinton thanked Carter for his role in achieving this breakthrough and welcomed the news that the North and South Korean presidents would soon meet. Answering a question on whether the United States had made concessions to North Korea to achieve the freeze, the president said no and offered this background information: "We know what the facts are. If you look at what we've done over the last year and a half, we have followed basically a two-pronged policy. We have worked as hard as we could to be firm, to be resolute, to bring our allies closer and closer together. And when I say our allies on this issue, I consider not just South Korea and Japan, but Russia and China to be our allies. All of us have the same interests and the same desires."[26]

An "Agreed Framework," negotiated by U.S. and North Korean representatives in Geneva, was announced by President Clinton in October and revealed that the United States, Japan, and South Korea had made important concessions to North Korea. The agreement envisioned the construction of two modern reactors in North Korea, at an estimated cost of over $4 billion, in return for inspections by the International Atomic Energy Agency and the eventual dismantling and removal of North Korea's nuclear facilities and associated materials. Clinton hailed the agreement as an

important step toward peace on the Korean peninsula, but critics
immediately charged him with bowing to North Korea's blackmail. Among these was the former secretary of state, James Baker,
who wrote: "Our policy of carrots and sticks gave way overnight
to one of carrots only—fuel oil to help run North Korea's belea-
guered economy, two new nuclear reactors, and diplomatic ties.
Moreover, Pyongyang has been given another five years to do
what they agreed to do in 1991—allow a full inspection of their
nuclear facilities. This agreement was an abrupt policy flip-flop, and
in the end, in my view, will prove to have been a mistake that will
make stability on the Korean peninsula less, not more, likely."[27]

Among the many uncertainties that followed the signing of
the "Agreed Framework" was the political impact of Kim Il-
Sung's sudden death in July 1994, a month after his meetings with
Jimmy Carter. His son, Kim Jong Il, was expected to succeed him
as leader of the Communist Party and of the country, but a leadership struggle could not be ruled out. The hiatus opened by the
North Korean leader's death delayed discussions on the nuclear
inspections issue well into 1995 and left it uncertain whether the
1994 agreement would in fact be implemented.[28]

Mexico's Financial Crisis

Getting Congress to ratify the NAFTA treaty with Canada and
Mexico, which President Bush had negotiated before leaving office, was one of President Clinton's highest priorities in 1993. As
had occurred with the Panama Canal treaties, which were negotiated in the Ford administration but were shepherded through
Congress by President Jimmy Carter in 1977, so the NAFTA treaty
had to be pushed through the Senate and House of Representatives
by Bill Clinton. It was not an easy task for him because organized
labor, a strong supporter of the Democratic Party during the 1992
election campaign, opposed trade concessions for Mexico because
it was convinced the treaty would result in the loss of good-paying
industrial jobs to lower paid Mexican workers. Environment
groups also opposed NAFTA because Mexican laws to protect
workers' conditions and the environment were far inferior to those
prevailing in the United States and Canada. Another factor was the
presidential campaign of billionaire Ross Perot, nominee of the
newly formed Reform Party, who had denounced the NAFTA plan
and aroused protectionist concerns among a large segment of voters. Nevertheless, with congressional Republicans supporting the

treaty and most Democrats going along with their president, Congress approved the North American Free Trade Agreement on November 23, 1993. The following week Congress gave its assent to another historic trade measure, the Uruguay round in the General Agreement on Tariffs and Trade (GATT), and to America's entry into the new World Trade Organization (WTO). These two international trade agreements represented the high-water mark in the United States' post–World War II willingness to accept tariff reduction pacts with the world's other trading countries.

Following ratification of the NAFTA trade pact, the government of Mexican President Carlos Salinas was very cooperative with the United States on a range of economic and political issues. However, during Mexico's 1994 presidential election year, that country was hit by a series of shocks that had the potential of destabilizing it politically. The first was the Zapatista uprising in the southern state of Chiapas. Poverty-stricken peasants rebelled against state and federal authorities and many joined a guerrilla organization that threatened to take root in other parts of Mexico. The Salinas government confined the violence in the state of Chiapas but did not succeed either in negotiating a peace arrangement or in fully stamping out the rebellion. A second shock occurred in April when the leading PRI (Institutional Revolutionary Party) candidate to succeed Salinas as president was assassinated. This touched off a major capital flight from Mexico and the political climate turned ugly. And third, Mexico was hit with inflation later in the year and a further flight of capital, just as the new PRI candidate, Ernesto Zedillo, had won the election as president. This inflationary wave resulted largely from the Salinas government's easing of credit in the economy to help Zedillo win. Following his inauguration, however, an economic crisis occurred that forced a substantial devaluation of the peso and opened the likelihood of default on the country's large foreign loans.

President Clinton quickly decided that Mexico was so important to U.S. interests in North America that it should not be permitted to go into bankruptcy, and perhaps throw its nearly 100 million people into economic and political chaos. As a result, Treasury Secretary Robert Rubin organized a financial rescue package for Mexico that included $20 billion in loan guarantees from the United States and another nearly $20 billion in credits and other assistance provided by international institutions, notably the IMF. This rescue effort was criticized in Congress, and some newspapers called it a "bailout for U.S. banks." A number of American financial institutions that had invested heavily in Mexico with hard currency loans were now threatened with default on repayment.[29]

In January 1995 when President Clinton announced his U.S. aid package, he emphasized that the danger Mexico faced posed a serious threat "to the economic future of the United States." He warned that if the United States failed to act, the crisis of confidence in Mexico's economy could spread in Latin America and in Asia. He claimed that the loan guarantees he was providing were not foreign aid and would not result in a charge to American taxpayers. He denied that this was a "bailout for Mexico." But the plan was unveiled at a difficult time for him politically because the Republicans had won the off-year congressional elections in November 1994 and now held a majority in the Senate and House of Representatives.

Clinton formally notified Congress on March 9 of the financial crisis in Mexico and of his plan to deal with it. The situation posed "unique and emergency circumstances" which U.S. law required him to justify in order to use the Exchange Stabilization Fund (ESF) of the Treasury Department. He cited a joint statement between him and congressional leaders, dated January 31, which showed, he said, that "we all agreed that such use of the ESF was a necessary and appropriate response to the Mexican financial crisis, and in the United States' vital national interest."[30] This represented a clear case of the president and congressional leaders agreeing that a vital national interest was at stake in Mexico.

Using the national interest matrix, Table 8 shows the level of

Table 8. Mexico's Financial Crisis, 1995

Basic interest	Intensity of interest			
	Survival	Vital	Major	Peripheral
Defense of homeland		Mexico	U.S.	Canada
Economic well-being		Mexico U.S.	Canada	
Favorable world order		U.S. Canada Mexico		
Promotion of values		U.S. Mexico Canada		

national interests held by Mexico, Canada, and the United States in the financial crisis in Mexico. It is apparent from this that the United States had a vital stake in three of its four basic interests, that Canada had a vital interest in two, and that Mexico had a vital level stake in all four categories. Despite some dissent, most members of Congress agreed with the Clinton administration that financial help for Mexico in this crisis was fully justified.

U.S. Military Intervention in Haiti

Haiti in the 1990s was the only country in the Western Hemisphere, other than Cuba, with an anti-democratic government. President Clinton's decision in 1994 to send 20,000 American soldiers there was his administration's first use of military force to support a U.S. foreign policy goal, in this case restoring a democratically elected president to power. A chaotic economic and political situation in Haiti had been inherited by Clinton from the Bush administration, which had decided in 1991 not to use force to restore President Bertrand Aristide to power after he was ousted in a military coup and forced into exile. Economic sanctions were imposed by Bush but had no effect on the ruling junta and further increased the misery of the Haitian people. As a result, thousands of Haitians took to sea in small boats and headed for the United States in hope of finding sanctuary, many of them perishing en route. The refugee flow became so large that the Bush administration set up camps at the U.S. base at Guantanamo Bay on the southern tip of Cuba, where the Coast Guard and Navy deposited most of the refugees. By 1994, however, the situation became intolerable when 21,000 Haitians were rescued at sea during a two-month period. The United States obtained a UN Security Council Resolution calling on member states to use all measures, including force, to restore President Aristide to power and end the military rule in Haiti. In September Clinton decided on intervention and persuaded some twenty other nations to join in the effort. But the president did not seek congressional authority for his action, citing as precedents Ronald Reagan's military intervention in Grenada in 1983 and George Bush's invasion of Panama in 1989 to support his view that envisaged a limited action of short duration to protect U.S. security interests. In an address to the nation on September 15, Mr. Clinton asserted that "for three years we and other nations have worked exhaustively to find a diplomatic solution, only to have the dictators reject each one. Now the United States must protect our interests, to stop the brutal atrocities that threaten tens of thousands of Haitians, to secure our borders, to preserve stability and promote democracy in our hemisphere, and to uphold the reliability of the commitments we make and the commitments others make to us."[31]

A crucial question for the White House was whether the military junta in Haiti, led by General Raoul Cedras, would voluntarily give up power and go into exile if it understood that military power was ready to invade their island. The alternative was for American and other troops to fight their way in. In this situation, President Clinton authorized former president Jimmy Carter to make a personal visit to Haiti to persuade Cedras and other military leaders to leave peacefully. He asked Senator Sam Nunn, chairman of the Senate Armed Services Committee, to accompany Carter, and he also asked General Colin Powell, former Chairman of the Joint Chiefs of Staff, to join the Carter team. Powell recalled that when the president called to explain the mission, he observed: "I took a chance on him [Jimmy Carter] in North Korea, and that didn't turn out too badly."[32]

General Powell records in his memoirs that even after Carter warned the Haitian leadership that an invasion was inevitable and that he hoped the arrival of U.S. forces would occur peacefully, General Cedras was adamantly opposed to giving up power. But when the junta learned the following day from their own sources that U.S. paratroopers at Fort Bragg were preparing to board aircraft, their view changed. Now Haiti's figurehead president, Emile Jonassaint, accepted the U.S. demand that the government resign by October 15. When American and other forces arrived on September 19, they encountered no opposition.[33]

The Haiti intervention showed that the Clinton administration was willing to use force in situations where it could support an important world-order interest—in this case the huge flow of refugees to U.S. shores—and a clear humanitarian objective. Haiti's military junta had provided the provocation, but there was widespread opposition in the public and Congress to the president's decision to intervene. He therefore announced his intention to end the military role in 1995 and turn over peacekeeping responsibilities to the United Nations. Although President Aristide was restored to power in October 1994, there was no indication that a real democratic government would soon emerge in this hapless country, or that the violence which had wracked it for decades would stop.

U.S. Military Intervention in Somalia

Political turmoil and civil wars continued in several African countries in the early 1990s, and U.S. policy was generally to let Britain
and France, the ex-colonial powers there, assume the primary role
in providing economic assistance. Few of these relatively new
countries had any semblance of democracy, and ethnic violence
plagued many of them. The situation in Somalia on Africa's east
coast was particularly appalling in 1992. Civil war among tribal
warlords had ruined the economy and left tens of thousands of
people starving. The humanitarian aspects of the conflict had become so chaotic that international food shipments were being hi-
jacked by armed thugs in the employ of the warlords. Grim
photos appeared on European and American television and
caused public outrage. President Bush decided during his last
month in office that the United States should intervene with
troops to ensure that food and medical assistance were delivered
to the starving population. He believed the mission could be accomplished in a few months, that the operation could then be
turned over to UN peacekeepers, and that the U.S. soldiers could
return home. On December 8 he dispatched 24,000 troops to Somalia, first to secure the port areas of its capital, Mogadishu, and
then to protect the food convoys to outlying towns and villages.
Operation Restore Hope, as the mission was called, was an immediate success in achieving its objectives, and when George Bush
left office the following month he could point to Somalia as an
example of the successful use of U.S. forces for humanitarian missions. He was less than realistic, however, in believing that such a
mission could be accomplished in six months and the troops withdrawn.

In the summer of 1993 President Clinton withdrew most of
the troops from Somalia, but he decided to leave about 4,000 to
assist the United Nations in peacekeeping and humanitarian missions. However, when UN peacekeepers came under sniper fire
from fighters supporting the Somali warlord Mohammed Farah
Aidid, the Security Council requested U.S. assistance in capturing
Aidid. The Pentagon reluctantly recommended that the president
send Army Rangers and the Delta Force, plus helicopter gunships,
a decision that Chairman of the Joint Chiefs of Staff General Colin
Powell later said he regretted. Eighteen Rangers were killed in a
shoot-out with Aidid's forces, and a film was carried on prime-
time television showing the body of a dead American soldier be-

ing dragged through the streets of Mogadishu, to the cheers of Somalis. The American public was outraged. Most of them had thought the troops were in Somalia to feed the starving people, not to fight in a civil war and hunt down a local warlord. As a result, Congress demanded the immediate withdrawal of U.S. forces. President Clinton complied during the next months.[34]

The clear lesson of the Somalia operation was that the law of unintended consequences takes over when the objectives of a mission are not carefully thought through and the potential costs are ignored. It was probably naive for the Bush administration to think that it could put 24,000 U.S. troops and transport planes into a country like Somalia, and then expect that it would do humanitarian work for a short time and leave. And it was folly for the incoming Clinton administration to think that it could successfully change a UN mission in Somalia's civil war from humanitarian assistance to one of nation building. Success in feeding people does not imply that a military force will also be successful in bringing warring tribes together at the peace table to work toward building a stable country. It was also doubtful whether the American public and Congress would support a long-term commitment to Somalia. This was a lesson that President Clinton took into account when he was pressed to send troops to the Balkans two years later.

Formation of the European Union

Three important issues faced Western Europe in the early 1990s, all of which directly affected U.S. national interests. These were progress toward economic and political unity among the twelve members of the European Community, relations with Russia and the successor states of the Soviet Union, and the deteriorating political situation in the Balkans.

After the Soviet Union's breakup in 1991, Europeans no longer worried about another great war on the continent, or about nuclear weapons. Instead, many were concerned about the future of a reunited Germany, whether this enlarged economic powerhouse in the middle of Europe would turn out to be a good European partner, or again try to dominate its neighbors.

The Maastricht Treaty of 1991 was named for the city in Holland that played host to twelve heads of government from the European Community countries who negotiated the final terms of a federal union to be accomplished by the end of the 1990s. This was a landmark achievement in postwar Europe's drive for economic and political unity and ranked with the fall of the Berlin Wall, German reunification, and the demise of the Soviet Union as fundamental changes in Europe during the final years of the twentieth century. In addition to agreeing to break down all barriers to the flow of goods, capital, and people among member states, the Maastricht agreement envisaged a common currency for the new federation, a radical idea which many observers doubted could be implemented by the end of the decade. Great Britain, for example, got an exemption to adopting the new currency, the euro, to replace the pound sterling. Germans too had doubts about giving up their strong deutsche mark until Chancellor Kohl produced an agreement that an independent European Central Bank would be established with headquarters in Frankfurt. It was also agreed that the European Monetary Union (EMU) would not come into effect until the principal partners brought their budgets under tight control and all but eliminated fluctuations among their currencies. Optimists thought the goal was achievable, and with a great deal of enthusiasm the European Commission set about preparing the groundwork.[35]

Western Europe's relations with Russia were conditioned to a considerable degree by the bilateral relationship between the American presidents, George Bush and Bill Clinton, and Russia's president, Boris Yeltsin. Their summit meetings, beginning in 1992, covered security concerns of the European countries, whose leaders were consulted regularly by Bush and Clinton and their cabinet members. German Chancellor Helmut Kohl, French President Francois Mitterrand, and British Prime Minister John Major all met individually with Yeltsin and reinforced the North Atlantic Alliance's policy of providing economic aid to assist Russia's political and economic reforms and efforts to dismantle nuclear weapons in accordance with treaties reached with the United States. The European, North American (United States and Canada), and Japanese governments also invited Yeltsin to participate in the annual meetings of the Group of Seven (G-7) industrialized nations at which heads of government discussed international economic and political issues. The German government, which wanted Russian troops withdrawn from its territory by 1994, was the most active in promoting investment and trade with Russia and encouraging private loans to Russia.

By the mid-1990s European and American leaders were also grappling with the issue of future European security arrangements, specifically whether continental defense would be enhanced in the twenty-first century if Poland, Hungary, and the Czech Republic were members of NATO. From Germany's standpoint, having Poland in NATO would ensure that it did not again become a political vacuum in eastern Europe and subject to competing interests of a resurgent Russia. Also, Poland's inclusion in NATO would ensure that the easternmost frontier of Europe's defense would be Poland's border with Ukraine and Belarus instead of the Oder River frontier between Germany and Poland. The United States supported this view, and President Clinton promoted it in his meetings with Yeltsin. But Yeltsin was adamantly opposed, seeing NATO expansion as a potential threat to his country's eastern European buffer zone. Britain was generally in favor of expansion, but France had deep concerns about alienating Moscow at a time when it needed reassurance of Europe's good intentions. In order to reduce Moscow's opposition, European and American leaders proposed a plan called Partnership for Peace in which all the East European states were invited to send representatives to, and participate in, discussions held at NATO headquarters in Belgium. This was considered as associate membership in the organization, and it encouraged regular consultations with Russia and East European governments without giving them access to the alliance's planning councils.

Another major security concern of Europe and NATO following the breakup of the Soviet Union was the fragmentation of Yugoslavia, made up of half a dozen religious and ethnic entities that had been brought together into one state after World I by the victorious Allies. Following World War II, Yugoslavia was held intact for thirty-five years by the iron rule of its Communist leader, Josip Broz Tito. After his death in 1980 the federation became dominated by its two largest entities, Serbia and Croatia. In 1991 the parliaments of Croatia and neighboring Slovenia declared their independence from Yugoslavia, and the unraveling of the country began. The parallel with the breakup of the Soviet Union that also occurred that year is noteworthy. Ethnic violence broke out between Croatia and Serbia, resulting in the deaths of thousands of civilians and ethnic cleansing of numerous cities. The German government granted diplomatic recognition to Croatia and Slovenia in December, and other EU countries followed Bonn's lead. In 1992 Bosnia-Herzegovina and Macedonia also were emboldened to declare their independence, and civil war quickly erupted in Bosnia. The minority Serb population then took up arms to merge the Serb-controlled parts of Bosnia with Serb-dominated Yugoslavia, which was headed by the ex-Communist strongman Slobodan Milosevic. The situation quickly became a humanitarian disaster. Even though the Bush administration decided it should not try to intervene, it nevertheless thought it could not remain passive while this humanitarian tragedy unfolded.

As a result, President Bush was persuaded by the State Department, over objections from the Defense Department, to launch a humanitarian relief effort using Air Force resources; but he was firmly opposed to deploying any U.S. ground forces because of expected strong congressional and public opposition. According to Secretary of State Baker, the only way a humanitarian nightmare could have been prevented in Bosnia in 1992 "would have been through the application of substantial military force early on" and with the full recognition that by intervening in Bosnia's civil war "the casualties would have been staggering." President Bush, Baker reported, therefore concluded that "our national interests did not require the United States to fight its fourth war in Europe in this century."[36] In essence, the Bush administration decided that although Bosnia was an important (major) national interest, it did not rise to the level of a vital interest and therefore did not justify the use of American forces in a combat role. Unlike the situation in the Persian Gulf two years earlier, Bosnia was viewed as a European regional problem, and Bush concluded that the European NATO countries should take the lead in dealing with it. The process by which the United States altered this view and determined that Bosnia was a vital interest is discussed in Chapter 9.

9
Toward the New Millennium, 1996–1999

The final years of the twentieth century saw unprecedented prosperity and economic growth in the United States. In 1999 the country recorded a lower inflation rate and less unemployment than at any time since the early 1970s. In addition, the federal government ran a budget surplus for the first time in thirty years and the Dow-Jones stock index rose to heights not dreamed of five years earlier. The United States surged ahead of Japan and Europe as the world's economic powerhouse. And in the 1990s the U.S. military, with superb training and highly sophisticated weapons, demonstrated in the Persian Gulf, in Bosnia, and in Kosovo a superiority over every other country in the ability to project power globally and to strike enemy targets anywhere. As a consequence of these factors, a Pew Research Center survey found in November 1999 that 81 percent of Americans were personally hopeful about the twenty-first century and that 70 percent thought the United States would do well.

However, an end to the Cold War and a decade of relative peace and prosperity had led Americans to show less interest in international affairs. Except for coverage of the Persian Gulf War in 1990–1991 and the Bosnian crisis in 1995–1996, the top news stories in major newspapers and on television news showed a significant decline in the public's attention to the world, in contrast to the 1980s when the media provided much greater coverage to events abroad. As a result, a gulf was emerging between the Clinton administration's determination to exercise vigorous American leadership in the new global environment and the public's waning interest in supporting foreign aid, the United Nations, and American peacekeeping operations abroad. This reality presented a major challenge to the White House as it sought to define broadly U.S. national interests for the new millennium and America's leadership role around the globe.[1]

The four-year period from 1996 through 1999 reinforced the notion that the post–Cold War international environment would be filled with serious economic challenges and threats to regional peace. A major crisis occurred in Bosnia at the end of 1995 and caused President Clinton to send 20,000 U.S. combat troops into the Balkans in 1996 as part of an international force designed to stop a civil war. Another dangerous situation occurred in U.S.-China relations in early 1996 when the government of China brought military pressure to bear on Taiwan to convince its leaders to stop their campaign to gain international status for Taiwan as a separate entity. Yet another threat occurred in Iraq in 1998 when Saddam Hussein's government expelled a UN inspection team that had been examining facilities that might be making chemical and biological weapons in violation of UN sanctions. American and British aircraft, which were already protecting Kurdish tribes with a no-fly zone in northern Iraq, were now ordered to bomb suspected Iraqi chemical and biological weapons facilities in Baghdad and elsewhere.

Two additional crises erupted in Kosovo and East Timor in 1999, focusing attention on this fundamental question regarding U.S. policy: Should the United States be willing to send its military forces just about anywhere to deal with humanitarian disasters if there is not a vital political (world order) interest at stake? The American public was deeply skeptical about having Washington take on peacekeeping missions abroad if they might entail the risk of military casualties and/or a significant rise in defense and foreign aid spending. Although President Clinton used his own authority to initiate a seventy-eight–day bombing campaign, with NATO support, against Serb forces in Kosovo, his desire to avoid casualties was a major limiting factor in the conduct of the air campaign. Policy makers were sensitive to what had happened in Somalia six years earlier, when the killing of eighteen American soldiers caused Congress to demand the withdrawal of all U.S. troops. A major problem for the administration when it deployed forces to Bosnia, and later in Kosovo, was its desire to accomplish political and humanitarian objectives without triggering a backlash from the public and Congress. It was a risky policy that called into question whether the White House had carefully calculated the costs and risks before deciding that there truly was a vital U.S. interest at stake that justified the commitment of American troops.

    This chapter discusses the most important challenges the
United States faced in its economic and world-order interests during the final four years of the twentieth century.

The Crisis in Bosnia

Civil war in Bosnia and the brutal ethnic cleansing of Muslims by
both Serb and Croatian factions in that country had caused deep
concern in the Bush administration and among NATO allies beginning in 1992. President Bush decided against intervention with
ground troops, and Bill Clinton adopted a similar view when he
became president in January 1993. By 1995, however, the atrocities inflicted by Bosnian Serbs against the Muslim population in
the eastern sector of Bosnia were so outrageous that the White
House could not ignore the nightly television photos inflaming
public opinion. At Srebrenica, for example, Serb forces ordered
UN peacekeepers aside, then rounded up and killed most of the
Muslim male population. With UN Security Council support,
President Clinton warned the Bosnian Serb leaders and their
backer, Yugoslav President Slobodan Milosevic, that he would
launch air strikes to force them to accept a cease fire and enter
peace negotiations. After Serb forces, in a test of Clinton's resolve,
shelled the main square of Sarajevo and killed many people, the
president ordered sustained air strikes on Serb positions.
Milosevic and the Bosnian Serb leaders finally agreed to lift the
siege of Sarajevo and accept an offer to hold negotiations in the
United States. Milosevic and Croatian President Franjo Tudjman,
along with the leaders of Bosnia's three ethnic factions, came to
the United States for talks at a U.S. military facility at Dayton,
Ohio. President Clinton's special representative and the chairman
of these negotiations was Ambassador Richard Holbrooke. Under
heavy U.S. political pressure, the five Balkan leaders accepted a
deal that included the introduction into Bosnia of a NATO-led
peace-enforcing mission comprised of some 60,000 military personnel. Clinton agreed to commit 20,000 American troops, which
were deployed in early 1996 despite terrible weather conditions.
By spring NATO had pacified the country without incurring any
battle casualties. In mid-1996 President Clinton could report that the
initial phase of the mission had been successful and hold open the
possibility that U.S. troops would withdraw by the end of the year.
    Sending 20,000 American forces to Bosnia, and to air bases in
Italy, to enforce the Dayton Agreement was a major political risk

for Clinton. Most members of the Senate and the House of Representatives, which were controlled by Republicans after the elections of 1994, were either opposed to the decision to intervene in Bosnia or expressed serious reservations about putting American GIs in harm's way in a part of Europe where the United States had no significant national interests. The president did not ask for a vote of approval from Congress, as George Bush had done in 1990 before launching the Desert Storm offensive in Iraq. Several Republican leaders, notably Senate Majority Leader Robert Dole and Speaker of the House Newt Gingrich, pledged to support the troops with whatever they needed to accomplish their mission, even as they disapproved of Clinton's decision. In effect, the Republicans played it both ways: they disagreed with the president's decision to send combat troops to Bosnia but supported the mission after it was underway. This was a situation reminiscent of 1991, when most Democrats in Congress refused to support President Bush in his request to use forces in the Persian Gulf, but supported the war once it had begun.

President Clinton's assessment of U.S. national interests and his justification for using combat forces in Bosnia in December 1995 is important to understand, as was the case when George Bush concluded in 1990 that U.S. interests in the Persian Gulf were vital. In a televised address to the nation on November 27, 1995, Clinton said he wanted to explain "why our values and interests as Americans require that we participate" in the UN-sanctioned intervention in Bosnia. He cited a need to help stop the killing of civilians, especially children, and emphasized that it was important "to bring stability to Central Europe, a region which he said was "vital to our national interests." He also made a strong case for the need for U.S. leadership: ". . . nowhere has the argument for our leadership been more clearly justified than in the struggle to stop or prevent war and civil violence. From Iraq to Haiti, from South Africa to Korea, from the Middle East to Northern Ireland, we have stood up for peace and freedom because it's in our interest to do so and because it is the right thing to do." He also cautioned that "America cannot and must not be the world's policeman. We cannot stop all war for all time, but we can stop some wars." He then emphasized the U.S. role: "There are times and places where our leadership can mean the difference between peace and war, and where we can defend our fundamental values as a people and serve our most basic, strategic interests." Appealing to the nation's sense of pride, he said: "My fellow Americans, in this new era there are still times when America and America alone can and should make the difference for peace. The terrible war in Bosnia is such a case. Nowhere today is the need for American leadership more stark or more immediate than in Bosnia."[2]

Clinton said that the reason he had not acted sooner to stop the slaughter of innocents in Bosnia was that "the United States could not force peace on Bosnia's warring ethnic groups." The Dayton Agreement now gave the United States the invitation it needed, he said, to "to bring about real peace" in that war-torn land. He justified his action by first citing the U.S. promotion of values interest: "Implementing the agreement in Bosnia can end the terrible suffering of the people, the warfare, the mass executions, the ethnic cleansing, the campaigns of rape and terror. Let us never forget a quarter of a million men, women, and children have been shelled, shot, and tortured to death." In addition to this emotional appeal to the humanitarian impulse of the American people, the president also emphasized the important world-order interest involved with this statement: "Securing peace in Bosnia will also help to build a free and stable Europe. Bosnia lies at the very heart of Europe, next door to many of its fragile new democracies and some of our closest allies. Generations of Americans have understood that Europe's freedom and Europe's stability is vital to our own national security." Having thus established important, although somewhat questionably vital, interests in the Bosnia crisis, Clinton outlined the policy instrument he planned to use to defend the interests: "The only force capable of getting this job done is NATO. . . . And as NATO's leader and the primary broker of the peace agreement [Dayton], the United States must be an essential part of the mission. If we're not there, NATO will not be there, the peace will collapse, the war will reignite." And a new conflict "could spread like poison throughout the region," he asserted, "eat away at Europe's stability, and erode our partnership with our European allies." Mr. Clinton was confident that once peace was restored, the refugees could return to their homes and begin to rebuild their lives, hold elections, and restore the multiethnic character of Bosnia. He expected international agencies to take the lead in the rebuilding process and said that the Europeans would bear most of the cost. He reported that the Joint Chiefs of Staff "have concluded that this mission should and will take about one year."[3] In this estimate, the president was being disingenuous.

Nowhere did the president cite an economic well-being inter-

est or a defense of homeland interest to support his view that
Bosnia was a vital U.S. interest requiring the deployment of U.S.
combat troops in a potentially hostile situation. Unlike in the
1990–1991 Persian Gulf crisis where President Bush emphasized
the area's oil as being vital to world markets, there was no similar
economic stake anywhere in the Balkans. Clinton's case for using
force there rested on his assessment that a vital world-order interest, i.e. support for peace and stability in Europe, was the key
motivating factor and that dealing with a humanitarian disaster
had become a vital promotion of values issue. The subsequent
decision by Boris Yeltsin's government to contribute a Russian
contingent to the peacekeeping force, to work with the Americans,
greatly facilitated Clinton's task of selling his policy at home.

By employing the national interest matrix, Table 9 shows how
the major participants—the United States, the European Union,
Russia, Yugoslavia, and Bosnia—probably assessed their interests
in the Bosnia crisis. For this purpose, Britain, France, Italy, and
Germany are combined under the heading "Euro-NATO." The
significance of this listing is that while the United States, the European Union, and Russia had vital world-order interests at stake
in the Bosnia crisis, Slobodan Milosevic's Yugoslavia did not. As a
result, Milosevic was in the end willing to compromise at Dayton

Table 9. The Bosnia Crisis, 1995-1996

Basic interest	Intensity of interest			
	Survival	Vital	Major	Peripheral
Defense of homeland	Bosnia		Yugoslavia Euro-NATO Russia	U.S.
Economic well-being		Bosnia	Yugoslavia Euro-NATO	U.S. Russia
Favorable world order		Euro-NATO U.S. Russia	Bosnia Yugoslavia	
Promotion of values		U.S. Euro-NATO Russia	Yugoslavia Bosnia	

and force his allies in Bosnia to accept what was clearly a defeat in terms to their goal: a Serb dominated Bosnia, or incorporation of the Serb parts of Bosnia into a Greater Serbia. Russia's willingness to join with the United States and the European Union countries resulted from its inability to play an independent role. Joining the other countries protected its vital interest in being involved as a participant.

America's intervention in Bosnia was a political risk for President Clinton because only one of the two basic interests at stake—promotion of values—seemed firmly at the vital level, despite his assurance that the U.S. world-order interest was as well. Whereas the humanitarian challenge was abundantly clear, this in itself would not have led to the sending of 20,000 combat troops to work with the European allies to end the violence. But the world-order interest, by the president's words, amounted to a derivative vital interest, flowing from an overriding U.S. interest in ensuring peace and stability in Western Europe. In reality, the Europeans had a higher world-order interest and a higher economic interest (Danube River commerce) in this Balkan conflict than did the United States. President Clinton had enunciated clearly that if the United States did not join with its NATO allies, the Europeans would not go in alone. His assertion that American leadership in this case was decisive was well founded, but the implications of an imbalance between the degree of Washington's interest in Bosnia and the size of its military and economic contribution raised the likelihood that Congress would question both the duration of the U.S. involvement and its cost. It had been all but certain from the beginning of the intervention that American troops would be in Bosnia far longer than the one year that Clinton had envisioned in his November 27, 1995, address. Indeed, in December 1996 their stay was extended for another eighteen months, and in 1998 a smaller force was deployed for an indefinite period.

Soon after the president announced that American forces would go to Bosnia, the key question raised by media commentators and members of Congress was what, beyond stopping the bloodshed, could be accomplished to bring long-term peace to that country. Some questioned whether the Dayton Agreement's emphasis on rebuilding a multiethnic society among the Serbs, Croats, and Muslims was realistic. They asked whether partition between Muslim-Croat sectors, which had been formed into a loose federation, and the Serb-controlled eastern sector might not be a preferred long-term outcome.[4] Richard Holbrooke, the mediator of the Dayton Agreement, responded that partition would cause more problems than it resolved. "While America's vital national interests are not directly at stake in every detail of Bosnia's political structure, it would be a significant setback to our overall position in Europe and within NATO if, after all we have accomplished in Bosnia, our successes thus far were undone by failure to finish the job. Partition, whether followed by dismemberment of Bosnia or not, could reopen other fragile international boundary issues in southeastern Europe and the former Soviet Union, unraveling the current peace in the region."[5] Like Clinton earlier, Holbrooke argued that peace in eastern Europe depended on securing a lasting peace in Bosnia.

In 1999 the Clinton administration decided to reduce the size of the U.S. contingent in Bosnia to about 4,000 personnel. The Pentagon concluded that the job of keeping the peace had been accomplished and that it was necessary to send a part of the Bosnia force to Kosovo, where NATO had assumed the job of pacifying that war-torn province of Yugoslavia (see below). By then, four years after the introduction of American and European forces into Bosnia, relative peace had returned to that country. But for all practical purposes, Bosnia remained divided into two distinct parts: a Muslim-Croat region in western and northern Bosnia and a Serb region adjacent to Yugoslavia in eastern Bosnia. Bosnia's economy and administration were in deplorable condition, with the result that it had become almost totally dependent on foreign assistance. In a 1999 article entitled "Dayton's Incomplete Peace," Ivo Daalder and Michael Froman asked whether it wasn't time for NATO and the UN to turn over the task of rebuilding Bosnia to the Bosnians. "So rather than insist that Dayton will have failed if Bosnia does not soon become a multiethnic democracy," they wrote, "it is better to accept reality and concentrate instead on safeguarding Dayton's biggest achievement—ending the bloodiest war in Europe since World War II. . . . Most important, this approach would place Bosnia's political and economic future where it belongs—firmly in the hands of the people themselves."[6]

The real significance of the 1996 Bosnia intervention by American and European forces lay not primarily in the task of bringing peace to the Balkans but in rebuilding an Atlantic Alliance that had seemed to be losing much of its mission after the Cold War ended and the Soviet Union collapsed. The fragmentation of Yugoslavia, the potential of old European rivals—France, Germany, and Russia—asserting competing national interests in the Balkans, and a United States that did not intend to be marginalized in the new Europe, these were the key factors that brought the NATO partners together in 1995 to face the threat that Slobodan Milosevic created by establishing a new Serb power base in the Balkans. Having lost the hope of keeping Croatia and Slovenia under his control, Milosevic dared the rest of Europe to deny his plan to retain control of Bosnia, Macedonia, Montenegro, and Kosovo. Although Macedonia had declared its independence in 1992, it had little chance of defending its borders without the presence of a U.S. peacekeeping force there as a warning to neighboring countries, including Greece, to avoid attacking this weak state.

Another important aspect of NATO's intervention in Bosnia was its determination to move ahead with plans to invite Poland, Hungary, and the Czech Republic to become members of the alliance, despite strong objections from Russian President Boris Yeltsin. (The prospective inclusion of Hungary and the Czech Republic in NATO greatly facilitated the movement of American troops stationed in Germany through those countries and into Bosnia in 1996.) The hopes of other East European states for an invitation to join NATO added to the diplomatic pressure that was exerted on Milosevic to accept the Dayton Agreement. Yeltsin was at that time fighting a fierce political battle at home for reelection and was not in a strong position to oppose either American pressure on Milosevic or its plans to enlarge NATO. After alliance leaders eventually issued invitations to Poland, Hungary and the Czech Republic in 1998, Russia acquiesced but insisted that no countries on its borders should be invited to join the alliance.[7]

Russia, and NATO Enlargement

At the beginning of 1996 Russia seemed to be headed toward a political and economic disaster. A two-year-old military operation against the separatist government in Chechnya had caused thousands of civilian and military casualties and countless more refugees from that unruly province in the southern Caucasus region. Russian interior ministry forces, backed by the army, had launched a poorly organized and implemented campaign against Chechen guerrillas in 1994 and a stalemate had developed. By early 1996, the Russian public turned strongly against the war and the United Nations was calling for a negotiated settlement. With Russia's presidential elections scheduled for June and his bid for reelection now in doubt, Yeltsin selected a popular military figure, General Aleksandr Lebed, to end the fighting on the best terms he could get. General Lebed did so by promising a semi-independent status for Chechnya. He achieved wide public acclaim for his success and decided to enter the race for president. Lebed's and Yeltsin's principal opponent in the presidential race was Gennady Zyuganov, leader of Russia's Communist Party, the largest in the State Duma. Yeltsin had lost much of his earlier popularity due to a serious decline in the Russian economy and the government's nonpayment of pensions and wages to its increasingly desperate citizens.

During the months leading up to the June election, Yeltsin used the powers of his office to institute a series of high-profile spending measures, including the payment of pensions, and social programs that were aimed at the provinces. This huge spending spree, along with vigorous campaigning and the cease-fire in Chechnya, raised Yeltsin's poll ratings and eventually produced his reelection in a July run-off. But the impact on the country's financial situation was costly. According to one expert, between March and May the central bank had to issue more than 25 trillion rubles and sell $3 billion of its scarce reserves to support the value of the ruble. In the months before the election, Yeltsin had issued forty-nine decrees implementing his expensive electoral program, with the result that Russia's budget deficit increased to 9.6 percent of GDP. Another 8 trillion rubles had to be paid out in inflation compensation to depositors of the country's largest savings bank.[8]

In effect, Yeltsin bought his reelection with massive new government spending. This caused dislocation to Russia's fragile economy, which brought on a further decline over the next two years. Another aspect of Yeltsin's reelection campaign was his political debt owed to a group of new capitalists, powerful "tycoons" as they were called, who received special favors from Yeltsin to establish themselves in positions of influence. These new capitalists became very powerful and rich as Russia struggled to revive its economy. In some ways, the economic situation in Russia following Yeltsin's election resembled the one that had developed in Mexico in 1995 after outgoing president Carlos Salinas inflated his currency in order to facilitate the election of Ernesto Zedillo. In that case, the United States and the international financial community took steps, with Zedillo's assistance, to help Mexico avoid default on its foreign debts. In the case of

Russia in mid-1998, when corruption and mismanagement had driven the economy to the point where a large IMF loan was required to avoid default, the IMF and Washington refused. The ruble quickly collapsed and Russia was forced to declare that it could not pay a portion of its international debt. International investment dried up and many businesses went bankrupt. The IMF and financial markets had in effect declared no-confidence in the Russian government's ability to put its financial house in order. Communist and nationalist parties in parliament now called for Yeltsin's resignation. He had been in poor health and observers thought he might not be able to remain in office, but President Clinton continued to show him support. From his standpoint, it was considered important that Yeltsin serve out his term to 2000 because both Clinton and the European leaders needed Russia's continuing participation in the peace-enforcing mission in Bosnia. They also wanted his acquiescence in granting NATO membership for Poland, the Czech Republic, and Hungary.

Clinton traveled to Moscow in September 1998 for a summit meeting with Yeltsin. They discussed Russia's financial crisis, NATO enlargement, and a looming crisis in the Yugoslav province of Kosovo. Their summit came at a crucial juncture politically for both because Yeltsin was facing great opposition in the Duma to his economic reform program and to his appointment of a prime minister, while Clinton had just admitted publicly what he had denied for months, namely, an illicit relationship with a young White House intern. He was also being investigated by Independent Prosecutor Kenneth Starr on a number of other matters that could lead to his impeachment. Both presidents were, therefore, in a weakened political position at home.

On September 2, 1998, after a lengthy meeting, Clinton and Yeltsin met with reporters in St. Catherine Hall at the Kremlin. They were in good spirits and declared their discussions a success, even though Yeltsin admitted there had been disagreements and that "our approaches have not always completely coincided." Continuing, he said: "Russia rejects the use of power methods as a matter of principle. Conflicts of today have no military solutions, be it in Kosovo or around Iraq or Afghanistan or others. Also we do not accept the NATO centrism idea for the new European security architecture. Nevertheless, our talks have been conducive to greater mutual understanding on these issues." Clinton addressed the crucial economic aid issue in a friendly but firm manner: "I know this is a difficult time, but there is no shortcut to developing a system that will have the confidence of investors around the world. These are not American rules or anybody else's rules. These are—in a global market, you have to be able to get money in from outside your country and keep the money in your country invested in your country. And if the reform process can be completed, then I for one would be strongly supportive of greater assistance to Russia from the United States and the other big economic powers, because I think we have a very strong vested interest in seeing an economically successful Russia that is a full partner across the whole range of issues in the world. I also think it's good for preserving Russia's democracy and freedom."[9]

On the issue of NATO's invitation to Poland, the Czech Republic, and Hungary to join the alliance, Yeltsin remained firmly opposed, although he was somewhat mollified by a recent agreement signed between Russia and NATO that pledged, among other things, that NATO troops would not be stationed in those countries. Yeltsin asserted: "We're not running away from the position which has been that we are against NATO expanding eastward. We believe this is a blunder, a big mistake, and one day this will be a historic error. Therefore, at this point in time, what we necessarily would like to do is to improve relations so that there be no confrontation. Therefore, we have signed an agreement between Russia and NATO. And in accordance with that agreement we want to do our part. However, no way shall we allow anybody to transgress that agreement, bypass that agreement, or generally speaking, put it aside. No, this will not happen." In response, Clinton admitted that "President Yeltsin and I have a disagreement about whether it was appropriate for NATO to take on new members or not. But I think there is a larger reality here where we are in agreement. . . . And if you look at what the NATO members will be discussing next year, they'll talk about how they can deal with regional security challenges, like in Bosnia . . . [that] we would not have solved the Bosnia war, or ended it, had it not been for the leadership of Russia and the partnership between NATO and Russia." Clinton then mentioned the growing problem of peace in Kosovo: "Similarly, we have got to work together in Kosovo to prevent another Bosnia from occurring." He referred to the importance of the Partnership for Peace program whereby some two dozen nations that were not NATO members were working together with NATO on issues such as terrorism and the spread of chemical and biological weapons "because they know that nation-states in the future are going to have common security problems and they will be stronger if they work together."[10]

The Moscow summit was essentially a damage control effort by the Clinton administration to keep open the lines of communication with Yeltsin's government in the wake of Russia's financial crisis and the impending enlargement of NATO. It may also have been designed to deflect public attention in the United States away from Mr. Clinton's political crisis, which threatened to bring about his impeachment in the House of Representatives. The impeachment proceedings did indeed occur the following month, and while that political drama was unfolding in Washington planning went forward in the administration and at NATO headquarters to confront Slobodan Milosevic over his expanding paramilitary operations in Kosovo (see below).

The Kosovo crisis in early 1999, which produced nearly three months of intensive NATO bombing in both Kosovo and Serbia, caused a serious situation in Moscow's relations with NATO and with Washington. The Russian cabinet, headed by Prime Minister Yevgney Primakov, was adamantly opposed to NATO's military intervention in Kosovo, even though it had supported tough UN sanctions against Belgrade for its refusal to stop its ethnic cleansing operations there. In March 1999, when it became clear that Milosevic would not be intimidated by NATO threats of bombing, Clinton sent Richard Holbrooke to Belgrade in a final effort to persuade Milosevic to back down, as he had previously done in 1995 in the Bosnian crisis. Primakov was flying to Washington for talks with Vice President Gore regarding economic matters when he learned that the Holbrooke mission had failed and that NATO would soon begin bombing Yugoslavia. The Russian prime minister ordered his plane to turn around and return to Moscow. Boris Yeltsin was outraged that his urgent personal pleas to Clinton had been dismissed and he withdrew the Russian mission to NATO headquarters in Belgium. Before the bombing commenced, Yeltsin conferred urgently with Clinton by phone and then went on Russian television to denounce the NATO plan. As bombing began, the Kremlin issued this statement in Yeltsin's name: "This is in fact NATO's attempt to enter the 21st century as global policeman. Russia will never agree to it."[11]

Moscow's opposition to the use of force against Yugoslavia stemmed from two factors: Serbia, the major province in Yugoslavia, had long been an ally of Russia, in czarist as well as soviet times; and Russia feared that military retaliation for a government's action *within* its recognized borders set a dangerous precedent. If NATO could use massive bombing against Serbia for its efforts to keep Kosovo within Yugoslavia, Russian officials asked, what might NATO do when rebellion again flared in Chechnya and Russia decided to use troops to put it down? The frayed relations were not helped when Clinton subsequently asked for Yeltsin's assistance in brokering a peace agreement with Belgrade that included a Milosevic pledge to withdraw Serb forces from Kosovo. Clinton offered to make Russia a part of the peace-enforcing presence in Kosovo, similar to the role that Russia had in Bosnia. This was a painful proposal for Yeltsin to accept. However, to avoid being marginalized in the Balkans, he agreed to send a mission to Belgrade, along with a delegation from Finland, to persuade Milosevic to evacuate Kosovo and permit NATO to supervise the withdrawal. Subsequently, Russian military leaders were so outraged that NATO refused to give Russia a separate occupation sector in Kosovo that, following the peace agreement but before NATO troops arrived from Albania and Macedonia, they sent a Russian contingent of 200 men through Serbia to take control of Pristina airport. This precipitated a tense standoff of several days before a suitable arrangement with NATO was worked out to share responsibility at the airport.

Meanwhile, the security situation in Russia's Chechnya province was again heating up. In August 1999 a series of bombings of apartment complexes occurred in Moscow and other cities, killing hundreds of civilians and wounding many more. Chechen guerrillas were accused of the bombing. At the same time their fighters were caught trying to destabilize the government of a neighboring province, Dagestan. Moscow charged that Chechens were trying to turn the entire Caucasus region against Moscow. After Yeltsin came under intense pressure from hard-liners in the State Duma and his generals, he appointed a new, tough prime minister, Vladimir Putin, and gave him a free hand to crush the resistance in Chechnya. Putin at first claimed that the ensuing large offensive was designed only to capture the rebel leaders. But it was soon obvious that the goal was to occupy the capital, Grosny, and impose military rule in the entire province.

When the leaders of over thirty European countries belonging to the Organization for Security and Cooperation in Europe (OSCE), including the United States and Canada, convened in Istanbul, Turkey, in November 1999, a major agenda item was the Russian offensive in Chechnya. Several European leaders declared that the bombing was needlessly killing and wounding civilians and called for peace talks. Being isolated in the midst of this gathering of European leaders, Yeltsin struck a defiant tone, claiming that Chechnya was a domestic matter and that the others had no right to interfere in what he declared was Russia's internal security problem. He used strong language to make his point: "You have no right to criticize Russia for Chechnya. As a result of the bloody ways of the terrorist acts that have swept over Moscow and other cities and towns of our country, 1580 peaceful inhabitants of our country have suffered. The pain of the tragedy has been felt by thousands of families in every corner of Russia. In the last three years terrorists have kidnapped 935 hostages, and these were not only Russians. They included also Britons, United States nationals, French nationals." Yeltsin directed his most pointed criticism at NATO for its actions in Kosovo eight months earlier: "Not all the ideas that have arisen in the course of the discussion about the future of Europe seem to us to be justified. I'm thinking in particular of the appeals for humanitarian interference—this is a new idea—in the internal affairs of another state, even when this is done on the pretext of protecting human rights and freedom. We all know already what disproportionate consequences such interference can cause. Suffice it to recall the aggression of NATO, headed by the United States, that was mounted against Yugoslavia. Now on the threshold of a new era, it is more urgently necessary than ever before that our principle [sic] commandment for our joint efforts in Europe should be, 'Do not harm.'"[12]

In a conciliatory response President Clinton agreed that "Russia has not only the right, but also the obligation to defend its territorial integrity." He acknowledged that "Russia has faced rebellion within and related violence beyond the borders of Chechnya." But he added that even though critics of Russia's policy "deplore the Chechen violence and terrorism and extremism and support the objectives of Russia," they fear that the means Russia chose would undermine its own efforts and not lead to a solution in Chechnya. He thought that Yeltsin should accept help from the OSCE and others to find a political solution. He also took issue with Yeltsin's criticism of NATO's action in Kosovo and compared it to the situation in Bosnia, "where the world community waited four years and we saw 2.5 million refugees and 250,000 deaths placed on the altar of ethnic cleansing." Unlike in Bosnia, he asserted, NATO acted more quickly in Kosovo and the refugees had mostly all been able to return home. "I believe we did the right thing. And I do not believe there will ever be a time in human affairs when we will ever be able to say we simply cannot criticize this or that or other action because it happened within the territorial borders of a single nation."[13]

While this conference was going on, Clinton met separately with four leaders from the Caspian Sea region—Georgia, Azerbaijan, Kazakhstan, and Turkey—to witness their signing of an agreement to build a $2.4 billion oil pipeline from Baku on the Caspian Sea to Ceyhan, Turkey, on the Mediterranean. The strategic significance was that Caspian oil reserves would eventually be open to world markets, perhaps in 2004, without traversing either Iranian or Russian territory. This agreement was a severe blow to Moscow's efforts to run Caspian oil through Russian territory to a port on the Black Sea, thereby benefitting the Russian economy. This news was further evidence, for Russian nationalists, that the United States was intent on isolating their country and preventing it from exerting influence in its own neighborhood. Like the expansion of NATO to Russia's west, the pipeline project was seen as America's enlargement of its economic power on Russia's southern border.

The confluence of these events in 1999—NATO enlargement, American and NATO bombing of Yugoslavia, and the building of a new Middle East oil pipeline without Russia's participation—marked the beginning of a dangerous nationalist backlash in Russia against the United States. The *New York Times*'s Moscow correspondent, Michael Wines, painted a grim picture of the new mood in his report: "Americans cannot truly imagine Russians' frustration at their imperial disintegration and economic collapse. But perhaps they can get a whiff of the emotional release Chechnya evokes among Russians by recalling how good it felt, after two decades of Vietnam, Watergate, Iran and Lebanon, to finally regain their military prowess—striking back first at Libyan terrorism in 1986 and then, far more dramatically, against Saddam Hussein."[14] David Hoffman, Moscow correspondent for the *Washington Post*, wrote of similar developments and described the soaring popularity of Prime Minister Vladimir Putin, whom Yeltsin reportedly had picked as his candidate in the June 2000 presidential elections. In only three months, Hoffman reported, Putin had "become Russia's most popular political figure." He wrote that even Russian liberals, who had denounced the war against Chechnya in 1995–1996, were now applauding Putin's hard-line approach to dealing with the province.[15]

China and Taiwan

Early in 1996 U.S. relations with China deteriorated to an alarming degree as a result of Beijing's decision to conduct military maneuvers in the Taiwan Strait to intimidate Taiwanese voters on the eve of their first presidential election. President Clinton had sought during 1995 to improve the dialogue with President Jiang Zemin, contending that "engagement" was the best way to get China's cooperation on political, economic, and security issues in Asia. Critics argued that "confrontation" with the communist regime over its aggressive military policies and suppression of dissent was a more realistic way to deal with this growing power in Asia. The debate was heightened in March when Taiwan's president, Lee Ten-hui, claimed that his nation had earned the right as a democratic, prosperous people to be treated as an important player in international relations, not simply as a province of China. This was viewed as outrageous talk by Beijing's leaders. To underscore their determination to bring Taiwan eventually under China's administration, the Chinese government overreacted by test firing missiles near Taiwan's harbors just prior to elections. This blatant use of power to influence a democratic election startled leaders in Washington, Tokyo, and other capitals. President Clinton thereupon sent two aircraft carriers to the Taiwan Strait as a warning that the United States would stand by its obligation to defend Taiwan against the use of force by China. This strong action caused Beijing to back away from a potential confrontation with the United States and led eventually to renewed efforts by the two governments to improve relations.

The Taiwan Strait confrontation produced a spate of U.S. newspaper editorials, op-ed columns, and journal articles that denounced China's aggressive intentions. One of these was written by Richard Bernstein and Ross Munro, two journalists who had lived in and done reporting from China. Under the title "The Coming Conflict with America," they argued that it was folly for the United States and other western countries to think that China could be dissuaded by trade and cooperative diplomacy to modify its plan to become the preeminent power in Asia. They argued: "Since the late 1980s, Beijing has come to see the United States not as a strategic partner but as the chief obstacle to its own strategic ambitions. It has, therefore, worked to reduce American influence in Asia, to prevent Japan and the United States from creating a 'contain China' front, to build up a military with force projection capability, and to expand its presence in the South China and East China seas so that it controls the region's essential sea lanes." They argued that "China's sheer size and inherent strength, its conception of itself as a center of global civilization, and its eagerness to redeem centuries of . . . weakness are propelling it toward Asian hegemony."[16]

A quite different view of China and of American policy was taken by Zbigniew Brzezinski, who had been the national security adviser to President Jimmy Carter. He recommended that the United States should accommodate China as the major regional power in Asia and work with Beijing to keep the peace. He proposed de-emphasizing America's strategic relationship with Japan and instead placing greater emphasis on a Sino-American partnership. Excerpts from his article, "A Geostrategy for Eurasia," provide the thrust of his thesis: "There will be no stable equilibrium of power in Eurasia without a deepening strategic understanding between America and China and a clearer definition of Japan's emerging role. That poses two dilemmas for America: determining the practical definition and acceptable scope of China's emergence as the dominant regional power, and managing Japan's restlessness over its de facto status as an American protectorate." U.S. policy, he said, "should be to divert Chinese power into constructive regional accommodation and to channel Japanese energy into wider international partnerships." He thought that Beijing's leaders needed to be told that "China's internal liberalization is not a purely domestic affair, since only a democratizing and prosperous China has any chance of peacefully enticing Taiwan." Brzezinski asserted that any "attempt at forcible reunification would jeopardize Sino-American relations and hobble China's ability to attract foreign investment."[17] Underlying this approach to America's strategic interests in Asia was his assumption that it was within Washington's power to persuade Japan, Korea, Taiwan, and the countries of Southeast Asia to accept China as the new power broker in East Asia.

In 1997 and 1998 the Chinese and U.S. governments made a serious effort to find accommodation regarding their major policy differences by arranging an exchange of state visits by President Jiang Zemin and President Clinton. Jiang traveled to Washington in October 1997 and Clinton made his return visit to China in June 1998. Both leaders demonstrated a willingness to pursue friendly dialogue in contrast to the rancor that had prevailed in 1995 and 1996. President Jiang told an audience at Harvard University that he and President Clinton had agreed to build a "constructive strategic partnership" to mark a new stage in U.S.-China relations. He recalled China's humiliation by "imperialist powers" in the nineteenth century and claimed that his country had now rebuilt itself and wished to be treated as a great power. President Clinton said in a news conference with Jiang following their meeting at the White House on October 27: "A key to Asia's stability is a peaceful and prosperous relationship between the People's Republic of China and Taiwan. I reiterated America's long-standing commitment to a one China policy. . . . I told Jiang that we hope the People's Republic of China and Taiwan would resume a constructive cross-strait dialogue and expand cross-strait exchanges. Ultimately, the relationship between the PRC and Taiwan is for the Chinese themselves to determine—peacefully."[18] Clinton reported that the leaders had agreed to "high-level dialogues between our cabinet officials on the full range of security matters" and that a presidential hot line would be established "to make it easier for us to confer at a moment's notice." He said the United States would do everything possible to bring China into the World Trade Organization, "provided China improves access to its market." He conceded that "we have fundamental differences, especially concerning human rights and religious freedom," but he was convinced that the best way to address them "is directly and personally, as we did yesterday and today." Clinton said the United States welcomed China's emergence as a "full and constructive partner in the community of nations."[19]

Clinton made a return state visit to China in June 1998 and spoke before student audiences as well as with government leaders. At a joint news conference on June 27 in the Great Hall of the People in Beijing, Jiang focused on the issue of Taiwan: "The Taiwan question is the most important and the most sensitive issue at the core of China-U.S. relations. We hope that the U.S. side will adhere to the principles set forth in the three China-U.S. joint communiques and the joint China-U.S. statement, as well as the relevant commitments it has made in the interest of a smooth growth of China-U.S. relations. The improvement and the growth of China-U.S. relations have not come by easily. It is the result of the concerted efforts of the governments and people of our two countries. So we should all the more treasure this good result."[20] Responding, Clinton stated simply, "I reaffirmed our long-standing 'one China' policy to President Jiang and urged the pursuit of cross-strait discussions recently resumed as the best path to a peaceful resolution." He also addressed what he called "the principal area of our difference in recent years . . . human rights questions" and reiterated the reasons why Americans felt strongly about these fundamental rights. In answer to a question, Jiang defended China's right to protect its internal security and reiterated China's version of events at Tiananmen Square in 1989: "I have stated our position that with regard to the political disturbances in 1989, had the Chinese Government not taken the resolute measures, then we could not have enjoyed the stability that we are enjoying today."[21]

It seemed clear from their lengthy news conference that the Chinese and American presidents had decided they would not permit ideological differences to get in the way of their efforts to foster a friendly working relationship between their governments and to improve the economic and political climate, including the matter of human rights. What was left unclear was how they planned to deal with the tough security issues involving the Taiwan Strait, the Korean Peninsula, and the South China Sea, all of which were considered by Washington to be vital U.S. interests.

The Clinton administration hailed the visit to China as a personal triumph for the president, but critics quickly attacked him for paying too high a price in terms of U.S. relations with other Asian states, particularly Japan and Taiwan. In a critique of Clinton's efforts to renew a close relationship with Beijing, after nine years of strained ties, Ted Galen Carpenter of the Cato Institute wrote in an article entitled "Roiling Asia: U.S. Coziness with China Upsets the Neighbors": "In trying to defrost its chilly relationship with China, the Clinton administration has overshot the mark. Its rapprochement with Beijing has sent political tremors through East and South Asia. The increasingly cozy U.S.-Chinese relationship—described by President Clinton and Secretary of State Madeleine K. Albright in terms like 'strategic cooperation' and 'strategic partnership'—has alarmed Taiwan, unsettled longtime U.S. allies Japan and South Korea, and prodded India to unveil its nuclear weapons program." Carpenter argued that even if American and Chinese security interests were reasonably compatible, "a strategic partnership is unduly optimistic." And if their interests are not compatible, he said, "the United States should be pursuing precisely the opposite course: encouraging other regional powers or groups of powers to counterbalance China."[22] The writer believed that the United States should avoid an overt strategic partnership with any Asian state and instead should encourage the emergence of several centers of power in Asia, including India.

It seemed clear that President Clinton was determined in 1998 that good relations with China were a vital national interest for the twenty-first century and that he was prepared to subordinate China's human rights abuses—promotion of U.S. values—to America's larger economic and world-order interests in Asia. His rapprochement with Beijing was deeply controversial at home, however. The policy was denounced by liberals in his own Democratic Party who claimed he had sold out on the human rights issue in order to promote American commercial interests, and by conservatives in the Republican Party who saw China as a strategic threat. Conservatives charged that he was downgrading U.S. alliances with Japan and South Korea. Both sides criticized him for downplaying China's repression of political dissenters. Although Clinton had hoped to follow up his China trip with renewed negotiations that would enable Beijing to join the World Trade Organization, he was severely hampered in this plan by startling revelations that China had stolen sensitive nuclear and missile secrets from U.S. laboratories. In addition, evidence was found that the Democratic National Committee had illegally received funds from Chinese sources during the 1996 presidential election campaign. These were later returned by the DNC.

In April 1999 Clinton invited Chinese Prime Minister Zhu Rongji to Washington to try to negotiate a comprehensive trade agreement that would open Chinese markets to American and other foreign goods and to take additional measures that would help China qualify for admission to the WTO. Being admitted to the WTO was a key objective of Beijing, and Zhu made far-reaching concessions in the negotiations. He also made a favorable impression on political leaders in Congress. However, the negotiations coincided with the release of a congressional report on Chinese spying in the United States and also with NATO bombing attacks on Yugoslavia, an action which China strongly protested. Clinton reluctantly decided to put off conclusion of a trade agreement with China, an action deeply embarrassing to Premier Zhu, who had expected to obtain an agreement and U.S. support for China's WTO membership. Relations with Beijing were further damaged in May when a U.S. B-2 bomber mistakenly destroyed the Chinese embassy in Belgrade, Yugoslavia, killing three people. China was outraged and recalled its ambassador to Washington.

Trade negotiations were suspended while the United States tried to mend diplomatic fences and make compensation.

In September 1999 Clinton sent his former secretary of the treasury, Robert Rubin, to Beijing to ascertain whether China was ready to reopen negotiations on a trade deal. Finding a favorable response, the president in November dispatched Trade Representative Charlene Barshefsky and a team of negotiators to Beijing to finalize an agreement that many in his administration and in the business community believed Clinton should have signed in April. After marathon negotiations, a far-ranging agreement was concluded that would, when fully implemented, open China's markets to international trade and commerce and institute the rule of law in China's commercial business dealings. In return, Beijing was assured that its membership in the WTO would go forward in 2000. Still, China had made no real concessions on human rights. In fact, while negotiations were proceeding a Chinese court sentenced four members of Falun Gong, a nonpolitical spiritual movement, to twelve years in prison for suspected anti-government activities. Clearly, Jiang Zemin and his regime were not about to let an important trade agreement with the United States be interpreted as bowing to Washington's demands on human rights. Trade negotiator Barshefsky summed up this point with a statement following the conclusion of this historic agreement: "We have to be realistic about the prospects for change in China because there are elements of the country that will never change. But what's the alternative? Let's punish China by not gaining access to its market? Who does that punish? I am cautious in making claims that a market-opening agreement leads to anything other than opening the market. It may—it could have a spillover effect—but it may not. And we've got to understand that."[23] The *New York Times* editorialized in a similar way: "There are critics who say that China will not live up to its trade promises, and that the trade organization is incapable of forcing it to do so. Perhaps. But with China outside the organization, the United States has no real leverage. With Chinese membership, the United States can marshal international sanctions for violations. Besides, the imposition of the rule of law on trade might strengthen the hand of domestic forces fighting for the rule of law for the rest of Chinese society."[24] A less favorable view was taken by *Washington Post* columnist Jim Hoagland, who charged that Clinton was paying too much attention to his legacy in foreign policy and not enough to facing the hard realities of China's long-range intentions. "U.S.

Chinese relations are in flux and on a downward path," he wrote. ". . . Clinton needs to put reality before legacy, national interests before vanity. This is when history needs him, not vice versa."[25]

The future of China-Taiwan relations and of U.S.-Taiwan security ties was not part of the negotiations conducted in Beijing in November 1999, but they were clearly on the minds of American officials and the leaders of Taiwan. In October the White House became alarmed that a bill known as the Taiwan Security Enhancement Act that was moving toward a vote in the House of Representatives might pass and generate enough publicity to jeopardize the upcoming trade negotiations with China. The bill, which had the support of both the Senate and House foreign relations committees, would require the Clinton administration to upgrade the U.S. military relationship with Taiwan, establish a new communications link between the American and Taiwanese armed forces, and encourage the sale of more advanced equipment to Taiwan, including a ballistic missiles defense system being developed by the Defense Department. The White House lobbied vigorously against the measure and threatened a veto it if it reached the president's desk. One administration official stated: "It moves us very close, if not all the way to a formal military alliance with Taiwan." He added that such a change would vastly complicate relations with Beijing and jeopardize the policies of numerous previous presidents to balance full recognition in relations with Beijing while caring for the security interests of Taiwan.[26]

The issue of Taiwan's desire to seek international recognition of its separate status, if not independence, flared in the summer of 1999 when its president, Lee Ten-hui, stated publicly that relations between his country and China could make progress only if China recognized Taiwan as an equal in negotiations, and not as a renegade province. He argued that Taiwan was a flourishing democracy with a strong economy and should be invited to join various international organizations, including the WTO. His view had wide support in Congress, particularly among Republicans. Later in the year Lee published an article in *Foreign Affairs* that summarized his views, adding fuel to the debate in Congress on whether the United States should support China's admission to the WTO.

In view of the likelihood that U.S.-Taiwan relations would be a foreign policy issue in the 2000 presidential election, Lee's views are recorded here in some detail: "Beijing continues to belittle Taipei as merely a local government. It has also sought to downgrade the status of the R.O.C. government in cross-strait exchanges and to insist on a hegemonistic interpretation of the 'one-China principle' to force Taipei to gradually acquiesce to a 'one country, two systems' formula. Simultaneously, Beijing has done its utmost to isolate the R.O.C. diplomatically. Consequently, the international community has become accustomed to Beijing's pronouncements while disregarding the obvious fact that each side of the strait is separately and equally ruled. . . . Cross-strait ties now form a 'special state-to-state relationship.'" Lee argued that the international community should appreciate the implications of Taiwan's democracy and accord it the "status and role it deserves."[27]

Some observers thought Lee would initiate a campaign in the United States to have Taiwan accepted as a member of the UN General Assembly and other international bodies, while leaving aside the issue of independence. That Taiwan's case would receive a welcome in the United States, particularly from Republicans, was underlined by a statement made by Governor George W. Bush of Texas, a Republican candidate for president, in which he supported the November trade agreement with China and hoped that Taiwan as well as China would be admitted to the World Trade Organization. Bush later stated that he supported the one-China policy that had been established in the 1970s.

North Korea, South Korea, and Japan

In August 1998 North Korea's military threat in Northeast Asia again burst upon the world when it launched a three-stage ballistic missile over Japan and into the Pacific Ocean to demonstrate that it now had the capability to hit targets in Japan and even Alaska. The Japanese government was stunned and imposed new sanctions on ties with North Korea. Washington too was surprised because its intelligence community did not believe that Pyongyang had developed a three-stage missile. The test firing was designed, experts believed, to force Japan and the United States to be more forthcoming in providing economic aid and food shipments for North Korea's impoverished population. The Clinton administration was sufficiently alarmed that the president appointed former defense secretary William Perry to lead a panel of experts to review U.S. policy toward the reclusive North Korean regime and recommend a course of action to deal with its new missile threat. Perry and his team consulted closely with Japan and South Korea and then proposed a two-track approach: first, comprehensive negotiations with the Pyongyang government to obtain a verifiable agreement that its nuclear weapons program and missile production had been stopped, as it had pledged four years earlier, in return for which the United States and its allies would reduce some economic sanctions that had been in effect since 1950; second, in the absence of an acceptable agreement, the United States, Japan, and South Korea would take specific steps to contain the threat from North Korea, although Perry did not suggest what these should be.

Negotiations with North Korea nearly broke down in mid-1999, and it appeared for a time that Pyongyang was preparing to test fire another long-range missile. All parties understood that such action would probably lead to retaliatory action by the United States. U.S. precision bombing in the Kosovo conflict that spring demonstrated that America had the capability to destroy North Korea's missile sites and production facilities as well as its nuclear plants. Negotiations between Perry and North Korean representatives took place in Berlin in August, and a tentative agreement was announced in September. North Korea agreed to suspend missile tests while the negotiations continued, and the United States agreed to reduce some of the existing sanctions. This agreement also permitted South Korean, Japanese, and American companies to do business in the North, but it appeared doubtful that much commerce would occur until North Korea enacted laws to protect foreign investors. Secretary of State Albright called the decisions to relax sanctions "a road that holds out the possibility of long-term stability and even eventual reconciliation on the Korean peninsula." She added that if circumstances required that the United States should follow another policy, "we will do so to defend our interests."[28]

Some members of Congress expressed outrage at what they considered to be a sellout to North Korea. The chairman of the House International Relations Committee, Benjamin Gilman, declared: "We are once again entering a cycle of extortion with North Korea." He called North Korea "one of the most significant threats to American national security in the world today."[29] Perry, who had negotiated the limited agreement, responded to this argument by acknowledging that some might argue that the deal amounted to "paying off the North Koreans," but that the alternative "of strengthening American forces along the Demilitarized Zone between North and South Korea would be far more expensive."[30]

In the following weeks, North Korea accepted visits from several South Korean businessmen and the South Korean government expressed guarded optimism that Pyongyang might finally be shifting toward accommodation. Skepticism in Washington was widespread, however, and reflected a view held by many that President Clinton was desperately trying, in the wake of his earlier Senate impeachment trial, to find foreign policy achievements to bolster his presidential legacy. Still, Perry's argument that a partial agreement with North Korea was better than the alternative—a new war on the Korean Peninsula—was accepted with relief in Washington.

In Japan, the political fallout from these events was significant. Japan's economy had been in recession for most of the 1990s, and Tokyo seemed unable to produce a stable, energetic government that could deal effectively with the serious economic problems. A new government headed by Prime Minister Keizo Obuchi instituted some banking reforms in 1998 and 1999 and undertook steps to stimulate the lagging economy. North Korea's missile launch in 1998 shocked Japan and caused its government to move closer to the United States on defense planning and to expand its defense role in Northeast Asia. Speculation grew about joining with the United States in the establishment of a missile defense shield against North Korea, but President Clinton's rapprochement with Beijing in 1998 caused some of Tokyo's politicians to question whether it was wise for Japan to depend solely on the United States for its security. In October 1999 one of these dissenters, Deputy Defense Minister Shingo Nishimura, was fired from his cabinet level job for voicing publicly his view that Japan should consider arming itself with nuclear weapons. Nishimura reflected a growing belief among Japan's younger political leaders that North Korea's nuclear threat required a reevaluation of Japan's non-nuclear stance and its complete reliance on the United States for defense. India's and Pakistan's testing of nuclear missiles in May 1998 had stimulated some interest in this view, but Nishimura was the only government official to state it publicly.

As 1999 drew to a close, it was apparent that the Clinton administration had decided to make accommodation in relations with the People's Republic of China the cornerstone of its East Asia policy. With China's help, Clinton believed the threat of North Korea could be contained. Japan would then remain an economic power and not become a military one, and the Taiwan issue could be defused by Washington's continuing to refuse support for the independence aspirations of President Lee. With a turnaround in the economies of the Southeast Asian countries in 1999, the Clinton administration also believed that economic and security problems there could be managed. It was an optimistic scenario that was based on the assumption that all of the parties in East Asia preferred peace and economic prosperity to war. It was a plausible calculation.

NATO's Intervention in Kosovo, and Its Aftermath

The U.S. decision, with NATO's support, to intervene militarily in the Serb province of Kosovo, a part of Yugoslavia, was probably the high-water mark of America's thrust into an international policeman's role during the 1990s. Unlike in Bosnia, which U.S., NATO, and Russian forces had pacified in 1996, the White House's decision on March 24, 1999, to begin bombing of Serb targets did not have support from the UN Security Council or Russia, and it caused deep misgivings in Congress. In fact, the bombing campaign against Serbia alienated both Russian and Chinese governments and caused serious doubts among some NATO allies about whether a U.S.-led bombing campaign would persuade Yugoslav President Milosevic to withdraw his forces from Kosovo and permit NATO to occupy that piece of Serb territory.

President Clinton's National Security Council concluded in the autumn of 1998 that Milosevic was starting an ethnic cleansing campaign in Kosovo to crush a guerrilla force, the Kosovo Liberation Army (KLA), which called for independence for Kosovo and was receiving arms and logistical support from neighboring Albania. NATO warned the Yugoslav leader that if his paramilitary forces continued their campaign to force the evacuation of civilians suspected of harboring KLA fighters, it might retaliate with bombing. The Belgrade government then entered into negotiations with NATO and tentatively agreed to give Kosovo, which was populated by ninety percent ethnic Albanians, a large degree of autonomy. But the condition was that the KLA gave up their arms and that Kosovo continued to be part of Serbia.

In February 1999 NATO's foreign ministers, including Secretary of State Madeleine Albright, met at Rambouillet outside Paris with representatives of the Kosovo Albanians as well as Serb and Russian foreign ministers. The task was to pressure both Albanians and Serbs to sign a U.S.-drafted document, supported by

NATO, that provided Kosovo with local autonomy, required the withdrawal of Serb forces and disarmament of the KLA, and authorized the introduction of some 50,000 NATO troops to enforce a cease-fire. The United Nations would then build a civil government and hold a referendum in three years to permit Kosovo residents to determine their future. This proposed settlement received the blessing of the UN Security Council, including Russia, and it had the general support of Congress. However, Russia adamantly refused to agree to using force to impose this solution, and it was in a position to block UN support for military action. After the U.S. exerted pressure on the Kosovar Albanians, they agreed to sign. But there was a question whether the KLA would relinquish its arms or agree on anything less than a promise of eventual independence. Serbia's foreign minister tentatively agreed to Kosovo autonomy and to the withdrawal provisions, provided the KLA was disarmed. But the Belgrade government firmly refused to agree to the introduction of NATO military forces to pacify the province. It also opposed a referendum. For Serbs, Kosovo was an important part of their country, and Milosevic, a strong nationalist, was not willing to let the province go. For Yugoslavia, this became a survival interest, the defense of its own territory.

Secretary of State Albright held a press conference at Rambouillet on February 23 following a final meeting with all sides to the Kosovo conflict. Serbia and the Kosovo leaders were now given two weeks by NATO to agree on what she called the "interim political settlement." In fact, NATO's foreign ministers had presented Milosevic with an ultimatum: either accept the U.S. and NATO peace plan or risk military action. One question asked of Albright at her press conference was whether it was clear that Serbia would be bombed if it did not accept the proposed agreement. The secretary of state answered: ". . . let me say that I believe that the linkage of force and diplomacy, as we have described it now so many times, did in the end move this process [negotiations] forward. I think it's important to remember that the threat of the use of force is often useful in diplomacy and it is a tool and not an end in itself." Her answer suggested that the threat of bombing had brought the Serbs to the negotiating table, as it had in the Bosnia crisis four years earlier when Milosevic stopped the fighting rather than risk war. She seemed confident that the threat to bomb would produce similar results in the case of Kosovo.[31] In reality, the United States and NATO were telling Milosevic that, in return for a Serb withdrawal from Kosovo and turning over control of the province to NATO, Serbia would retain sovereignty for three years, until the referendum was held. It was not the kind of deal that a tough leader such as Milosevic was likely to accept, even at the risk of war.

When it was clear by mid-March that Milosevic would not agree to the military parts of the Rambouillet proposal, President Clinton called congressional leaders to the White House for an urgent briefing. He also held a news conference and warned the nation that the Kosovo crisis "threatens our national interests." He said that "if we and our allies do not have the will to act, there will be more massacres" and that "in dealing with aggressors in the Balkans, hesitation is a license to kill."[32]

The congressional leaders had told the president that most Americans didn't even know where Kosovo was and that if he intended to use force he needed to make a strong public case. A few days earlier the House of Representatives had narrowly supported a U.S. contribution to a peacekeeping force for Kosovo, provided all the parties agreed to the settlement. In view of the new information the president had given them, Speaker Dennis Hastert stated that the House vote no longer applied. "We're on the brink of a very grave situation," the Speaker warned. Other congressional leaders, particularly Republicans, were wary of giving the president their support for war without a full congressional debate. Answering a charge that he was rushing to bomb Serbia without sufficient provocation, the president assured the lawmakers that Milosevic's refusal to accept U.S. and allied peace efforts had given him and NATO "all the justification needed" to launch air attacks: "I think they have acted first. They have massed their troops, they have continued to take aggressive action . . . and have killed a lot of innocent people." (Clinton didn't explain that Serb forces were operating on Serbia's territory.) Still, Representative Tillie Fowler, a member of the House Armed Services Committee, raised this concern: "I'm afraid we're unleashing the dogs of war and escalating the conflict instead of stabilizing it." Senate Majority Leader Trent Lott told the press after the White House meeting that there was a strong feeling in both parties that it was important for Congress to vote on whether to support the president in his plan to use the armed forces.[33]

On March 22, when the bombing assault in Serbia seemed imminent, the Senate held a full debate on the president's plan. Strong sentiments were expressed on both sides. Senator Joseph Biden, ranking Democrat on the Senate Foreign Relations Committee, challenged Republican members' assertions that the U.S. had little if any stake in the Balkans. He asserted the struggle threatened NATO's credibility with a "massive tide of refugees" that could destabilize neighboring countries. "The national interests of the United States are directly threatened," Biden asserted, "by the continued aggressive actions of the Yugoslav government in Kosovo." Republican Senator Kay Bailey Hutchinson argued that "we're now picking sides in a civil war where the United States' interests are not clear. Moreover, the administration has no post-bombing policy. Before we go bombing sovereign nations we ought to have a plan." Democratic Senator Byron Dorgan was opposed to the whole debate idea, warning that the dissension on the bombing issue "could lead the Serbs to doubt American resolve."[34] A motion in the Senate to give the president authority to commence air strikes in Yugoslavia passed later that day by a vote of 58 to 41, with some Republicans joining with Democrats to give the president their support.

That evening Secretary of State Albright appeared on CNN television's "Larry King Live" and was asked by King whether a vote of 58 to 41 was a sufficient mandate for the president to engage in warfare in Kosovo. She replied: "Well, I think that there are [people] who, I believe, do not see the national interest in this. Everybody has their own views. But we worked this very hard. President Clinton has been meeting with members of Congress, both houses, and we feel very strongly that this is the right thing to do and are pleased by the support that we have." King asked whether ground troops were contemplated, as the Senate vote had not authorized that. She responded: "We have made very clear that the only ground troops that would be used would be to implement a peace agreement, and we have no plans to use ground troops in an aggressive way—only to implement a peace agreement." In answer to a question as to how long she expected the bombing to last, the secretary said that "it is going to be a sustained attack and it is not something that is going to go on for an overly long time."[35]

On the evening of March 24 President Clinton addressed the nation regarding the commencement that day of air strikes in Kosovo. He outlined what he saw as the important national interests involved: "We act to protect thousands of innocent people in Kosovo from a mounting military offensive. We act to prevent a wider war, to diffuse [sic] a powder keg at the heart of Europe that has exploded twice before in this century with catastrophic results. And we act to stand united with our allies for peace. By acting now we are upholding our values, protecting our interests, and advancing the cause of peace." He elaborated this point in another part of the address: "Do our interests in Kosovo justify the dangers to our Armed Forces? I've thought long and hard about that question. I am convinced that the dangers of acting are far outweighed by the dangers of not acting—dangers to defenseless people and to our national interests." He also cited the challenge to NATO: "Imagine what would happen if we and our allies instead decided just to look the other way, as these people were massacred on NATO's doorstep. That would discredit NATO, the cornerstone on which our security has rested for 50 years now." He believed that if he did not act now, it would "let a fire burn in this area, and the flames will spread. Eventually key U.S. allies could be drawn into a wider conflict, a war we would be forced to confront later, only at far greater risk and greater cost."[36]

President Clinton in this address seemed to base his decision to intervene in Kosovo on two of the basic U.S. national interests: humanitarian considerations (values), and concerns about a wider war, with implications for NATO (world order). Of these two interests, he voiced more concern for the humanitarian factor because the moral issue was likely to influence the public more than fear of a wider war in the Balkans. These were the same arguments he had used to justify American intervention in Bosnia in 1995–1996, but in that case he had the support of Russia and China. In Kosovo he did not have the support of Moscow, which vehemently objected to using force instead of additional diplomacy. As a result, the president could not get support from the UN Security Council, and this situation made Kosovo a more difficult intervention legally for him to justify. In any case, Milosevic defied the NATO bombing assault and sent his army in force into Kosovo with the goal of forcing the ethnic Albanian population to flee into Macedonia or Albania, and potentially to destabilize those neighboring countries. Kosovo suddenly threatened to become a larger and costlier war.

Using the national interest matrix, Table 10 suggests how the principal countries viewed their interests in Kosovo in March 1999. This breakout of interests suggests that Yugoslavia had the highest interest—survival—at stake, while the United States and the Euro-NATO countries appeared to have vital world-order interests. It should have been predictable, therefore, that Yugoslavia would fight instead of agreeing to a dismantling of its country. It

Table 10. The Kosovo Crisis, 1999

Basic interest	Intensity of interest			
	Survival	Vital	Major	Peripheral
Defense of homeland	Yugoslavia	Macedonia Albania Russia	Euro-NATO Greece	U.S.
Economic well-being		Yugoslavia Macedonia Greece	Euro-NATO Albania	U.S. Russia
Favorable world order		Euro-NATO U.S. Macedonia Russia Greece Albania	Yugoslavia	
Promotion of values		Euro-NATO U.S. Yugoslavia Russia	Greece Albania Macedonia	

was probably predictable also that Russia and Greece, both of which had historical and religious ties to Serbia, would strongly object to NATO's use of force, though the Greek government did reluctantly acquiesce in NATO's decision. Macedonia and Albania, two neighboring countries that had absorbed a massive influx of Kosovo refugees when the bombing commenced, also had vital interests at stake. Finally, the European NATO countries, as well as the United States, had a high, perhaps vital, humanitarian (values) interest in stopping Serbia's ethnic cleansing, and a vital world-order interest in preventing the spread of this conflict.

What is not obvious, however, is whether Kosovo ever reached the vital interest level for the United States, even though the president acted as if it had. To qualify as a threat at the vital national interest level, there must be a dangerous situation at hand that directly threatens the security and well-being of the country. Such a case could be made for most of the European NATO countries because of their proximity to the crisis. But it was a stretch for President Clinton to claim that America's security interests in Western Europe were severely threatened by Slobodan Milosevic's harsh retaliation against ethnic Albanian guerrillas who were threatening the security of his territory. A similar issue surfaced later in 1999 in Russia when Boris Yeltsin's government decided to fight the guerrillas in Chechnya who were determined to detach that province from Russia. However, in this case neither the European NATO countries nor the United States made any serious claim that fighting guerrillas in Russia was a cause that should require sanctions or intervention by NATO peacekeepers. In reality, Clinton talked as if a vital U.S. interest were at stake in Kosovo because he believed this would persuade Milosevic to withdraw instead of fight.

The Clinton administration's handling of the Kosovo crisis, particularly its assumption that a short period of bombing would bring Milosevic to accept the Rambouillet plan, proved to be seriously flawed. Within a week the war turned into a humanitarian disaster as Serb troops engaged in one of the largest ethnic cleansing operations since World War II, forcing nearly a million people to flee Kosovo and seek refuge in Macedonia and Albania. No advance preparations had been made by NATO for this contingency. When it became clear after a week that bombing Serb targets in Kosovo was not having the expected effect, the bombing was intensified and NATO's military command was authorized to start bombing in the Serb heartland, including the capital, Belgrade. Also within a week the first talk of sending NATO ground troops was heard, based on the growing realization that bombing alone was probably not going to end Serbia's hold on Kosovo. The White House continued to say that the president did not favor ground troops. He probably had two important reasons: first, public opinion at home was not ready for an enlarged war in the Balkans; and second, several European allies, notably Germany and Italy, were opposed to a ground war. However, when NATO heads of government came to Washington at the end of April to celebrate the fiftieth anniversary of the signing of the North Atlantic Pact, it appeared that preserving the credibility of NATO had now become a principal war aim. British Prime Minister Tony Blair lobbied for consideration of sending ground forces to Kosovo because he and others were persuaded that bombing alone would not force Milosevic to withdraw. NATO Supreme Commander U.S. General Wesley Clark shared that view. In May President Clinton, who was coming under increasing pressure from some members of Congress to take steps to ensure that NATO succeeded in its objectives, authorized the Pentagon to be-

gin planning for a ground invasion of Yugoslavia. Suddenly the
stakes in Kosovo had grown, and worry about "not losing" began
to drive U.S. policy. In early June talks were held with Milosevic
by high level Russian and Finnish emissaries. These eventually
produced a cease-fire and a peace agreement between NATO and
Yugoslavia whereby all Serb forces would be withdrawn from
Kosovo and NATO forces and UN civilians would take over control of the province. There was no mention of holding a referendum in three years, and Kosovo officially remained part of Serbia.

On June 10 President Clinton addressed the nation and
claimed that a great victory had been achieved because NATO had
remained united and air power had done its job. "The result will
be security and dignity for the people of Kosovo," he said. "This
victory brings a new hope that when a people are singled out for
destruction because of their heritage and religious faith and we
can do something about it, the world will not look the other way."
He took pleasure in restating that no American combat deaths had
resulted from seventy-eight days of intensive bombing. He
pledged that the United States would contribute about 7,000 of the
50,000 foreign troops that would be sent to Kosovo by nearly
thirty countries. Clinton ended his address with this vision of the
future: "We have sent a message of determination and hope to all
the world. Think of all the millions of innocent people who died
in this bloody century because democracies reacted too late to evil
and aggressions. Because of our resolve, the 20th century is ending not with helpless indignation but with a hopeful affirmation
of human dignity and human rights for the 21st century."[37]

There was strong criticism of the administration's handling of
the Kosovo crisis from segments of the press, Congress, and various foreign policy research organizations. Even though everyone
was relieved that the war had ended without American forces
having to fight Serb troops in the Yugoslav mountains, strong
words were voiced against American diplomacy. Charges were
made that misjudgments at the State Department and White
House had led to an unnecessary war with Milosevic and to the
alienation of two key UN members, Russia and China. Clinton
was also faulted by some, notably Senator John McCain, for his
early statements that he did not intend to use ground forces. This
was an invitation, critics said, to Milosevic that he should hold out
for a better deal on Kosovo than the one offered him in March by
Secretary Albright and other NATO leaders. Moreover, the humanitarian disaster that resulted in Kosovo once the bombing had

commenced was cited as a major unintended consequence of the administration's erroneous assumption that a few days of bombing would bring Milosevic to his senses.

One of the harshest attacks on Clinton and Albright was by Professor Michael Mandelbaum, a foreign policy specialist at Johns Hopkins University. In an article entitled "A Perfect Failure," he observed: "Every war has unintended consequences, but in this case virtually all the major political effects were unplanned, unanticipated, and unwelcome. The war itself was the unintended consequence of a gross error in political judgment. Having begun it, Western political leaders declared that they were fighting for the sake of the people of the Balkans, who nevertheless emerged from the war considerably worse off than they had been before. The alliance also fought to establish a new principle governing the use of force in the post–Cold War world. But the war set precedents that it would be neither feasible nor desirable to follow." He charged that "relations with two large, important, and troublesome . . . countries, Russia and China, were set back by the military operations in the Balkans." The effect, he said, was "to worsen relations with the only two countries in the world that aim nuclear weapons at the United States." The U.S. scholar argued that although NATO had promised Russia that it would be a full participant in European security affairs, the war against Serbia showed that pledge to be hollow: "NATO initiated a war against a sovereign state that had attacked none of its members, a war to which Russia had objected but that Moscow could not prevent."[38]

During a press conference on June 25 President Clinton acknowledged for the first time that he had underestimated Serbia's ability to withstand the NATO bombing campaign. Clinton said he had believed that Milosevic would submit to allied demands after "a couple of days" of bombing and stop the Serb assault on Kosovo. He added that once he realized that the Yugoslav leader would not submit easily, he determined that the bombing would continue for many weeks until the increasing damage would cause him to relent.[39] The president's admission confirmed what critics had said for two months, namely, that the Kosovo crisis had been bungled and that overconfidence had led the administration into a serious error of judgment regarding a crucial issue in diplomacy and war: Never underestimate your enemy.

At the end of 1999 the U.S. military was constructing one of its largest bases abroad, in the eastern part of Kosovo. It was apparent that the 6,000 U.S. service personnel who were there would be replaced by countless others, and that American forces would probably be stationed in that part of the Balkans indefinitely. This was an extension of American power and influence into a part of the world where it had not been engaged prior to 1996. For those Americans who believed that the United States should not be the world's policeman and that Europe should take over responsibility for policing the Balkans, the presence of this major U.S. base in Kosovo suggested that the outward thrust of Pax Americana had not yet ended.

A New European Union

One of the most significant historical events in the latter half of the twentieth century was the formation of the European Union (EU), which brought together fifteen of Europe's most developed countries. By 1999 this embryonic federal system was nearing full integration of the economies of Europe and was fostering political collaboration among the member nations. As a result, the EU had the potential to become a new world power center in the twenty-first century. The movement toward full integration of the European economies and the EU's decision to proceed with the European Monetary Union (EMU) gained impetus in the late 1990s when nearly all of the EU countries elected left-of-center governments. Tony Blair's British Labour Party held a large majority in parliament, which gave his government considerable freedom to advance ideas for coordinated defense and foreign policies among EU members. Lionel Jospin's Socialist Party won a narrow electoral victory in France because the conservative parties were deeply split. In Germany a coalition of Social Democrats and Greens, headed by Social Democratic leader Gerhard Schroeder, formed the first leftist government since 1982. And in Italy the Social Democrats, led by Massimo D'Alema, were in a coalition government with the restructured Communist Party. Smaller EU countries also had elected left of center governments. In 1998 the Council of Ministers (heads of the member governments) appointed a new management-oriented executive, Romano Prodi, as head of the unwieldy European Commission. The Council also decided to move rapidly to full economic integration with a new currency, the euro, which was introduced in 1998 for banking purposes and would replace the various national currencies in 2002. Britain and Denmark reserved their option to join the EMU at a later date. By the end of 1999 twelve additional countries, all of them in eastern Europe, had applied for EU membership. Of these, Poland, the Czech Republic, Hungary, Slovenia, and Estonia were expected to be admitted by 2004. Other eastern countries, including Turkey and Cyprus, were hopeful of gaining membership by 2010.

The emergence of a united Germany, Europe's largest country and strongest economy, as a fully integrated partner in the new Europe provided the basis for proceeding toward European unification. With the Soviet threat to Europe removed, the future for a united, democratic, and economically prosperous Europe looked very promising. But in 1999 the Council of Ministers faced this fundamental question: how could Europe speak as a more united entity in world affairs unless it also coordinated its foreign policies and eventually established an independent defense force? The event that crystallized the thinking of Europe's leaders was NATO's military intervention in Kosovo in March 1999 and the huge disparity that was displayed between America's high-tech military capability and the less sophisticated equipment used by the European countries. Britain, Germany, France, and Italy also suddenly recognized that not only were their air forces not in the same league with that of their American allies, but they could not come close to matching the U.S. in mobility and air lift capability. It was estimated, for example, that American air power, both Air Force and Navy, accounted for nearly 80 percent of all missions flown over Kosovo and Serbia in a nearly three-month period. This disparity in contribution to the war effort gave Washington the decisive voice on political and military strategy during the Kosovo conflict, to the discomfort of European leaders. Prodded by the British and French, the EU decided at a June meeting of its Council of Ministers in Cologne to begin coordinating their military weapons budgets and investing more in military research and development. This move was taken in order to address a growing realization that the EU might otherwise become a permanent protectorate of the United States and be obliged before long to purchase American military equipment. The EU also decided to appoint a foreign policy representative, Javier Solana, who had been NATO's secretary general. He would serve as the EU's chief spokesman on foreign policy issues, a step toward eventually giving him the role of a foreign minister. EU leaders also agreed to create an autonomous European defense force with the capability to act independently of the United States when the latter decided that its vital interests were not at stake, but when the Council of

Ministers believed that military action was required. Britain and France took the lead in pressing for the establishment of a "Rapid Reaction Force" of some 60,000 troops, to be available for action if NATO—meaning the United States—chose not to be involved. As the *Economist* observed in its special survey on Europe in 1999: "The strategic argument says, in essence: 'You never know.' America is a foreign country and a long way away. . . . However sound transatlantic relations may be at any given time, a prudent Europe cannot pursue a long-term policy of dependence on America because Europe cannot possibly have any guarantees about the future direction of American policy. Hostility is highly unlikely. Indifference or incomprehension are perfectly possible. So if Europe can provide for its own security, it should do so. And if America approves, so much the better."[40]

The Kosovo crisis was also an awakening to European leaders that they were in danger of losing control of their foreign policy options to the American president and secretary of state if they were not united both politically and in terms of defense. A large part of responsibility for the trend toward U.S. domination of Europe's foreign and security policy was the failure of the Europeans themselves to take decisive action to deal with the Bosnia crisis in the early 1990s, and then permit the Americans in 1998 to control the diplomacy with Yugoslav President Milosevic on Kosovo. Had Britain, France, Italy, and Germany been able to enunciate a European policy on dealing with the tough Serb leader and then back it with the threat of EU intervention, Washington might well have accepted a supporting role. As it was, the Europeans, principally Britain and France, did not coordinate their policies. Richard Holbrooke, in the case of Bosnia, and Madeleine Albright, in the case of Kosovo, seized the policy reins within NATO and pressed the U.S. viewpoint. In the case of Bosnia, Holbrooke's tough diplomacy worked. On Kosovo, Albright's pressure on Milosevic to accept the U.S.-drafted NATO ultimatum issued at Rambouillet failed completely to resolve the crisis, resulting in a bombing war that did not remove Milosevic from power and that left Kosovo in a physical and economic shambles.

Washington's reaction to Europe's efforts to assert an independent voice in foreign policy and defense matters, and to establish the euro as a competitor reserve currency to the dollar, was generally positive. But some viewed the new trend as putting Europe into a much stronger competitive relationship to the United

States for influence in the world. C. Fred Bergsten of the Brookings Institution believed that there were dangers inherent in the launch of the euro as a serious rival to the dollar and that it would take much cooperation and wisdom on both sides of the Atlantic to avoid additional protectionist measures being applied by the European Union and the United States.[41] On the question of an independent European defense force operating outside NATO, it was too early to say at the end of 1999 how militarily significant the new force would be or how the Pentagon would respond. One expert, Richard Medley, writing in October 1999, thought that on balance this was a good idea for Europeans: "First, it assures them of the kind of personal historical legacy that European heads of state still crave. With EMU firmly on track, constructing an EU defense pillar would put them at the center of history in a way that tucking in the corners of monetary union never could. Second, military union moves Europe one giant step closer to political parallelism with the United States."[42]

In December 1999 the EU heads of government met in Helsinki, Finland, and finalized arrangements to form a 60,000-member Rapid Reaction Force by 2003 and to make Europe a strategic player that other powers, including the United States, would have to reckon with. The EU leaders pledged that Europe's new military strength would not detract from the effectiveness of the NATO alliance but would instead contribute to the alliance's cohesion. French Defense Minister Alain Richard said in an interview that "if Europe takes on more responsibility by building up its military strength, that will contribute to the long-term equilibrium of the alliance." In response, U.S. General Wesley Clark, NATO's top military commander, was generally supportive of the European initiative: "I think anything that increases the overall capabilities of the members of NATO in the defense area is commendable and we should be pushing it. We've got to make sure the institutions, as they emerge, and the linkages, as they emerge, in fact do that."[43] In a commentary on the Rapid Reaction Force, entitled "The EU Turns its Attention from Ploughshares to Swords," *The Economist* wrote: "Post-Kosovo Europe is sounding keen on a joint defence force that is less reliant on America. Its actions have yet to match its words." It continued: "The French present these ideas in one way, as an opportunity for Europe to assert itself as a 'separate civilization' from North America. The British have another view. European-only defence efforts, they reckon, will work best for tasks that are endorsed by the American administration but fail to arouse enough enthusiasm from Congress to warrant direct American involvement. In other words, a more robust Europe would be doing America a sort of favor."[44]

Europe will undoubtedly remain a vital national interest of the United States in the new century, and the EU's movement toward political and economic integration should not diminish that interest. Europe's defense, economic well-being, participation in maintaining a favorable world order, and promotion of western values in the world—these are all reasons why Europe will continue to rank at the top of U.S. global interests. Although there may be strong economic competition from EU countries and disagreement on some important international political issues, the bonds that have grown across the Atlantic between 1945 and 2000 are firm and are not likely to be cast aside as Europe becomes a major power center. However, the United States will need to accept the notion that Europe has the capability and the will to chart its own course in the twenty-first century. This would be the culmination of a dream that post–World War II U.S. leaders hoped would one day come true, a United States of Europe capable of standing on its own feet.

Prospects for Peace in the Middle East

The United States became heavily involved in the Middle East as a result of Britain's retrenchment after World War II, the discovery of vast oil reserves in the Persian Gulf, and creation of the state of Israel in 1948. Britain's withdrawal left a power vacuum that the United States slowly and reluctantly filled. The cost of that extension of U.S. interests into the area escalated considerably in the 1990s. Iraq's invasion and occupation of Kuwait led to a major expansion of America's military presence in the Gulf and the establishment of bases in Saudi Arabia, Kuwait, and Bahrain. In the late 1990s Iran and Iraq, the largest countries in the Gulf, remained implacable adversaries of the United States, and Washington maintained economic sanctions against both. However, Russia and France, largely for commercial reasons, pressed for the easing of the sanctions and hoped thereby to increase trade with these oil-rich countries and, perhaps, to influence the direction of their authoritarian regimes. The Clinton administration refused to lift the trade restrictions, contending that any change regarding Iraq should result from a real shift in its policy or the end of Saddam

Hussein's rule. In the case of Iran, Washington held some hope
that moderate forces surrounding Muhammed Khatami, the new
head of government, would eventually prevail against the conservative heirs of Ayatollah Khomeini, who led the 1979 Islamic
Revolution. In sum, the level of U.S. interests in the Persian Gulf
did not change after 1991: both its economic well-being interest
and its world-order interest remained at the vital level.

Three countries in the eastern Mediterranean area also were
fundamental to U.S. interests. These were Turkey, Israel, and
Egypt. Although Turkey was allied with the United States in
NATO, neither Israel nor Egypt had a formal alliance with Washington. However, both emerged as U.S. vital world-order interests
in the 1970s because of their strategic location and their pro-West-
ern governments. In the case of Israel, a vital promotion-of-values
interest also existed because of the strong sentimental attachment
that Americans have to the need of a homeland for the Jewish
people. Israel and Egypt also became the largest recipients of U.S.
economic and military aid, and Turkey was high on the aid priority list. In 1998 Israel and Turkey concluded a military cooperation agreement that enhanced the security of both countries
against Syria and Iraq and gave support to Turkey's special interest in the nearby island state of Cyprus. Turkey had occupied the
northern part of Cyprus in 1974 to protect the minority Turkish
Cypriot population against a plan by the majority Greeks to merge
the country with Greece. As a result of the growing security links
among the United States, Turkey, Israel, and Egypt, the United
States entered the new millennium as the undisputed major
power in the eastern Mediterranean.

The most difficult problem the United States faced in the
Middle East at the end of the 1990s was how to bring about a lasting peace between Israel and the 2 million Palestinians who demanded a homeland of their own, including a return of refugees
to areas that were occupied by Israel in 1967: the Gaza Strip, West
Bank territory, the Golan Heights, and East Jerusalem. Israel had
moved toward an accommodation with Yasser Arafat's Palestine
Liberation Authority when Yitzhak Rabin was prime minister in
the early 1990s. But Rabin's assassination by an Israeli extremist
placed the peace process, which had been started at the Madrid
conference in 1991, on hold until May 1999. In that month Israeli
elections brought to power a coalition led by Labor Party leader
and former general Ehud Barak. He had pledged to carry out
Rabin's 1994 initiative to reach a peace settlement with the Pales-

tinians. Soon after forming a new moderate government Barak conferred with President Clinton and Egyptian President Hosni Mubarak, as well as European leaders, to enlist their support for a final settlement. He envisioned turning over occupied lands to the Palestinians and negotiating the terms of a Palestinian state, but not relinquishing any part of Jerusalem. In September 1999 Barak and Arafat announced their intent to complete a "framework agreement" by February 2000 and thereafter to negotiate a final settlement, hopefully before the end of that year. Many observers thought this was highly ambitious, given the stakes involved. Barak also carried out provisions of the Wye agreement, which had been negotiated a year earlier by his predecessor, Binyamin Netanyahu, but not implemented. These included a land corridor for Palestinians traveling between Gaza and the West Bank, a turnover of additional territory to the Palestinian Authority, and the release of hundreds of Palestinian political prisoners. When Barak, Arafat, and Clinton met in Oslo, Norway, in November 1999 to commemorate the death four years earlier of Yitzhak Rabin, the three leaders implicitly accepted the idea that, at the end of the peace process, a Palestinian state would be proclaimed and receive international support. Nevertheless, there was no indication of an understanding about Jerusalem, even though President Clinton remarked that he was hopeful that an Israeli-Palestinian peace settlement could be accomplished during his final year in office. He said that helping the peace process along was his highest foreign policy priority, and it was clear that his administration would go all out to accomplish that goal.

In mid-December another breakthrough in the peace process occurred when Syrian President Hafez al-Assad agreed to have Foreign Minister Farouk Charaa meet in Washington with Prime Minister Barak to discuss a settlement of the Golan Heights issue. There had been secret talks between the Israeli and Syrian governments, and a tentative understanding had apparently been reached to end Israel's occupation of the Golan Heights in return for security guarantees and normal relations between the two countries. The meeting took place on December 15, with President Clinton opening the session. After this initial meeting Barak and Charaa agreed to resume deliberations in January 2000. Earlier *The Economist* had commented: "The tight timetable that Mr. Barak has insisted on imposing on the [peace] process is risky but may turn out good for concentrating minds."[45] It appeared that the Oslo accord had indeed concentrated the minds of Syria's leaders, who seemingly did not wish to be left behind if Israel and the Palestinians reached their peace settlement.

Summing Up

As the twentieth century closed, the United States was at the zenith of its power and influence in the world. It had mended relations with its potential adversary in Asia, China, and it had defused, momentarily at least, the nuclear threat of North Korea. Japan remained an economically strong ally, despite a prolonged recession, and Southeast Asia was quiet following the economic turmoil of 1998 and the uncertain changes in government in Indonesia, including its relinquishment of East Timor to UN administration. In Europe, the U.S. and NATO had subdued for a second time in five years the ruthless president of Yugoslavia, and Washington had maintained an open, if contentious, relationship with Boris Yeltsin's Russia. An uneasy peace prevailed in the Persian Gulf, backed up with American and British military power. And the prospects for a comprehensive peace between Israel and its Arab neighbors seemed promising. Yet, the price of this worldwide extension of America's power had not been fully grasped by the American public and by many members of Congress; for if the United States planned to continue expanding its global reach in the twenty-first century, it was clear to some observers that the size of the armed forces and the Defense Department's budget would need to be increased substantially and that small conflicts in Asia and Africa would have to be handled primarily by the United Nations, the European Union, or other coalitions of countries. At the close of the century the American public seemed to be saying to leaders in Washington: "You can play the world policeman's role as long as it doesn't increase my taxes or cause casualties to our troops." That divergence of views between policy makers who seek to "make the world safe for democracy" and a public that doesn't wish to be disturbed was a challenge that would confront the new president in 2001.

10
Role of the Aloof but Vigilant Superpower

As the United States entered the twenty-first century it faced a fundamental choice regarding its attitude toward other regions of the world and the role it wished to play in shaping the international environment during the next decade. Simply put, Americans needed to decide whether their government should take on the role of international hegemon or accept the less grandiose role of aloof but vigilant superpower. A hegemonic role implies that the U.S. government is willing to intervene regularly, with military forces when necessary, to create an international order that enhances regional security around the globe and, in addition, makes the world "safe for democracy." The aloof but vigilant superpower role suggests that the United States will be involved politically and economically in the world with a large array of policy tools (see Chapter 1, Table 5) to influence events, but will not intervene militarily just anywhere to stop civil wars and regional violence unless its own vital interests are at stake. This includes defending allies against attack and protecting vital natural resources whose availability in world markets is deemed to be vital to U.S. economic well-being. International hegemony implies willingness to use force to stop governments from brutalizing their own citizens as well as those of their neighbors, whereas the aloof superpower stance reserves decisions to use force against such regimes only if they pose a dangerous threat to an entire region, the Persian Gulf for example. Obviously, most foreign policy decisions fall somewhere between these two poles, and this discussion focuses on the propensity of political leaders to favor one direction or the other.[1]

A mood of "triumphalism," as some called it, seemed to characterize the American public's mood at the end of 1999 and was epitomized by the cover of newsmagazine *U.S. News and World*

Report in a December issue. It featured an attractive drawing of smiling Uncle Sam with this bold headline: "Man of the Century." The magazine's cover story commented: "At the dawn of the new millennium now, one may look back at the old and find it impossible not to recognize an indelible American imprint in virtually every area of human endeavor—in science and medicine, business and industry, arts and letters—it has been Uncle Sam's century." Continuing, it observed: "Over the years, America has been criticized by friend and foe for a dominance both real and perceived. But there is no gainsaying the fact that, if nations were people, Uncle Sam would be the man of the century."[2]

In the late 1990s an archetype of the hegemon outlook in foreign policy was Secretary of State Madeleine Albright, whose family background reflected Europe's confrontations with both fascism and communism. Dr. Albright views the world as an arena where dictators need to be curbed or ousted before they bring great harm to their own people and their neighbors. Her public crusade against Yugoslav President Slobodan Milosevic over his aggressive policies in Bosnia and Kosovo was carried out under the banner of "human rights and democratic values." Unlike her predecessor, the reserved Warren Christopher, Albright engaged daily in public diplomacy, both in the United States and abroad. She constantly lectured other countries and leaders on their responsibilities to uphold human rights and democratic values. In February and March of 1999 she was the Clinton administration's spokesperson for a tough policy against Milosevic, bluntly warning him that if he did not accede to NATO's plan to detach Kosovo administratively from Yugoslavia his country would face U.S. military action. When the Kosovo war ended and Milosevic remained in power, she took the lead in encouraging opposition groups within Serbia to rise up and oust him, holding out the promise of economic aid if they succeeded.

In an article in *Foreign Affairs* at the end of 1998 Secretary Albright had this to say about the goals of American foreign policy: "To guard against overextension, we must insist that others do their share. We must differentiate between the essential and the merely desirable. We must skillfully use every available foreign policy tool, from the mildest demarche to the use of force. . . . To protect our interests, we must take action, forge agreements, create institutions, and provide an example that will help bring the world closer together around the basic principles of democracy, open markets, law, and a commitment to peace." She asserted that "the United States cannot persuade others to act if we are not willing to do so ourselves. Effective coalitions are a consequence of, not an alternative to, U.S. leadership."[3] Implicit in these words is the willingness to use force, if other measures fail to persuade recalcitrant regimes to accept the American view of the "basic principles of democracy." They also made clear that she believed America's allies were not willing to confront troublemakers unless the United States took the lead, the implication being that only the United States had the capability and willingness to be the world's policeman. It was the voice of an aspirant to the role of hegemonic superpower.

A different view of America's role in the twenty-first century, one that supported the more limited "aloof superpower" course, was offered by Harvard University scholar Samuel Huntington under the title "The Lonely Superpower." Huntington observed: "American officials quite naturally tend to act as if the world were unipolar. They boast of American power and American virtue, hailing the United States as the benevolent hegemon. They lecture other countries on the universal validity of American principles, practices, and institutions." He cited Albright's claim that the United States is the world's "indispensable nation" and criticized her boast that "we stand tall and hence see further than other nations." He went on: "This statement is true in the narrow sense that the United States is an indispensable participant in any effort to tackle major global problems. It is false in also implying that other nations are dispensable—the United States needs the cooperation of some major countries in handling any issue—and that American indispensability is the source of wisdom."[4] Huntington further charged that American officials were "peculiarly blind to the fact that often the more the United States attacks a foreign leader, the more his popularity soars among his countrymen who applaud him for standing tall against the greatest power on earth." He cited Slobodan Milosevic and Fidel Castro as examples and concluded that "Neither the Clinton administration nor Congress nor the public is willing to pay the costs and accept the risks of unilateral global leadership." In this view, no matter how much the "foreign policy elites may ignore or deplore it, the United States lacks the domestic political base to create a unipolar world." The result, Huntington observed, is "a foreign policy of rhetoric and retreat and a growing reputation as a hollow hegemon."[5]

At the end of 1999 it was unclear which of these two views of an internationalist foreign policy would prevail in the United

States. It was a crucial issue that was likely to be debated during the 2000 presidential election campaign.

U.S. National Interests in the Twenty-First Century

Using the national interest framework described in Chapter 1, how should U.S. national interests, especially vital interests, be defined for the international arena that exists at the beginning of 2000? If one accepts the view that the United States does not possess the domestic political base required to take on the role of hegemonic superpower, what national interests should guide the makers of foreign policy during the coming decade? Comparing the four basic national interests that are described earlier, the following is my evaluation of U.S. interests in 2000.

Defense of Homeland Interests. For the next decade the United States does not face a threat of massive destruction on its territory. Even though Russia has a limited capability to launch ICBMs against the United States, it will not have the will to do so because the costs, in both physical and economic terms, would be horrendous. China does not yet have such capability and is not likely to risk destroying its impressive economic gains by provoking a major war with the United States. North Korea, Iraq, and Iran might try to employ possession of nuclear and other weapons to extort political and economic concessions, but their leaders are not likely to risk full-scale retaliation by launching nuclear or other mass destruction weapons against U.S. territory or that of a U.S. ally. Nevertheless, it remains a vital interest for the United States to exert strong efforts against nuclear proliferation by any potential enemy that aspires to acquire these weapons. The United States also has a defense of homeland interest in building a credible nuclear shield to protect itself from rogue states that might acquire these weapons and threaten to use them. Though Russia and China currently oppose altering the 1972 ABM treaty, this strategic defense program should be completed over the next decade, even if this involves concessions to satisfy Moscow's and Beijing's national interests.

Terrorism, another kind of threat to the defense of homeland interest, is difficult to defend against because its country of origin in often unknown. The deep concern about a millennial terrorist attack in America at the end of 1999 focused public attention and was indicative of the sense of fear that affects the country when a

New York Trade Center–type disaster occurs and foreign terrorists are apprehended. Although American federal and local law enforcement agencies are now well trained to deal with these potential emergencies, there is a strong likelihood that serious incidents will occur in the next years as additional countries and terrorist groups are moved to take what they see as retaliatory actions against Americans and U.S. territory. The rise of the terrorist threat is an inevitable consequence of the United States being perceived abroad as a hegemonic superpower.

Economic Well-being Interests.   At the beginning of the twenty-first century the United States is the world's economic superpower, boasting an economy that has outpaced all of its rivals and that gives promise of growing steadily in the coming decade. U.S. government support for free trade around the world has richly benefited both U.S. citizens and peoples in many other countries where the principles of market choices and sound banking are practiced. Globalism, supported by instantaneous communications around the world, seems to be firmly established as a basic fact of life for international commerce. One of the most exuberant testimonials to the power of the global economy was a 1999 book by Thomas Friedman, a columnist for the *New York Times,* entitled *The Lexus and the Olive Tree.* Friedman argues that free markets are inevitable everywhere and that leaders and countries resisting their pressure will be swept aside. But he also suggests that the global market system will not work without strong U.S. leadership, including the occasional use of military force, to pressure recalcitrant countries into line. The book is an implicit call for the United States to be the hegemonic superpower.[6]

A crucial question is, therefore, which economic issues will rise to the level of vital economic challenges in the future. Clearly, protecting the high American standard of living against threats from abroad is a vital economic interest. But how do policy makers define "high standard of living," and what price should Americans pay to ensure it? For example, in 1973 the Nixon administration was faced with an oil embargo by Arab oil-producing countries that were furious with the president for supporting Israel militarily during its October war with Egypt. Americans were forced to cut back drastically on their driving, and long lines appeared at gas stations around the country. President Nixon had to determine whether this oil crisis threatened a vital interest of the country, with the implicit need of military force to intervene in the Middle East, or whether the issue was a major national interest entailing dislocations to the economy that, while painful, were not so dangerous to the nation that he needed to take drastic action to break the oil embargo. Nixon decided the issue was major, not vital, and the country learned to cope with an oil shortage, aided by increased imports from Iran, Venezuela, and Mexico. On the other hand, in 1991 America and other countries used force in the Persian Gulf to prevent an Iraqi dictator, Saddam Hussein, from occupying not just oil-rich Kuwait, but potentially also Saudi Arabia and the Gulf Emirates. Throughout the 1990s Persian Gulf oil was viewed as a vital economic interest. To defend it the United States stationed nearly 10,000 U.S. military personnel in and around the Gulf area to reassure friendly countries that they would not be attacked and that their oil would continue to flow to world markets.

In the coming decade the United States will need to come to grips with this crucial issue: Is Persian Gulf oil so vital to America's and the world's economy that U.S. air, navy, and army forces should be stationed there indefinitely and be prepared to go into action to protect it against not only aggression, but also against revolutions of the kind that engulfed Iran in 1979? In short, should the Gulf area remain a vital economic interest of the United States? In my view, Persian Gulf oil is very important to the U.S. and the world economy, but it is not a vital interest. This view results from two factors: first, the world possesses other major sources of oil: in Mexico, Venezuela, western Africa, the Caspian Sea, Russia, and Southeast Asia. This reality challenges the claim that Saudi Arabia's and Kuwait's reserves are crucial to America's standard of living and must be protected. A second reason is that the Gulf states producing the oil are not likely suddenly to stop selling it even if a war occurred. In the 1980s and in 1990–1991, the Strait of Hormuz was a "choke point" for the passage of oil tankers to the Indian Ocean. In 2000, however, there are pipelines across Saudi Arabia to the Red Sea, and a new one has been proposed to bring Caspian Sea oil to world markets through Turkey, bypassing both Iraq and Iran. In sum, diplomacy, economic pressure, and market competition constitute a better means than American military power to ensure a continuing flow to world markets of Persian Gulf oil.

Some observers suggest that the European Union, with its new common currency, the euro, and its emerging political and military cohesiveness, will pose a serious challenge to American economic supremacy. In some sectors European competition may indeed harm industrial and commercial interests in the United States, but the so-called economic threat from Europe is not likely to be more than a major level danger to the U.S. economy. In fact, many American and European corporations are already so linked that it is difficult to show whose national interests are being affected by the ebb and flow of international commerce. In Asia, Japan, South Korea, Taiwan, and China are all important to the economic well-being of the United States, but none of them is crucial (vital) in the sense that the American economy could not sustain a serious disruption in trade with any or even most of them. The Asian economic crisis of 1997–1998 was a serious test, and the U.S. financial markets were only slightly affected. In the Western Hemisphere the United States cemented free trading relationships with Canada and Mexico through the NAFTA arrangement, and it is expanding trade and financial relationships with several South American countries, notably Chile, Brazil, and Argentina. Although critics deplored the refusal by Congress to give President Clinton renewed "fast track" authority to negotiate additional free trade agreements similar to the one that led to Mexico's inclusion in NAFTA, this has not dampened efforts to negotiate bilateral agreements elsewhere in the hemisphere. The benefits of free trade are now so clear that it is probably only a matter of a few years before the United States will be willing to open negotiations to expand the NAFTA agreement southward.

A new and potentially damaging threat to the entire U.S. economy and international economic system appeared in early 2000 in the form of an electronic virus that infected millions of personal and commercial computers using the internet for communications. The so-called love bug virus launched by internet hackers in the Philippines quickly spread around the globe and caused an estimated $8 billion in damage to U.S. businesses. Building detection mechanisms and countermeasures against future electronic threats will be a major task for the federal government and U.S. businesses in the future.

World-order interests. With the Cold War over and the Soviet Union dismantled, the United States had a unique opportunity in the 1990s to reassess its world-order interests. It could decide which of the many commitments it had made over the previous forty years to defend numerous countries remained truly vital in the post–Cold War era. The Bush administration, which

was in office during the breakup of the Soviet Union, had to deal
with new challenges to regional power balances in the Persian
Gulf, the Balkans, and Northeast Asia. It concluded that some security commitments could be downgraded while others needed
to be reinforced. In general, the reassessment made by President
Bush was in the direction of considering fewer countries and issues to be vital world-order interests. In Asia Bush downgraded
the importance of Southeast Asia and closed important air and
naval bases in the Philippines. However, he reinforced defense
cooperation with Japan and South Korea and worked with China
to defuse a potential nuclear threat from North Korea. In Europe
his administration encouraged governments there to take additional responsibility for dealing with the security concerns of
countries in Eastern Europe. President Bush showed much concern over the regional threat to the Balkans posed by Yugoslav
President Milosevic but concluded that the threat did not rise to
the level of a vital interest requiring him to intervene. In the Persian Gulf, however, Bush decided that reversing Iraq's invasion
of neighboring Kuwait was indeed a threat to vital U.S. interests.
He also pressured Israel and its Arab neighbors to negotiate peace
in Palestine because he concluded that it was vital to U.S. interests to prevent renewed war, which would adversely affect
America's relations with countries throughout the Middle East.

After President Clinton came to office in 1993, his NSC reas-
sessed world-order interests in a more expansive manner. In Somalia he tried to exert military pressure to help build a politically
stable government to replace the warring factions that had devas-
tated the country. In Haiti he used American troops to oust a military regime and restore an elected president whose subsequent
policies could hardly be called democratic. In Bosnia Clinton decided to seize the leadership role from the faltering European
NATO allies and forge a coalition that intervened to stop ethnic
cleansing and restore the country's multiethnic society. He also
pressed for expanding NATO's membership eastward to include
Poland, the Czech Republic, and Hungary, despite strong objections from Russia. He did this on the grounds that it was vital for
world order reasons to have these states inside the western security zone in order to preclude their becoming pawns in a future
European power struggle. Clinton agreed with Bush's assessment
of the U.S. interest in building cooperative relations with China,
and he reiterated his policy that there was only one China. Clinton
deepened U.S. commitments and military presence in the Persian

Gulf region, and he embraced Bush's and Secretary of State Baker's earlier pressure on Israel and the Palestinians to make peace.

In sum, one might plausibly argue that prior to 1999 there was not a significant difference between the Bush and Clinton administrations in the assessment of U.S. world-order interests, even though Clinton showed more willingness than Bush to take on responsibility for stopping a civil war in Bosnia.

It was the Kosovo intervention in March 1999 that clearly distinguished Bill Clinton's view of world-order interests from that of George Bush. The contrast between the way Bush handled the 1990–1991 Persian Gulf war and how Clinton dealt with the Kosovo crisis is instructive. Bush demonstrated that he was prepared to liberate Kuwait from Iraq's aggression if other countries in Europe, the Middle East, and Asia were willing to support a full military intervention. He also insisted upon getting a United Nations Security Council authorization to use force against Iraq, and he asked for a formal vote from both the Senate and House of Representatives before he launched an air and land war.

In contrast, Clinton's view of the national interest in Kosovo made the confrontation with President Milosevic appear to be an American effort to impose its will on a Balkan bully. There was no UN authorization for the use of force because Russia and China objected, even though both had supported economic sanctions. Firm support in Congress was lacking, although the Senate, in a close vote, gave its assent to a limited bombing campaign. The NATO allies were divided, with Italy and Greece not favoring sustained bombing and Germany deciding that it would not support a ground invasion. Unlike Bush, who fought the Gulf War with ground troops as well as air forces, Clinton was persuaded that air power alone could succeed. He correctly feared a domestic backlash if significant casualties resulted. In sum, Clinton conducted the military campaign as if it were a high major interest, not a vital one needing to be fought with all available resources in order to prevail.

How should the United States assess its vital world-order interests in the coming decade? In my view Europe, Northeast Asia, and North America (including the Caribbean) will continue to be the core world-order interests of the United States, with the Eastern Mediterranean area occupying the border line between a major and a vital interest. China, Russia, North Korea, and Iran are potential threats to these core interests, and the United States must carefully monitor their actions in order to determine whether accommodation of their national interests is feasible or whether confrontations are likely to occur. All of the remaining areas of the world are at the major or peripheral level, not the vital one that could require the use of U.S. forces. If this assessment is reasonably correct, it may be argued that the United States is today substantially overcommitted in terms of the disposition of its armed forces abroad and of the array of countries to which it is pledged to provide military and economic aid. The number and size of U.S. diplomatic missions in many countries is excessive, particularly in the number of military personnel attached to U.S. embassies and military assistance groups that are located in nearly one hundred countries.

Promotion of Values Interests. This is the basic national interest on which the Clinton administration departed significantly in its rhetoric, and occasionally its actions, from the Reagan and Bush administrations. Clinton and his secretary of state redefined human rights and democratic government as U.S. vital interests that should be defended with American troops "wherever possible," as he declared in 1998 and 1999. His and Secretary of State Albright's view was consistent with the policies of previous Democratic presidents—Woodrow Wilson, Franklin Roosevelt, John Kennedy, and Jimmy Carter—in emphasizing the idealistic content of American foreign policy. This altruism is, of course, as old as the American republic, beginning with the Declaration of Independence. What was new with the Clinton administration, however, was the president's stated willingness to use military forces to support promotion of values in the absence of other vital interests, for example, in humanitarian crises in Central Africa, Kosovo, and East Timor. In effect, Clinton raised promotion of values to a level that even Jimmy Carter, who had emphasized human rights as an important part of his foreign policy, did not suggest, namely, using force to impose American values abroad.

In the coming decade, the degree to which human rights and democracy will be a guiding principle in formulating U.S. foreign policy may be influenced by the presidential election of 2000. History suggests that a Republican president would place less emphasis on promotion of values abroad, in the belief that America will earn more respect abroad if it conducts itself like a great power instead of as a missionary promoting its own way of life.

Alternative Foreign Policy Courses

At the beginning of 2000 the United States has three alternative courses that it can follow in foreign policy. Two of them are real possibilities whereas the third, neoisolationism, is not. These alternatives tend to reflect the views expressed by the principal presidential candidates of the Reform, Democratic, and Republican parties but, do not coincide with them. They are discussed here according to the extent of the three parties' desired U.S. involvement in the world.

Alternative 1: Neoisolationist Bastion. Despite the prevailing majority view at the turn of the century that the United States should continue to play a major world role, a significant minority of Americans do not share that view. These dissenters believe that the government has sacrificed too many good-paying industrial jobs at home in its global pursuit of free trade. The NAFTA arrangement with Mexico is cited as a prime example. Neoisolationists think that America's military forces are now spread around the world because of too many U.S. defense commitments and Washington's propensity to assume ever greater peacekeeping responsibilities. They complain that Congress squanders money on foreign assistance and on funding for UN peacekeeping operations that have little to do with U.S. interests. They also charge that the United States has relinquished its sovereignty to international organizations, such as the United Nations and the World Trade Organization. They view it as a gross mistake to have handed over the Panama Canal in 1999 to what they see as a corrupt Panamanian government. In sum, neoisolationists see no reason for the United States to bear the major costs of keeping the peace everywhere and of building the economies of the world's developing countries. With the Cold War over, they say, this country should concentrate its efforts on improving living conditions at home, including making America a safer place in which to live.

An isolationist inward-looking policy has not prevailed within either of the two major political parties since Dwight Eisenhower defeated Senator Robert Taft for the Republican Party's presidential nomination in 1952. But neoisolationism has resurfaced from time to time as third-party candidates were able to capture public attention in the 1960s and 1990s. A former Alabama governor, George Wallace, ran for president in 1968 as leader of the American Independent Party with a populist, nationalist message. He captured forty-six electoral votes that year. In 1972 he ran again but was crippled by an assassin's bullet before the election and dropped out of the race. In 1992 a billionaire entrepreneur, Ross Perot, formed the Reform Party with an anti-internationalist platform and won 18 percent of the national vote for president. Many of his supporters, who might otherwise have voted Republican, were attracted by his criticism that President Bush's free trade policies, especially NAFTA, would lead to the loss of good-paying jobs to developing countries, specifically Mexico, that had lower wages. Some observers thought Perot's isolationist appeal to middle class voters cost Bush his reelection in 1992. Perot ran again in 1996 but captured less than half the votes he received in 1992.[7]

The drive to inform the electorate about the value of an antiglobalist foreign policy will be pressed in 2000 by two important political organizations: Perot's Reform Party and the powerful AFL-CIO labor organization. The latter will lobby within the Democratic Party for policy statements that limit the president's authority to conclude trade agreements harmful to organized labor in the United States. These organizations will be joined by certain environmental interest groups whose members believe the U.S. government gives far too much attention to large business and financial interests when negotiating international trade agreements, and too little attention to the environmental impact of its globalist policies.

Ross Perot's likely successor as nominee of the Reform Party, Patrick Buchanan, will forcefully articulate the party's neoisolationist viewpoint. A long-term Republican activist, Buchanan left that party in 1999 because, he asserted, it had forsaken its traditional conservatism in foreign policy and entered a broad consensus with the Democrats on pursuing globalist policies that had seriously harmed U.S. workers. In the fall of 1999 Buchanan came in for intense criticism over his new book, *A Republic, Not an Empire*, in which he argued, among other things, that the United States should not have entered World War II. Britain would have made peace with Nazi Germany, he asserted, and the United States could have managed quite well by focusing its national interests on the Western Hemisphere. Buchanan defended his isolationist view of history with a commentary in the *Washington Post* entitled "The War that Didn't Need Waging."[8] Despite his acknowledged rhetorical skills, neoisolationism does not appear to have much chance to gain ground in the 2000 elections.

Alternative 2: International Hegemon. This foreign policy course is essentially the one pursued by Bill Clinton from 1995 through 1999. It began with his decision to intervene with 20,000 American troops in Bosnia to stop an ethnic cleansing campaign sponsored by the governments of Serbia and Croatia. This policy was expanded in Iraq at the end of 1998 when U.S. air power was used against Iraqi targets in order to force Saddam Hussein's regime to cooperate with UN arms inspectors and, implicitly, to cause its overthrow. The bombing was supported by Great Britain but was opposed by France, Russia, and China, the other permanent members of the UN Security Council. In 1998 and 1999 the Clinton administration expanded the hegemonic role by forging a NATO ultimatum to the government of Yugoslavia to withdraw from Kosovo or face NATO bombing. When President Milosevic refused to bow to this pressure, NATO bombed Yugoslav territory for seventy-eight days.

In its economic policy, the Clinton Treasury Department used its enormous influence within the IMF and World Bank to pressure Russia to adopt economic reforms and accept the expansion of NATO countries eastward. In East Asia the State Department used economic and political influence in Indonesia to force the resignation of President Suharto and the country's evacuation of East Timor. Washington used its veto power on membership in the World Trade Organization to pressure China to accept major changes in its economic system and to improve its record in human rights, which Beijing refused to do. By the end of 1999, the United States was seen increasingly by the rest of the world as pursuing a unilateral hegemonic foreign policy whereby Washington called the shots on all the important international issues and its allies and other states were then expected to follow obediently along. One high French official, in frustration over U.S. policy, called the United States the "hyperpower."

The exercise of an international hegemon's role necessitates that the United States have available large amounts of foreign aid to encourage developing countries to accept Washington's policies. It also requires powerful military forces that are on call whenever the president decides that America must take the lead in dealing with troublemakers anywhere in the world. In 1999 Congress objected to the size of the administration's foreign aid budget after it became clear during the Kosovo intervention that U.S. armed forces had been stretched beyond their safe limits in order to provide trained military personnel for their numerous peacekeeping and peace-enforcing missions around the world. Clearly, a significant mismatch was developing between President Clinton's interventionist policies and Congress's reluctance to pay the increased costs.

A full public debate about Clinton's hegemonic foreign policy did not occur in Congress in 1999 or register with the general public for two reasons: first, the U.S. economy was so robust that Americans did not seem to care about costs and risks. The few casualties that had occurred in Bosnia in 1996 and Kosovo in 1999 convinced the public that military interventions abroad were "casualty-free." Foreign aid, which formerly was a rallying point for opponents of an internationalist foreign policy, no longer aroused real opposition because the federal budget by 1999 was not in deficit and the amount of foreign aid appeared to be relatively small compared with defense appropriations and other federal expenditures. A second factor shielding Clinton's interventionist policy was the reluctance of Republican congressional leaders to fully debate the question, even though they had expressed serious concern when he dispatched troops to Haiti, Bosnia, and Kosovo.

Vice President Albert Gore, the likely nominee of the Democratic Party for president in 2000, has been an intimate confidant to President Clinton on foreign policy from the time the administration came to office in 1993. He attended National Security Council meetings at which major foreign policy decisions were discussed, including the military interventions. He had a central role in formulating administration policy toward Russia and represented the president on numerous foreign policy missions abroad. In sum, there is no reason to think that Mr. Gore, as president, would depart significantly from the interventionist proclivities of the second Clinton administration. He might soften the State Department's rhetoric on human rights, free markets, and democracy, but there is scant indication at the beginning of 2000 that this loyal vice president would depart significantly from Clinton's worldview, namely, that the United States has a "unique opportunity" in history to shape the world essentially in its own image.

Alternative 3: Aloof but Vigilant Superpower.   Like the international hegemon role, the aloof superpower course adheres to the internationalist foreign policies that every president since World War II has followed. On the broad issues of national defense, enhancing the economy in the global marketplace, supporting allies, confronting aggressors, and promoting the principles of democracy and human rights, these basic U.S. interests have been supported by Democratic and Republican presidents alike, beginning with Harry Truman and his successor, Dwight Eisenhower. Where the parties and their presidents have often diverged is around two of these basic national interests: world order and promotion of values. On world order, the issue has been to what extent the United States should be involved militarily in establishing order (policing) around the globe and in using American troops to stop local wars (combat). On promotion of values, the issue has been how high a priority the State Department should give to emphasizing human rights and democracy, particularly when this interest is in conflict with U.S. economic well-being and world-order interests, as in the case of China.

It was possible at the beginning of 2000 to see the general outlines of the foreign policy views of Governor George W. Bush of Texas, the front-runner for the Republican nomination for president. His public statements during the primary campaign suggested that he tended toward the aloof but vigilant superpower role. He favored strengthening U.S. military forces by providing a substantial increase in funding for the Defense Department and building a limited nuclear defense shield to deal with "defense of homeland" threats. On world order issues, Bush expressed concern about China's long-term intentions in Asia, but reiterated the "one-China" policy initiated by President Nixon. However, he seemed firm in demonstrating that the United States would oppose an attempt by China to force Taiwan to accept unification. Bush supports China's entry into the World Trade Organization and normalizing U.S. trade relations with Beijing. However, his efforts to bring about human rights improvements in China, as well as other countries with authoritarian governments, would be made primarily in private discussions with their leaders, instead of through public statements that have little impact, particularly in China.[9] On NATO, both Bush and Gore believe that America's allies should accept more responsibility and pay a larger share of the costs of maintaining peace in the Balkans and in the Persian Gulf.

A test of how far a Republican president in 2001 would depart from the Clinton administration's foreign policy will be his response to the unresolved humanitarian issues in Bosnia and Kosovo, and to the next regional crisis in Asia, Africa, or the

Middle East. If a Republican president resists pressure at home and abroad for America to take the lead in stopping civil wars in just about any part of the world, this would suggest he favors the "aloof superpower" role. There may, of course, be some cases where a vital interest is at stake but the timing and/or the means to deal with it are not positive and a decision should be put off. This situation occurred in the Bosnia crisis in 1992 when the Bush administration decided that neither public opinion nor the means to deal with this civil war was favorable to supporting a large-scale intervention. President Clinton waited three years and concluded that both public opinion and the means were available to support an armed intervention in Bosnia.

Another test will occur if President Clinton's strenuous efforts to bring about a peace settlement between Israel and Syria are successful. The president reportedly was prepared to ask Congress to provide $5–10 billion to pay for the costs of implementing such an agreement. U.S. troops might be required to monitor a demilitarized zone along the Golan Heights, which Israel planned to return to Syria as part of a comprehensive settlement. If this occurs, even a Republican Congress would likely conclude that the financial cost of facilitating peace between Israel and Syria, although high, was manageable in light of America's vital interest in promoting peace in the eastern Mediterranean area.

Bipartisanship on continuation of Clinton's overall foreign policy was not probable, however. The Senate's rejection in October 1999 of his request for ratification of an international nuclear test ban treaty was a stunning foreign policy defeat for the Clinton-Gore administration. The treaty required a two-thirds affirmative vote in the Senate but fell far short of that requirement. The debate and outcome signaled that Senate Republicans and some Democrats objected to an "international hegemon" role which many lawmakers believed Clinton had inaugurated by making war on Yugoslavia. At a news conference the president blasted Republican senators as "new isolationists" who were threatening national security. "By this vote," he charged, "the Senate majority has turned its back on 50 years of American leadership against the spread of weapons of mass destruction."[10] Clinton's aides compared the defeat to the Republican Senate's rejection in 1920 of President Wilson's proposal for the United States to join the League of Nations, an action that ushered in two decades of isolationism and led, they claimed, to World War II. Republicans vigorously denied the charge, arguing that the test

ban treaty was seriously flawed and would harm national security. *Washington Post* columnist Charles Krauthammer charged
that the Clinton administration had used the term to divert public
and world attention away from its own "meandering through the
world without a hint of strategy," and accused it of "wading
compassless in and out of swamps from Somalia to Haiti to Yugoslavia." The columnist asserted that a wise foreign policy should
always be "guided by American national interests and security
needs."[11]

This foreign policy confrontation between the Democratic
president and Senate Republicans signaled that the 2000 presidential race might produce a serious debate about the interventionist
policies of the Clinton administration and the more cautious superpower stance followed by the Bush administration. There was
little evidence, however, to conclude that the Republican Party
would be anything other than an internationalist party in the tradition of Eisenhower, Nixon, and Bush.

Toward the end of 1999 a prominent journalist and media
commentator, Alan Murray of the *Wall Street Journal,* made this
observation regarding the mood of the country: "The great irony
at the end of the century, I believe, is that our relative position in
the world has never been stronger, yet the public attitude toward
the very institutions that brought us to that position has never
been poorer."[12]

This lack of public trust in American leaders and government
institutions is, in my view, a recipe for serious political trouble
ahead. Given the general attitude of the public, which pays far too
little attention to international affairs, it is essential that our national leaders have the trust of the American people in order to
lead the country effectively. Franklin Roosevelt had that trust in
1941–1942 and used it to rally the nation during World War II.
Harry Truman had the public's confidence when he warned in
1947–1948 about the dangers of Soviet expansionism. And Ronald
Reagan had it when he decided in the 1980s to confront the Soviet
leadership on the futility of their continuing to pursue the Cold
War. At the beginning of the twenty-first century the country
needs national leaders in whom the public has confidence to deal
effectively with the great international challenges that lie ahead.

Americans could look back in 2000 on a century of extraordinary achievements in a broad range of endeavors, both foreign
and domestic. A crucial question in the new century is whether
the United States should attempt to remake the world essentially

in its own image, or accept the reality that America is probably incapable of being a hegemonic superpower. In our democratic system the electorate decides long-term national interests, and in early 2000 its preference seems to be the aloof but vigilant superpower role.

Notes

Introduction, 1989: A Transition Year in World Politics

1. Quoted in *Washington Post*, May 13, 1989, p. A15.
2. See Felix Rohatyn,"America's Economic Dependence," *Foreign Affairs*, 1988–1989, pp. 53–65.
3. See David P. Calleo, Beyond American Hegemony: The Future of the Western Alliance (New York: Basic Books, 1987), chap. 12.
4. Paul Kennedy, The Rise and Fall of the Great Powers (New York: Random House, 1987), chap. 8.
5. *Washington Post*, January 18, 1989, p. A4.

1. Defining U.S. National Interests

1. National Security Strategy of the United States, Special White House Report, January 1987, p. 4.
2. For a comprehensive survey of writers on "national interest," see Elmer Plischke, *Foreign Relations: Analysis of Its Anatomy* (Westport, Conn.:Greenwood Press, 1988), chaps. 2–3.
3. Paul Seabury, *Power, Freedom, and Diplomacy* (New York: Random House, 1963), p. 87.
4. Donald E. Nuechterlein, *United States National Interests in a Changing World* (Lexington: Univ. Press of Kentucky, 1973), chap. 6: "Changing Perceptions of U.S. Interests in Southeast Asia—A Case Study."
5. James M. Rosenau, *The Scientific Study of Foreign Policy*, (New York: Free Press, 1971), p. 248.
6. The first version of this matrix was published in my article "National Interests and Foreign Policy: A Conceptual Framework for Analysis and Decision-Making," *British Journal of International Studies*, Oct.1976, p. 247.
7. Caspar Weinberger, Fighting for Peace: *Seven Critical Years in the Pentagon* (New York: Warner Books, 1990), chap. 6.
8. These sixteen criteria are discussed in more detail in Nuechterlein, *America Overcommitted: United States National Interests in the 1980s* (Lexington: Univ. Press of Kentucky, 1985), pp. 18–25.
9. Ibid., see chap. 2, "Instruments of Foreign and National Security Policy. "
10. Excerpted from Donald E. Nuechterlein, "National Interests and National Strategy: Are There Parallels with U.S. International Corporate Interests?" in Herbert L. Sawyer, ed., *Business in the Contemporary World* (New York: Univ. Press of America, 1987), pp. 197–220.

2. Era of American Preeminence

Sources

Acheson, Dean. *Present at the Creation*. New York: Norton, 1969.
Ambrose, Stephen E. *Eisenhower the President*. New York: Simon & Schuster, 1984.
Ball, George W. *The Discipline of Power*. Boston: Little, Brown, 1968.
Bescholoss, Michael R. *Mayday: Eisenhower, Khrushchev, and the U-2 Affair*. New York: Harper & Row, 1986.
Cooper, Chester L. *The Lion's Last Roar: Suez, 1956*. New York: Harper & Row, 1978.
Ferrell, Robert H. *The Eisenhower Diaries*. New York: Norton, 1981.
Kamow, Stanley. *Vietnam: A History*. New York: Viking, 1983.
Kennan, George F. *Memoirs*. Boston: Little, Brown, 1967.
Kennedy, Robert E. *Thirteen Days: A Memoir of the Cuban Missile Crisis*. New York: Norton, 1969.
Pogue, Forrest C. *George C. Marshall: Statesman, 1945–1959.*New York: Viking Press, 1987.
Schlesinger, Arthur M. Jr. *A Thousand Days: John E Kennedy in the White House*. Boston: Houghton Mifflin, 1965.
Truman, Harry S. Memoirs: Years of Trial and Hope. Garden City, N.Y.: Doubleday, 1956.

3. Time of Reassessment

Sources

Brzezinski, Zbigniew K. *Power and Principle: Memoirs of the National Security Adviser, 1977–1981*. New York: Farrar, Straus, & Giroux, 1983.
Carter, Jimmy. *Keeping Faith*. New York: Bantam Books, 1982.
Cooper, Chester L. *The Lost Crusade: America in Vietnam*. New York: Dodd, Mead, 1970.
Hoopes, Townsend. *The Limits of Intervention*. New York: McKay, 1969.
Johnson, Lyndon B. *The Vantage Point*. New York: Holt, Rinehart & Winston, 1971.
Kamow, Stanley. "Giap Remembers: Hanoi's Legendary General." *New York Times Magazine*, June 24, 1990, p. 22.
Kissinger, Henry. *The White House Years*. Boston: Little, Brown, 1979.
Kissinger, Henry, and Cyrus Vance. "Bipartisan Objectives and American Foreign Policy." *Foreign Affairs*, Summer 1988, pp. 899–921.
Nixon, Richard. *RN: The Memoirs of Richard Nixon*. New York: Gossett & Dunlap, 1978.
Nuechterlein, Donald E. *National Interests and Presidential Leadership*. Boulder, Colo.: Westview, 1978.
Rusk, Dean. *As I Saw It, as Told to Richard Rusk*. New York: Norton, 1990.

4. Resurgent American Power

1. Quoted in *New York Times*, Jan. 30, 1981, p. A1.

2. Ibid.,Feb. 3, 1981, p. A16.

3. Alexander M. Haig, Jr., *Caveat: Realism, Reagan, and Foreign Policy* (New York: Macmillan, 1984), pp. 128–29.

4. Donald T. Regan, *For the Record* (New York: St. Martins Press, 1988), pp. 327–28.

5. Ibid., p. 333.

6. *Time*, Nov. 5, 1990, pp. 42, 44.

7. Quoted in *Washington Post*, May 13, 1989, p. A15.

8. See Chapter 5 for a discussion of U.S.-Canada relations.

9. See Donald E. Nuechterlein, "United States National Interests in the Middle East: Is the Persian Gulf a Bridge Too Far?" *Naval War College Review*, Winter 1989, pp. 114–19.

10. Presidential Documents 18, no. 35 (6 Sept.1982): 1082.

11. Alexander Dallin and Gail Lapidus, "Reagan and the Russians: American Policy Toward the Soviet Union," in Kenneth L. Oye, ed., *Eagle Resurgent? The Reagan Era in American Foreign Policy* (Boston: Little, Brown, 1987), p. 224.

12. Bob Woodward, *Veil: The Secret Wars of the CIA, 1981–87* (New York: Simon & Shuster, 1987), pp. 457–65, 426; Casey quoted p. 462.

13. Stephen Rosenfeld, "The Guns of July," *Foreign Affairs*, Spring 1986, pp. 698–99.

14. Quoted in *New York Times*, April 28, 1983, p. A12.

15. Robert W. Tucker, "Reagan's Foreign Policy," *Foreign Affairs*, January 1989, pp. 15, 16, 26–27.

16. Weinberger, *Fighting for Peace*, p. 442.

17. The Persian Gulf crisis in August 1990 (see Chapter 8) was a test of the U.S.-Soviet detente relationship. Moscow and Washington worked closely in the UN Security Council to bring international pressure on Iraq to withdraw its troops from Iraq. But Moscow was reluctant to condone the use of force to support sanctions, and this caused some U.S. officials to question the solidity of the relationship with respect to dealing with security threats in the Middle East.

18. Quoted in *Washington Post*, Dec. 4, 1989, p. A1.

19. James Baker, "A New Europe, a New Atlanticism: Architecture for a New Era," *Current Policy* (Department of State), 1989, No.1233, p. 2.

20. Ibid., p. 5.

21. For a critical analysis of Reagan's economic policies, see Kevin Phillips, *The Politics of Rich and Poor: Wealth and the American Electorate in the Reagan Aftermath* (New York: Random House, 1990). See also his article on the same subject in *New York Times Magazine*, June 17, 1990, p. 26.

22. In 1990 the political climate in South Africa was greatly improved when the Pretoria government released from prison Nelson Mandela, leader of the African National Congress. He later became president of South Africa.

5. U.S. Interests and Policies in North and South America

1. After a week of negotiations in June 1990, Prime Minister Mulroney and the ten provincial premiers agreed on a revised version of the Meech Lake Accords, but it was not ratified by Manitoba and New-foundland. (See later in this chapter for a fuller discussion.)

2. David Frum, "Would Two Northern Neighbors Be Better Than One?" *Wall Street Journal*, Jan. 12, 1990, p. A13.

3. Joel Garreau, *The Nine Nations of North America* (New York: Avon Books, 1981), chap. 1.

4. In September 1990 the New Democratic Party won the provincial elections in Ontario and formed a government there for the first time in history. Party leader Bob Rae became the province's premier.

5. See Chapter 8 for a discussion of the NAFTA pact. When Canada's minister of trade, John Crosby, announced in October 1990 the government's decision to join the United States in its negotiations with Mexico, strong protests were registered by the Liberal and New Democratic parties, which earlier had opposed the FTA, and by many trade unions, which feared competition from cheap Mexican labor. NDP leader Audrey McLaughlin called the proposed agreement "morally wrong" because, she claimed, Mexican laborers were treated unjustly. Despite its misgivings, the Canadian government decided it could not risk being excluded from an agreement reached between the two other major North American economic powers.

6. The Canadian government, for financial reasons, withdrew its forces from Germany in 1994. However, Canada joined other NATO countries in peace-enforcing missions in Bosnia and Kosovo.

7. For an analysis of historical, cultural, and political relationships between Americans and Canadians, see Seymour Martin Lipset, *Continental Divide: The Values and institutions of the United States and Canada* (Toronto: C.D. Howe Institute, 1989). See also Nuechterlein, op-cit, *America Overcommitted*, chap. 3: "North America: The Neglected Heartland."

8. Quoted in Graham Fraser, *Playing for Keeps: The Making of the Prime Minister, 1988* (Toronto: McClelland & Steward, 1989), p. 339.

9. Quoted in Ibid., pp. 289–91.

10. Turner was not considered an effective leader of his party in 1988, and during the campaign there was some talk among Liberals about replacing him. Even though he gained in stature following his TV debates with Mulroney and also energized Canadian nationalists, he did not appeal to Quebec's voters, as Mulroney clearly did.

11. Quoted in Fraser, *Playing for Keeps*, p. 368. In 1991 Bouchard left the Conservative Party, formed the Bloc Quebecois, and later became the premier of Quebec province.

12. For a fuller analysis of the Meech Lake Accords, see Ronald L. Watts, "An Overview,"in Peter M. Leslie and Ronald L. Watts, *Canada: The State of the Federation, 1989* (Kingston, Ont.:Queen's University, 1989), pp. 11–18.

Notes to Pages 130-144

13. See special report "Stepping Back From the Brink," *Maclean's*, Nov. 20, 1989, p. 22.

14. Thomas Courchene, *What Does Ontario Want?* (Toronto: ECW Press, 1989), p. 40.

15. Early in 1990 New Brunswick had finally ratified, but Newfoundland had carried out its threat to rescind.

16. *Globe and Mail*, Sept. 21, 1990, p. A19.

17. Canada, parliament, House of Commons, Debates, Nov. 1, 1990, pp. 5004, 5005, 5006.

18. *Whig Standard* (Kingston), Jan. 4, 1990, p. 6.

19. A poll published by the *Globe and Mail* on Oct. 30, 1990 (pp. Al, A8) and the Canadian Broadcasting Corporation on the same date found that 63 percent of Quebec respondents said that the province was likely eventually to separate from Canada. Non-Quebeckers were less positive, with 41 percent believing that separation was likely. On the question of whether Quebec should separate totally, retain some links to Canada, or remain as a province of Canada, the response of Quebeckers was revealing: totally separate, 13 percent; retain some links, 48 percent; retain status quo, 37 percent.

20. David Frum, in "Canada? Who'd Want It:" (*Wall Street Journal*, May 17, 1990), argues that the Atlantic provinces are so depressed economically and so dependent on aid from Ottawa that they should be refused admission to the United States. The issue of Quebec became more pressing in October 1995 when a new referendum showed that 49.4 percent of the population was in favor of independence.

21. The astonishing loss of popular support suffered by the Sandinista Party in the February 1990 elections is discussed below.

22. *Washington Post*, May 3, 1990, p. A9; May 4, 1990, p. A3.

23. Larry Rohter, "Can He Save Mexico," *New York Times Magazine*, Nov. 20, 1988, p. 84

24. *Christian Science Monitor*, July 25, 1989, p. 1.

25. Canada was not entirely pleased with the idea of Mexico's becoming part of the North America Free Trade Agreement. Many Canadian firms and most labor unions feared that cheap Mexican labor would compete with Canadian labor and force many Canadian firms to close.

26. Alan Riding, *Distant Neighbors* (New York: Vintage Books, 1986), pp. 458, 460.

27. *Washington Post*, April 26, 1990, p. A22.

28. Noriega took refuge in the Vatican Embassy in Panama City, from which he bargained with U.S. authorities. After fruitless efforts to persuade Washington to permit him to go into exile, he surrendered to the U.S. military and insisted he be treated as a military officer.

29. David Broder, "Panama: An Intervention That Made Sense," *Washington Post*, Jan. 14, 1990, p. B7.

30. Quoted in *Washington Post*, Jan. 6, 1990, p. A14.

31. *Economist*, Jan. 20, 1990, p. 24. Despite much speculation to the contrary, the U.S. withdrew its remaining forces from Panama in December 1999.

32. President Bush outlined his ideas for an inter-American free-trade zone in a Washington speech entitled "Enterprise for the Americas Initiative," June 27, 1990. For its text, see Current Policy (State Department), No. 1288.

6. U.S. Interests and Policies in East Asia

1. After a civil war and United Nations pressure, East Timor was granted independence in 1999.

2. President Suharto resigned in 1998 and a new democratically-elected government, headed by Abdurrahman Wahid, took power in 1999.

3. Quoted in "Change and Response in Japan: International Politics and Strategy" (prepared text from workshop, "Change in Northeast Asia— International Implications for the 1990s," sponsored by Australian National University, Canberra, Feb. 7–8, 1990).

4. Nevertheless, after the Philippine government failed to renew the bases agreement in 1991, the U.S. evacuated all of its military forces and the Navy was relocated in Japan. The U.S. made an arrangement with Singapore for ship visits and repairs.

5. For a discussion of U.S. involvement in the Middle East and Persian Gulf in the 1980s, see Donald Nuechterlein, "U.S. National Interests in the Middle East," *U.S. Naval War College Review* (Winter, 1989), pp. 114–19.

6. In 1998 both India and Pakistan test fired nuclear missiles for the first time. India said it wanted to be admitted to the "nuclear club."

7. A.D. Gordon, "India: Nation, Neighborhood, and Region," in Coral Bell, ed., *Agenda for the Nineties* (Melbourne: Longman Cheshire, 1990), p. 196.

8. For a detailed analysis of Australia's economic relationships with Japan and other industrialized Asian states, see Ross Garnaut, *Australia and the Northeast Asian Ascendancy* (Canberra: Australian Government Printing Service, 1989), esp. chap. 3, "Trade and Growth."

9. Australia's reaction to Britain's withdrawal from "East of Suez" in 1971 and the U.S. withdrawal from Vietnam in 1973 is discussed at length in Coral Bell, *Dependent Ally: A Study in Australian Foreign Policy* (Melbourne: Oxford Univ. Press, 1988), chap. 9, "East of Suez and the Guam Doctrine."

10. *The Defence of Australia, 1987* (Canberra: Australian Government Printing Service, 1987), p. 1.

11. It is noteworthy that in September 1999 Australia took the lead in sending UN-sanctioned military peace-enforcing troops to East Timor to arrange the withdrawal of Indonesian police and militia units following a favorable vote for independence by East Timor's population..

12. Gareth Evans, *Australia's Regional Security* (Canberra: Department of Foreign Affairs and Trade, 1989), p. 46. It is noteworthy that Minister Evans's introductory statement of Australia's national interests came strikingly close to naming the four basic U.S. interests described in Chap-

ter 1 of this book: "The four main priorities of Australian foreign policy have been identified in a recent Ministerial speech as: Protection of Australia's security through the maintenance of a positive security and strategic environment in our region [defense of homeland]; pursuing trade, investment and economic co-operation [economic well-being]; contributing to global security (to the extent that we can, through alliance-related activities like our hosting of the Joint Facilities and multilateral efforts like our chemical weapons initiatives) [favorable world order]: and contributing to the cause of good international citizenship (reflecting our need, and capacity, to contribute to the resolution of global-scale problems like the environment, human rights and refugees) [promotion of values]."

13. Although the Philippine economy declined somewhat after the U.S. withdrawal in 1992–1993, it soon turned the Subic Bay naval facility into a profitable commercial venture.

14. Richard Cheney, text distributed by U.S. Embassy, Tokyo, Feb. 23, 1990.

15. Ibid.

16. The United States was represented at the APEC meeting by four cabinet members: Secretary of State James Baker, Secretary of Defence Richard Cheney, Secretary of Commerce Robert Mosbacher, and U.S. Trade Representative Carla Hills. For an analysis of Australia's interest in APEC and regional economic cooperation, see Stuart Harris, "Pacific Economic Cooperation: Benefits for Australia," *Current Affairs Bulletin*, Oct. 1989, pp. 22–27.

7. U.S. Interests and Policies in Europe and the U.S.S.R.

1. Quoted in *New York Times*, June 5, 1990, p. 1.

2. President Bush proposed a revision of NATO nuclear policy to a summit meeting of allied leaders in London in July 1990. A new strategy would view nuclear arms as "weapons of last resort" in case of war in Europe. He also proposed the withdrawal from Europe of all U.S. nuclear-tipped artillery shells, resolving a contentious issue between Washington and Bonn (*Washington Post*, July 2, 1990, p. Al).

3. In December 1990, the GATT countries postponed a decision to conclude the Uruguay Round of negotiations.

4. *Economist*, June 30, 1990, p. 46.

5. Later, the U.S. and NATO agreed to remove all nuclear weapons from Germany in the early part of the decade.

6. Some experts have viewed the EDC idea, which the Eisenhower administration supported in the 1950s, as a potential alternative to NATO's defense structure. See Jim Hershberg, "A Pan-European Military?" *Washington Post*, Outlook, June 17, 1990, p. D3.

7. Quoted in "Bush Sees Revamped NATO as Core of Europe's Power," *New York Times*, May 5, 1990, p. A5.

8. "U.S. Asks NATO to Consider New Multinational Units," *Washington Post*, May 23, 1990, p. A33.

9. The U.S. promotion-of-values interest was highlighted by Secretary of State James Baker in "Democracy and American Diplomacy," an address to the World Affairs Council of Dallas on March 20, 1990; see *Current Policy* (Department of State), No. 1266.

10. In late 1991, as the U.S.S.R. was collapsing, Latvia, Lithuania, and Estonia all declared their independence.

11. "Shevardnadze Seeks Curbs on Forces in New Germany," *New York Times*, June 23, 1990, p. A4.

12. Quoted in "Presidents' Joint News Conference," *Washington Post*, June 4, 1990, p. A23.

13. *New York Times*, June 23, 1990, p. A1.

14. Ibid., June 30, 1990, p. A9.

15. See Chapters 8 and 9 for the impact of the U.S.S.R.'s dissolution on Russia's domestic and foreign policies.

16. In May 1990 the Defense Department decided not to upgrade the short-range Lance missile in Germany because of the persuasive argument that its warhead would strike only German soil following the German reunification. This decision resolved an issue raised in Washington by the Kohl government in April 1989 (see Introduction.)

17. This was a task also for President Bush and Prime Minister Thatcher in 1990; however, neither of them faced as strong a neutralist-pacifist movement as the one in West Germany.

18. Helmut Kohl, "A United Germany in a United Europe," text distributed by the German Information Center (GIC), New York, June 4, 1990.

19. Hans-Dietrich Genscher, "The Future of a European Germany," text distributed by GIC, New York, April 10, 1990.

20. Genscher, text of statement distributed by GIC, May 14, 1990.

21. Genscher, text of speech distributed by GIC, May 26, 1990.

22. Kohl, text of speech made available by GIC, June 7, 1990.

23. Quoted in Time, June 25, 1990, p. 36.

24. In recognition of Kohl's extraordinary achievement in bringing about German economic union, the *Economist* for June 30, 1990, titled its cover picture of him "Wunderkohl."

25. Quoted in Survey of *Current Affairs* (Foreign and Commonwealth Office, London), April 1990, p. 130.

26. "A Tale of Three Cities," *Economist*, June 2, 1990, p. 24.

27. "France—Still on Guard," *Washington Post*, July 12, 1990, p. A23.

28. Jeane Kirkpatrick, "It's Time Now to Influence Events in Europe," *Washington Post*, June 25, 1990, p. All.

29. Ronald Steel,"Germany in NATO? Not Important," *New York Times*, June 28, 1990, p. A25.

30. The NATO summit meeting in London in July 1990 accepted President Bush's and Chancellor Kohl's new NATO strategy, designed to reassure Soviet leaders and undercut antinuclear sentiment in Germany. Prime Minister Thatcher and President Mitterrand reportedly were not entirely pleased with the Washington-Bonn plan. See "Bush's NATO Success Advances U.S. Goals," *Washington Post*, July 7, 1990, p. A18.

8. Post–Cold War Challenges to U.S. Interests

1. President Carter said in his State of the Union message on January 23, 1980: "Let our position be absolutely clear: An attempt by any outside force to gain control of the Persian Gulf region will be regarded as an assault on the vital interests of the United States of America, and such an assault will be repelled by any means necessary, including military force" (*Keeping Faith*, p. 271).

2. See Weinberger, *Fighting for Peace*, chap. 8,"The Persian Gulf Success Story."

3. Quoted in *Washington Post*, Aug. 16, 1990, p. A33.

4. Department of State news release dated September 12, 1990. The quotations cited here are from a text of the address issued by the U.S. Embassy, Ottawa, entitled "'Iraqi Aggression Will Not Stand,' President Says," pp. 1-2, 5.

5. George Bush and Brent Scowcroft, *A World Transformed* (New York: Knopf, 1998), p. 486.

6. Ibid., pp. 491–92.

7. Ibid., pp. 514–15.

8. Ibid., p. 504.

9. James A. Baker, *The Politics of Diplomacy* (New York: Putnam, 1995), pp. 563, 564.

10. Michael Mandelbaum, "The End of the Soviet Union," *Foreign Affairs: America and the World 1991/92*, p. 169.

11. Robert M. Gates, *From the Shadows"* (New York: Simon & Schuster, 1996), p. 554.

12. Ibid., p. 552.

13. Bush and Scowcroft, *A World Transformed*, pp. 564, 565.

14. Baker, *Politics of Diplomacy*, p. 625.

15. Dimitri Simes, "The Return of Russian History," *Foreign Affairs* (January/February 1994): p. 73–74.

16. "Press conference in Moscow of Presidents Clinton and Yeltsin," *1995 Presidential Documents Online via GPO Access*, vol. 31, no 19, pp. 792–99.

17. Bush and Scowcroft, *A World Transformed*, p. 89.

18. Ibid., p. 106.

19. Ibid., pp. 108–11.

20. Ibid., 276.

21. Baker, *Politics of Diplomacy*, p. 324.

22. "Press Conference at the White House,"*1995 Presidential Documents Online via GPO Access*, vol. 21, no. 32, p. 1423.

23. Kenneth Lieberthal, "A New China Strategy," *Foreign Affairs* (November/December 1995): pp. 46–47, 49.

24. The political fallout from Japan's Persian Gulf policy was addressed by Edward Desmond, *Time Magazine* correspondent in Tokyo, in "Ichiro Ozawa: Reformer at Bay," *Foreign Affairs* (September/October 1995): pp. 117–31.

25. Baker, *Politics of Diplomacy*, p. 596.

26. "Remarks on North Korea and an Exchange with Reporters," *1994 Presidential Documents Online via GPO Access,* vol. 30, no. 25, pp. 1327–28.

27. Baker, *Politics of Diplomacy,* p. 598.

28. For a sober analysis of the future of North-South Korean relations, see Byung-joon Abn, "The Man Who Would be Kim," *Foreign Affairs* (November/December 1994): pp. 94–108.

29. For a critical view of the Mexican government's record in dealing with financial crises, see Jorge G. Castaneda, "Mexico's Circle of Misery," *Foreign Affairs* (July-August 1996): pp. 92–105.

30. "Message to Congress on the Financial Crisis in Mexico," *1995 Presidential Documents Online via GPO Access,* vol. 31, no. 10, p. 390.

31. "Address to the Nation on Haiti," *1994 Presidential Documents Online via GPO Access,* vol. 30, no. 37, p. 1779.

32. Colin Powell, *My American Journey* (New York: Random House, 1995), p. 598.

33. Ibid., pp. 598–602.

34. See Powell, *My American Journey,* p. 584, for a discussion of the Somali intervention and its consequences.

35. For an analysis of the prospects for a European monetary union, see Rudi Dornbusch, "Euro Fantasies," *Foreign Affairs* (September-October 1996), pp. 110–24. Enlargement of the European Union (EU) to include six eastern European states was agreed to at the EU's meeting in Helsinki in December 1999. The six states that would be admitted in 2002 were Estonia, Poland, Hungary, the Czech Republic, Slovenia, and Cyprus. Seven additional countries, including Turkey, were given candidate status.

36. Baker, *Politics of Diplomacy,* p. 651.

9. Toward the New Millennium

1. See Garrick Utley, "The Shrinking of Foreign News," *Foreign Affairs* (March/April 1997): pp. 2–10.

2. "Address to the Nation on Implementation of the Peace Agreement in Bosnia-Herzegovina," *1995 Presidential Documents Online via GPO Access,* vol. 31, no. 48, p. 2060.

3. Ibid., p. 2062.

4. See Radha Kumar, "The Troubled History of Partition," *Foreign Affairs* (January/February 1997): pp. 22–34.

5. Richard Holbrooke, "Letter," *Foreign Affairs* (March/April 1997): p. 172.

6. Ivo Daalder and Michael Froman, "Dayton's Incomplete Peace," *Foreign Affairs* (November/December 1999): p. 113.

7. For a discussion of the political and economic costs of NATO expansion, see Amos Perlmutter and Ted Galen Carpenter, "NATO's Expensive Trip East," *Foreign Affairs* (January/February 1998): pp. 2–6.

8. See Daniel Treisman, "Why Yeltsin Won," *Foreign Affairs* (September/October 1996): pp. 64–77.

9. Both statements are contained in "The President's News Confer-

ence with President Boris Yeltsin of Russia in Moscow,"*1998 Presidential Documents Online via GPO Access*, vol. 34, no. 36, pp. 1686, 1688.

10. Ibid., pp. 1691, 1692.

11. "Moscow Recalls NATO Delegate to Protest Raids," *Washington Post*, March 25, 1999, p. A30.

12. "In Words of Yeltsin and Clinton: Examining Terrorism and Human Rights," *New York Times*, November 19, 1999, p. A13.

13. Ibid.

14. "Russia Pines For a New Savior: Victory," *New York Times*, November 21, 1999, section 4, p. 1.

15. "Russia's Steely Premier Ruling to Popular Beat: Putin's Star Rising in Presidential Race," *Washington Post*, November 22, 1999, p. A17.

16. Richard Bernstein and Ross Munro, "The Coming Conflict with America," *Foreign Affairs* (March/April 1997): p. 19.

17. Zbigniew Brezezinski, "A Geostrategy for Eurasia," *Foreign Affairs* (September/October 1997): pp. 58, 59.

18. "The President's News Conference with President Jiang," *1997 Presidential Documents Online via GPO Access*, vol. 33, no. 44, p. 1673.

19. Ibid., pp. 1674, 1675.

20. "The President's News Conference with President Jiang in Beijing," *1998 Presidential Documents Online via GPO Access*, vol. 34, no. 27, p. 1246.

21. Ibid., p. 1250.

22. Ted Galen Carpenter, "Roiling Asia: U.S. Coziness with China Upsets the Neighbors," *Foreign Affairs* (November/December 1998): pp. 2, 6.

23. "A Deal That America Just Couldn't Refuse," *New York Times*, Nov. 16, 1999, p. A10.

24. "Opening China's Markets," *New York Times*, Nov. 16, 1999, p. A30.

25. "Reality Before Legacy," *Washington Post*, November 14, 1999, p. B7.

26. "White House Opposes Bill on Taiwan," *Washington Post*, October 3, 1999, p. A26.

27. "Understanding Taiwan," *Foreign Affairs* (November/December 1999): pp. 12, 14.

28. "Trade Sanctions on North Korea Are Eased by U.S.," *New York Times*, Sept. 18, 1999, p. 1.

29. Ibid., p. 4.

30. Ibid.

31. Department of State, Office of the Press Spokesman, Paris, France, "Press Conference of Secretary of State Madeleine K. Albright," Rambouillet, France, February 23, 1999.

32. "Clinton Says U.S. Has Stake to Justify Strikes on Serbia," *Washington Post*, March 20, 1999, p. A1.

33. Ibid., p. A16.

34. "Senate Considers Barring Airstrikes," *Washington Post*, March 23, p. A13.

35. Department of State, Office of the Press Spokesman, "Secretary of

State's Interview on Serbia on CNN's *Larry King Live*," Washington, D.C., March 23, 1999.

36. "Address to the Nation on Airstrikes Against Serbian Targets in the Federal Republic of Yugoslavia (Serbia and Montenegro)," *1999 Presidential Documents Online via GPO Access*, vol. 35, no. 12, pp. 516, 517.

37. *1999 Presidential Documents Online via GPO Access*, vol. 35, no. 23, pp. 1075, 1076. The president did not mention in his address what was cited widely as a major reason for the total lack of casualties during the intensive bombing campaign: U.S. planes stayed above 15,000 feet in order to avoid Serb antiaircraft missiles. This restriction limited to some extent the accuracy of the bombing missions.

38. Michael Mandelbaum, "A Perfect Failure," *Foreign Affairs* (September/October 1999): pp. 2, 7.

39. "Clinton Underestimated Serbs, He Acknowledges," *New York Times*, June 26, 1999, p. A6.

40. "A Survey of Europe: A Work in Progress," *The Economist*, October 23, 1999, p. E11.

41. C. Fred Bergsten, "The Dollar and the Euro," *Foreign Affairs* (July/August 1997): pp. 83–95.

42. Richard Medley, "Europe's Next Big Idea: Strategy and Economics Point to a European Military," *Foreign Affairs* (September/October 1999): p. 19.

43. "Military Posture of Europe to Turn More Independent," *New York Times*, December 13, 1999, p. A1.

44. "The EU Turns Its Attention from Ploughshares to Swords," *The Economist*, November 29, 1999, p. 54.

45. "Back to Oslo, even Camp David," *The Economist*, November 6, 1999, p. 48.

10. Role of the Aloof but Vigilant Superpower

1. Robert Ellsworth, a former U.S. ambassador to NATO, and Dimitri Simes, head of a Washington think tank, used the term "benign superpower" in their call for a less interventionist U.S. foreign policy. However, "benign superpower" implies a lack of interest, even neglect, whereas an "aloof but vigilant superpower" role envisions an active, involved U.S. foreign policy. See "Imposing Our 'Values' by Force," *Washington Post*, December 29, 1999, p. A17.

2. Michael Barone, "The American Century," *U.S. News and World Report*, December 27, 1999, pp. 39–40.

3. Madeleine Albright, "The Testing of American Foreign Policy," *Foreign Affairs* (November/December 1998): pp. 53, 62.

4. Samuel Huntington, "The Lonely Superpower," *Foreign Affairs* (March/April 1999): p. 37.

5. Ibid., p. 40.

6. *The Lexus and the Olive Tree* (New York: Farrar, Straus, Giroiux, 1999), pp. 352, 373–75.

7. The nationalist, isolationist political strain in American history and

foreign policy was analyzed by Walter Russell Mead in his article "The Jacksonian Tradition and American Foreign Policy" in *The National Interest* (Winter 2000), pp. 5–29.

8. Patrick Buchanan, "The War That Didn't Need Waging," *Washington Post*, October 11, 1999, A25.

9. For an insight into how Governor George W. Bush, as president, might view foreign policy, see Condoleezza Rice, "Promoting the National Interest," and Robert B. Zoellick, "A Republican Foreign Policy," in the January/February 2000 issue of *Foreign Affairs*. Both writers were senior officials during the George Bush presidency and are foreign policy advisers to Governor Bush.

10. "Clinton Says 'New Isolationism' Imperils U.S. Security," *New York Times*, October 15, 1999, p. A1.

11. Charles Krauthammer, "The Phony Battle Against Isolationism," *Washington Post*, October 29, 1999, p. A31.

12. From Murray's remarks at the University of Virginia's Miller Center of Public Affairs, September 24, 1999.

Index

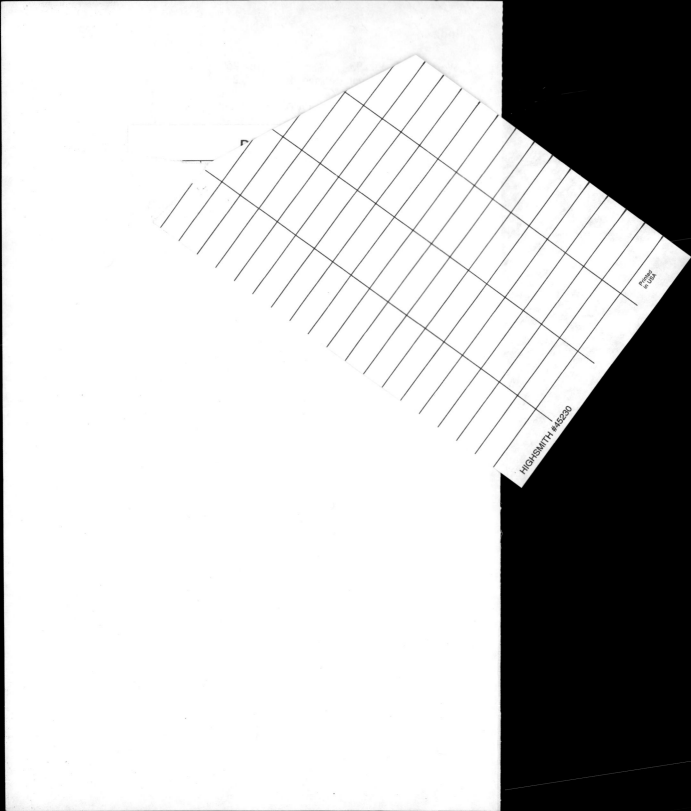